The Queen's House

The Queen's House

A SOCIAL HISTORY
OF BUCKINGHAM PALACE

Edna Healey

Carroll & Graf Publishers, Inc.
New York

To my husband and family
with gratitude for
their constant encouragement

Text copyright © 1997 by Royal Collection Enterprises Ltd and Edna Healey
Illustrations copyright © as on List of Illustrations page xi

First published in England by Fourth Estate Limited

First Carroll & Graf edition 1998

Carroll & Graf Publishers, Inc.
19 West 21st Street
New York, NY 10010-6805

Library of Congress Cataloging-in-Publication Data is available.
ISBN: 0-7867-0565-5

Manufactured in the United States of America

Contents

Acknowledgements

I am deeply grateful to Her Majesty The Queen for gracious permission to quote from documents and letters in the Royal Archives, and for giving me the privilege of access to Buckingham Palace.

I am indebted to HM Queen Elizabeth The Queen Mother for allowing me to publish some of her hitherto unpublished letters now in the Royal Archives. I am particularly grateful that she spared time to see me. HRH Princess Margaret also kindly gave me some valuable insight into the history of Buckingham Palace.

I am deeply indebted to Lady de Bellaigue, the Registrar of The Queen's Archives, and to Oliver Everett, Assistant Keeper of The Queen's Archives, for their guidance and assistance.

I give my grateful thanks to the librarians and their colleagues of the House of Lords Library, the British Library, the Westminster City Library and Archives and the East Sussex County Library. As always, I owe a great debt to the librarian and staff at the London Library. Jessica Rutherford, Director of the Royal Pavilion, Brighton, has been particularly helpful.

I have been given every encouragement from many members of Her Majesty's Household. I am most grateful to the Lord Chamberlain, the Rt Hon. the Earl of Airlie; Her Majesty's Private Secretary, the Rt Hon. Sir Robert Fellowes; the Master of the Household, Major General

Sir Simon Cooper; the Director of Finance and Property Services, Michael Peat; and the former Press Secretary, Charles Anson, and other members of the Royal Household for their friendliness and unfailing courtesy.

I am deeply conscious of my debt to Hugh Roberts, Edward Hewlett, Christopher Lloyd and Sir Oliver Millar, and all the members of the Royal Collection, not only for the time and encouragement they have given me but also for their written works. They have contributed superb introductions to the catalogues of exhibitions in The Queen's Gallery, many of them modestly unsigned. I am aware that in this book I have been able only to touch the surface of subjects to which they have given long years of profound study. They bear no responsibility for my shortcomings.

I am most grateful to all at my publishers, Michael Joseph Ltd, particularly to my editors, Susan Watt and Anne Askwith, for their patience, constant support and encouragement, and to my picture researcher, Lily Richard. Barbara Peters has given me invaluable advice and assistance.

My secretary, the late Mary Morton, continued to work with dedication until her untimely death. Cheryl Lutring has competently finished her work.

List of Illustrations

12. Chelsea porcelain service (1763) (The Royal Collection)

13. *Fanny Burney* (Frances D'Arblay) (*c.* 1784–5) by Edward Francis Burney (1760–1848) (By courtesy of the National Portrait Gallery, London)

14. *Queen Charlotte* (1797) by Sir William Beechey (1753–1839) (The Royal Collection)

15. *Mrs Jordan and Two Children* (1834) by Sir Frances Chantrey (1781–1841) (The Royal Collection)

16. *The Family of George III* (1783) by Thomas Gainsborough RA (1727–88) (The Royal Collection)

17. *George IV* (1791) by George Stubbs (1724–1806) (The Royal Collection)

18. *Queen Victoria and Prince Albert and the Bal Costumé of 12 May 1842* by Sir Edwin Landseer (1803–73) (The Royal Collection)

19. *Queen Victoria's Sitting-Room* (1848) by James Roberts (1800–67) (The Royal Collection)

20. *The New Ballroom at Buckingham Palace* by Louis Haghe (1806–85) (The Royal Collection)

21. *The Family of Queen Victoria* (1887) by Laurits Tuxen (1853–1927) (The Royal Collection)

22. *The Queen's Garden Party 26 June 1897* by Laurits Tuxen (The Royal Collection)

23. *King Edward VII in Garter Robes* (1907) by Sir Arthur Cope (1857–1940) (Private Collection – photo: Nathan Kelly)

24. *Queen Mary* (1911–13) by Sir William Llewellyn (1858–1941) (The Royal Collection)

25. *George V and Queen Mary Enthroned at the Great Coronation Durbar, Delhi, 12 September 1911* by George Percy Jacomb-Hood (1857–1927) (The Royal Archives, Windsor Castle)

26. *George V with Princesses Elizabeth and Margaret* by T. P. Earl (1874–1947) (The Royal Collection)

27. The Duke of Edinburgh marches on the fiftieth anniversary of VJ Day, 15 August 1995 (PA News)

28. HM Queen Elizabeth The Queen Mother (1948) by Cecil Beaton (1904–80) (Camera Press)

All Royal Collection photographs are reproduced © Her Majety Queen Elizabeth II

Prologue

On 4 June 1763, in the third year of his reign, George III celebrated his twenty-fifth birthday at St James's Palace. Two days later his young Queen, Charlotte, staged her own surprise present. She had persuaded her husband to remain at St James's Palace from Saturday 4 June until Monday 6 June while she completed her preparations at their new home, Buckingham House. The King had bought the red-brick mansion at the end of Pall Mall in 1763* from Sir Charles Sheffield, who had possessed it since 1742, and they had spent the last year watching over the rebuilding and refurbishment.

Now, on a warm June night Queen Charlotte took her husband through the darkened great house up the grand staircase to the Queen's rooms overlooking the garden. Then, at a signal, the shutters were opened and below them the terrace and lawns were suddenly, amazingly, revealed, brilliant in the light of 4,000 glass lamps. Over the shining long canal, a delicate bridge had miraculously appeared. Pavilions and a splendid colonnade had arisen, and graceful figures linked huge screens lit from behind, like magic lanterns, showing images of the King bringing peace to the world, and his enemies, envy, malice and destruction falling headlong to perdition. The Queen had commissioned the architect

* Negotiations began in 1760 but the contract was not finally signed until April 1763.

Robert Adam to design this magnificent display, which dazzled the throng of glittering guests and delighted the King.[1]

Queen Charlotte's German band played 'God Save The King' and then, while the band played music by George Frideric Handel, the King and Queen joined the assembly for a 'supper of a hundred cold dishes followed by an illuminated dessert'. Apparently at this party a new court dress was introduced, of stiff-bodiced gowns and bare shoulders. 'The old ladies will catch their deaths,' the gossip Horace Walpole wrote maliciously. 'What dreadful discoveries will be made, both of fat and lean. I recommend to you the idea of Mrs Cavendish going half stark!'[2]

There have been many parties since then in the gardens of Buckingham Palace, as Buckingham House is called today, but probably none has pleased a monarch more. 'The King', so it was said, 'was delighted with this unexpected testimony of his consort's love and respect.' It was no small achievement for a nineteen-year-old girl, recently and unexpectedly plucked from the obscurity of a small German dukedom, Mecklenburg-Strelitz.

The King, in love and gratitude, gave Buckingham House to Queen Charlotte; the gift was officially confirmed by Parliament on 26 April 1775. During her lifetime it was known as 'the Queen's House' and here twelve of their fifteen children were born.

The palace on this site was to be rebuilt and altered many times, but it has remained at the centre of the royal family's life and, since 1837, has been the monarch's official London residence.

CHAPTER ONE

The Duke of Buckingham

'Sic situ laetantur lares'
[The Household Gods delight in such a situation]

Inscription around the roof
of the Duke of Buckingham's house[1]

Palaces and Predecessors

George III was the first monarch to take up residence in Buckingham House, but the site had had royal connections since the Tudors and each of his predecessors had added something to the history of Buckingham Palace.

Every king or queen, past and present, has had a different concept of the purpose of a palace: an outward sign of power and dominance, a symbol of mystical status, or an expression of the monarch's own whims and fantasies. George III, essentially a simple man, wanted, in addition to his official residence, St James's Palace, a family home where he could live with his adored young wife, bring up a family and lead the life of a cultured country gentleman with his books, his pictures and his music.

Henry VIII was the first monarch to acquire the land adjoining the site of the Palace. His father, Henry VII, had made the medieval Palace of Westminster* both home and royal headquarters. His law courts and Parliament were here and here he held Court in the Painted Chamber, his great bedroom.†

---

* He had many other palaces outside London: he built Richmond Palace and extended Greenwich Palace, where three Tudor monarchs were born.

†Traditionally Somerset House on the banks of the Thames had been assigned to the monarch's consort as a dower house. Charles I's wife, Henrietta Maria, had lived

Henry VIII had been king for only three years, when in 1512 fire destroyed much of the old palace. In 1529, when Cardinal Wolsey fell from grace, the King took the opportunity to seize York Place, the Cardinal's magnificent palace on the bank of the River Thames. The Palace of Westminster still housed Parliament and the law courts but was no longer the royal residence. It has retained, however, the old name and is still the Palace of Westminster. York Place became the Palace of Whitehall and for a century and a half was the headquarters of the Court until it, in turn, was destroyed by fire.

Henry VIII, with his superabundant energy, expected his palace to be more than a seat of state and a symbol of dominance: it was also to be a place of frolic and entertainment. He looked across Whitehall to a stretch of wasteland and saw it as a perfect hunting ground conveniently close to his palace. So in December 1531 he acquired from Roger Lupton of Eton College the 185 acres stretching from Whitehall to the site of the present Buckingham Palace. The land was, at this time, reedy marshland watered by two streams, the Westbourne and the Tyburn. Henry VIII drained the marshes, channelled the streams into a lake and laid out gardens. The area was to become St James's Park, named after a twelfth-century hospice there, dedicated to St James the Less, which had originally been endowed by the citizens of London for the care of 'fourteen leper maydens'.[2] Since then monks and 'maydens' had brought scandal to the Hospital of St James, and plague and neglect

there, and in 1761, by Act of Parliament, it had been settled on Queen Charlotte. On 12 April 1775, Lord North brought a message from the King to Parliament asking that 'more suitable accommodation be made for the residence of the Queen should she survive his majesty'. On 26 April Parliament agreed that 'the Palace in which His Majesty resides, lately known by the name of Buckingham House & now called the Queen's House be settled on the Queen in lieu of Somerset House, in case she should survive His Majesty. That . . . the said Palace be annexed to, & vested in the Crown of Great Britain.' Somerset House was to be 'vested in His Majesty, his heirs and successors for the purpose of erecting & establishing certain public offices'. The King was granted £100,000 towards the purchase and improvements of the Queen's House and in consideration of the new use of Somerset House. (Source: *Parliamentary History of England*, House of Lords, vol. 18, 15–17.)

had emptied the decaying buildings, which in 1449 Henry VI gave to Eton College. The Master of Eton kept the Hospital of St James as his town house but provided for the upkeep of four poor women there. In 1536 Henry VIII took it over, dismissed the four women with a pension of £6 13s. 4d. a year, demolished it and built a hunting lodge in its place. Later, enlarged and rebuilt, it became St James's Palace. So, where once bell and clapper had sounded, the woods rang with hunting horns when Henry VIII and Queen Anne rode out on a May morning with 'a goodly company to the fields of Kensington'.[3]

Henry VIII acquired the land adjoining the site on which Buckingham Palace is built, but it was James I who first cultivated it. In 1608 he paid £935 for the 'walling, levelling and planting thereof of mulberry trees' on four acres of adjoining wasteland near the site of the north wing of the present Buckingham Palace. Impressed by the wealth created by the French silk industry, James I had decided to outshine the French King. In 1607 he appointed William Stallinge, an employee at the Customs House with experience of breeding silkworms, 'to research and publish a book' on 'Instructions for the planting and increase of mulberry trees, breeding of silkworms and the making of silk'. He also instructed deputy lieutenants to require landowners in their counties to 'purchase and plant ten thousand mulberry trees at the rate of 6 shillings per thousand'.[4]

Alas, Stallinge and, later, his son Jasper were to spend many years and thousands of pounds of the King's money in the vain attempt to persuade silkworms to thrive on the leaves of the black mulberry trees they had planted. They had failed to realize that though the black mulberry produces delicious fruit, its leaves are rough and silkworms prefer those of the white mulberry.

So in 1625 James I and Stallinge both died without embellishing the kingdom with the silk that the King so much desired: his scheme of a great English silk industry had never materialized. Stallinge's son Jasper being equally unsuccessful, on 4 July 1628 Charles I granted his friend Lord Aston the right to 'keep his mulberry gardens at St James with a yearly fee of £60 during his life and that of his son'.[5] But when in 1635 Lord Aston was made ambassador to Spain all pretence of supervising the breeding of silkworms was abandoned and the weaving sheds and outhouses were neglected.

There were, however, sharp men who realized that there were fortunes to be made not in silk but in property. As London expanded, a site in a rural setting with easy access to the Palaces of Westminster, Whitehall, St James and Kensington was of great potential value, and there were three men in particular who were eager to seize it: Lionel Cranfield, James I's Treasurer, Hugh Audley, the most formidable property lawyer in London, and William Blake, his man of business. The story of the involvement of these men and others in the establishment of the site of Buckingham Palace was to continue for years, through civil war, the Commonwealth and successive reigns, and through a maze of complicated litigation.

The Mulberry Garden was outside the walls of St James's Park and was part of the freehold of Ebury Manor, an area which stretched from the present Oxford Street through to Chelsea. Henry VIII had acquired the freehold for the Crown, but Queen Elizabeth I had granted a long lease to Sir Thomas Knyvett which ran until 1675. He in turn had assigned his lease to two London merchants. When James I came to sell Ebury Manor, the Mulberry Garden was specifically excluded. These four acres were to remain Crown property throughout all the vicissitudes of the century, except for a short period when Cromwell sold it together with the rest of King Charles's property.

When in 1618 and 1622 the two leases for Ebury Manor owned by the merchants came on the market, Cranfield moved swiftly and secretly to buy them, using the names of two of his servants, although as the King's Treasurer he ought to have bought them for the Crown. It was easy, he thought, to cheat James I in the last years of his dissolute life. A clever but unscrupulous minister who had risen from grocer's apprentice to be the King's financial adviser, Cranfield finally overreached himself and in May 1624 was impeached by Parliament for 'bribery, extortion, wrong & deceit'. He was heavily fined, imprisoned and disgraced.

Hugh Audley, who had picked up much property from such disasters, saw vultures gathering and pounced. Before Cranfield was imprisoned, he used his knowledge of his secret to blackmail him into selling Ebury

Manor. On 1 March 1626 Audley paid him £9,400 for the whole Ebury leasehold, using William Blake as one of his trustees. Although there would be many tenants on and around the future site of the Palace in the coming years, Hugh Audley held the leasehold of Ebury Manor until his death in 1662.

While William Blake was negotiating the purchase of Ebury Manor for his employer Audley, he was engaged in property speculation on his own account. Outside the south-west wall of the Mulberry Garden was half an acre of wasteland, the site of the old hamlet of Eyecross and the future site of part of the forecourt of Buckingham Palace. Blake illegally acquired it and built a simple house there for his son and daughter-in-law, to be named Blake House. Thanks to Audley's patronage, Blake flourished: in 1626 he bought himself a knighthood and somewhat dubious title deeds to the new property, having avoided the law forbidding new building on the grounds that there had been dwellings there before.

James I was succeeded by his son, Charles I. Sir William Blake entered the new reign an apparently prosperous citizen, with a house in Kensington and another on a site that the new King's friend, Lord Goring, coveted. In fact Blake was deep in debt and after his death in 1630 his heir negotiated the sale of Blake House to Lord Goring, completing the sale in 1633.

George Goring and Goring House

George Goring was a survivor. He had served four monarchs: he was a favourite at the Court of Queen Elizabeth I. James I knighted him in 1608, and two years later made him a Gentleman of the Privy Chamber to his second son Charles, who entrusted him with the negotiations in France for his marriage to Henrietta Maria, daughter of Henry IV of France. When she became Queen, Lord Goring became her Vice-Chamberlain and Master of the Horse. This close association with the Queen proved useful during the Civil War: it was Goring who was chosen to conduct the Queen to her old home in France. He served and fought for Charles I and lived to see Charles II restored to the throne. In his time he played successfully many parts: buffoon and statesman, lady's man and tough soldier.

His sturdy loyalty was rewarded, and he became exceedingly wealthy, well able to afford to build himself a handsome house on the site he had bought, though he ran himself into debt in the process. Instead of demolishing the existing building he appears to have enlarged and embellished Blake's original house. From a contemporary print it would seem to have been a solid brick house – plain and unpretentious like its owner. Unlike the present Buckingham Palace, it faced south. He also appropriated more 'waste' land in order to extend his courtyard entrance and enlarge his garden. He had built, according to a contemporary survey, 'a fair house and other convenient buildings and outhouses and upon the other part of it made the Fountain Garden, a Tarris [terrace] walk, a courtyard and a laundry yard'.[6]

While Goring was establishing himself in his comfortable villa at one end of the royal estate at St James's, Charles I, in the Palace of Whitehall on the bank of the Thames, was treading his disastrous political road to the scaffold. His Palace was then, in the words of historian Thomas Macaulay, 'an ugly old labyrinth of dirty brick and plastered timber'. It was a huddle of disparate buildings: richly decorated apartments for the royal family, houses with low, dark rooms for courtiers and servants, and the great high-ceilinged Banqueting House, designed in 1619 by architect Inigo Jones in the Palladian style. There were galleries displaying statues and paintings, privy gardens where men and women of rank could walk unchallenged.

Politically incompetent and uncomprehending though Charles I was, he had excellent artistic taste and during the first decade of his reign assembled a most spectacular collection of paintings.

He owed some of his talent to the example of his mother, the shadowy Anne of Denmark, who was said to have cared more for paintings than for men, and who took great pleasure in the acquisitions of her royal predecessors, including the tapestries and Hans Holbeins of Henry VIII, and Elizabeth I's exquisite miniatures. Charles I's elder brother,

Prince Henry, who had died of typhoid in 1612 aged eighteen, had also inherited a scholarly interest in art and had started his own collection.

Charles I, according to the painter Peter Paul Rubens, even before his accession was 'the greatest amateur of paintings among the princes of the world'. His passion had been fired by his visit to Madrid in 1623, when he travelled in disguise on a mission to Spain to woo Philip IV's sister. He returned without a bride but inspired by Philip IV's great art collection in Madrid.

When he became King he sent his agents to bargain, and his ambassadors to look for great paintings. He bought through them the cartoons of Raphael, Leonardo da Vinci's *John the Baptist* and many other treasures. His greatest triumph was the purchase in 1626 of the collection of the Gonzaga family in Mantua – 'so wonderful and glorious a collection that the like will never again be met with' – which included works by Andrea Mantegna, Raphael, Titian, Tintoretto and Rubens.

A generous patron, Charles I commissioned Rubens to paint the great ceiling in the Banqueting House in honour of his father, James I. It was finished in 1634. He commissioned Rubens's pupil, Sir Anthony van Dyck, to paint some of the greatest paintings in the Royal Collection today: 'The Greate Peece': *Charles I and Henrietta Maria with Their Two Eldest Children*, Charles and Mary, dominates the Picture Gallery. He brilliantly portrays the unmartial character of the King, his diffidence and melancholy, and his spirited French wife, the Catholic Henrietta Maria, who was to fight tenaciously on the King's behalf throughout the Civil War. She shared his love of art; and it was to her that paintings came as gifts from the Papacy, knowing that they would be passed to her husband. In 1636 the Pope's nephew, Cardinal Barberini, sent her a batch of paintings including ones by Leonardo and Andrea del Sarto.

While the King and Queen were filling their Palace of Whitehall with superb paintings, George Goring was enlarging the grounds of Goring House. He bought two large fields, known as Upper and Lower Crow, of twenty acres, from Audley, though he never completed payment for them. By 1634 Goring owned most of the land on which the present

Buckingham Palace was built except the four acres of Mulberry Garden and the area now occupied by the eastern forecourt. In spite of the great fortune he made through the patronage of the King, he was constantly in debt and mortgaged Goring House to his wife's relatives. Nevertheless he hankered after the Mulberry Garden, finally bought the lease after Lord Aston's death in 1639 and at last, in July 1640, he persuaded the King to grant him the freehold, but the agreement never received the confirmation of the Great Seal. In 1642 the Civil War had begun and Charles I had more pressing worries. During the Civil War, Goring lost everything. He could not keep up payments to Audley, and left Goring House, which was requisitioned by Parliament. Charles I took his own Court to Oxford, and by 1643 Goring House was fortified by Oliver Cromwell's troops. There was a large fort at Hyde Park Corner and 'a redoubt and battery . . . at the lower end of Lord Goring's wall'. For a while troops were stationed in Goring House; afterwards it was repaired and Parliament decided that the Speaker, William Lenthall, should be allowed to live there.

Meanwhile in 1642 Goring joined the King's army. He had made a fortune in his royal service and was now prepared to spend it and his life for the King. He sent for his son to join the King's army, writing to his wife, 'had I millions of crowns or scores of sons, the King and his cause should have them all'.[7] Charles I repaid him by creating him Earl of Norwich on 28 November 1644. He was captured during the Civil War and imprisoned at Windsor Castle. On 10 November 1648 the House of Commons voted for his banishment, but on 6 March 1649 he was sentenced to death. However, he was reprieved by the influence of Speaker Lenthall, who interceded on his behalf.

In January 1649, while the new Earl of Norwich was imprisoned, facing trial and possibly death, his master Charles I had been condemned. On 30 January 1649 he took his last cold walk from St James's Palace to the Banqueting House in the Palace of Whitehall. He wore extra warm clothing in case the people should think he shivered from fear not cold. As he climbed to the scaffold outside the first-floor window, did he glance up to the great Rubens ceiling he had commissioned? It would have brought him some consolation if he could have seen into the future. When the great fire of 1698 destroyed the Palace of Whitehall, the Banqueting House and its Rubens was all that was saved.

After the execution of the King, Parliament ordered a commission to be appointed to arrange the sale of the King's property to pay his debts. The sale of his pictures, a total of 1,570, lasted from October 1649 to the middle of the 1650s. So one of the world's greatest art collections was scattered. The paintings were eventually dispersed among private buyers, and are now in museums in France, Spain, Austria and the USA, and elsewhere. Cromwell, however, kept some for the empty walls of Hampton Court Palace – among them, significantly, the pride of the collection, Mantegna's *Triumphs of Caesar*.

The houses and land of Charles I were also sold, including the Mulberry Garden, which was still Crown property, and as such it was sold to Sir Anthony Deane, who in turn sold it to a Mr Chipp, who turned it into a place of entertainment. It was described in the Parliamentary survey of 1651, made when the King's estates were sold, as including 'a bowling alley, a part planted with several sorts of fruit trees and another part planted with whitethorn in the manner of a wilderness or maze walk'. Throughout the Commonwealth and Protect-orate, 1653–60, when other places of entertainment were closed, the Mulberry Garden behind its high red-brick wall remained open – and notorious. It was often referred to in Restoration plays: for instance, in his play *The Mulberry Garden*, Sir Charles Sedley's hero says, 'These country ladies . . . take up their places in the Mulberry Garden as early as a citizen's wife at new play.'[8] Sedley's granddaughter was to become the chatelaine of the house and gardens he made famous.

The diarist John Evelyn reported in his journal on 10 May 1654:

My Lady Gerrard treated us at Mulberry Gardens, now the only place of refreshment about the Town for persons of the best quality to be exceedingly cheated at: Cromwell and his partisans having shut up and closed Spring Gardens which until now had been the usual rendezvous for the Ladies and Gallants of this season.[9]

Throughout the Protectorate, and after the Restoration of Charles II in 1660, the Mulberry Garden continued to flourish until it was finally closed in 1675. During that time Mr Chipp created there a number of small booths, perfect for picnicking or courting. The diarist Samuel Pepys visited the garden in May 1668 and found it 'a very silly place, worse than Spring Gardens, and but little company, and those of a rascally, whoring sort of people, only a wilderness that is somewhat pretty but rude'. The next year in April he took a party and enjoyed 'a new dish called Spanish olio', which was specially prepared for them in one of the eating booths. This mixture of meat and vegetables was so tasty that he asked the cook to keep it 'till night' when, after a walk, they returned 'to supper upon what was left at noon . . . and we mighty merry'.[10]

The merriment cannot have been very agreeable to the tenants of Goring House on the other side of the high brick wall. Battered by the troops who occupied it during the defence of London in the Civil War, and its gardens wrecked by the fortifications dug around it, the property had been abandoned by the Earl of Norwich, who, on his release from prison after the execution of Charles I, had gone into exile with his young King. Nevertheless Hugh Audley, a major creditor of Norwich and owner of the freehold, had kept an eye on the property and seen the fabric of the house decay. He undertook some repairs and refurbishments and by the Restoration Goring House appears to have been rented out for social events. Pepys took his wife there in July 1660 to 'a great wedding of Nan Hartlib to Mein Herr Roder, which was kept at Goring House with very great estate, cost and noble company'.[11]

Two years later, on 23 November 1662, Hugh Audley died, leaving, as Pepys recorded, 'a very great estate', which included the freehold of much of the present Palace site, except the Mulberry Garden. The Ebury estate went to one of his great-nephews, Alexander Davies, and after him to his daughter. All that is now remembered of the powerful lawyer and his heiress Mary Davies are the London streets named after them. (Mary married Sir Thomas Grosvenor in October 1677, and between them they founded the great property empire now belonging to the Duke of Westminster.)

After the Restoration, Norwich had returned from Holland and tried to regain possession of Goring House. Failing in this, he begged Charles

II at least to recognize the hurried, and unsealed, grant of the Mulberry Garden that his late lamented father had agreed in 1640. The King was about to compromise and grant him a lease of the garden when Mr Chipp appeared on the scene with his title, which had been bought in good faith. It is possible that Charles II welcomed an excuse not to part with such a useful parcel of land. George Goring, 1st Earl of Norwich, died at Brentford in January 1663. His son, the 2nd Earl of Norwich, continued the legal battle but the King announced he would retain the freehold and compensate anyone who could prove a right to it. No one could. Mr Chipp continued to run his 'entertainment' business, but now he paid rent to his landlord, the King. Charles II's decision to keep the freehold of the four-acre Mulberry Garden would later have important consequences.

On 29 March 1665, John Evelyn, then a civil servant, recorded in his diary, 'Went to Goring House, now Mr Secretary Bennett's, ill built . . . but the place capable of being made a pretty villa.'[12]

'Mr Secretary Bennett' had leased Goring House after his first attempt to buy it had failed, owing to the early death of Alexander Davies in the plague epidemic of 1665. The new owner was the young Mary Davies. Her inheritance was in trust, so selling any part of it was difficult. Bennett was to build on the site of Goring House, not a villa but a palatial mansion.

The Earl of Arlington and Arlington House

When Charles II and his courtiers returned after the Restoration they brought with them French taste in architecture, furnishings and landscape gardening. Influenced by the French King Louis XIV's great gardener, André Le Nôtre, Charles II redesigned St James's Park. Now the occupants of Goring House could look out over the forecourt to a long, straight canal bordered by shady avenues. Here the King played the game 'pall-mall' or wandered with his courtiers and yapping spaniels to inspect his aviaries in Birdcage Walk. St James's Park had ceased to be a hunting ground, and it was now the stage on which that most visible of kings could play his own distinctive royal role.

The new owner of Goring House, Mr Secretary Bennet, at this time was one of the wealthiest and most influential men at the Court of Charles II. Henry Bennet, later made Baron with the title Lord Arlington, was educated at Westminster School and studied theology at Christ Church, Oxford, where perhaps he acquired the pompous manner for which he was later mocked. He fought with Charles I in the Civil War, and was wounded. Afterwards he always wore a black patch on his nose, perhaps as a reminder to the King of his loyal cavalier service. He escaped to the Continent and made himself a master of languages and foreign affairs. In 1657 he was knighted by the exiled Prince and the next year was sent by Prince Charles as ambassador and agent to Madrid, where he remained until after the Restoration. There he made many useful contacts who were only too ready to pay him handsomely for his services as a Spanish agent.

When Charles II returned to the throne, Bennet turned to politics, becoming MP for Callington in Cornwall in 1661; the following year he became Secretary of State and a close adviser to Charles II. In 1665 the King created him Lord Arlington. In the same year he married a rich Dutch wife, Isabella de Broderode, who was the granddaughter of the illegitimate son of Prince Henry Frederick of Orange.

His power grew, and with it came immense wealth. As his influence grew, so did the hatred of his enemies. The 2nd Duke of Buckingham called him an 'arrant fop from head to toe'. But he was much more than that. The historian Thomas Babington Macaulay summed him up:

he had some talent for conversation and some for transacting ordinary business of office. He had learned during a life passed in travel and negotiating, the art of accommodating his language and deportment to the society in which he found himself. His vivacity in the closet amused the King; his gravity in debates and conferences imposed on the public, and he had succeeded in attaching to himself, partly by services, partly by hopes a considerable number of personal retainers.[13]

According to the Comte de Gramont, Arlington assumed to perfection the gravity and solemn mien of the Spaniards, a scar across the bridge of his nose, which he covered with a little lozenge shaped plaster, gave a secretive and mysterious air to his visage . . . he had an overwhelming anxiety to thrust himself forward which passed for industry . . . and an impenetrable stupidity which passed for the power to keep a secret.[14]

But in fact, as Macaulay judged, he had the art 'of observing the King's temper and managing it beyond the men of his time'.

Through his influence with the King, Arlington had secured the lease of Goring House and in 1677 a ninety-nine-year lease of the Mulberry Garden, which he later closed. The 'rascally whoring sort of place' was no fit neighbour for the King's Secretary of State.

In modern terms he was more than a millionaire but even so he was often in debt. His wife, Isabella, was as extravagant as her husband and soon filled Goring House with sumptuous furnishings, pictures and ornaments. Arlington's mansion was becoming a palace fit for the entertainment of a king, and grand enough to impress the great nobles and foreign ambassadors who came to consult him, and sometimes to pay him. 'Ambassadors using so noble a House with so much freedom, gives cause to conclude that they paid dear for it,' wrote the anonymous author of a tract in 1671.

Pepys, then a civil servant in the Admiralty, came to report to the minister at Goring House on 12 July 1666. Apparently Arlington was 'not up being not long since married, so after walking up and down the house, being the house I was once at at Hartlib's sister's wedding, and it is a very fine house and finely finished'.[15]

In 1667 Arlington acquired another vast mansion at Euston, near Newmarket, Suffolk, where he could entertain the King, his courtiers and mistresses during race meetings. On 23 June 1667 Pepys reported that a friend was 'concerned by my Lord Arlington in the looking after some buildings that he is about in Norfolk, where my Lord is laying out a great deal of money . . .'[16]

It was here that the King was to bring his new French mistress, Louise de Kéroualle, for a mock marriage.

In his two houses, Euston and Goring House, Arlington is said to have employed 1,000 servants. According to Pepys, there was 'nothing almost but bawdry at court from top to bottom': an ambitious man had to accommodate himself to the times. Even the upright Evelyn watched with fascination the King's frolics at Euston and Goring House. Arlington was, Pepys observed, the confidant of the King's 'pleasure and much in favour with one of the King's mistresses', Barbara Villiers, Countess of Castlemaine (later Duchess of Cleveland), the imperious beauty who dominated Charles II for many years. It was this close connection with both the King and his mistress that provided Arlington with his greatest political coup. On 1 August 1672 the King gave his natural son by the Countess of Castlemaine as husband to Arlington's only daughter and sole heir, Isabella. Isabella was only five years old at the time and her husband Henry Fitzroy, 1st Duke of Grafton, was nine, a rough, though handsome boy. Evelyn watched the marriage ceremony with concern and disapproval.

I was at the marriage of Lord Arlington's only daughter (a sweet child if ever there was any) to the Duke of Grafton, the King's natural son by the Duchess of Cleveland; the Archbishop of Canterbury officiating, the King and all the grandees being present. I had a favour given me by my Lady but took no great joy of the thing for many reasons.[17]

Seven years later, when Isabella had reached the age of consent, the marriage was confirmed. On 6 November 1679 Evelyn was

this evening at the remarriage of the Duchess of Grafton to the Duke ... she being now twelve years old. The ceremony was performed in my Lord Chamberlain's (her father's) lodgings at Whitehall by the Bishop of Rochester, His Majesty being present. A sudden and unexpected thing (when everybody believed the first marriage would have come to nothing) ... I was privately invited by my Lady her mother to be present. I confess I could give her little joy and so I plainly told her; but she said the King would have it so, and there was no going back: & this sweetest, hopefulest, most beautiful child, and most virtuous too, was sacrificed to a boy that had been rudely bred, without anything to encourage them but His Majesty's pleasure. I pray God the sweet child find it to her advantage who if my augury deceive me not will in a few years be such a paragon as were fit to make the wife of the greatest prince in Europe. I stayed supper where His Majesty sat between the Duchess of Cleveland (the incontinent mother of the Duke of Grafton) and the sweet Duchess the bride.

My love to Lord Arlington's family and the sweet child made me behold all this with regret. Though as the Duke of Grafton affects the sea, to which I find his father intends to use him, he may emerge a plain, useful, robust officer and were he polished, a tolerable person for he is exceeding handsome, by far surpassing any of the King's other natural issue.[18]

The Duke of Grafton did in fact turn out as Evelyn hoped. He had rough manners but had spirit and was a brave soldier. In the Monmouth rebellion of 1685 he fought for his uncle, James II, against the rebels near Bristol, distinguishing himself in that campaign. However, later on he deserted the Royal Stuart Standard, having fallen completely under the influence of John Churchill (later 1st Duke of Marlborough) and joined the army of William of Orange in Ireland. In 1690, on 29 September, he was wounded at the Battle of Cork and was carried home dying. He died on 9 October.

The Duchess of Grafton, too, fulfilled Evelyn's prophecy. On 26 October 1683 he went to see her 'lying in of her first child a son . . . she was become more beautiful if it were possible, than before and full of virtue and sweetness. She discoursed with me on many particulars, with great prudence and gravity beyond her years.'[19]

While her husband was at the wars, Isabella lived with her parents in Goring House, now one of the finest in London. Lady Arlington sent to Paris 'for the finest Venice brocatelle' to make hangings for an ante-room and covers for twelve chairs, bed curtains in green damask and coverings of the same stuff for a sofa.

On 17 April 1673 Evelyn visited Goring House and saw Lady Arlington's 'new dressing room with the glasses silver jars and vases cabinets and other, so rich furniture as I had seldom seen'. Evelyn also admired the paintings Arlington had acquired, and the

incomparable piece of Raphael's, being a Minister of State dictating to Guicciardini, the earnestness of whose face looking up in expectation of what he was next to write, is so to the life, and so natural, as I esteem it one of the choicest pieces of that admirable artist. There was a woman's head of Leonardo da Vinci: a Madonna of old Palma, and two of Vandyke's, of which one was his own picture at length, when young, in a leaning posture; the other an eunuch singing.[20]

But nemesis was waiting. Arlington had become too proud and powerful and his enemies now moved in to diminish him. On 15 January 1674 he was impeached for popery, with some justification. In addition to receiving bribes from the Spanish, his wife, so they said, was in the pay of the French. But the King could not afford to desert him: Arlington knew too much, so he was not convicted. He did, however, resign as Lord Chamberlain. To recover from the stressful months, he went to Bath. In September 1674, while he was away, his splendid house was totally destroyed by fire.

On 21 September 1674, Evelyn went to see

the great loss that Lord Arlington has sustained by fire at Goring House, this night consumed to the ground, with exceeding loss of hangings, plate, rare pictures and cabinets; hardly anything was saved of the best and most princely furniture that any subject had in England. My Lord and Lady were absent at Bath.[21]

Arlington, as tenacious as ever, retreated to his country estate at Euston, and meanwhile rebuilt Goring House more splendidly than before.

In 1677 Arlington was finally able to buy from the trustees of Hugh Audley's estate 'The ... mansion called Goring House lying near St James Park wall, and all that garden having therein a terrace walk, and a mount set with trees.' The mount was, presumably, part of the Civil War fortifications. There were also kitchen gardens 'lying beside the Highway leading to Chelsea [the site of today's Royal Mews], a great yard and pond enclosed with a brick wall and a flower garden'. In addition there was 'that Great Garden adjoining to the premises and enclosed round with a brick wall'.[22] The site of the old Mulberry Garden still belonged to the Crown.

Newly furnished after the great fire, Arlington House, as it was now called, was again a splendid mansion fit for the entertainment of great men of influence and the King himself. The new house had an additional advantage, one that would be of great importance in the future: Arlington realigned it so that, instead of facing south as the preceding houses had done, it now faced east, and his main rooms now looked over St James's Park towards the Palaces of St James, Whitehall and Westminster.

The poet John Dryden described Arlington House and gardens in ecstatic verse – a long Latin poem, translated into a florid jingle by a contemporary versifier. Arlington, a classical scholar, would have appreciated the subtle flattery of Dryden's Latin.

> Here wondering crowds admire the owner's state,
> And view the glories of the fair and great;
> Here falling statesmen Fortune's changes feel
> And prove the turns of her revolving wheel.

Arlington certainly lost political favour but he never lost the King's friendship. He retired from politics and enjoyed the delights of his house and garden.

John Evelyn, as Arlington's friend, adviser and man of taste, and who had seen the potential in Goring House, would certainly have had a hand in planning the new Arlington House. It was he who had discovered the woodcarver Grinling Gibbons at work in his cottage and had introduced him to Arlington and Charles II. Evelyn was also an expert on arboriculture and would have advised Arlington on the planning of the gardens at Arlington House, as he did at Euston.

The gardens were idyllic. Dryden described them in verse which reads better in his Latin than in translation.

> Here watch the fearful deer their tender fawns
> Stray through the wood, or browse the verdant lawns.
> Here from the marshy glade the wild duck springs
> And slowly moves her wet, incumber'd wings.

Charles II, his courtiers and his ladies were frequent visitors, strolling round the parterres filled with

> A thousand flowers of various form and hue.
> There spotless lilies rear their sickly heads,
> And purple violets creep along the beds;
> Here shews the bright jonquil its gilded face,
> Join'd with the pale carnation's fairer grace;

> The painted tulip and the blushing rose
> A blooming wilderness of sweets compose.

The wilderness and the maze were haunted by nightingales whose descendants would enchant George III and his young Queen. In fact this idyllic setting was one of the main reasons for George III's choice of a home.

Here at Arlington House Charles II held secret political meetings, met his natural son, the Duke of Monmouth, or bargained with his opponents in support of his brother, James.

Dryden's sycophantic hymn of praise concluded:

> Here, Arlington, thy mighty mind disdains
> Inferior earth, and breaks its servile chains,
> Aloft on Contemplation's wings you rise,
> Scorn all below, and mingle with the skies.

It went on to describe how this paragon among politicians, having resisted the calls of Glory and Ambition, received Jove's final accolade:

> Thy only daughter, Britain's boasted grace,
> Join'd with a hero of the royal race;
> And that fair fabrick which our wondering eyes
> So lately saw from humble ruins rise,
> And mock the rage of the devouring flame!
> A nobler structure, and a fairer frame!
> Whose beauties long shall charm succeeding days,
> And tell posterity the founder's praise.

Venus blessed 'the united happy pair':

> The aweful father gave the gracious sign,
> And fix'd the fortunes of the glorious line.[23]

Nothing gave Arlington more pride in his last years than the thought of his 'glorious line' continuing through the ages in his splendid new mansion at the end of the Mall.

At the end of his life Arlington possessed a fine mansion with groves and bowling greens, a 'Dwarf tree garden . . . the very extensive orange houses with the Bagnio, Bathing cisterns and the like'. There were stables for at least thirty horses, and offices for a large retinue of servants. 'There were 8 rooms on the ground floor besides the Chapel', whose seats were lined with purple velvet and the floor was made of black and white marble. On the first floor were six rooms and a 'long gallery of nine sash windows towards the Park . . . a chimney piece of blue marble . . . fifteen pictures at full length with gilt frames'. Here Arlington spent his retirement, looking out over the newly planned gardens of St James's, and admiring his paintings as he walked up and down his long gallery, where at the end 'was a small frame of olive wood with holes and pins for the exact computation of walking a mile'.[24]

On 6 February 1685, Charles II died, and in July Arlington followed his master. Both had concealed to the end their true faith. When death approached, Arlington, like his King, recognized that the time of dissimulation was over and sent for a Roman Catholic priest.

Apart from making provision for his wife, Arlington left his entire estate to his son-in-law, the Duke of Grafton, and his daughter, Isabella, who also inherited his title. After her husband's death, she retired with her seven-year-old son, Charles, now 2nd Duke of Grafton, to their mansion at Euston and let Arlington House to the Duke of Devonshire. He took little care of the property and once again it was damaged by fire. On 14 October 1694 Isabella took as her second husband Sir Thomas Hanmer. Trustees took care of the young Duke's inheritance. The next tenant of Arlington House was John Sheffield, Earl of Mulgrave and Marquess of Normanby, who in 1703 was to become the Duke of Buckingham. In 1702 the Trustees granted him permission to buy the house and gardens, but it took two years to disentangle the legal ownership of the estate, since the Mulberry Garden was still Crown property.

Isabella lived until 1722 – long enough to see a new magnificent mansion, Buckingham House, rise on the ruins of her old home.

So the present Buckingham Palace was named, not after the ambitious Arlington, nor even the enchanting Duchess of Grafton. That honour was reserved for one who, like Arlington, had royal connections. In 1705 the Duke of Buckingham married the formidable Katherine, widow of the Earl of Anglesey and natural daughter of James II. Throughout the next centuries, however, the Grafton family was to remain close to the Court. Today the Queen's Mistress of Robes is the Duchess of Grafton.

The Duke and Duchess of Buckingham at Buckingham House

The Duke of Buckingham was born John Sheffield, in 1647, the son of the 2nd Earl of Mulgrave, to which title he succeeded at the age of ten. William III created him Marquess of Normanby in 1694; and in 1703 Queen Anne made him Duke of Normanby and then Duke of Buckingham. Until 1703 he was generally known as Mulgrave.

Like the Duke of Grafton, he was one of the young courtiers whom Charles II made captains of ships and commanders of army troops – a practice which infuriated the regular sailors and soldiers, as civil servants like Pepys and Evelyn reported. Macaulay cites Mulgrave as an example:

any lad of noble birth, any dissolute courtier, for whom one of the king's mistresses would speak a word, might hope [for] a ship of the line . . . If in the interval of feasting, drinking and gambling, he succeeded in learning the names of the points of the compass, he was thought fully qualified to take charge of a three decker. In 1666, John Sheffield, Earl of Mulgrave, at seventeen years of age, volunteered to serve at sea against the Dutch. He passed six weeks on board, diverting himself [with] young libertines of rank and then returned home to take command of a troop of horse. After this he was never on the water till the year 1672 when he was appointed Captain of a ship of 84 guns, reputed the finest in the navy. He was then 23 years old . . . As soon as he came back from sea, he was made Colonel of a regiment of foot.[25]

Though Mulgrave was a typical Restoration rake, he had ability and immense self-confidence and charm. In 1673 Charles II made him a Gentleman of the Bedchamber and he was already earning himself the nickname 'Lord Allpride'. His levees were held with all the panache of the Restoration Court and were attended by courtiers and ambassadors from home and abroad.

It was this overweening pride that for a while brought him down. He had the temerity to woo, and perhaps to win, Princess Anne, daughter of the King's brother, the Duke of York, later to be James II. For his presumption, Charles II banished him, but later reinstated him and in 1685 he had followed the late Lord Arlington as Lord Chamberlain and was living as a tenant in Arlington House.

Even his enemies acknowledged him to be a man of distinction. 'In parliamentary eloquence,' as Macaulay wrote, he was 'inferior to scarcely any orator of his time'.[26] As a writer and poet he was praised and imitated by Pope and Dryden. As a collector of fine paintings he had the advice and approval of John Evelyn.

After Charles II's death his political power grew. Although, unlike Arlington, he had no real belief in Roman Catholicism, he won James II's approval and was seen attending him to Mass. In 1679 Charles II made him Lord Lieutenant of the East Riding of Yorkshire and he became the leader of the Tory party in the Lords.

When William of Orange landed, Mulgrave attempted to hold the line for James II by keeping the Lords in session; but finally he voted for William of Orange and his wife Mary. Like Grafton, he was one of the first to take the oath of allegiance: while Grafton carried the King's crown at the Coronation of William III and Queen Mary, Mulgrave carried the Queen's. But unlike Grafton he did not leap into battle on William's behalf. The new King had to win his support and William was shrewd enough to bribe him. In 1694 he made Mulgrave a Privy Councillor with a pension of £3,000 a year – though he did not in fact consult him. But there were limits to Mulgrave's flexibility. He retained some loyalty to the 'King over the water' and refused to support William III's attack on Jacobites. William III, who also had his limits, therefore dismissed him as a Privy Councillor.

However, when Queen Anne came to the throne in 1702, she showed that she had not forgotten her former lover. One of her first acts was to create Mulgrave Lord Privy Seal and in 1703 she made him Duke of the county of Buckingham and Normanby. But the Whig influence was growing, and as a leading Tory Buckingham, as we must now call Mulgrave, was increasingly unpopular. The Crown no longer had its old power: Queen Anne could not protect him and in 1705 he lost all his appointments.

Now all his ambition and considerable talents were centred on the new house which was rising from the rubble of Arlington House and which he renamed Buckingham House. In 1705 he took a new wife – his third – who was to make him even more ambitious. He had failed to win the hand of Anne, James II's legitimate daughter by his wife Anne Hyde; but now he married Katherine (the divorced wife of the Earl of Anglesey), James's natural daughter by his mistress, the plain but clever Catherine Sedley (created Countess of Dorchester), whose wit was inherited from her father, the brilliant and licentious Sir Charles Sedley, the author of the Restoration comedy *The Mulberry Garden*.

The new 'Lord Allpride' had met his match. The new Duchess of Buckingham had fire and brilliance in her blood through her mother's side as well as the royal blood of which she was inordinately proud. She was a fanatical Jacobite: every year on the anniversary of Charles I's execution, she and her whole court went into the deepest mourning. Buckingham House was to become the centre of Jacobite intrigue until her death, and Birdcage Walk became known as 'Jacobite Walk'.

Buckingham House, in her eyes, was to be an alternative palace to outshine the dingy St James's Palace along the Mall. What Queen Anne thought as she saw her former lover's magnificent new home rising from the ashes of Arlington House is not known. But she was gracious enough to receive the new Duchess and, even more important, she gave Buckingham verbal permission to take a strip of St James's Park to improve his entrance.

The new house was built not on the old foundations but close to them – nearer to Green Park – and partly on the Mulberry Garden, whose leasehold still had seventy years to run. It faced east, overlooking St James's Park, and Buckingham saw that, with the extra land and new alignment, it would appear that St James's Park was part of his estate. In fact, he took over an acre of extra land from St James's Park and the common highway, and pulled down the entrance lodge to the Park and a length of wall in order to give him a spacious forecourt and carry the road round his enclosure. The total acreage of his estate was now '1 Rood 6 Perches' (thirty-three acres). Queen Anne was furious at his presumption but did nothing about it.

One of the architects employed was Captain Winde. An old soldier, elderly at this time, a man of some mettle, he was said to have taken the Duke to the roof of Buckingham House to admire the view and then threatened to throw himself – and the Duke – off the roof if he was not paid. Buckingham paid.

Begun in 1705 and finished three years later, Buckingham House was described as a

graceful palace, very commodiously situated at the westerly end of St James's Park, having at one view a prospect of the Mall & other walks, and of a delightful and spacious canal; a seat not to be condemned by the greatest monarch. It consists of a mansion house, & at some distance from each end of that, conjoined by two arching galleries, are the lodging rooms for servants on the south side of the court, & opposite, on the north side the kitchen & laundry.

The walls were brick with two ranges of pillars, of the Corinthian and Tuscan orders.

Above these

an acroteria of figures, standing erect and fronting the court: they appear as big as life and look noble. Mercury . . . Secrecy . . . Equity . . . Liberty . . . Truth holding the sun in his right hand and treading on a globe and Apollo with his lyre.

On the west face were 'Spring, Summer, Autumn and Winter'. There were four Latin inscriptions in 'capital gold characters: *Sic situ laetantur lares; Rus in urbe; Spectator fastidiosus sibi molestus;* and *lente suscipe, cito perfice*'.[27]*

---

*The Latin may be translated as: the household gods delight in such a situation; the country in the town; the too fastidious critic harms chiefly himself; and be slow to undertake an obligation, and quick to discharge it.

On its easterly side, facing the Park, was a spacious court, enclosed by a wall and a beautiful iron gate with the Duke's coronet exquisitely represented in wrought iron. It was a place to satisfy even the proud Duchess.

Eccentric the Duchess may have been, but she managed her difficult husband well. In a letter to the Duke of Shrewsbury, he described his contented life at Buckingham House:

I rise now in summer, about seven o'clock in a very large bedchamber (entirely quiet, high and free from the early sun) to walk in the garden or, if raining in a Salon filled with pictures, some good, but none disagreeable; There also, in a row above them, I have so many portraits of famous persons . . . as are enough to excite ambition in any man less lazy, or less at ease, than myself.

He loved the garden, not because it had any 'vanities' but because of the situation: 'the noblest that can be, presenting at once to view a vast Town, a Palace & a magnificent Cathedral'. He took some exercise to make himself

fitter for either business or pleasure . . . I see you smile, but I confess myself so changed . . . as to my former enchanting delights, that the company I commonly find at home is agreeable enough to make me conclude the evening on a delightful Terrace.

'Only one thing I forgot,' he concluded,

though of more satisfaction to me than all the rest . . . and 'tis the little closet of books at the end of that green house which joins the best apartment, which besides their being so very near, are ranked in such a method, that by its mark a very Irish footman may fetch any book I want.

Under the windows 'is a little wilderness full of blackbirds and nightingales'.[28]

It is the best description of the Buckingham House that George III was to buy.

Buckingham's political ambition faded, although when the Tories returned to power in 1710, he was made Lord President of the Council and reinstated as a Privy Councillor. When Queen Anne died in 1714, however, he was removed from all his posts.

He died at Buckingham House on 24 February 1721, and was outlived by the Duchess for twenty-two years, during which time she became more 'fantastical' than ever.

She arranged a pompous funeral and a tomb in Westminster Abbey for him, preparing her own wax effigy which she wanted to be placed by his side. After his death, the Duchess made some alterations to Buckingham House, but it was still grand enough to attract George III's grandfather when he was Prince of Wales. The Duchess, however, demanded too high a price, so he neither bought nor rented it.

In a letter to a Mrs Howard, the Duchess named the amount of purchase-money which she required for the property:

If their Royal Highnesses will have everything stand as it does, furniture and pictures, I will have £3,000 per annum, both run hazard of being spoiled, and the last, to be sure, will be all to be new bought whenever my son is of age. The quantity the rooms take cannot be well furnished under £10,000; but if their Highnesses will permit the pictures all to be removed, and buy the furniture as it will be valued by different people, the house shall go at £2,000 – If the Prince and Princess prefer the buying outright, under £60,000 it will not be parted with as it now stands, and all His Majesty's revenue cannot purchase a place so fit for them nor for a less sum – The Princess asked me at the drawing room if I would sell my fine house. I answered her smiling, that I was under no necessity to part with it; yet, when what I thought was the value of it should be offered, perhaps my prudence might overcome my inclination.[29]

In 1735, when she took her ailing son to Rome, she caused a sensation by demanding to be treated in France and Rome as royalty. The nineteen-year-old boy, the second legitimate offspring of the Duke of Buckingham, died in Rome in October 1735.

Walpole saw her in December 1741: 'The Duchess of Buckingham, who is more mad with pride than any mercer's wife in Bedlam, came the other night to the opera "en princesse", literally in robes, red velvet and ermine.'[30]

On 14 March, Walpole gossiped 'Princess Buckingham is dead or dying ...' The diarist Lord Hervey wrote spitefully of 'cette folle la Duchesse de Buckingham'. Obviously Hervey did not know that she had left Buckingham House to him in her will. However, he did not live long enough to enjoy it: he died a few months after the Duchess.

The Duchess was determined to be remembered in death as in life. As she lay dying, she sent for the funeral ceremony to check it and insisted that her staff should remain standing 'until she was quite dead'. She must have approved the eulogy written about her before her death by her friend the poet Alexander Pope. When her husband died he wrote, 'It seemed as tho' his spirit was breathed into her to fulfil what he had begun to perform.'[31]

Since there was no legitimate heir to the Buckingham estate, between £3,000 and £4,000 per annum of it went to the Crown, and the rest to Charles Herbert, the Duke's natural son by a Mrs Lambert, on condition that he took the name of Sheffield; he was made a Baronet in 1755. Clearly he could not cope with so grand an inheritance: in 1754 he tried to sell Buckingham House to the trustees of the British Museum, who were looking for a new home. His letter suggests that he had not inherited his father's literary ability.

My Lord
In persuance to your commands I have considered what value to put upon my House, Gardens and Fields for which I hope if it should suit Sr Hans Sloane's Trustees they wont think Thirty Thousand Pounds to [sic] much; it having cost the old Duke twice that Sum but Fifty years ago and Mr Timbill [?] the Builder who was always reckoned an Honest able Man in his Profession valued it at more than [I ask] four years ago, since when I have layd out several Hundred Pounds in Repairing and Adorning it and I am with great Respect
    Your Lordship's
        Most obedient
            And humble servt
                [?] Sheffield

The trustees, however, turned down his offer.

That the said Committee to the Number of 15 having met on the 16th Feb^ry at Northumberland House, thought proper to waive any particular consideration of the proposal made of such Buckingham House, on the General one of the Greatness of the Sum demanded for it, the inconvenience of the situation, and other circumstances, therefore proceeded to the other offer of Montagu House . . .[32]

The trustees therefore decided to purchase Montagu House in Bloomsbury, on the site of the museum today.

Eventually in 1761 Sheffield accepted George III's offer of £28,000.* And so at last the house at the end of the Mall became the home of the royal family.

---

*The negotiations for the sale took some months. Arlington and the Duke of Buckingham had incorporated the old Mulberry Garden into their estate. These four acres were Crown Property and it took some time to establish the boundaries. Arlington had never acquired the freehold: when his hundred years lease expired, this land would return to the Crown. Realising that this would make the sale more difficult, Sheffield agreed a reasonable price.

CHAPTER TWO

George III and Queen Charlotte

'Rus in urbe'
[the country in the town]

Inscription around the roof of the
Duke of Buckingham's house [1]

'The Queen's House'

On the morning of 25 October 1760, George II died at his palace at Kensington. He had outlived his wife, Caroline of Anspach, and his son Frederick, Prince of Wales, who had died nine years earlier. So it was his grandson, Prince George, who, at the age of twenty-two, became King. The young man, idealistic and dedicated, was determined to make a clean break with his predecessors. George I and George II had remained solidly German, spoke little English and were happy in Hanover at their palace of Herrenhausen. For them, possession of the English throne meant an extension of their military power in Europe. On the whole they were content to leave the running of the English government to their ministers. Both kings were openly immoral in their domestic lives. George I had divorced his wife and locked her away for life in a remote German castle, and consoled himself with his plain German mistresses. George II married a clever wife, who accepted her husband's infidelities and led her own interesting life in her dower house, Leicester House, where she entertained writers, painters and politicians, and at Richmond.

The new King had never known his grandmother, Caroline, but the echoes of violent family rows had reverberated through his childhood, as his father Frederick, Prince of Wales, had been detested with a paranoiac bitterness by both his own parents. He had been brought up

28

by his mother, Augusta, dowager Princess of Wales, who had come from Germany as a young bride and had also suffered the hatred of the King and Queen. He had been tutored by a serious-minded Scot, John Stuart, 3rd Earl of Bute, his counsellor and 'dearest friend'.

George III was to make a double break with the past. First, unlike his grandfather and great-grandfather, he was proud to consider himself British. He spoke German fluently and looked Hanoverian, being tall, well built and fair-haired, but he was rooted in England. In fact, although being Elector of Hanover, he never visited his German kingdom. Second, there would be no mistresses in George III's palace.

Among the many problems that faced the young King at the beginning of his reign there were two personal concerns to be dealt with: he had to choose a wife and a home.

The young King was handsome and virile but he had reached the age of twenty-two without attracting scandal – a remarkable feat at that time. His mother had kept a watchful eye on him and Bute, who was himself happily married, regarded it as his duty to guide the King not only politically but also in his domestic life. He became George III's chief minister and he steered him away from what he considered would be an unfortunate marriage. So the King regretfully resisted the temptation to propose to a delectable young woman, Lady Sarah Lennox, in favour of a traditional dynastic marriage with a foreign princess.

Royal marriages were affairs of state, arranged to establish alliances and suit the political needs of the time. So many a young bride left her country to live 'amid the alien corn'. If they were lucky they spoke the language of their new home or could bring some of their own people with them.

George III's mother, a princess of Saxe-Gotha, had come to England as a girl of sixteen still clutching her doll. James I had married Anne of Denmark; his son Charles I had strengthened his relations with France by marrying Henrietta Maria, daughter of Henry IV. Charles II had married Catherine of Braganza; his brother James took as his second wife Mary of Modena. Dutch William of Orange married James II's elder daughter, Princess Mary, and his younger daughter, Princess Anne, had married George of Denmark. The Hanoverians looked to

Germany for their wives and mistresses. So an international network spread, each marriage bringing different traditions to the palaces of Britain.

Prince George's mother and grandfather had argued over the merits of princesses from different families in the small states that constituted what is now modern Germany. In 1761 George was to choose for himself. Guided by Lord Bute and with the advice of the Hanoverian minister in London, Baron Philip Adolphus von Munchhausen, he considered the list of possible candidates among the German Protestant princesses. No Roman Catholic could be considered. One by one the princesses were rejected, some, like the princesses of Anhalt Dessau, because of a reputation for 'galanterie'. Princess Augusta's favourite, her niece Princess Frederica of Saxe-Gotha, was said to be marked by smallpox and deformed. Princess Philippina of Brandenburg-Schwedt was opinionated and unattractive; Princess Caroline of Hesse-Darmstadt had a foul temper. Finally the choice fell on seventeen-year-old Princess Sophie Charlotte of Mecklenburg-Strelitz. In the royal European network she was his third cousin. Further enquiries were made and it was reported that she was healthy, pleasant, with '*le meilleur coeur du monde*'. No one claimed that she was a beauty, but she played the harpsichord well and sang and danced '*à la merveille*'. She spoke no English but had some French and had received a plain education in the Protestant convent at Herford, Westphalia. Bute now sent his friend and fellow Scot, Colonel David Graeme, to make a final assessment and to arrange the marriage. The colonel was charmed by the girl, who 'fixed the love and esteem of everyone who is acquainted with her'.

Princess Charlotte's father, the Duke of Mecklenburg-Strelitz, had died eleven years earlier and had been succeeded by her brother Charles. When Graeme arrived at the little castle in the remote north German dukedom, the family were in great distress. Princess Charlotte's mother was dying, but in her last conscious moments she was able to give her consent. The Princess's agreement was taken for granted. It was not every day that a proposal from the King of England dropped from the skies.

The King now moved 'in a great hurry' with a characteristic impatience. On 8 July he called a Privy Council and informed them of his decision; emphasizing the fact that Charlotte's family had shown the firmest zeal for the Protestant religion.

Since his Coronation had already been planned for 22 September, he was relieved that Duke Charles did not allow his mother's death to delay the marriage long. On 16 August Princess Charlotte presided over a farewell banquet in the Palace of Neustrelitz. Those who had feared that Princess Charlotte, in her inexperience, would be unable to uphold the dignity of her new status were surprised to see her easy composure. The next day she set off on a rugged journey and storm-tossed crossing that would test her endurance further. It was not until Monday 7 September that she landed at Harwich, rested a night at Lord Abercorn's house at Witham and then was rushed with a splendid cavalcade through crowded London streets to be received at the garden gate of St James's Palace by the King and royal family. She was to be married at ten o'clock that same night.

On the night of her arrival the King took Princess Charlotte to see an Aladdin's cave of fabulous jewels, among them those she was to wear at the marriage ceremony, 'a stomacher of diamonds, worth three score thousand pounds'; 'a little cap of purple velvet quite covered with diamonds, a Diamond aigrette in form of a Crown, 3 dropped diamond ear rings & Diamond necklace'. George II had bequeathed the Hanoverian jewellery to be shared between George III and his brother, the Duke of Cumberland, and the King had bought the Duke's share.

So, arrayed in a gown of white and silver, weighed down on a stifling hot night by 'an endless mantle of violet coloured velvet, lined with ermine, fastened on the shoulder by a bunch of large pearls' and accompanied by ten bridesmaids glittering in gowns of white silk embroidered with diamonds, Princess Charlotte was led by the King's brothers, the Duke of York and Prince William, later Duke of Gloucester, to meet her bridegroom, a handsome figure in 'a stuff of a new manufacture, the ground silver with embossed plate and frosted silver'.[2]

She had come through three disturbing months, during which she had endured with astonishing equanimity the death of her mother, her farewell to her home, her stormy voyage and now the glittering Court at the Palace of St James. Not surprisingly she trembled on her arrival. '*You* may laugh,' she whispered to the Duchess of Hamilton, one of her Ladies of the Bedchamber; 'you have been married twice; but it is no joke to me.'

Even that well-informed old gossip Horace Walpole was impressed. In a letter to his friend, the British Envoy at Florence, he praised her good sense and charm.

Is this bad proof of her sense? On the journey they wanted to curl her toupet. 'No, indeed,' said she, 'I think it looks as well as those of the ladies that have been sent for me: if the King would have me wear a periwig, I will; otherwise I shall let myself alone.' The Duke of York gave her his hand at the garden-gate: her lips trembled, but she jumped out with spirit. In the garden the King met her; she would have fallen at his feet; he prevented and embraced her, and led her into the apartments, where she was received by the Princess of Wales and Lady Augusta: these three Princesses only dined with the King. At ten the procession went to chapel, preceded by unmarried daughters of peers, peers, and peeresses in plenty. The new Princess was led by the Duke of York and Prince William; the Archbishop married them; the King talked to her the whole time with great good humour, and the Duke of Cumberland gave her away. She is not tall, nor a beauty; pale, and very thin; but looks sensible, and is genteel. Her hair is darkish and fine; her forehead low, her nose very well, except the nostrils spreading too wide; her mouth has the same fault, but her teeth are good. She talks a good deal, and French tolerably; possesses herself, is frank, but with great respect to the King. After the ceremony, the whole company came into the drawing-room for about ten minutes, but nobody was presented that night.[3]

In three short months Charlotte had been transformed from a quiet and plain princess of an obscure and remote German dukedom to be Queen of England, with her own two dower houses, Somerset House in London and the White House at Kew.

She had an immense household of her own. The Duke of Manchester was her Lord Chamberlain, the Duchess of Ancaster her Mistress of the Robes. She had

two vice-Chamberlains, two Gentleman Ushers of the Privy Chamber, three gentleman ushers daily waiters, three gentleman ushers quarterly waiters, two pages of the Presence Chamber, four pages of the backstairs, physicians, surgeons and apothecaries, 'an operator for the teeth', six Ladies of the Bedchamber, six Maids of Honour and six Women of the Bedchamber.[4]

Her 'mistress laundress, sempstress & starcher' was an elderly daughter of a nobleman.

Since Queen Charlotte spoke no English, it was with great relief that she turned to the two ladies she had brought from Germany, the ferocious Elizabeth Schwellenberg and Louisa Hagedorn. Although the King had discouraged the introduction of foreign attendants, he did allow her to bring one of her household, Frederick Albert. This highly intelligent and cultured man was to remain her faithful servant for the rest of his life.

It was an exceptionally happy marriage, for which the King thanked his 'dearest friend' Bute most effusively. Now it was Queen Charlotte who took his old mentor's place. After a brief, unsuccessful spell as the King's Prime Minister, Bute retired and the Queen gave the King the warm companionship that his affectionate nature demanded. Years later, during the black period of his ill health, he could say, 'The Queen is my best friend.' And though, when illness loosened his tongue, he revealed a suppressed lust for Lady Pembroke, whom he called Queen Esther, he remained steadfastly faithful and doting.

The King's choice of a palace was equally happy – at least for the first years. There were a number of alternatives. There had been, in the past, plans to build a new palace in St James's Park – one architect even suggesting diverting the canals around Buckingham House so that there could be a ceremonial water approach. The old Whitehall Palace on the Thames had been destroyed by fire in 1698, and only the Banqueting House remained, and it could have been rebuilt; Somerset House on the Strand, with a superb terrace overlooking the Thames, the traditional dower house for royal consorts, could have been enlarged. As a bachelor the King had lived at Savile House next door to his mother's mansion in Leicester Square, and his father, when Prince of Wales, had also bought Carlton House in London. Then there was Hampton Court, beloved of William III and Queen Mary, but George III, it was said, had never forgotten unhappy times there when his grandfather, George

II, had boxed his ears. Windsor Castle was not in good condition at this time, as a visitor reported on 16 August 1766: 'the castle furniture was old and dirty, most of the best pictures removed to the Queen's Palace and the whole kept so very unneat that it hurts one to see almost the only place in England worthy to be styled our King's Palace, so totally neglected'.[5]

The same was said of the official London royal residence, St James's Palace, which George III disliked intensely: he said it was a 'dust trap', and 'too near the road'. And there were so many disturbing echoes from the past: those 'leper maydens', the tragic Anne Boleyn whose initials were still there, entwined with Henry VIII's in the brickwork. From here Charles I had taken his last walk through the park to his execution in Whitehall. The Palace had been neglected since the death of his grandmother, Queen Caroline; the room in which she had died was still untouched, the dead wood still in the grate. George II's mistress, the Hanoverian Countess Walmoden, still lived in the room next to the old King's. This was no home for a young bride.

But it had to serve for the first year. The King pensioned off the Countess, turned her room into his library and refurbished a suite of rooms for Queen Charlotte in delicate blue and white. Their first child, Prince George – later George IV – was born at St James's Palace (Prince Alfred, their youngest son, and Princess Amelia were born at Windsor, but the rest of their fifteen children were to be born at Buckingham House). Henceforward St James's Palace was used for official entertaining – for the levees and drawing rooms that were regular features of Court life. Foreign ambassadors are still today accredited to the Court of St James.

Then the King gave all his attention to their new home, the elegant, red-brick Buckingham House at the end of the Mall. He wanted a new home away from his official residence. Buckingham House, he hoped, would be his retreat, his *'rus in urbe'*, where he could live the life he really wanted – that of a cultured gentleman with books, paintings, music and gardens, amid a large, happy family.

In the first two years of their marriage the King and Queen slipped away as often as possible to supervise the refurbishment of Buckingham House, or 'the Queen's House', as it was now called. Horace Walpole wrote to a friend: 'The King & Queen are settled for good & all at Buckingham House: and are stripping the other palaces to furnish it . . . they have already fetched pictures from Hampton Court, which indicates their never living there.'⁶

When George III bought Buckingham House it was much as it had been left by the Duchess of Buckingham. Contemporary illustrations show the elegance of the entrance to the red-brick house. As Buckingham had described:

The Avenues to the house are along St James's Park, through rows of goodly elms on one hand and gay flourishing limes on the other, that for coaches, this for walking; with the Mall lying between them. This reaches to my iron palisade that encompasses a square court, which has in its midst a great basin with statues and water works.

Two wings enclosed the courtyard, which joined the house by corridors supported on Ionic pillars. These wings were for kitchens and storehouses with rooms above for servants. 'On top of all a leaden cistern holding fifty tuns of water, driven up by an engine from the Thames, supplies all the waterworks in the courts and gardens, which lie quite round the house . . .' The roof of the house, 'which being covered with smooth mill'd lead, and defended by a parapet of ballusters . . . entertains the eye with a far distant prospect of hills and dales, and a near one of parks and gardens'.

It was this rural site that Dryden had praised and that so attracted the King. The gardens at the rear were as the Duke had left them: formal in the French manner, with avenues and arbors and a long canal bordered by limes. At the rear of the garden was a terrace,

400 paces long, with a large Semicircle in the middle, from whence are beheld the Queen's two parks, and a great part of Surry; then going down a few steps you walk on the banks of a canal 600 yards long and 17 broad, with two rows of Limes on each side.

On one side of this Terrace a Wall covered with Roses and Jassemines [sic] is made low to admit the view of a meadow full of cattle just under it, (no disagreeable object in the midst of a great city) and at each end a descent into parterres with fountains and water-works.

Inside all was magnificence. From the courtyard, as the Duke of Buckingham had written,

we mount to a Terrace in the front of a large Hall, paved with square white stones mixed with dark-coloured marble, the walls thereof covered with a sett of pictures done in the school of Raphael. Out of this, on the right hand, we go into a parlour 33 foot by 39, with a niche 15 foot broad for a Buvette, paved with white marble, and placed within an arch, with pilasters of divers colours, the upper part of which as high as the ceiling is painted by Ricci.

From hence we pass through a suite of large rooms, into a bedchamber of 34 foot by 27, within it a large closet which opens out into a green-house.

The King was to take the ground floor for himself, giving Queen Charlotte the whole of the first floor. As the Duke described, it was reached by

eight and forty steps, ten foot broad, each step of one entire Portland stone. These stairs, by the help of two resting places are so very easy there is no need of leaning on the iron balluster. The walls are painted with the story of Dido.

The roof of this staircase, which is 55 foot from the ground, is of 40 foot by 36, filled with the figures of Gods and Goddesses. In the midst is Juno, condescending to beg assistance from Venus, to bring about a marriage which the Fates intended should be the ruin of her own darling Queen and People . . .

From a wide landing place on the stair head, great double doors opened into a succession of rooms, some overlooking the gardens at the rear with a distant view of Chelsea fields, others with a splendid view from the front of St James's Park, the Banqueting House and Westminster Abbey.

The first room on this floor has within it a closet of original pictures [the Duke of Buckingham's], which as yet are not so entertaining as the delightful prospect from the window. Out of the second room a pair of great doors give entrance into the Saloon, which is 35 foot high, 36 broad and 45 long. In the midst of its roof a round picture by Gentileschi, 18 foot in diameter, represents the Muses playing in concert to Apollo, lying along a cloud to hear them. The rest of the room is adorned with paintings relating to the Arts and Sciences; and underneath divers original pictures hang all in good lights, by the help of an upper row of windows which drown the glaring.

Above were rooms for children and servants, 'the floors so contrived', wrote the Duke, 'as to prevent all noise over my wife's head'.[7]

The King had chosen well. The site alone was well worth the £28,000 he had paid and was to be one of the main attractions of Buckingham Palace in years to come. Though George III was to alter and rebuild, the core of Buckingham Palace today is the Duke of Buckingham's house.

Unfortunately Buckingham House had never been designed for a large family, each with a household of its own – as Queen Victoria would later discover. Year after year, Queen Charlotte produced another prince or princess with astonishing ease, and before long she and the King would go further afield for their country air, to Kew and Richmond and later to Windsor.

'The Apollo of the Arts'

Now, though, with great enthusiasm, the King began furnishing and rebuilding his new house. Though he was young, he had been unusually well prepared for this work. His parents had encouraged his love of the arts. His father, the much-maligned Frederick, Prince of Wales, had been a discriminating collector. His mother, Augusta, Princess of Wales, an intelligent and cultured woman, had helped to create the pleasure gardens at Kew, and had supervised the rebuilding of Carlton House, which stood on the Mall on the site now occupied by the Athenaeum Club, the Institute of Directors and the road between them, and which Prince Frederick had bought in 1732.

As tutor Lord Bute was to have a profound effect on George III and a lasting effect on Buckingham Palace itself. Introduced to Prince Frederick in 1747, Bute, a dedicated botanist, was appointed to supervise the gardens at Kew; later he was to encourage Queen Charlotte in her serious botanical studies. As tutor to Prince George from 1755, he gave him a lasting love not only of the arts, music and literature but also of science. He made sure that Prince George was prepared for kingship, inspiring him with a high idealism. Bute has often been criticized for his lack of political judgement, and his profound influence on the intelligent King has been underestimated.

Bute brought to George III men of talent whose influence would be lasting. Many of them were Scots, such as Thomas Coutts, the banker of Coutts & Co., who are still the royal bankers; and Allan Ramsay, who became the King's official artist. Robert Adam was to be one of the two architects appointed to rebuild the Queen's House. Sir William Chambers, the other appointment, was even more important: some of his work can still be seen today in Buckingham Palace.

William Chambers was born in Sweden to parents of Scottish descent who, like many seventeenth-century Scots, had emigrated to Sweden. After his education at Ripon in England, he began a career in the Swedish East India Company. On their behalf he visited India, journeyed to China several times and developed a profound interest in Chinese culture and gardens, and particularly in their art and architecture. This inspired him to change his career. He studied architecture in Paris, and spent some years in Italy, meeting Robert Adam in Rome. He was not impressed by the cocky young Scot: he found his work superficial and too pretty for his own strongly classical taste. When he returned to England his unusual knowledge of Chinese architecture and gardening brought him to the attention of Lord Bute. In 1757, Princess Augusta appointed Chambers as tutor in architecture to George, who, after the death of his father in 1751, had become Prince of Wales.

An inspiring tutor and a congenial companion, Chambers shared Prince George's taste for classical simplicity. He taught him for three mornings a week and gave him a lifelong love of architecture, which was to be his favourite hobby. In later years his disturbed mind was often quietened by the discipline of making architectural drawings or planning castles in the air.

When Prince George became King he appointed Chambers as his architect for work on the Queen's House, with Robert Adam as his colleague. In the event, Adam made little contribution to the Palace, although Queen Charlotte chose him to design her spectacular garden party for the King's birthday. He also designed the chimneypiece for the Saloon and a ceiling for her Crimson Drawing Room. Neither Chambers nor the King appreciated Adam's delicate arabesques. As the King later said, his work 'had too much gilding which puts one in mind of gingerbread'.

Chambers was now the architect in charge, but the King kept a close eye on the alterations, offering his own drawings for doorcases and windows. The King liked simplicity, so Buckingham's ornate railings were taken down and plain ones now enclosed the courtyard. The east façade was simplified, giving the house a more restrained classical outline.

The King's greatest pride was in his libraries. George II, who had no taste for books or art, had, in 1757, given the old royal library of some 65,000 books to the newly founded British Museum. George III planned to add to his own considerable collection.

Between 1762 and 1772 a series of library rooms were built on to the south-west corner, as well as a new bedroom for the King, which linked the library to the main block of the house. In 1767 Sir William Chambers's superb Octagon Library was completed with a great octagonal table in the middle. It was characteristic of the King's generosity that he allowed scholars to use his library, and he instructed his agents never to bid against a scholar, a professor or any person of moderate means who desired a book for his own use.

John Adams, first American minister to Britain, admired the King's library in 1783. 'The books were in perfect order . . . chosen with perfect taste and judgment, every book that a King ought always to have close at hand.'[8]

We hear of Dr Johnson, in February 1767, absorbed reading by the fire, surprised by the silent entrance of the King, who had instructed his librarian to let him know when the Doctor visited; of the famous voice, undiminished by awe of royalty, booming through the building; and of the old Tory, who usually had no good word for the Hanoverians, going away delighted with his conversation with a literate King.

George III's new library rooms were much needed; he was to accumulate a collection of 67,000 volumes. He sent his librarian, Richard Dalton, to Italy in search of books, Old Master drawings, medals and coins for his collection. His favourite cabinetmakers, William Vile and John Bradburn, made exquisite bookcases and cabinets for the coins and he took a close personal interest in the work. His love of books is illustrated by his establishment of a fine Royal Bindery in 1786.

The King had inherited a collection of paintings, many of which were lying neglected in Windsor Castle. He now brought pictures for the Queen's House from his other palaces, and bought paintings and commissioned contemporary artists. Bute, an enthusiastic collector himself, must have assisted the King with great pleasure.

The King's greatest purchase was the collection of Joseph Smith, the British Consul in Venice. Bute's younger brother, James Stuart Mackenzie, British envoy to Turin, negotiated the sale in 1762 for £20,000.

The collection included Italian drawings, and seventeenth- and eighteenth-century paintings, among them charming Italian villa scenes by Sebastiano and Marco Ricci. There were some Flemish and Dutch works, including the luminous *A Lady at the Virginals with a Gentleman* by Jan Vermeer, but the prize of the collection was the fifty paintings and one hundred and forty drawings by Canaletto. Smith had been for many years the patron of the artist.

At the same time the King's agent, the architect James Adam, bought on the King's behalf from Cardinal Albani a collection of 300 drawings, including some by Domenichino, Maratta and Nicolas Poussin. These had belonged to Pope Clement XI.

The King's haul landed early in 1763. Dalton and Mackenzie supervised the loading of the consignment from Livorno, Italy, in February 1763. The excitement of the King and Queen Charlotte can be imagined as the sun-lit Canaletto landscapes were unpacked in the cold spring London light. The King supervised every detail of the hang of the pictures, drawing plans of their proposed positions, undoubtedly guided by Chambers, who worked on the alterations of the Queen's House until 1773.

There would be changes over the years, but from drawings and a 1792 inventory it is possible to get an idea of the hang of the pictures in the King's rooms on the ground floor and in the Queen's rooms on the floor above. The entrance hall was illumined by Canalettos and Zuccarellis from the Smith collection. The hall led in to an enfilade of rooms looking on to the garden. To the right, at the end, was the King's Dressing Room, on three walls of which were Canaletto landscapes; the fourth, the window wall, looked on to the garden. It was a landscape room of a kind becoming popular in the eighteenth century. Next to it the King's Warm Room was vibrant with seven historical paintings by one of the King's favourite painters, Benjamin West. There were paintings by van Dyck, Rubens and Titian in the next rooms, the Passage Room and Drawing Room. In the King's Closet twenty-four pictures were closely hung. Next came the King's Bedchamber, adorned by twelve canvases by Luca Giordano, representing the story of Cupid and Psyche. In the Great Octagon Library more Venetian pictures were hung above the bookcases.

Some of the greatest pictures were in the Queen's rooms on the first floor. The famous Raphael cartoons were brought from St James's Palace in 1763 and hung in her Saloon against wall coverings of green damask. The Queen's Breakfast Room was dominated by the two superb van Dycks – *Charles I with Monsieur de St Antoine* and *Charles I and Henrietta Maria and with Their Eldest Two Children*. George III was fascinated by the Stuarts and this painting would have been a constant reminder that, though he was a Hanoverian, he was also descended from Charles I's sister, and of the heavy price of kingly pride.

This seems to have been a favourite room, which Queen Charlotte used for music. The Queen shared many of the King's interests. She was not a 'dim girl', as she has been called. Over the years she was to study botany conscientiously and, though one must make allowances for flattery of royalty, she was acclaimed by leading botanists. The vivid exotic flower *Strelitzia reginae*, brought from the Cape of Good Hope in 1773, was named after her. Serious academics also dedicated their works to her.

Queen Charlotte developed a genuine interest in art. It was she who, in 1772, was to commission Johann Zoffany's famous painting of the great room in the gallery in Florence, *The Tribune of the Uffizi*.

The King, too, was a patron of contemporary artists. He founded the

Royal Academy in 1768 'under our immediate patronage and protection' and continued to interest himself very much in its success.

'He has given unlimited power to the Treasurer to draw on his Privy Purse for whatever money shall be wanted for the Academy.'⁹ Although Sir Joshua Reynolds wrote this with gratitude he was never in the King's favour, even though he became the Academy's first president. When the King was asked to sit for Reynolds he replied, 'Mr Ramsay is my painter.' Allan Ramsay was commissioned to paint the Coronation portraits of the King and Queen. Perhaps no one has succeeded so well in capturing the charm and intelligence of a lady whom no one considered beautiful. Thomas Gainsborough, too, was a favourite and was chosen in 1782 to paint fifteen oval portraits of the royal family.

The King enjoyed chatting with his artists, accepting their eccentricities with good-humoured tolerance. So we see him in the Queen's House patiently suffering as the sculptor, Joseph Nollekens, pinched his nose while measuring it with his callipers, and listening with amusement to the sculptor's odd explanations for failing to keep his appointments.

The King chose the best craftsmen and women at a period when the standards of workmanship were very high indeed.

The elegant carved bookcase that today is in the 18th-Century Room at the Palace was made in the workshops of Vile & Cobb. Cobb, the master upholsterer, appears in J. T. Smith's life of Nollekens, strutting through the Queen's House in all his pompous self-importance. He was, apparently,

a singularly haughty man, the upholsterer. One of the proudest men in England, he always appeared in full dress of the most superb and costly kind, whether strutting magnificently through his workshops, giving orders to his men, or on some errand at the 'Queen's House', where the King who smiled at his pomposity frequently employed him for cabinet work of an elaborate and expensive sort.

Cobb himself became immensely wealthy, living in some great state himself. When Nathaniel Dance painted his picture he nobly sent the painter home in his own carriage.

Smith records an occasion in

His Majesty's library at the Queen's House when giving orders to a workman whose ladder chanced to stand before a book required by the King, His Majesty desired Cobb to hand him the work. Instead of obeying, Cobb called to his man, 'fellow, give me that book!' The King with his usual condescension rose and asked Cobb for his man's name. 'Jenkins, your Majesty,' answered the astonished upholsterer. 'Then,' observed the King, 'Jenkins. You shall hand me that book.'[10]

William Vile, a cabinetmaker of distinction, had worked for Horace Walpole in his remarkable house at Strawberry Hill. The King gave large orders to Vile & Cobb in the years 1760–4 and their workshop at 72 St Martin's Lane must have been extremely busy. The street was much frequented by artists and wealthy patrons – Thomas Coutts, the King's banker, had a house there at this time. William Vile supplied to the Queen music desks and 'a very handsome jewel cabinet' for £138 10s. at the beginning of her reign in 1761, 'mahogany [sic] stands for birdcages, 2 mahogany houses for a Turkey monkey'.

It was William Vile to whom was entrusted the delicate work in 'the conversion of the late Japan room into the new Japan room'. This entailed removing the black and gold 'japanned' panels from the Duke of Buckingham's Saloon and refitting them in the Queen's Breakfast Room; and making a 'quantity of new Japan to make out the new'. William Vile was succeeded by the equally distinguished cabinetmaker, John Bradburn, who provided delicate and elegant furniture for the Queen's House between 1764 and 1767.

Most tantalizing are the references to Mrs Naish, joiner, who apparently not only carved the most elaborate bedsteads, but could also turn out square boxes for beds for Queen Charlotte's little dogs and innumerable commodes for all the palaces. Mrs Naish was the daughter of the joiner Henry Williams, who had worked for the King's father, Frederick, Prince of Wales. We know that she was given many commissions.

Some of the Queen's most elaborate furniture was made by Eastern craftsmen. Mrs Warren Hastings gave her a carved ivory sofa with a canopy of white satin.

Many craftswomen stitched away during these years of refurbishment at the Palace. Mrs Priscilla MacEwan, presumably a Scot, was paid the immense sums of £3,778 14s. as well as £225 18s. 6d. for feathers. Queen Charlotte, herself an accomplished needlewoman, became the patroness of the 'Royal School of embroidering females', where poor girls learned embroidery. There was also a 'lacewoman for Flanders point lace'[11].

Not since Charles II, who encouraged men like Grinling Gibbons, had a king and queen taken such an interest in the work of craftsmen and women. In George III's reign traditions were established that were carried on by families of craftsmen for generations. The Crace firm, for example, was founded in 1768 by Edward Crace, who worked for George III in many capacities. Son of coachmaker John Crace, Edward Crace was apprenticed to an artist and 'set up his business' as a decorative house painter to the nobility and gentry. The most famous example of his work in this field was in 1770 on the spectacular interior of the Pantheon in Oxford Street. George III had been much impressed by the decoration of the Pantheon and also by the obvious quality of Edward Crace's work. He therefore sent his librarian, Richard Dalton, to engage Edward Crace for the cataloguing and care of the paintings in the Royal Collection – and he remained in the King's service until his death in 1799.

The King and Queen occasionally looked in to watch the cleaning and revarnishing of the collection. Edward Crace also worked on the King's paintings at Hampton Court and Windsor Castle. He was succeeded by his son, John, who became the greatest of the family. He worked as a decorator and upholsterer – amongst his bills are one for the supply of '39 yards of yard wide Morone Chintz', and another for 'A turkey pattern Brussells Carpet with a neat border'. According to his son, Frederick, John Crace introduced 'Imitation of marbling and graining of woodwork' into English decoration during the 1790s. Frederick Crace was taken up by the Prince of Wales – 'being first noticed by the Prince of Wales and Mrs Fitzherbert being at work upon gilding the iron railing of the staircase'.[12] The Prince of Wales was to employ John and Frederick Crace to work on the chinoiserie interior of the Royal Pavilion in Brighton and at Carlton House.

In 1765 the firm Wedgwood made an exquisite green and gold service for Queen Charlotte, named Queen's Ware in her honour. Mr Josiah Wedgwood, who recorded his visits to the Palace, was charmed by the Queen and instructed his partner Bentley to smarten himself up for the visits to the Queen's House. The delicate service of Chelsea china which, early in the reign, the Queen sent to her brother the Duke of Mecklenburg-Strelitz was given back to Queen Elizabeth (now the Queen Mother) in 1947, and is now displayed in glass-fronted cabinets in the Bow Room at Buckingham Palace, through which thousands of visitors to the royal garden parties pass each year.*

The King took great interest in acquiring furniture for the Palace. In 1781, he attended an auction.

On Monday his Majesty passed by West Thorpe House near Marlow, the seat of the late Governor Winch [sic]. He sent one of his Equerries to enquire whose goods were selling by auction; when Mr Christie requested his most dutiful respects might be presented to his Majesty for he wished to show him some very curious ivory chairs and a couch that were to be disposed of.

His Majesty turned back, they were shown him on the lawn opposite the house and he liked them so well that he ordered them to be purchased for the Queen ... the chairs cost 14½ guineas each, the couch 48 guineas and two small cabinets 45 guineas.[13]

Governor Wynch had ordered this furniture in 1770 to be made at Madras by native craftsmen from English models. Deposed in 1775 by the Court of the East India Company, he returned to England, where he died in May 1781.

We know of other furniture acquired by Queen Charlotte from the sale of her collection in 1819. James Christie, son of the 'Mr Christie' who had sold this lot to George III, offered in his Great Room, Pall Mall,

A rare and costly sopha, veneered with ivory, with carved back, arms and feet, engraved with devices of serpents and tiger's heads, with cane bottom.

A set – 1 corner armchair and 8 square back chairs veneered with ivory.[14]

---

*The King and Queen surprised visitors by their knowledge of the manufacture of china. On a holiday in Cheltenham in 1788, they visited Worcester and toured the pottery there.

Two sofas made £106 12s., two sets of chairs £171 5s. 6d., two miniature cabinets £55 2s. 6d. The Prince Regent bought these at the auction and placed them in the Corridor or the Long Gallery at the Royal Pavilion, Brighton; they were brought to Buckingham Palace in 1847. Some of them are now in the Principal corridor at Buckingham Palace.

George III's own rooms were uncarpeted and simply furnished, but his extravagance was his collection of clocks. Some are still to be seen in Buckingham Palace. He particularly admired the work of Benjamin Vulliamy, a member of another family that served the Crown for generations. A German lady, Sophie von la Roche, met Vulliamy's father in the Queen's House in 1786.

Mr Vulliamy, senior, also showed us one of his eldest son's inventions, which cannot but interest a British sovereign with affection for his subjects. For on a large semi-sphere set in the wall, he can follow which parts of the world are affected if a heavy gale is sweeping England; while the weather-vane on this house, with its eminent situation, calculates and records so accurately on this sphere that the king can conjecture how his fleet is faring. I told Mr Vulliamy that I thought him a very lucky father.[15]

Typically, the King was not content to be a mere collector: he made a study of the clocks' workings. In a memorandum in his handwriting he shows how to take a watch apart and put it back together. With the help of his architect, Sir William Chambers, he even designed a domed case in gilt and tortoiseshell for an astronomical clock by Christopher Pinchbeck and others. In 1765 he acquired a four-sided astronomical clock by Eardley Norton for his Octagon library. He also encouraged new talent, granting £100 to John Arnold, a young Cornish watchmaker, to help him in his researches. In 1764 he was rewarded: on his birthday Arnold presented him with the smallest repeating watch ever made, set in a ring, for which the delighted King gave him 500 guineas.

Sir William Chambers was not only the King's architect, surveyor and clock designer: he also designed his state coach. Commissioned in November 1762, it cost a prodigious £7,587 19s. 9½d. The well-known sculptor, Joseph Wilton, was paid £2,500 for the carving, G. B. Cipriani painted the panels and the wheels were copied from an ancient triumphal car. Three cherubs perched on the roof represented the genius of England, Scotland and Ireland. Horace Walpole saw it:

There is come forth a new state coach which has cost £8,000. It is a beautiful object, though crowded with improprieties. Its supports are Tritons, not very well adapted to land carriage, and formed of palm trees, which are as little aquatic as Tritons are terrestrial.[16]

The Queen's House was splendidly furnished, and infinitely more magnificent than other great town houses such as Marlborough House and Devonshire House.

It is fortunate that we have a rare description of the interior of the Palace in the early days of the King's reign by an acute and experienced observer. Mrs Philip Lybbe Powys seems to have spent her life inspecting great houses and her greatest triumph was on 23 March 1767 when she 'went to see what is rather difficult to see at all, the Queen's Palace'. It is worth reproducing her account in full.

The hall and staircase are particularly pleasing. The whole of the ground floor is for the King, whose apartments are fitted up rather neatly elegant than profusely ornamental. The library consists of three rooms, two oblong and one octagonal. The books are said to be the best collection anywhere to be met with. The Queen's apartments are ornamented as one expects a Queen's should be, with curiosities from every nation that can deserve her notice. The most capital pictures, the finest Dresden & other china, cabinets of more minute curiosities. Among the pictures let us note the famed cartoons from Hampton Court & a number of small & beautiful pictures; one room panelled with the finest Japan. The floors are all inlaid in the most expensive manner, and tho' but in March, every room was full of Roses, carnations, hyacinths etc, dispersed in the prettiest manner imaginable in jars & different flowerpots on stands. On her toilet, besides the gilt plate, innumerable knick-knacks. Round the dressing room, let into the crimson damask hangings in a manner uncommonly elegant, are frames of fine impressions, miniatures etc. It being at that time the coldest weather possible we were amazed to find so large a house so warm but fires, it seems, are kept the whole day, even in the closets, and to prevent accidents to furniture so costly from the neglect of the attendance, there is in every chimney a lacquered wire fire board, the cleverest contrivance that can be imagin'd as even the smallest spark cannot fly through them, while you have the heat & they are really ornamental.

By the Queen's bed was an elegant case with twenty-five watches, all highly adorned with jewels.[17]

Both the King and the Queen shared a deep love of music. Even as a boy, George III had been enchanted by the music of Handel, who, alas, did not live to see his young admirer crowned. Queen Charlotte took singing lessons from Johann Christian Bach, youngest son of the great composer. A room in the palace was fitted up as a music room with an immense organ, elaborately carved in 1764. Three new harpsichords were bought for the Queen. The King would sometimes accompany her on his flute. It was here that the seven-year-old Wolfgang Amadeus Mozart came to enchant them: Queen Charlotte sang, accompanied by the young prodigy on the organ. In her honour Mozart composed four sonatas.

Perhaps at no other time has the Palace been such a centre of creative activity and excitement, except in the early years of Queen Victoria's reign. Throughout the reign of George III, the King's own enthusiasm, and his tolerant acceptance of the oddities of the artistic world, are remarkable.

'The King's account'

It is impossible to estimate the exact cost of the rebuilding and furnishing of Buckingham House, but enough details are recorded to indicate the vast scale of the expenditure. Apparently £13,885 14s. 6½d. was spent on rebuilding in the years 1762–3 and later additional sums of £10,197 and £9,757. Since 1697 such expenditure was paid for out of the 'Civil List', voted by Parliament, at the beginning of each reign, and allotted for the expense of civil government. (The King was not expected to cover the cost of defence – the Navy, the Army, and a provision for foreign affairs were the responsibility of Parliament.)

In 1714 George I was granted £700,000 per annum and £100,000 for the Prince of Wales. Sir Robert Walpole secured a better deal for George II, who was given the full sum and its profits. George III's father, Frederick, Prince of Wales, was granted £500,000 per annum and an extra £100,000 upon marriage.

However, because he followed the Hanoverian pattern of the son's political opposition to his father, in 1747 Frederick, Prince of Wales, pledged that when he became king he would take only a fixed sum of £800,000 per annum. George III felt duty-bound to honour his father's pledge, and the first legal Act of his reign was the granting of a Civil List of £800,000 fixed income. Had he adopted his grandfather's system he would have become extremely wealthy, but because this was an age of inflation, and he had much greater responsibilities than his grandfather, the King was often in debt.

Out of the Civil List, the King was expected to pay for government expenses (apart from the armed forces), the running of the Court and allowances to the royal family. His private and personal expenses came out of the Privy Purse, for which he was allowed £48,000 per annum, increased in 1777 to £60,000. This came out of the Civil List, but was private: he was not answerable to the Treasury for details of this expenditure.

For the first three years of George III's reign Lord Bute was Keeper of the Privy Purse. With the advice of Bute, the King appointed Thomas Coutts as his banker: 'Coutts in the Strand is my banker,' the King wrote; later he made him a Gentleman of the Privy Chamber. Totally discreet,* Thomas Coutts remained one of the King's financial advisers until the political activities of his radical son-in-law, Sir Francis Burdett, infuriated the government and the King removed his account. George III's sons, however, remained as customers, plaguing the upright banker with their debts. Loyally, Thomas Coutts destroyed his records of the King's Privy Purse, so we shall never know exactly how this money was spent. But it is assumed that a large proportion was spent on

---

* He was sent by the King to visit the Cardinal Duke of York, the last of the Stuarts in Rome; his bank arranged the King's pension to the Duke.

private charities, the King being parsimonious in his own personal expenditure.

Out of the Civil List the King had also to pay allowances to his three brothers when they came of age, dowries to his two sisters when they married, the Coronation expenses and the Queen's allowance.

As his family grew, so did his expenses; and in spite of his careful management, by 1769 he was in debt and asked Parliament for an additional grant of £573,000. In 1777 he had to ask again for an increase of the Civil List to £900,000. This Parliament reluctantly granted, reminding the King that this was a time of great distress and unrest. The opposition, as will be seen, constantly attacked the waste of money on King and Court.

'The King's on the road!'

Delighted though the King and Queen were with the Queen's House they soon found it to be inadequate for their growing family. Queen Charlotte had been seven months pregnant with her second child at the time of the housewarming party, and an elegant nursery had been prepared. Princes George and Frederick – later George IV and the Duke of York – slept in identical, beautifully carved beds made by the joiner, Mrs Naish, and studied at identical little desks, establishing a lifelong empathy. But as each year brought a new baby, the Queen's House became no longer suitable.

An infant Prince of Wales, as in 1763, would require a governess, a subgoverness, a dry nurse, a wet nurse, a necessary woman and two rockers.

An adult Prince of Wales might have a hundred officers and servants on strength. He would need four gentlemen, half a dozen grooms and four pages to see him to bed the year round. Besides a Chancellor, a Master of the Horse, Equerries and so forth he would require an Attorney-General, a Solicitor-General, two 'Counsel learned in the law' and a whole string of watermen.[18]

There was, besides, a restlessness in the King's nature, symptomatic of his later illness, and once he had arranged the Queen's House in London to his satisfaction he wanted to move on. So as the years went by he and the Queen, and their family, spent more and more time at their other homes at Kew and later Windsor, and their visits to Buckingham House became a duty, to be hurried through as quickly as possible so that the King could rush back to the country. In 1785 he wrote that he was hardly ever at the Queen's House. As the King's coaches rattled from palace to palace, the households went too, requiring transport, rooms and offices at each stage.

As the family and their entourages increased, new houses had to be built at Kew until there was quite a village round Kew Green. The King was always closely involved, and with the advice of his old teacher, Sir William Chambers, he planned the building and refurbishing with a frenetic excitement. In the 1760s he was planning a new palace at Richmond. In 1776 he had moved on to Windsor, planning the renewal of the Castle.

There were still duties and ceremonies in London. Each new birth meant an elaborate christening, when the Queen received her guests in Mrs Naish's splendid bed, under a velvet canopy in a cloud of exquisite lace. Each child's birthday was celebrated in elaborate fashion and new clothes were *de rigueur* for the children and courtiers. The King's birthday on 4 June was always celebrated in high style. In the early years there were drawing rooms once a fortnight, when the Queen entertained ladies in the hot and stuffy rooms at St James's Palace, and when the King gave levees for gentlemen, standing the day long, sometimes without food, talking, talking, questioning with his famous 'What? What? What?' and listening. As foreign observers noted, it was so unlike the cold formality of the French court.

At least the concerts given at the Queen's House twice a week were a relaxation. J. C. Bach's wife, the famous singer Galli, and their pupils often performed, and there were private quartet parties twice a week when the great flautist Johann Christian Fischer played. But all these occasions were time-consuming and exhausting, for the King involved himself entirely in everything he did. He allowed himself little rest:

concerned to keep down his weight, he would often ride out from the Queen's House for a three-hour gallop before breakfast.

He began to tire of a London now increasingly dirty and smokeladen. The great gale of 1779 gave him an excuse to spend more time in the country. As the writer Mrs Papendiek (daughter of the Queen's page) remembered,

It took off the upper corner of the Queen's House. This was the room next to the one in which the Princes Ernest, Augustus & Adolphus slept, which was over the bedroom of their majesties. The King was up, and with his children in a moment. The ceiling was falling fast & had already broken the bedstead of the elder Prince . . . but no harm happened to them.[19]

So the whirling, restless years went by, with the King, his family and household rushing from concerts and levees, or leaving London late at night to be at Windsor for the next morning's hunt, or at Kew for supervision of the newest building project.

At the Queen's House they often entertained visiting Germans – some distinguished, others, such as Sophie von la Roche, obscure. Writing in 1786 she recalled her visit.

The noble simplicity of the furnishings, the order and neatness, were marks of the character of the owner – marks of the wise humility upon the throne.

The library occupies the largest apartment and embraces the entire treasure-house of human knowledge. Three rooms are given up to it [there were in fact four rooms]. Two are much larger and finer than the Versailles ones. Fine pictures by Van Dyck, a large number by Claude Lorrain, Guido Reni, Del Sarto, masterpieces by Angelica [Kauffmann] and some excellent miniatures render these simple damask hangings very valuable.

In a small cabinet off the bedroom are the portraits of the fourteen royal children – thus the first waking moments are dedicated to this sight and the emotions of true motherhood. May theirs be the reward of such tenderness, my heart softly murmured.

In one apartment I saw Raphael's famous cartoons. Above the library is a room which the king, the Prince of Wales, the relatives of the Gibraltar Eliot must cherish very much since ports of such importance to England as Plymouth and Portsmouth are excellently modelled there, with all their buildings and gardens and ships and their manifold industries; Gibraltar's rocky fastness, the Spanish encampment, all on a table ten feet long . . .

The concert hall contains a large organ, and this not merely because England happens to be particularly fond of this instrument, but also because the royal family holds private prayers to an organ accompaniment; for it has always been mainly associated with church music.

The audience chamber is devoid of all splendour: one cabinet, however, is enhanced by the queen's tapestry-work. In a side room looking on to the garden an artist was at work; and there, too, we found two lovely portraits of the youngest princesses . . .

There is a colonnade in the vestibule worthy of the dignity of this small palace's mistress; but since it originally belonged to the Buckingham family, whose name, Buckingham House, it still bears, it also shows that the builder had a taste for greatness and nobility; since the stairs are also decorated with frescoes . . .

The choice of site for this palace is perfect, as it takes in the gradual incline, from which the royal park of St James's and Green Park can be completely overlooked, and at the back of it a pleasant garden has been laid out in which to take a solitary stroll. The towers of Westminster Abbey, the coronation and burial-ground of British monarchs can be seen from here as well as from St James's Palace.

We rejoiced on passing through the suites of apartments at being able to enumerate a series of virtues and accomplishments common to the lofty souls of the proprietors of this residence. While marvelling at the delightful order and simplicity reigning everywhere, Mr Vulliamy said, 'The eye of the queen spreads this elegance in Buckingham's house, just as her heart allows the king to savour the sweet happiness of purest love.'

Sophie von la Roche was not only conducted round the Queen's House by Vulliamy senior: she also counted herself lucky to be received by the King and Queen. On Tuesday, 19 September 1786, she wrote,

I was full of excitement without feeling in the least afraid, for the queen was famed for her kindness and virtue; this made me just as confident as I was awed. The idea that I was to see and speak to Queen Charlotte of England, whom I had so long admired, at close quarters upon English soil, kept me awake for quite a long while.

She need not have feared: the King and Queen put her immediately at ease.

The king, a most distinguished and handsome man, listened with kind attention while I spoke with his worthy consort, and addressed me very graciously, adding, however, that as 'an authoress they should not speak to me in German.' I replied that 'I rejoiced for my Fatherland that their Majesties still loved its language.' Thereupon he laid his hand upon his breast with fine, manly frankness, saying, 'Oh, my heart will never forget that it pulses with German blood. All my children speak German.'

At that moment the princesses approached. Her eldest Highness, a really lovely princess; Princess Augusta, lively and attractive; the two youngest ones very innocent and sweet. They all addressed me in German; are all kindly disposed, and their beauty proves that they are children born of purest love.[20]

Queen Charlotte was happiest in the country; when at the Queen's House, she longed for her quiet flower garden in the country lane at Kew, or for the informality and easier clothes of Windsor, where they could drop in on their subjects casually. One contemporary, Lieutenant Colonel Phillip, remembered the Queen calling on Mrs Garrick at her home in Hampton without notice. 'Mrs Garrick was much confused at being caught in the act of peeling onions for pickling. The Queen however, would not suffer her to stir; but commanded a knife to be brought . . . & actually sat down . . . & peeled onions.'[21] She could not have done this at the Queen's House in London.

There was little rest – a day or two among her flowers and then the headlong rush. Her household would pack up her gowns, Mrs Naish would pack the close-stools and the chamber pots, and the younger children would be bundled into carriages. The cry would go up: 'The King's on the road!' and his subjects would flatten themselves against the hedges as the royal cavalcade swept by at breakneck speed.

The King was indeed 'on the road' – a road that would eventually, in 1788, lead to a complete mental breakdown. It is tragic that George III is remembered chiefly as the King who went mad (as it was then thought he was; his illness is now thought to have been the side effect of the metabolic disorder porphyria). In fact Court life for the first three decades of his reign was more culturally and intellectually rich than at almost any other period in our history.

Court Life

It is fortunate that we have the memoirs of two intelligent women who brilliantly portray the pleasures and pains of Court life in the reign of George III. The Queen had appointed Fanny Burney, a distinguished novelist (author of *Evelina*) much admired by Dr Johnson, as Keeper of the Robes, and she was with the Queen during the nightmare period of the King's first spell of apparent madness.

The other was Charlotte Papendiek, the daughter of Frederick Albert, the German page whom the Queen had persuaded to come with her from Mecklenburg-Strelitz, where originally he had served as hair-dresser/barber. Charlotte married Christopher Papendiek, a German page in the King's entourage, and in the late 1830s, wrote her autobiography under her married name. It covers the period from before her birth in July 1765 to 1792. Her father, a fine, cultured man, and a competent musician, had sent her at the age of six to be educated at Streatham, south London, where she was well taught by two ladies, friends of Mrs Thrale and Dr Johnson. She, too, like Fanny Burney, had been flattered by Johnson. Her father, who had hoped that her training would qualify her to become one of the Queen's household, unwillingly allowed her to become the wife of a courtier, knowing what a difficult life that was, as generations of courtiers' wives have discovered. Mrs Papendiek flourished in the cultural life of the Court and eventually took Fanny Burney's place, remaining with the Queen until her death.

Unlike Mrs Papendiek, Fanny Burney withered at Court and retired, broken in health. She had lived, she recorded, 'in the service of Her Majesty five years within ten days from July 17 1786 to July 1791'. She had counted the days.

During her term of office, she spent most of her time with the Queen in the country, though she had a room in St James's Palace and another in Buckingham House, where she slept when the royal family were in London. Unfortunately she gives little description of the Queen's House in her journals – in any case Miss Burney was extremely short-sighted and Court etiquette did not allow her to wear glasses; but she is an admirable witness of life among the courtiers, which was much the same in all the palaces. Unlike Mrs Papendiek, who was bred to Court life and accepted the discomforts with cheerful resignation, Miss Burney could never rid herself of the sense of the indignity of her position. To be summoned by a bell, like a servant, was a 'mortifying mark of servitude. I always felt myself blush, though alone, with conscious shame at my own strange degradation.' Though she was charmed by the tact and gentleness of the 'sweet queen', she was uncomfortable in the ritual of dressing her. The Queen's maid 'hands the things to me and I put them on. 'Tis fortunate that I have not the handling of them . . . embarrassed as I am, and should run a prodigious risk of giving the gown before the hoop, and the fan before the neck-kerchief.' She was affronted, too, by the ferocious Mrs Elizabeth Schwellenberg, who had also come with the Queen from Germany and dominated the Queen's household, and bullied and patronized Fanny Burney. But her pride was most hurt when Mrs Schwellenberg came to her in great secrecy, saying, '"The Queen will give you a gown! The Queen says you are not rich." . . . There was something . . . quite intolerable to me & I hastily interrupted her with saying: "I have two new gowns by me, & therefore do not require another."'

Such ingratitude was incomprehensible to Madame – but Miss Burney was adamant. 'To accept even such a shadow of an obligation upon such terms I should think mean & unworthy; and therefore I mean always, in a Court as I would elsewhere to be open & fearless in declining such subjection.' The Queen was 'all sweetness, encouragement & gracious goodness to me, & I cannot endure to complain of her old servant . . . I could not give up all my own notions of what I think everyone owes to themselves.'

Nevertheless she continued to suffer the bullying, as when, on long coach journeys, Madame insisted on keeping the windows open, so giving Fanny a swollen face. Miss Burney endured the 'slavery' for the same reason that she had accepted the honour. Her father, Dr Burney, a distinguished musicologist who had observed royal patronage of musicians in his travels through German courts, was writing a history of music. She hoped he might, through her influence, gain some preferment at the English Court.

No one has caught better than Miss Burney the atmosphere of life among the courtiers, its longueurs and miseries. Generations of equerries have sympathized with her friend, Colonel Goldsworthy.

'What a life it is? Well! it's honour, that's one comfort; it's all honour, royal honour! One has the honour to stand till one has not a foot left; & to ride until one's stiff, & to walk till one's ready to drop – & then one makes one's lowest bow, d'ye see, and blesses one's self with joy for the honour.'

'After all the labours,' cried he, 'of the chase, all the riding, the trotting, the galloping, the leaping, the – with your favour, ladies, I beg pardon, I was going to say a strange word, but the – perspiration, – and – and all that – after being wet through over head, and soused through under feet, and popped into ditches, and jerked over gates, what lives we do lead: Well, it's all honour! that's my only comfort! Well, after all this, fagging away like mad from eight in the morning to five or six in the afternoon, home we come, looking like so many drowned rats, with not a dry thread about us, nor a morsel within us – sore to the very bone, and forced to smile all the time! and then after all this what do you think follows?'

To his horror the King offered him

'Barley water in such a plight as that! Fine compensation for a wet jacket, truly! – barley water! I never heard of such a thing in my life! barley water after a whole day's hard hunting!'

'And pray did you drink it?'

'I drink it? – Drink barley water? no, no; not come to that neither! But there it was, sure enough! – in a jug fit for a sick-room; just such a thing as you put upon a hob in a chimney, for some poor miserable soul that keeps his bed! just such a thing as that! – And, "Here, Goldsworthy," says His Majesty, "here's the barley water!"'

'And did the King drink it himself?'

'Yes, God bless His Majesty! But I was too humble a subject to do the same as the King!'

Fanny Burney's 'directions for coughing, sneezing or moving before the King and Queen' were sent to her mother Mrs Burney – a wry commentary on the miseries of Court life.

In the first place, you must not cough . . . you must choke . . . but not cough. In the second place you must not sneeze . . . you must hold your breath – . . . if the violence . . . breaks some blood vessel, you must break the blood vessel – but not sneeze . . . If a black pin runs into your head you must not take it out . . . if the blood should gush from your head . . . you must let it gush. If however the agony is very great . . . you may bite the inside of your cheek . . . if you even gnaw a piece out, it will not be minded, only be sure to swallow it, or commit it to a corner of your mouth until they are gone – for you must not spit.

Protocol remained the same at Buckingham House, Windsor and Kew, though life was more relaxed in the country. Clothes were plainer at Windsor and even simpler at Kew. Later the royal family could be even more relaxed on their holiday expeditions. They could stroll down the promenade at Cheltenham, Gloucestershire, or sit and sew in the bathing machines at Weymouth, Dorset, although even there the King might be surprised by a loyal band, in a nearby bathing machine, playing 'God Save The King' as he popped his head out of the water.

Fanny Burney watched Court protocol with the curious eye of one observing strange customs in a foreign land. You did not knock at royal doors, you rattled the keys; you did not pass the open door of a room where royals were; you did not sit in the royal presence, unless especially invited; and you never turned your back on the royal family. Fanny Burney learned with difficulty the art of walking backwards, without 'treading on my own heels, or feeling my head giddy'. In an Oxford college she watched with admiration a wonderful example of the 'true court retrograde action'. Lady Charlotte Bertie, a Lady-in-Waiting, trapped with the King at the head of a long room, had to retreat.

She therefore faced the King, and began a march backwards – her ankle already sprained, and to walk forward, even leaning upon an arm, was painful to her: nevertheless back she went, perfectly upright, without one stumble, without ever once looking behind . . . and with as graceful a motion, and as easy an air, as I ever saw . . .

It was a feat worthy of a skilled circus performer.

It was on this very tiring visit to Oxford that Miss Burney observed the discreet camaraderie among courtiers. Not allowed to eat in the King's presence, and famished, the 'untitled attendants' watched in an envious semi-circle while the Princess Royal sat down to a splendid collation.

Major Price & Colonel Fairly seeing a very large table close to the wainscot behind us, desired our refreshments might be privately conveyed there . . . while all the group backed very near it, one at a time might feed, screened by all the rest.[22]

But through all the pains and longueurs of Court life Miss Burney retained her affection for the King and Queen – she, 'full of sense & graciousness . . . speaks English perfectly well . . . though now & then with a foreign idiom & frequently a foreign accent'. She had not only read Miss Burney's books but was generally well read, delighting in finding old books on bookstalls. As for the King, 'he speaks his opinion without reserve . . . His countenance is full of inquiry, to gain information without asking it . . . All I saw of both was the most perfect good humour, good spirits, ease & pleasantness.' Yet at the end, Miss Burney was to discover the insensitive side of the 'sweet Queen'. When, broken by stress and ill-health, she wanted to retire, she found the Queen unsympathetic and unwilling to let her go. Even then she excused her – it was not unkindness but lack of experience.

Mrs Papendiek's view of Court life was different. It was she, not Miss Burney, who was in a foreign country: though born in England, her father, mother and husband and many of their friends were German. But she was bred to Court life, and the Queen was at ease with her old Mecklenburg-Strelitz acquaintances. Her father, Frederick Albert, and husband, Mr Papendiek, both cultivated, intelligent men, could count as friends some of the most distinguished artists, scientists and musicians of the time. Educated as she was to hold her own, Mrs Papendiek flourished. 'Art & science hovering round us . . . attracted others & we became the centre of a charming coterie.'[23]

In the pages of her memoirs the hierarchy of George III's Court is seen with German eyes. She accepts with cheerful resignation their position. 'People in our rank do not travel with servants,' she writes. 'Nor do they serve ices or have fine china.'

But in their circle at George III's Court, there was a cultural richness rarely met at other courts and to which she had an access. Through her words the famous names become human. Here are painters Reynolds and Gainsborough eyeing each other's work warily; 'Pretty little' Angelica Kauffmann and the eccentric Henry Fuseli were guests at her hospitable table; the painter of exquisite miniatures, Jeremiah Meyer, and his wife were close friends; Benjamin West, the President of the Royal Academy, often dropped in, and his handsome son was a particular close friend. Mrs Papendiek tried in vain to help Sir Thomas Lawrence in his early unsuccessful attempts to gain royal favour. The wives of the famous told their life stories to her sympathetic ear: Mrs Zoffany, the artist's wife, confessed how she had been his mistress at the age of fourteen. She admired the long-suffering Mrs Meyer, whose difficult husband sent their children away to a miserable school, and who generously gave his exquisite miniatures to the sitters after his death.

She was equally popular with scientists such as Sir Joseph Banks and Sir William Herschel, who became the King's Astronomer. She heard the history of his life from the time when he came to England, a deserter from the Hanoverian army, with a shilling in his pocket, before making his way to fame through his music and his skill in making telescopes. He, his brilliant sister and his wife were welcome visitors at her own home.

Fanny Burney's encounter with Herschel confirms the generosity of the King and the breadth of his patronage. Herschel came to Windsor to show 'His Majesty and the royal family the new comet lately discovered by his sister, Miss Herschel'. Miss Burney went into the garden where Herschel 'showed her "the first lady's comet", and some of his new discovered universes, with all the good humour with which he would have taken the same trouble for a brother or sister'.

His success, she observed,

He owes wholly to his majesty . . . he was in danger of ruin, when his . . . great & uncommon genius attracted the king's patronage. He has now not only his pension . . . but . . . licence from the king to make a telescope according to his new ideas . . . that is to have no cost spared in its construction, and is wholly to be paid for by his majesty.[24]

There was much at Court to excite Miss Burney's intellectual interest, but she was never at ease, unsure of her place in the social hierarchy.

But no one enjoyed the cultural life of the Court more than the daughter of the Queen's page. Though she might listen to the grand concerts at the Queen's House from the next room, she never felt, as Miss Burney did, uncertain of her place or outside the pale. She, her husband and her father were part of the royal family, secure in their position among 'people of our rank'.

Mrs Papendiek took advantage of free tickets to theatres and operas, and was the friend of singers such as the great Mara, and actors and actresses including Mrs Siddons, Miss Farren, David Garrick and Roger Kemble. But it was among the musicians that she was most at home. Her father, Frederick Albert, played many instruments, and Mr Papendiek was an accomplished flute player. 'We must have Papendiek on his flute,' George III exclaimed when they were discussing a forthcoming concert at Westminster Abbey. The Prince of Wales, no mean performer himself, often sent for him to accompany him in his musical evenings, but both her husband and father firmly refused to take part in the Prince of Wales's wild evenings. As for Johann Christian Bach, he and his wife were for many years an important part of their lives. He taught her to sing and she never forgot the enchantment of his musical parties on the river at Richmond. She mourned his sad later years when he was neglected and wept with his wife at his death. Mrs Papendiek was a competent pianist herself, playing with great pleasure Bach's compositions on the new grand piano – which they acquired when the King rejected it for Windsor. She gave balls in her kitchen and concerts in her sitting room to which some of the most talented men and women of the time were delighted to come. The German impresario, Johann Peter Salomon, was a frequent guest at her musical evenings. He gave her tickets to the concerts he organized for Franz Joseph Haydn's 'London' symphonies.

Her memoirs illustrate perfectly the atmosphere of the Court of a king and queen who encouraged the arts and sciences as perhaps no other monarchs have done. As a writer in the *London Chronicle* of May 1764 recognized, 'The fine arts, hitherto too much neglected in England, seem now to rise from oblivion, under the reign of a monarch, who has a taste to perceive their charms, and a propensity to grant his royal protection to whatever can embellish human life.'[25]

'Uneasy lies the head that wears the crown'

Unfortunately this renaissance did not last. The autumn of 1788 brought a chill wind: the King suffered a serious mental breakdown. He had had an earlier illness, believed to have been similar, in 1765, from which he soon recovered. He recovered from the 1788 breakdown in the next year but it was the harbinger of a gathering storm, which eventually by 1810 was to destroy the King's sanity. George III, who had been hailed as the 'Apollo of the Arts', slowly dwindled into a sad old man, blind and deaf, shut away at Windsor.

The history of the King's 'madness' can be sketched only lightly here. The current theory that he suffered from porphyria might well be true, but it is worth pointing out that even without it, the pressures weighing on him were enough to strain his mental health.

During his reign he was battered by a succession of public and private tragedies, and he lost early the support of the man on whom he had completely relied. The Earl of Bute was an excellent tutor and his good influence in the education of George III should not be underestimated. But Bute, like many academics before and since, was out of his depth in the harsh world of politics. Besides, Bute was a Scot, and the 1745 rising of the Young Pretender (Bonnie Prince Charlie) was not forgotten – Buckingham House was called 'Holyrood House' by the satirists. The King made Bute his Chief Minister but in 1763 he resigned, leaving his pupil to stand on his own two feet and make his own decisions at a critical time. Bute retired to a house at Kew, where he wrote his botanical works and encouraged the Queen and her daughters in their studies and flower painting. In vain the young King searched for a substitute. Chief Ministers succeeded each other in rapid succession: George Grenville followed Bute in 1763, Rockingham followed Grenville in 1765 and Grafton followed Rockingham in 1766. The only minister of great stature, the elder Pitt, 1st Earl of Chatham, whom the King, after initial hostility, came to respect, suffered a nervous breakdown in 1767. Had he still been in charge, the waste and folly of the conduct of the American War of Independence might have been avoided. As it was, the King was guided through the years of war by the ineffectual Lord North, who, though painfully aware of his own inadequacy, could not persuade the King to allow him to retire. To a king with a deep sense of royal duty, losing the American colonies was a bitter blow.

The pressures on George III were all the more heavy because, even had he been willing to delegate responsibility, after the resignation of his adored Bute there was no one he could trust. He felt he must oversee everything, from the hanging of pictures to the personal supervision of the defence of London during the Gordon riots.

The Gordon riots, named after Lord George Gordon, were provoked by a move to relax the intolerant laws against Roman Catholics. In the summer of 1780 drunken mobs were wrecking the City of London, setting on fire houses belonging to anyone sympathetic to the Catholics. Several thousand troops were quartered in the grounds of the Queen's House, and the King spent the night with his men, as Henry V had before the Battle of Agincourt. Finding that they were sleeping on the ground, he promised them that 'straw would be brought for the next night & my servants will instantly serve you with a good allowance of wine & spirits'. His grandfather, George II, had been the last king to lead his troops into battle, at Dettingen, Germany, and George III had the same Hanoverian courage. It was claimed that it was his decisiveness in calling up the troops that stopped the riots.

Then there was the eternal problem of Ireland, which some of his ministers wanted to solve by granting Catholic emancipation, which the King believed would mean breaking his Coronation oath to preserve his Protestant inheritance. An invasion of the French into Ireland in 1789 doubled the threat.

The French Revolution of 1789, culminating in the death by guillotine of the French King and Queen, sent a flood of refugees to Britain, bringing hair-raising tales of bloody massacre. The British monarchy itself was under threat. It was a dangerous world, deeply disturbing for a king with a profound sense of royal duty.

'Burke's blast'

The troubles that beset George III in foreign affairs were made more difficult by the increasingly hostile opposition at home. The new radicals found the contrast between royal extravagance and public misery infuriating. The Queen's House, now so little used, was expensive to maintain and such expenditure proved offensive. Angry questions in Parliament were followed by a brilliant speech by the statesman Edmund Burke. In 1779 he had propounded a 'Plan of Economic Reform', which proposed, among other things,

the overhaul of the Royal Household and the abolition of scores of offices, notably those of treasurers, comptrollers and cofferers; the partial extermination of sinecures; a reduction of secret pensions; and a curtailment of redundant offices in the independent jurisdictions of Wales, Cornwall, Chester and Lancaster. He said: 'There is scarce a family so hidden and lost in the obscurest recesses of the community which does not feel that it has something to keep or to get, to hope or to fear, from the favour or displeasure of the Crown.'

On 11 February 1780 Burke made one of his greatest speeches – a bitter attack on the corruption in the royal Household.

Our palaces are vast inhospitable halls. There the bleak winds, there 'Boreas and Eurus and Caurus and Argestes loud', howling through the vacant lobbies and clattering the doors of deserted guard-rooms, appal the imagination and conjure up the grim spectre of departed tyrants – the Saxon, the Norman and the Dane; the stern Edwards and fierce Henrys – who stalk from desolation to desolation through the dreary vacuity and melancholy succession of chill and comfortless corridors.

The Household, Burke claimed, still retained 'Buttery, Pantry and all that rabble of places which, though profitable to the holders and expensive to the State, are almost too mean to mention. Why not put the catering out to contract, as the King of Prussia did?' There were superfluous offices: 'Why could not the Lord Chamberlain take over the Great Wardrobe – a department which in a few years had cost the Crown £150,000 for "naked walls or walls hung with cobwebs".'

So many Offices were sinecures, given to MPs and others.

Why maintain an Office of the Robes when the Groom of the Stole held a sinecure? These establishments, useless in themselves, had three useless Treasurers – 'two to hold a purse and one to play with a stick'. Why pay a man £100 a year, with an assistant also at £100 a year, to regulate some matter not worth twenty shillings? Everybody knew the answer; that these dignitaries were paid for their vote in Parliament, not for their diligence in administration, cookery or catering.

Then in a passage of ringing rhetoric he savaged the 'principle that one person should do the work, while another drew the emoluments'.

The King's domestic servants were all undone; his tradesmen remained unpaid, and became bankrupt – because the turnspit of the King's Kitchen was a Member of Parliament. His Majesty's slumbers were interrupted, his pillow was stuffed with thorns and his peace of mind entirely broken – because the turnspit of the King's Kitchen was a Member of Parliament. The judges were unpaid; the just of the kingdom bent and gave way; the foreign ministers remained inactive and unprofited; the system of Europe was dissolved; the chain of our alliances was broken; all the wheels of government at home and abroad were stopped; because the turnspit of the King's Kitchen was a Member of Parliament.[26]

Burke did not win the vote, but he won the argument and his arrows struck home. The King secretly looked to private bankers to service his debts.

Nathaniel Wraxall, a contemporary, noted the effect of Burke's blast.

Many persons of high rank reluctantly disappeared from about the King's person and Court in consequence of Burke's Bill. The Earl of Darlington quitted the Jewel House and Lord Pelham the Great Wardrobe; the first of which offices owed its institution to Elizabeth, while the latter remounted to the times of the Plantagenets. The Earl of Essex laid down the Stag Hounds, as did Lord Denbigh the Harriers.

Many other sinecures were blown away.

Treasurer of the Chamber, Cofferer of the Household and six clerkships in the Board of Green Cloth. The valuables of the Jewel House and Great Wardrobe were put in the care of the Lord Chamberlain. From this year, too, the appointments of Lord Chamberlain and Lord Steward ceased to carry cabinet rank. Mysteriously, the Master of the Buck Hounds survived the purge.[27]

And economies were made in the royal Household, much to the indignation of the higher ranks among the equerries. Mrs Papendiek watched with anger, as cheaper newcomers were employed 'who felt no interest – neither duty nor respect; and as to fidelity, such was not understood'. She wrote:

It is a dangerous expedient to call the attention of the public to economies practised in the Royal Household. It degrades every regulation and as the inferior classes always look with a jealous eye upon the great, any changes that may be deemed absolutely necessary should be accomplished as quietly and privately as possible. It is not improbable that the wonderful change in our Royal Household was brought on by Edmund Burke's reform in the Civil List; and that this led through many trifling channels to the destruction of the French king, for in his country also the cry for economy was raised and soon spread far and wide.[28]

'The Damnedest Set of Millstones'

Added to the King's political difficulties was the deep disappointment and concern that his family caused him. The Prince of Wales in particular was almost as hostile to him as his father had been to George II. The

Prince's wild extravagance, debts and mistresses had caused the King great distress from when the Price was sixteen and even more so when he came of age and moved from the Queen's House to his own residence, Carlton House. Here his riotous behaviour and his alternative court were a constant humiliation to the abstemious King, who had hoped to bring in a reign of virtue. The pain was even greater when the Prince lured the King's favourite son, the Duke of York, into his circle. When the Prince secretly married the charming Mrs Fitzherbert he was doubly breaking the law – by marrying a Roman Catholic, forbidden by the Act of Settlement, and by marrying against George III's law forbidding any royal marriage without the King's permission. Furthermore the Prince, seduced by the politics of the King's enemy, Charles James Fox, actively canvassed in elections for the Whigs.

During these years there were other family worries. On 17 September 1767, the King's brother, Edward, Duke of York, the much loved companion of his youth, died at Monaco. The Duke, a 'silly and frivolous' young man, had lost the King's favour; so much so that when, in 1765, the King was drafting a Regency Bill in case of his death, he deliberately left out the Duke, appointing the Queen as Regent. Nevertheless, the King was deeply distressed at his death and 'cried his eyes out'.

The death of the King's mother in 1772 was yet another sharp blow. She had been an important influence in his early life, and even after his marriage he had kept closely in touch.

Then he was deeply concerned about his sisters. Princess Augusta was unhappily married to the difficult and unfaithful Hereditary Prince of Brunswick. She was widowed in 1806 and the King brought her back to England and settled her in Blackheath, and she died at her rented house in Hanover Square in 1813. Her daughter, Princess Caroline, was to become the scandalous wife of the Prince of Wales, and for the sake of his sister, the King and Queen made great efforts to have patience with that difficult lady.

Another sister, Princess Caroline, was even more tragic. She was married at fifteen to her cousin, the diseased and wretched Christian VII of Denmark. She consoled herself with the Court doctor, Struansee, was condemned for adultery and was banished to a fortress, after being forced to watch the execution of her lover. George III persuaded the Danes to allow her to go to Celle in Hanover, where she died in 1775 at the age of twenty-four. She is remembered in Denmark as 'the Queen of Tears': portraits of her and her husband hang in Buckingham Palace today – a sad reminder of the harsh fate of many royal brides.

The King's brothers, the Dukes of Gloucester and Cumberland, had offended him by making secret marriages, causing him to introduce in 1773 the Royal Marriages Act.

The deaths of the King's own children, Prince Alfred in 1782, aged nearly two, and Prince Octavius in 1783, aged four, were successive hammer blows: he had said he did not wish to go to Heaven if Octavius was not there. In the scale of grief, the death of this much-loved son ranked with the loss of a continent.

'I fear I am not in my right mind'

It is worth remembering the appalling strain on the royal Household during the time of the King's madness. They watched the King, for whom they had affection, beaten and confined in a straitjacket, lose his prized dignity and self-control and sink into degradation. Both Miss Burney and Mrs Papendiek describe these harrowing times. 'The depth of terror during that time no words can paint,' wrote Miss Burney, who was bid 'to listen to hear what the King was saying in his delusions . . . Nothing could be so afflicting as this task . . . even now, it brings fresh to my ear his poor exhausted voice.'[29]

Mrs Papendiek's father and husband bore much of the burden at this time. The cutting of the King's beard was a dangerous task which Frederick Albert could not face – though he had come from Germany as the King's barber. Instead Mr Papendiek sent for sharpened razors and performed the delicate operation, chatting easily in his comforting German voice. It took two hours, while the Queen, hidden, watched in terror.

It was Mr Papendiek, too, who tactfully dealt with the King when, in his madness on Christmas Day 1788 at Kew, he got under the sofa to 'converse with his saviour'. His daughter wrote that her father 'got under to him, having previously given orders . . . that the sofa should be lifted straight up . . . He remained lying by his majesty, then by pure strength lifted him in his arms and laid him on his couch, where in a short time he fell asleep.'

Mrs Papendiek noted with understandable disappointment that the equerries and pages were not rewarded for their extra work and stress during the King's madness. Their 'perquisites' were cut, as Mrs Papendiek wrote, 'as part of the economies brought on by Edmund Burke's reform in the Civil List'. Burke had not realized how much the pages and equerries relied on perquisites as part of their wages. For example, Bedchamber women had a share of the Queen's clothes worth £200 per annum. Mrs Papendiek's father was allowed

table cloths, stove candles and pitcher wine; and from the Princesses' rooms wax candles . . . and the remains of any meal served to them separately, with wine . . . Mr Papendiek observed the same rule with my father: whatever remained untouched he took, but anything that had been tasted, he allowed the page's man to take.[30]

Some disappointed members of the Household left the King's service, including Mr Fortnum, who resigned to open up a grocer's store in Piccadilly, now known as Fortnum & Mason.

In the years following his recovery from this bout of madness, the King tried to avoid excessive stress. He took frequent holidays in Weymouth and elsewhere and avoided as much as possible the strain and the formalities at the Queen's House. Indeed they were rarely there.

But the political pressures remained. The war with France was renewed on land and sea. In 1805 the news of the victory at Trafalgar brought relief, but he had a relapse in 1806. Once again it was grief in the family that finally broke his mind. His beloved daughter Princess Amelia died on 2 November 1810. From then on he became hopelessly insane, never to recover. After much argument and acrimony, on 5 February 1811 the Prince was sworn as Regent at a Privy Council.

'The Queen's House'

The Queen was given the 'care of the King's royal person' and his Household was to be managed by her. She was to be assisted by a Queen's Council of eight Privy Councillors headed by the Archbishops of Canterbury and York. She was granted an increased allowance, and when in February 1812 the Regency Act was renewed, her four daughters were allowed an annuity of £6,000 each, for which they were immensely grateful. Princess Sophia wrote to thank the Prince Regent for his kindness to 'four old cats' – wondering that he 'did not put them in a sack and drown them'.

The Queen's House was now entirely just that, since the Prince Regent held court at Carlton House or at the Royal Pavilion, Brighton. Now that the Queen and Princesses had more money, they could refurbish the Queen's House, which had been neglected during the last twenty years. Even in 1802, a reporter from the *Gentleman's Magazine* was surprised that, in spite of the grandeur of the Duke of Buckingham's frescos still on the walls, the King's floors were 'cold and hardrubbed' and 'without a carpet, a luxury of which his majesty denies himself in almost every room'. Princess Elizabeth had painted the velvet curtains 'in shades of brown and maroon' and embroidered delicate flowers on white satin chair covers. But the tables and chairs 'are of a very plain and old fashion'. Even the materials

are not always so . . . good, seldom so beautiful as would be required in the houses of many opulent individuals. Though old, the furniture bears no stamp of venerable antiquity. The damask of the curtains and chairs is much faded: the mahogany . . . is not beautiful: it is even so dull that it much resembles walnut; and the latter are made with curving legs, and clump or rather knob feet, not well carved.[31]

The writer contrasts the Queen's House with the 'gold-mouldings, satin lined compartments and stately mirrors' of the 'opulent nobility'. In fact, he considered that many 'opulent tradesmen would not envy these apartments'. The reporter, however, tried to make a virtue out of what he obviously considered a shabby house. Now that 'fortunes are wasted' in show, it 'may be beneficial to many individuals to see ... how much more easily their Sovereign is satisfied'. If the Queen's House was shabby in 1802, how much worse it must have been in 1811 after years of neglect.

Fortunately, in 1819 W. H. Pyne produced his *Royal Residences*, illustrated with glowing paintings of the Queen's state rooms at this time, so we can see the results of the refurbishment. Pyne describes the courtyard and entrance hall in 1818 still very much as the Duke of Buckingham had left it. 'On the ground floor the suite of His Majesty's apartments are remarkable for their plainness.' He describes the paintings throughout the House: the Canalettos, and in the King's Breakfast Room portraits of William III and Queen Mary by Sir Godfrey Kneller, one of Queen Charlotte by Benjamin West, 'a Vandyke portrait of James I' and two 'full length portraits of ladies by Lely'. More Sir Peter Lely ladies were in the King's Dining Room, together with the Zoffany portraits of Queen Charlotte and George III, and the famous Charles I by van Dyck.

In the Saloon stood the 'superb throne of Her Majesty of crimson velvet with embroidery and fringe of gold',[32] which had come from St James's Palace during the Regency.

The doors opened to the Crimson Drawing Room, where the walls were hung with crimson satin and gilt chairs and sofas were covered with the same. Next was the Blue Velvet Room, more in the cool, elegant style of the younger Queen Charlotte, the walls hung with pale blue silk, the curtains, chairs, sofas and table covers all in blue velvet. Here were landscapes by Claude Lorrain and Rubens of winter and summer.

It was in the Green Closet on walls hung with green silk that Queen Charlotte had placed her favourite Gainsboroughs: a collection of portraits of thirteen of her children – their heads only. Like the Blue Velvet Room, this room had matching green velvet curtains and chair and table covers.

The Queen's Breakfast Room was still panelled with japan, as the main Saloon had been in the time of the Duke of Buckingham. This room, warmly carpeted in red, was Queen Charlotte's Music Room:

here was her 'fine toned organ with the bust of Handel'. From the windows of this room she and the King had watched the 'brilliant scene' on the June night in 1763 at her surprise housewarming party.

On the ground floor the King's Octagon Library was still lined with books. But now his voice was silent and Dr Johnson's voice boomed no more.

The Queen was seldom now at her London house but there were happy occasions when the old splendour was revived. On 22 July 1816 her daughter, Princess Mary, married her cousin William, Duke of Gloucester, son of the King's brother. The marriage ceremony was held in the Saloon at the Queen's House, now richly furnished with crimson velvet, before a temporary altar draped with old lace and heavy with massive silver communion plate. Staff attendants, ambassadors in full ceremonial dress, the great officers of state and an immense glittering throng swept up the Grand Staircase past the Yeomen of the Guard to the brilliantly illuminated Salon. A contemporary described it in detail:

The foreign Ambassadors, with their ladies, entered the saloon first, then followed the Cabinet Ministers and their ladies, and proceeded to the right. The great Officers of State, and those of the Royal Households, went to the left. The Queen took her station at the left side of the Altar, where was a state chair placed for her, the Princesses Augusta and Elizabeth, the Duchess of York, Princess Sophia of Gloucester, were on her left and their female attendants after them; while the Prince Regent was on the right side of the Altar, and his Royal brothers near him.

Everything being arranged and ready, the Lord Chamberlain retired, and introduced the Duke of Gloucester and presented him to the Altar. He then retired again, and with the Duke of Cambridge, introduced the Princess Mary, and the Royal Duke presented her Royal Highness to the Prince Regent, who gave her away in marriage to the Duke of Gloucester.

Her Royal Highness was dressed with her usual simplicity; she wore no feathers, but a bandeau of white roses fastened together by light sprigs of pearls. Her neck was ornamented with a brilliant fringe necklace, her arms with bracelets of brilliants formed into flowers, and her waist with a girdle to correspond with her bandeau.[33]

Princess Charlotte: the Lost Heiress

There had been many disagreements between the Queen and her eldest son, especially over the Regency Bill. But in her last years the Prince of Wales was once more her favourite son. Surprisingly, she was fascinated by the Royal Pavilion at Brighton, but then she had always loved the spectacular. She spent Christmas there in 1815 and enjoyed the celebrations for Princess Charlotte's birthday on 7 January 1816.

This was a particularly happy party and one with great consequences for the future of the monarchy. It was here that the heiress to the throne, next in line after the Prince Regent, Princess Charlotte, announced her engagement to Prince Leopold of Saxe-Coburg. Blissfully happy, Princess Charlotte, the daughter of impossible parents, the Prince Regent and Caroline, could not wait to escape from her lonely and unsettled life. She wrote enthusiastically of her settlement, 'The income is to be 50,000 a year. My pin money is to be 10,000 out of wh. I am to pay my ladies, maids etc.' She was to have three or four ladies and 'give them 500 a year each – which is enormous . . . and 8 footmen, town and country carriages, riding coachmen etc.'. As for Leopold, he was 'very much talented with a 1000 resources – musick [sic], singing, drawing, agriculture farming and botany, besides all he is a capital Italian scholar so I have everything almost I could wish and desire'.[34]

Prince Leopold was to be much involved in the history of the royal family and of Buckingham Palace. He and his friend Stockmar were to be major influences for decades to come on the lives of Queen Victoria, the Prince Consort and even on Edward VII. Prince Leopold was at this time an extremely handsome and popular young man of twenty-five. He had shown interest in Princess Charlotte two years earlier when he was in London with the Tsar Alexander I, in whose army he was at that time serving. One of his sisters had married the Tsar's brother, giving him an entrée into the Russian Imperial Court, where he was apparently a great favourite; another sister was Princess Victoire, who was to become the mother of Queen Victoria. When he met her, Princess Charlotte's affections were otherwise engaged; but disappointed in that love, she now in 1816 accepted with enthusiasm Prince Leopold's offer. The Prince Regent, who had wanted Princess Charlotte to marry Prince William of Orange, overcame his reluctance and gave his consent. The Queen very much desired the match and enjoyed preparing her trousseau.

The year 1816 was one of hope. Queen Charlotte was delighted when, on 2 May 1816, her namesake, Princess Charlotte, married Prince Leopold. The Regent somewhat reluctantly gave his daughter away at a ceremony at his magnificent Carlton House and the wedding breakfast was held there in his extravagant style. Princess Charlotte and Prince Leopold settled most happily after the honeymoon at the charming country house, Claremont, near Esher in Surrey, where Prince Leopold enjoyed replanning the garden and estate.

With them at Claremont was his friend and adviser, Baron Stockmar. Stockmar was the son of a Coburg lawyer. His mother, a woman of great sense and intelligence, was a great influence in his life. His happy, secure childhood gave him the stability for which he became renowned. He had trained as a doctor, fought against the French and set up his own military hospital in Coburg, where he insisted on treating all soldiers alike, whether they were allies or enemies. Prince Leopold had been impressed by this fellow citizen, and on a visit to Coburg had persuaded him to give up his medical career and join him as a friend and adviser. So the quiet, small figure, in his comfortable, uncourtly garb, was always there, ready with wise advice whenever it was needed.

This year, Prince Leopold would later remember, was the happiest of his life. He had the adoring love of Princess Charlotte and the steady friendship of his counsellor, Stockmar. Their happiness was a bright light in Queen Charlotte's darkening days.

The Queen visited the King regularly in his sad isolation at Windsor. Did she try to cheer him with the news of Princess Charlotte's engagement? He would have been glad: but the news of the rackety life her mother, Princess Caroline, was leading would have filled him with despair. The Prince Regent's estranged wife was now scandalizing the courts of Europe with her wild behaviour. Fortunately for his peace of mind, the King could not know of the Prince's continuing extravagant life, his debts, his drinking and his mistresses. Queen Charlotte had to endure the shame of it all alone.

Did she try to tell him of the world outside as the years passed? Perhaps she tried to penetrate the mists of his mind with news of the Duke of Wellington and his victory over the French at the Battle of Waterloo in 1815. But he was beyond caring: wars and domestic troubles, unemployment, riots, all belonged to a world he had left.

In November 1817 came heartbreaking news which she certainly would have kept from the King. Princess Charlotte – the heiress to the throne, the hope of the future – died in childbirth on 6 November. After fifty hours of agonizing labour she was delivered of 'a fine, large, dead boy'. Stockmar had been there but medical protocol prevented him from interfering in another doctor's case. He never forgot Princess Charlotte's desperate last moments, recording later:

During her agony the doctor had said 'Here comes an old friend of yours.' She stretched out her left hand eagerly to me and pressed mine twice vehemently. I went out of the room, then the rattle in the throat began. I had just left the room, when she called out loudly 'Stocky, Stocky.' I went back, she was quieter but the rattle continued. She died at 9pm.

In old age Leopold was to say he 'never recovered the feeling of happiness which had blessed his short married life'.[35]

'The passing of a "very kind spirit"'

As Queen Charlotte walked with difficulty through her state rooms, there were too many poignant memories of her own happy days of early marriage. The King's rooms on the ground floor were much as he had left them: on the walls of his Dining Room still hung Zoffany's portraits of herself, young and elegant, wearing the miniature by Meyer, set in a bracelet, that the King had sent to her in Mecklenburg before her marriage; and of the young King, painted so handsome and upright – it was unbearable to think of the blind old man shuffling around his closed world at Windsor, lost to her for ever.

Now the great staircase was hard to climb: she had told the Prince Regent on 19 December 1817 that she was 'well in health but continue to puff when I go up and down stairs'.[36] Upstairs in her long suite of rooms there were too many mirrors: she could not escape the image of the stout little lady with the tragic eyes. Beechey had caught the sad look, though his portrait on the walls of the Saloon was kinder than the mirrors. She could laugh wryly at her 'fat figure', but she thought of the cruel satires and cartoons in the popular press with pain.

Most poignant of all, as she made her slow progress through her rooms, were the paintings by Gainsborough in the Green Closet of the heads of thirteen of her children, in all their shining innocence. What had become of all that hope and promise? The Prince Regent was trapped in a disastrous marriage, deep in debt, his dissolute lifestyle earning him hatred and ridicule. Frederick, Duke of York, the King's favourite, had been caught up in the scandals of his mistress's arraignment for bribery; his marriage to the eccentric Frederica had produced no children. William, Duke of Clarence, had lived for more than twenty years with his actress mistress, Mrs Jordan, by whom he had ten children. Edward, Duke of Kent, had had a similarly comfortable long 'marriage' without the blessing of the Church, with Madame de St Laurent – his 'old French lady', as his sisters called her. Ernest, Duke of Cumberland, the black sheep of the family, according to gossip which she must have heard, was accused of every imaginable vice. Adolphus, Duke of Cambridge, had been something of a comfort and his marriage to Augusta of Hesse Cassel welcomed. Augustus, Duke of Sussex, however, had had a marriage to Lady Augusta Murray, which finished in separation in 1801. But most tragic were the two little boys who had died young – Prince Alfred and Prince Octavius: she could sigh over the painting by Benjamin West, *The Apotheosis of Prince Octavius*, describing their ascent to heaven, which hung on the walls (it still hangs there) – and Princess Amelia, whose death in 1810 had pushed the King over the brink into his final breakdown. But at least her other daughters had given her love and comfort even if there had been spectacular rows –

understandable, considering their confined and frustrated lives. Charlotte, the Princess Royal, had married Frederick I, the Hereditary Prince of Württemberg, on 18 May 1797 and Princess Mary was at last settled.

Queen Charlotte never gave up hope that one day the King would regain his senses. So, in her refurbished apartments she held drawing rooms, and received delegations and diplomats, wearing her fabulous diamonds, silks and old lace as he would have wished. Richard Rush, American Minister to the Court of St James, remembered one such occasion, when a thousand guests thronged the great staircase, which, as he recorded in his diary on 17 February 1818,

branched off at the first landing . . . The company ascending took one channel; those descending, the other, and both channels were full . . . The openings through the old carved balusters, brought all under view at once, and the paintings on the walls were all seen at the same time . . . Four rooms were allotted to the ceremony. In the second, was the Queen. She sat on a velvet chair and cushion, a little raised up. Near her were the Princesses and ladies in waiting . . . The Prince Regent was there and Royal Family . . . The doors of the rooms were all open . . . You saw in them a thousand ladies richly dressed . . . I had already seen in England signs enough of opulence and power – now I saw on all sides, British beauty.[37]

In 1817 the Queen was struck to the heart by the death of her grandchild, Princess Charlotte, whom she had come to love. After the funeral at Windsor, she went to Bath to take the waters. Here she met again Madame d'Arblay – whom she had known as Fanny Burney. The novelist was shocked at the appearance of the Queen but nevertheless saw her making her

round of the company . . . with a Grace indescribable, and, to those who never witnessed it, inconceivable; for it was such as to carry off Age, Infirmity, sickness, diminutive and disproportioned stature and Ugliness! – as to give her . . . a power of charming and delighting that rarely has been equalled.[38]

Other commentators were more cruel, but Fanny Burney's praise was echoed by others who saw her at the Queen's House fulfilling her duties. On 25 February 1818, in the last year of her life, Richard Rush, the

American Minister, was equally charmed by the grace with which she received his letters of credence in all the splendour of the great Saloon at the Queen's House. She, who had followed the American War of Independence with passionate and partisan interest, now received the Republican envoy with 'a very kind spirit', asking intelligent questions about Rush's home town Philadelphia, and about America in general. He found her 'gentle voice' and the 'benignity of her manner attractive and touching'.

The same strength that had supported her as a young girl at Court now steeled her to battle on, though she was often in pain.

In her last year there were still duties to perform and there were weddings to celebrate. On Tuesday, 7 April 1818 her daughter, the intelligent Princess Elizabeth, married Frederick, the future Landgrave of Hesse-Homburg. The Queen and Princess Elizabeth had often quarrelled. The Princess had once claimed that 'the King had spoiled her [the Queen] from the hour she came, and we have continued doing so from the hour of our birth'. But now they were reconciled and the Saloon at the Queen's House was once more transformed into a chapel, the temporary altar covered in red and gold. The guests stood for the ceremony, but Queen Charlotte, in pain, sat on her throne, and Princess Elizabeth knelt to receive her blessing. Richard Rush was there, full of praise for the Queen: he noticed that she wore a miniature of the King around her neck.

There was one more drawing room on 14 April, but this was her last. There was another wedding: the Duke of Cambridge had married, at Cassel, Princess Augusta of Hesse-Cassel, sister of the Grand Duchess of Mecklenburg-Strelitz. Now on 1 June they were remarried in the Queen's Saloon in her presence. Queen Charlotte welcomed with pleasure the bride with Mecklenburg connections.

She hoped to return to the King at Windsor, but she was too weak to travel. The iron gates around the Palace forecourt were closed: the rattle of carriages disturbed her.

On 20 June she left the Queen's House for the last time. She managed to get as far as Kew. In the drawing room of the Dutch House she witnessed two of her sons' double wedding: William, Duke of Clarence, married Princess Adelaide of Saxe Meiningen, and Edward, Duke of Kent, married Princess Victoire, widow of the Prince of Leiningen and sister of Prince Leopold. The Duke of Kent had supported Prince Leopold in his pursuit of Princess Charlotte: he, in turn, had encouraged this marriage of the Duke with his sister, Victoire. Two faithful ladies had been put aside to make these royal marriages. Mrs Jordan was dead and the Duke of Kent's long and happy relationship with Julie, Madame de St Laurent, had to be ended.

After the death of Princess Charlotte there were no legitimate heirs to the throne in the younger generation and it seemed that the monarchy was in danger, but the royal Dukes, elderly but, it was hoped, still fertile, had hastily come to the rescue. In fact, none of the Duke of Clarence's legitimate children were to survive, but he was to become William IV and the Duke of Kent was to be the father of Queen Victoria.

Queen Charlotte had not long to live. She was not able to make the journey on to Windsor and after months of suffering, on Tuesday, 17 November 1818 she died.

Her daughters, Princesses Mary and Augusta, had 'witnesssed sufferings I can never describe and I trust we shall never forget, the example of fortitude and mildness and every virtue'. The Prince Regent, her favourite son, was there at the end, her hand tightly clasped in his. Queen Charlotte had been through much rough weather since she had crossed the stormy North Sea to her wedding, but she had kept the faith as she saw it; and had maintained the dignity of the Crown through a generation of scandal. At the end she had the comfort of the love of her family: as her daughter Princess Mary wrote, 'Hers was a long life of trials. Religion and her Trust in God supported her under all her various misfortunes that brought us all together . . . we must feel the want of her every hour.'[39]

Queen Charlotte was buried in St George's Chapel at Windsor, a grieving Prince Leopold the most affected of the mourners.

Did they tell the King at Windsor of her going? Or was he too far away in his timeless world where past and present were mingled? He would have approved the choice of the music of Handel as her Requiem, saying, as he often did, 'The King had loved it when he was alive.'

'And farewell King'

The cold January of 1820 brought unexpected tragedy to the Kents and long-awaited release for the King. On 23 January the Duke of Kent died of pneumonia at Sidmouth, Devon, by the sea. He and his wife Victoire, Duchess of Kent, and Princess Victoria, their six-month-old baby, had been staying at Claremont with the Duchess's brother, the widower Prince Leopold. They had come to Devon for a Christmas break and here the Duke caught the cold that killed him. His death took everyone by surprise – he had been the strongest of the King's sons. It happened that the ubiquitous Stockmar was with him at the end, and sensibly urged him to make his will and appoint executors, one of whom was his equerry, John Conroy – a character who was to cause trouble in the future. Prince Leopold came to the Duchess of Kent's rescue, persuaded her to stay to bring up little Princess Victoria in England, and made her an allowance.

Six days later, on 29 January 1820 at eight o'clock at night, George III died at Windsor, the Duke of York at his bedside. For a moment he had seemed to regain his sanity, saying, 'Frederick, give me your hand.' As the Duke told Princess Lieven, wife of the Russian ambassador, 'he was allowed to fade out quietly, he was given no remedy and he did not suffer at all'.

Many who had been most critical now sighed at the passing of the 'good old King'. Even the cynical and waspish Princess Lieven slipped into elegiac mood. She wrote to the Austrian statesman, Prince Metternich:

There is something poetic in the picture of this old, blind King, wandering about in his castle among his shadows, talking with them; for he lived his life among the dead – playing on his organ and never losing his illusions. I really believe that, for the last nine years of his reign, he was the happiest man in his kingdom; the saddest of all infirmities – blindness – had become the source of all his pleasures. Nothing could call him back to the world of reality, and his ideal world was full of all the pure joys that a gentle and pious fancy could invent.[40]

So in his mind he could wander again through the Queen's House, admire his pictures, remember the artists and listen to the music of Handel. Now he could dream of his wonderful clocks and listen to their ticking in a world outside time.

CHAPTER THREE

George IV

'I am too old to build a palace . . . If the public wish to have
[one] . . . I will have it at Buckingham House . . . There are early associations
which endear me to the spot.'[1]

GEORGE IV

The Age of Fantasy

When George IV acceded to the throne, his first concern was to plan
the most extravagant of coronations, bringing back old traditions. Herb
strewers walked before the King, a Champion rode into Westminster
Hall on his grey horse, wine flowed and thousands of candles shone.
There were onlookers who remembered the hunger and poverty outside
and did not know whether to laugh or cry. The sight of the horse
that refused to walk backwards from His Majesty's presence certainly
provoked disrespectful merriment. Many were furious at the indignity
suffered by George's Queen, Caroline, who, though she [tried all] the
doors of the Abbey, was refused entry to the Coronation. When soon
after the King heard the news of her death, there was no grief for a wife
he had come to hate.

His next concern was to provide himself with a London residence.
From the first years of his adult life he had been possessed by a mania
for building, and each new home had reflected his changing moods,
expressions of his world of fantasy. In the Royal Pavilion, Brighton, he
was an oriental potentate; in Carlton House, he wanted to outshine the
French King; at Windsor Castle, he was a knight of battles, convincing
himself that he had fought at the Battle of Waterloo.

By the time George IV became King, his passion for creating palaces
was waning: his fantastic Pavilion at Brighton was losing its charm, and

he was becoming tired of the 'Mahomet's Paradise' he had created in Carlton House. A lifetime of self-indulgence had left its mark: crippled by gout, increasingly obese, he had become the butt of satirists and cartoonists. His extravagance in times of war and poverty, and his treatment of his eccentric wife, Queen Caroline, had made him deeply unpopular. To his enemies Carlton House, his London home, had become the symbol of the decadence of the British monarchy.

Carlton House had been bought by the King's grandfather, Frederick, Prince of Wales, and his grandmother, Princess Augusta, had lived there until her death in 1772. When Prince George came of age in 1783 he was given Carlton House: for the next thirty years, with the help of five successive architects, the Prince had spent vast sums, altering and improving, furnishing and refurnishing with manic energy, forever changing his plans. The waste and extravagance had been scandalous, although it must be said that he accumulated a superb collection of paintings and a priceless hoard of treasures and furniture, silver, china and *objets d'art*, many of which grace Buckingham Palace today.

He must have sorely tried his first architect in 1783 – Sir William Chambers – who was succeeded in the next year by Henry Holland. Nevertheless Chambers's love of Chinese art and architecture left a lasting impression on the Prince. Four years later, he created a Chinese Room at Carlton House. Thirty years later its furniture was to be transferred to the Prince's second and even more fantastic palace, the Brighton Pavilion.

When, in 1811, the Prince became Regent, Carlton House became the centre of Court life, where he held his levees, receptions, and fabulous fêtes to celebrate victories in the Peninsular War, and in honour of Louis XVIII on his return to France after the Battle of Waterloo. In July 1814 an even more extravagant celebration was held in honour of the Duke of Wellington. John Nash, appointed in 1813 as architect for Carlton House, created mirror-lined tents and pavilions in the garden for these festivities.

However, by 1819, the Prince was growing tired of Carlton House: there was not enough room for his vast assemblies, and it had no gallery suitable for his growing collection of paintings – over 250 had to be stored on the attic floor.

George IV was one of the great Royal collectors, comparable with Charles I. He undoubtedly was genuinely interested in art and showed real discrimination in his purchase of paintings. However, he accumulated pictures with obsessive greed, buying and selling almost until his death. But he was a generous patron: he bought pictures from Reynolds, Gainsborough, Beechey and Hopper, and commissioned many more, including narrative paintings from David Wilkie. George Stubbs was a particular favourite. Eighteen of his pictures, now in the Royal Collection, belonged to George IV.

During his Regency he had collected mainly Dutch and Flemish seventeenth-century pictures. Perhaps their cool order brought peace to his restless mind. Surprisingly the extravagant Regent took pleasure in van Ostade's painting of a child being fed in a cottage. This was part of a collection of eighty-six paintings he bought from the banker Sir Thomas Baring in 1814: also included were Jan Steen's rollicking *Twelfth Night Feast: the King Drinks* and a luminous evening landscape by Aelbert Cuyp.

Now that he was King he could find a new home not only for his paintings, but for his richly decorated French furniture, his chandeliers and massive candelabras, his clocks and Sèvres porcelain.

However, he could not at first decide what kind of palace he wanted. There were many suggestions offered. The architect Sir John Soane had already produced detailed plans for a splendid residence for the new King. Mrs Arbuthnot, wife of the Commissioner for Woods and Forests, Charles Arbuthnot, records that at a house party at Stratfield Saye in October 1825, Colonel Trench MP had shown the Duke of Wellington his own plans for a new building.

Colonel Trench wants to have a palace in the Park on what is called Buck Vine Hill, and the execution of his plan would cause half Hyde Park to be occupied by buildings, courts and gardens. It is the worst plan of a house I ever saw, and quite colossal, for he proposes a statue gallery 500 feet long, a drawing room 190, and other rooms in proportion. It is the most ridiulous plan I ever saw for, added to it, is the idea of a street *200 feet wide* extending from the end of

Hyde Park opposite the New Palace to St Paul's!! The King and the Duke of York are madly eager for this plan; but the former says he supposes his d—d ministers won't allow it... Colonel Trench has persuaded him that Buckingham House will always be a damp hole unfit for him to live in; and the ministers, in consequence of the King's determination to have no other place, during the last session obtained money from Parliament, obtained the King's approval of the plan and immediately set to work to build there for him. All the rest of us laughed at Col. Trench and his plans; we advised him to put his palace in Kensington Gardens and not to touch the 'lungs of the people of England', as the newspapers call the parks.[2]

However, the King, rejecting all alternative plans, decided to rebuild Buckingham Palace and demolish Carlton House. The Riding School next door was converted into a store for his furniture and possessions.

The King solved the problem of storing at least some of his vast collection of paintings: he lent 164 in 1826 and a further 185 in 1827 for exhibition in the British Institution in Pall Mall, of which he was the patron. The foreword in the catalogue recorded His Majesty's 'desire to interest the public feeling in the advancement of the fine arts'. When Prince Regent he had shown a genuine interest in supporting British artists and took great interest in the proposal for a National Gallery. Ten Corinthian pillars from the front of Carlton House were saved and, according to Clifford Smith, used in the façade of the new National Gallery when it was built in 1838.

Nash had already given much thought to a new palace and tried to persuade the King to build higher, in line with Pall Mall. He did not like Buckingham House's northern aspect, and rightly considered it too low and damp. However, the King was adamant. In the presence of Lord Farnborough he warned Nash not

at his peril ever to advise me to build a Palace. I am too old to build a Palace. If the Public wish to have a Palace, I have no objection to build one, but I must have a pied-à-terre. I do not like Carlton House standing in a street, and moreover I tell him that I will have it at Buckingham House; and if he pulls it down he shall rebuild it in the same place; there are early associations which endear me to the spot.[3]

He had had a happy childhood there with Queen Charlotte.

The idea that George IV would be satisfied with a *pied à terre* was preposterous. His feet were never wholly on the ground. Even in 1819, before he became King, he had considered rebuilding Buckingham House on a grand scale. But, as he told the Prime Minister, Lord Liverpool, that would cost around £450,000. The government, however, had refused to allot anything more than £150,000. These were days of distress and riots. So it was not until 12 July 1821 that the King told his Surveyor-General Stephenson 'to put all plans relating to Buckingham House in the hands of Nash', and work did not begin until 1825.

If the new King did not know what he wanted, John Nash did. The new palace should be part of his grand scheme for London. He had already designed Regent's Park and the great sweeping arc of Regent Street leading from the Park down to Carlton House. Now he was planning to clear away the jumble of little streets round the King's Mews on the site of the present Trafalgar Square and create an open space where the Battle of Trafalgar could be commemorated, reveal the church of St Martin's-in-the-Fields, unite the roads from Whitehall, the Mall and the Strand, and link with the great road to Regent's Park. Buckingham Palace would then be the climax of the long avenue, the Mall. He also had plans for a West Strand development, but by this time he was fully engaged in his work on the palace, so the building with the round turrets that he designed, now the bank of Coutts & Co., was built by other architects. In many respects his vision was realized: Trafalgar Square was created and Regent Street and Regent's Park remain an elegant monument to him. The King's Mews was removed to the Grosvenor Place end of the palace garden.

In June 1825 a bill was passed in the House of Commons authorizing work to begin on the 'repair and improvement of Buckingham House' with a grant of £200,000.

On 23 January 1826 *The Times* reported:

The new palace is to be called 'The King's Palace in St James's Park'. A large artificial mound has been raised near the lower end of Grosvenor Place to hide the stables, behind it a fish pond will be constructed. The centre will remain as a parallelogram, from each side of which a circular range of buildings will end in pavilions.

The entire pile will be of immense magnitude.

All the principal and state apartments will face west.[4]

This is one of the earliest references to the 'Palace'.

In May 1826 *The Times* reported that, on the advice of his doctors, His Majesty was not to return to Brighton and that the Pavilion was to be stripped inside and out; some items were to be used at Buckingham Palace. The truth was that the King was no longer the Prince Charming of his youth, and he had grown so immensely fat that he was unwilling to be seen in public. The house and garden at the end of the Mall would be a retreat, a '*rus in urbe*', again. But the retreat was to become an 'immense pile', thanks to the co-operation of a king who could not rid himself of the *folie de grandeur*, and an architect who was only too ready to oblige him.

'Nash, the state rooms you have made me are so handsome that I think I shall hold my courts there'

It is time to take a closer look at John Nash, the architect mainly responsible for the Palace we see today, although there would be major alterations and additions in the reigns of Queen Victoria and King Edward VII. It is important to remember that in 1825 Nash was seventy-three and was still an extremely busy architect, the Palace being only one of many projects in which he was concerned.

His early life is obscure, but it appears that he was born in Lambeth of Welsh parents in 1752. His father and cousins were millwrights and engineers with relations still working in Wales. Apparently his father was sufficiently prosperous to take a house in Spring Gardens, near Charing Cross, where he died when Nash was seven years old. Their neighbour Robert Taylor was one of the most successful architects of the day and may have taken an interest in the bright little boy. Certainly he took him as an assistant, possibly in 1766 or 1767; and with him he would have served a seven years' apprenticeship. It is a pity we know so little of Nash's years with Taylor, for his influence was to remain with him all his life. Robert Taylor began in his father's trade as a mason and sculptor, studied in Rome and on his return found wealthy patrons in the city. He switched early from sculpture to architecture and became famous for his solid classical buildings, in town and country. He became architect to the Bank of England, received a knighthood and made a fortune, which he left for the teaching of foreign languages at the University of Oxford. This eventually resulted in the foundation of the Taylorian Institute. In Taylor's office the young Nash had an excellent grounding in the principles of classical architecture, and the energy which drove him all his life would have been harnessed and disciplined by a master who worked hard and demanded accuracy.

It is said that Nash was 'a wild irregular youth' and his biographer, William Porden, records that he drove Taylor into a frenzy, upon which Taylor would 'pinch John's ears and perform some sort of jigs with cries of "harum scarum"'. The qualities that marked his later work were obviously present as a boy – the talent and the energy which on one occasion drove him to stay up all night to complete a job which his colleagues said could not be done. Above all, if Robert Taylor could have looked down in after life at his pupil's work for the 'Palace in the Park' he would have shaken the walls of heaven with his 'harum scarum'.

There are various and differing accounts of the next stage of Nash's life, but some facts seem to be established. According to Porden, after 'the term of his articles expired' Nash retired to a small country estate, where he led the life of 'a gentleman keeping the best company of Bon Vivants'. In short, this was said to be a period of 'harum scarum'. In April 1775 Nash married Elizabeth Kerr, a surgeon's daughter, by whom he had a son, baptized on 10 June 1776; and, it would appear, they lived in Lambeth.

His first building ventures – speculative building in Bloomsbury Square – set a pattern he would follow with the same mixture of success and failure in Regent Street and Carlton Gardens. The stucco for his buildings was supplied by the firm of Robert, James & William Adam, who reappear in the history of Buckingham Palace later on. He lived in one of the houses and moved on to Great Russell Street. In 1782 he left his wife for a Welsh lady, became involved in a court case, and, in 1783, became bankrupt, describing himself as 'John Nash, Carpenter, Dealer and Chapman'. He retreated to Wales and gradually established himself as an architect responsible, among other things, for Carmarthen Gaol. From then onwards he pursued an uneven course upwards, raising classical buildings and experimenting with iron work in construction. In 1795 the graceful iron bridge he built at Stratford-on-Teme collapsed.

Attracted by his lively personality and intelligence, the Prince drew him into his circle. He began to rely on Nash, not only as his architectural surveyor but also as a political supporter, intelligent enough to be sent on delicate missions to Westminster. Almost his first action as Regent was to set in motion again work on the Brighton Pavilion and when James Wyatt, his Surveyor-General, died in September 1813, he appointed Nash as Deputy Surveyor. For the next two years Nash concentrated on his work for Carlton House and London. For the peace celebrations of 1814 he was commissioned to build a fantastic pagoda over a bridge in St James's Park. It was brilliant but, like his bridge, was doomed: it caught fire and collapsed.

From 1815 to 1823 Nash was in charge of the Brighton Pavilion, a monster of a building that changed its shape as the Regent became possessed by a new fantasy. The cost was prodigious, paid for, supposedly, out of the Regent's Privy Purse. By 4 May 1820 the estimates totalled £134,609 16s. 5d. But Nash exceeded these by £11,109. There were also constructional problems, which sometimes occurred in Nash's buildings: the roof of the Pavilion, covered in his experimental 'Delhi Mastic', leaked. However, it was repaired and by 1823 the Brighton Pavilion, in all its oriental mad glory, was finished. Many mocked, but its sheer exuberance would amaze generations of visitors to come. Typically, George IV – as he now was – lost interest and he rarely visited the Pavilion after 1823.

In the first years of his reign he had other things on his mind. His estranged wife, Queen Caroline, returned to England, determined to attend the Coronation and take her place as Queen. The King's enemies welcomed her, and the mobs cheered her and booed the King, whose extravagance and self-indulgence made him unpopular. Queen Caroline's eccentric career ended in tragedy. Barred from Westminster Abbey on the day of George IV's Coronation, 19 July 1821, she returned home in deep distress, was taken ill on 30 July and died on the night of 7 August 1821.

The King now turned his attention to the deserted Queen's House. When in 1821 Nash was commissioned by the King to 'repair' the Queen's House Nash was fully extended. He was getting old, but he had not lost his phenomenal energy. He led the life of a hospitable country gentleman at the castle he built at East Cowes on the Isle of Wight, where in 1817 the Prince Regent visited him. He was described by one of his guests, Mrs Arbuthnot, as 'a very clever, odd, amusing man . . . with a face like a monkey's but civil and good humoured to the greatest degree'.5 John Nash certainly knew how to charm the ladies.

The Queen's House was in fact in the area allotted to one of the King's other architects, Sir John Soane, who was at this time building a new entrance to the House of Lords but expected to be the architect for the new Buckingham House. Nash's amusing and conciliating letter of 18 September 1822 is typical of a man whose gift for laughing at himself could disarm opponents.

. . . it occurred to me that our appointments are perfectly constitutional, I the King, you the Lords, and *your* Friend Smirke [Sir Robert Smirke, the third of the King's architects], the Commons, and the blood instantly rushed to my face seeing or fancying that you wanted to dethrone me. It then struck me that you wanted to be both King and Lords and in fancy I heard you cry out – 'Off with his head, so much for Buckingham', and I sighed 'why should he so long for my empty chair when a few years would give him that without offence which has occasioned in him so offensive an act,' for I am old, but feeling my head on my shoulders I marched off to Buckingham House.

He concluded:

. . . I have your figure now before my eyes, a thick black shadow standing on the foundation walls of the new arcade . . . Oh . . . that some friend could describe my thick, squat dwarf figure, with round head, snub nose and little eyes in such an act of contemplation, but I must be shot flying.[6]

He addressed it to 'J Soane Esq. Architect to the whole Peerage of England'.

In May 1825 readers of *The Times* were informed:

Buckingham House is to be converted into a palace, for the residence of the King. The centre building will ostensibly remain, but the interior of it will be entirely renovated. Two magnificent and tasteful wings, which have been projected by His Majesty himself, upon a very large scale will be added to the centre. The domestic offices, suited to the luxury of these times, and replete with every convenience, will be concealed from the public eye by an ingenious artifice. The workmen have already commenced their labours; the whole will be finished in 18 months.[7]

In June *The Times* reported again:

In consequence of the extensive alterations that are [being made] in this palace there are nearly 400 artisans of every description at work on the premises, amongst whom there are no fewer than 120 carpenters. These men are satisfied with the usual pay of 5 shillings a day, and accordingly they have given offence to their fellow-workmen who have struck for an increase. On Tuesday a number of these non-contents surrounded the palace, and threatened the men unless they left their work. They were provided with sticks, and one who was armed with a sword flourished it about in a menacing manner. Finding they could not prevail upon the men to quit their work, they entered the building, where they repeated their threats to the workmen . . . Mr Firth the superintendent had to call in a party of the Coldstream Guards to force them to leave.[8]

In June 1825 the work was proceeding. Nash appointed an old friend, William Nixon, as general Clerk of the Works, with three clerks under him, each responsible for one third of the work, to be carried out at the same time. The Treasury obligingly agreed his estimate of £200,000 for 'repairs' – before it knew what it was getting. Nash had still not presented his complete estimate, nor had he finished the plans. Parliament was taking him on trust, as it later learned to its cost.

The problems that were to concern future monarchs had their roots at the beginning of the rebuilding of the Palace. The trouble was that the King and his architect were two old men in a hurry. In 1825, the King's health was poor; he knew he had not many years ahead and he still did not know what he wanted. Nash had not the time, nor, for that matter, the inclination to work out careful plans.

But the fatal flaw in the construction was that the King could never decide the purpose of the Palace. Though at first he had thought of it as a *pied à terre*, when he saw how splendid Nash's rooms were becoming, he changed his mind. 'Nash,' he cried, 'the state rooms you have made me are so handsome that I think I shall hold my courts there.' Nash complained that the original plan had been to build a residence, and there were no more rooms planned for a queen nor offices for the Lord Chamberlain and Lord Steward. The King replied, 'You know nothing about the matter; it will make an excellent palace, and Lord St Helens and myself have arranged the use of several apartments.'[9] They could meet the cost by pulling down St James's Palace, which he disliked. Instead, he took the decision to raze Carlton House and build mansions on the site. Being so near the Palace they could be let at enormous profit, or so he claimed.

As the Palace grew grander, the King saw it as a great monument to the victors of Trafalgar and Waterloo. In this Lord Farnborough encouraged him. He had been in Paris as an official during the peace negotiations and was impressed by the nobility of the French state buildings, the elegance of the work of French architects and Napoleon's arch in the Tuileries. Nash was delighted to design a great Marble Arch for the front courtyard, a Roman victory arch which would dominate the vista from the end of the Mall. On 4 September 1826 *The Literary Gazette* described the plans with awe: 'This is a portico of two orders of architecture, the lower is Doric copied from the Temple of Theseus at Athens. The upper is Corinthian like the Pantheon in Rome.'[10] Originally Nash had planned it to be, like the exterior of the Palace, made of Bath stone, but, carried away by enthusiasm, sent to Italy for the finest Carrara marble, to be chosen by his agent, Joseph Browne. It came by sea, was landed at Pimlico on the Thames and hauled to the Palace in great wagons.

The sculptor Sir Francis Chantrey was commissioned for 9,000 guineas to execute a statue of His Majesty to crown the Arch. Nash had intended to have three panels on the parapet commemorating Trafalgar, and a continuous frieze representing Waterloo. The sculptors engaged for the marble work were E. H. Baily and Richard Westmacott, and the estimate for the whole was some £50,000.

It was this vision that was enthusiastically described in *Fraser's Magazine* in 1830.

The whole of this gorgeous pile will, when finished, be about sixty feet high. The gates are to be of mosaic gold, and the palisade which is to connect it with the wings of the Palace are to be spears of the richest workmanship that has yet been executed for such a purpose in that superb metal.[11]

Those splendid gates, wrought by Samuel Parker and costing 3,000 guineas, were nearly ruined by last-minute penny-pinching. The beautiful semi-circular head was damaged during its transportation in a 'common stage wagon'.

The Arch always looked out of place, jutting up like some great rock in a bay, but it remained in front of the Palace until 1850, when it was taken down and rebuilt on its present site at Marble Arch.

The Building of the New Palace

During the years from 1825, when the work on the new Palace began, to 1837, when it was finally completed, the peace of St James's Park was shattered. Buckingham's house could no longer be described as '*Rus in urbe*'. The air was thick with dust as Buckingham House was rebuilt and Carlton House demolished. The park resounded with the crash of falling masonry. Wagons laden with precious furniture or heavy with slabs of marble, loads of rubble, pillars and pediments rumbled along the Mall.

To add to the babel, St James's Park was undergoing a major transformation: sweeping curves were dug out, widening the old formal canal. In 1764 George III had appointed Lancelot 'Capability' Brown as his landscape gardener. His plans for a romantic lake bounded by sweeping banks, with an island in its midst, had never been adopted. Now George IV gave Repton (son of Humphrey Repton) the opportunity to reshape the Park. The gardener had worked closely with Nash for many years – indeed Nash often called him his 'partner'.

St James's Park became part of Nash's vision of the new London, a romantic counterpart to Regent's Park linked by a graceful street. The new Park owed much to Brown's original plans, but Repton also widened the Mall to accommodate a carriage drive in a direct line to the Palace. The gardens at the rear of the Palace were transformed from 'a meadow with a formal dingy canal . . . into a cheerful . . . pleasure ground'.[12] Redesigned in the new 'picturesque' fashion, there were now winding walks and a serpentine lake. The earth excavated was used to build a great mound at the end of the garden.

Nash's plan followed the lines of the Duke of Buckingham's house. The main block was still flanked by two wings, but these were now changed and moved further out, giving an enlarged courtyard (and making more room for the servants). Sadly the Duke's graceful fountain was no longer there and the comfortable red brick was now clad in Bath stone. A flight of stone steps still led up to the entrance under the classical portico.

The design on the garden side of the Palace was simple and elegant. The long line of the house was relieved by a graceful central semi-circular bay and above it a corresponding dome. This latter was to be much mocked and later removed. Nash had not intended it to be seen from the front of the house, where it popped up like an upturned cup. Later he would cheerfully admit to a Commission of Enquiry that he had not realized how wrong the wings in the front courtyard would appear, nor how absurd the dome on the garden front would appear when seen from the front.

A wide terrace before the garden front was to be flanked by four garden pavilions, although eventually only three were built.* Today

---

* One was later removed to Kew, and one transformed into a chapel in Queen Victoria's reign; the third eventually became the swimming pool.

visitors to the Queen's annual garden parties can still admire what Professor Richardson has called the terrace's

simple yet regal grandeur ... The level lines of the façade emphasise the projecting curves of the central bow. Touches here and there, for example the ellipsoids with ornamental surrounds beneath the projecting portions of the cornice, recall the elegances of the Louis XVI style and pay a compliment to Sir William Chambers.[13]

The two frieze panels on either side of the bow were sculptured in Coade stone.   Inside the building there were major alterations. The Grand Hall and sweeping staircase follow much the same plan as that of the Duke's old house, but Nash lowered the floor of the Hall, making more dramatic the flight of stairs with its elegant wrought balustrade.

The garden side of the house was greatly altered. Queen Charlotte's long enfilade of state rooms opening off each other was swept into one long, wide gallery, and beside it Nash created a new line of state rooms looking on to the garden. Nash had admired galleries like this for paintings or statuary in the great country houses he had visited. In fact, he had built one for his own house in Regent Street.

As Nash's biographer, John Summerson, has written, he 'was not and never had been a great interior designer ... but to be faced now at seventy-six with the creation of a set of Royal Apartments of the greatest possible dignity and richness might have daunted a Mansart or an Adam'.[14] He succeeded: each salon had a 'marked stylistic character'. It is not surprising that the King found the state rooms 'handsome'.

In the Green Drawing Room and the Throne Room on the courtyard side the eye is drawn up by tall pillars to the intricate beauty of the coved ceilings. On the garden side, in the dignified White Drawing Room once again pillars with carved capitals support a ceiling of delicate design. Next is the Music Room, which is quintessential Nash: five tall windows overlook the garden and ten massive pillars support a ceiling where the half dome over the bay window sings in counterpoint with the dome in the centre. In describing Nash's work it is a musical analogy that comes most frequently to mind.

Although his work has all the grace of the period, Nash was prepared to experiment. All the pillars throughout the state rooms were made of scagliola in rich, vibrant colours. Scagliola was an Italian technique which had been used in England since Charles II's time. It had a base of wood, covered with coarse grained plaster undercoat, which could be painted to look like marble of many colours. Sir William Chambers described the new process of manufacture:

first basic layer plaster – then finer paste with less marble 1.5″ thick, and after having beat it for some time then strew in bits of marble of different kinds and beat them into the paste, then when dry put on paste made of powder of tites, lime and soap water – this lay on the thickness of sheet of paper and smooth and polish it with polished towel before it dries then rub it with linseed oil and a woollen cloth.[15]

Nash also used the artificial stone made by Mrs Coade for sculptures and friezes on the exterior of the Palace. The remarkable lady who invented it deserves her place in the history of the Palace. As the author of her obituary in *The Gentleman's Magazine* of 1821 wrote,

Eleanor Coade was the sole inventor and proprietor of an art which deserves considerable notice. In 1769 a burnt artificial stone manufactory was erected by Mrs Coade at King's Arms Stairs, Lambeth . . . Coade stone resisted frost and consequently retained 'that sharpness in which it excels, every kind of stone sculpture and even equals marble'.[16]

Mrs Coade was obviously a formidable character who ran her 'manu-factory' with great efficiency. She was a stalwart supporter of her local Baptist church and left most of her considerable wealth to charity.

In her biography of Mrs Coade, Alison Kelly describes Coade stone as:

a material, [that] although composed of various ingredients may be described as a species of terracotta. It combines in one mass pipe-clay, flint, sand and glass and stoneware, that had already passed the furnace. These are ground to a very fine powder, and are mixed in the proper proportions and the whole is well kneaded together by means of the addition of water. In this state it forms a kind of paste which has the ductility of the clay usually employed in modelling. It is now wrought into the form desired . . . and when finished it is left to dry gradually. When thoroughly desiccated the performance is placed in a kiln, where it undergoes an intense white heat; and being allowed to cool it is now complete.[17]

In her last years Eleanor Coade employed a distant relation of her aunt, William Croggan, as her manager and after her death he bought the business. It was he who was employed at Buckingham Palace, supplying not only Coade stone but also scagliola. He worked on the Duke of York's mansion, now Lancaster House. Croggan went bankrupt in 1833, and died two years later.

Nash also tried new methods in the construction of the Palace chimneys. As *The Times* reported on 10 March 1826:

The chimnies [sic] of the new palace building in St James's Park for the King, are being built upon a new construction, to avoid the nuisance of smoke, and the necessity of climbing boys to sweep them, agreeably to Mr Hiort's patent for an improvement in the architectural construction of chimnies.

Apparently Mr Hiort, who was an architect in the Office of Works, had given a lecture to explain his invention. He wrote that he had never met anyone who had actually thought of seriously eliminating smoke. Evidently no one in the Ministry had read Evelyn's treatise *Fumigorium*, which had impressed Charles II more than a century earlier. 'His new chimneys were to be of patent bricks glazed inside which need less cleaning and have no need of climbing boys. All sharp angular turns and other impediments had been eliminated.'[18]

There was still concern about climbing boys a year and a half later. *The Times* reported in 1827 that

Joseph Glass, the mechanical chimney-sweeper, patronised by the Society for superseding climbing boys, was sent for last week to make trial of his newly-invented machine in some of the most difficult flues in the building, and succeeded in passing the machine through them with great ease. Several surveyors were present and expressed great admiration at the facility with which it was apparent that the cleansing of the flues might be effected, and the prospect of a total abolition of the barbarous climbing boy practice.[19]

Samuel Parker designed the intricate balustrades on the main staircase and the bronze capitals of many of the pillars; George Seddon worked the exquisite marquetry of the floor of the Music Room; Richard

Westmacott, William Pitts and Charles Ross modelled much of the charming detailed plasterwork. Joseph Theakston, the sculptor who carved the monumental chimneypiece that dominates the Grand Hall, is remembered with affection. William Jeakes made the grates and the steel and brass firedogs in the Throne Room, and an immense iron spit which still hangs on the wall of the kitchen over gleaming modern appliances. He makes a tantalizing appearance in the letters of the novelist Charles Dickens as a skilled engineer, 'ingenious in his trade', who made a washing machine for him to be sent to Florence Nightingale when she was a nurse in the Crimea.

'The End of the Imperial Dream'

There is a pathos and some bathos in the King's last years. His other dream palace, Carlton House, was a pile of rubble, an oriental fantasy, like Prospero's dream, now faded from his mind. But there was still Buckingham Palace, which he would never occupy, but which was to reflect so much of his personality in the fabulous possessions he left behind: the exquisite furniture, mirrors and chandeliers, gilded fittings, priceless china and vases, and superb collection of paintings that had been removed from Carlton House were later to be transferred to the new Buckingham Palace.

When the sad old King's last days are forgotten he can at least be remembered as one of the great collectors, rivalled only by Charles I. Many of the paintings he bought are still to be seen in Buckingham Palace. He is justly praised for his artistic discrimination; however, one cannot help reflecting that it is easy to be a great collector if you can spend vast sums of money that you do not possess. The King collected great paintings: he also collected great debts. In partnership with Nash he brought elegance and grace to the streets and parks of London. Above all he encouraged Nash to create in Buckingham Palace some of his finest work.

At the last, he hid away in his splendid robes either at Windsor or at his last refuge, Virginia Water. Here was a magical Chinese pavilion: across the lake he built Roman ruins, and rode under the broken arch with his commander, the Duke of Wellington. The victor of Waterloo, often impatient with his impossible master, listened with a wry smile. But he also later remembered, with pleasure, days quietly fishing with the King from the barge on the lake.

At the end of his life the King's fantasies were imperial; here at Buckingham Palace he would be remembered – triumphant in battle. Had he not, at least in his dreams, fought at Waterloo? Through the Marble Arch he could ride forth like a Roman emperor: his victories, Trafalgar and Waterloo, were to be engraved there. Immortal in marble he would be a hero, remembered with Nelson and Wellington. The other entrance gates, he mused, could be for visitors, but this 'would be for us'.*

In the last years of his life, the King, who had once been the 'first gentleman of Europe', was a sad wreck living as a recluse at Windsor Castle. Increasingly large doses of laudanum mixed with cherry brandy eased his gout but confused his mind. His ministers, Wellington and Peel, wanted him to sign the Catholic Relief Bill, a measure that he obstinately refused to accept, believing it conflicted with his Coronation oath. Finally he agreed, but the struggle left him exhausted. On 12 April 1830 he took his last drive and early in the morning of 26 June he died. He was buried in St George's Chapel, Windsor.

*In 1816 the Prince Regent had bought for 500 guineas three superb models of Roman arches constructed of white marble and gilt bronze by Giovacchino and Pietro Belli in 1815. The Arch of Constantine was surmounted by the Emperor in a white marble chariot drawn by four gilded horses and crowned by victory.

CHAPTER FOUR

William IV

'The King never calculated upon the use of
Buckingham Palace for any purpose of state.'[1]

LORD HOLLAND

The Palace at Pimlico

With the death of George IV on 26 June 1830, Nash lost his strongest
supporter: now there was no hope of the knighthood he so longed for.
On 22 October 1830 Nash was suspended from the office of Architect
to the Board of Works. As Prime Minister the 'Iron Duke', the Duke
of Wellington, had been stringent enough; now Nash could expect even
less generosity from the Whigs who won the elections in November.
In fact the waste and extravagance of the 'Palace in Pimlico' was exactly
the kind of corruption they had been elected to root out.

Lord Grey, the new Whig Prime Minister, appointed a Select Committee to investigate the Palace affair. It was particularly concerned
about the structural safety. It must have galled Nash to hear of his old
colleagues, Smirke and Soane, being appointed to judge the safety of
his building. They found this difficult: without ripping up the floors it
was not possible to judge, because of what they called 'the extensive and
peculiar use of iron'. Nash had been one of the pioneers of cast-iron
construction and was so confident of its strength that he suggested that
they should bring in the Army to march on every floor. The Committee
did not share his confidence but could not prove his cast-iron work
faulty. Indeed their conclusion was that, though Nash had been guilty
of 'inexcusable irregularity and great negligence', he had committed no
crime and was not to be prosecuted. In December the brief report of

the Committee was published and their Lordships directed that Nash's appointment as architect responsible for the work on the Palace be withdrawn.

The full report of October 1831 was damning. Not only were there complaints of incompetence, but the Committee had also received suggestions of malpractice. Nash had sent Joseph Browne to Italy to purchase Carrara marble for the Marble Arch: his account was questioned. There had been 'no fair competition' for the purchase of iron.

Upon the whole, my Lords see in the paper before them no justification of Mr Nash's conduct. The estimate submitted to and sanctioned by Parliament has been exceeded to a large amount; the progress of such excess has been concealed from my Lords and their earlier interposition therefore prevented. My Lords feel it incumbent upon them to mark their sense of such conduct by every means in their power.[2]

There were still criticisms of the use of cast-iron and the Committee considered that some of the constructional defects which 'at present render the building ineligible as a royal residence' could be remedied. However, they still regretted the site chosen; they thought it might have been cheaper to have built on a new site. As Nash's biographer, Sir John Summerson, has calculated, 'The cost of converting Buckingham House into Buckingham Palace estimated in 1826 at £252,690 had increased to £331,973 in 1827, to £432,926 in 1828, to £496,169 in 1829, and now stood at £613,269. It would cost still more to finish the work.'[3]

During his last years, Nash spent most of his time at his castle on the Isle of Wight, leaving his London office to the care of his wife's cousin, James Pennethorne. This young man, who was destined to play an important part in the Palace improvements in Queen Victoria's reign, had great talent. Nash started him off in his own office and then paid for his further training, first as a pupil of the architect, A. C. Pugin, and then two years' study abroad. Through Nash he met many of the talented artists and architects of the day; he travelled from the mainland with Turner when the great artist came to stay at the castle. He must have been closely concerned with Nash's final work for the West Strand improvements and for the building of Clarence House, and certainly would have been consulted by Blore on the work at Buckingham Palace. Pennethorne owed much to Nash and never forgot his great debt.

Nash was harassed in his retirement by his creditors, for though he had amassed a fortune, much was invested in property. He died in 1835 and was buried in the churchyard at East Cowes. Buckingham Palace was Nash's creation. He was an architect well trained in the classical tradition but a visionary with a fertile imagination: a risk-taker, an innovator, a gambler with a lofty disregard for accounts, he certainly merited Taylor's furious rebuke, 'harum scarum'. But his energy, fun and charm intrigued even his critics; and there is an underlying harmony that graces most of his work. A new wing now encloses the forecourt and hides Nash's impressive façade. But today the visitor to Buckingham Palace has only to look up to Nash's ceilings to appreciate the astonishing imaginative vitality of his work. He was, in the words of *John Bull*, 'in fact a most extraordinary man'.

The Uninspired Blore

William IV was perfectly comfortable at Clarence House, rebuilt for him as Duke of Clarence, and did not want Buckingham Palace. He was essentially a simple man with nothing of his brother's *folie de grandeur*. He immediately understood that it was not the time to spend money on palaces.

When King William came to the throne the battle for Parliamentary reform was at its height. Finally in 1832 and with great difficulty, Lord Grey and the Whigs managed to get the Reform Bill through Parliament and to persuade the King to give his assent. At a time like this the King had the sense to realize that Whigs and radicals would fiercely oppose extravagant expenditure on the Palace. William IV's sympathies lay more with the Tories but he tried to keep above party politics, although he had great difficulty in restraining his ultra-Tory wife, Queen Adelaide. He told Lord Holland that 'the expense of his brother's coronation had been £250,000 . . . a wasteful display . . . it was prudent nay incumbent upon persons in his situation . . . to advise every means of curtailing useless expense and unnecessary parade'.[4]

As the contemporary historian, Robert Huish, wrote, 'The representatives of the people could not be brought to vote any further sum for the completion of this palace, and it now stands as a monstrous insult upon the nation, and a monument of the reckless extravagance of its projector.'

The King had determined he would never make it his home and 'he never calculated upon the use of Buckingham Palace for any purpose of state'. Huish considered that:

This cumbrous pile now hangs as a dual weight upon the nation. It is never intended to finish it as a royal residence, and, like York House, it may one day become the residence of some opulent nobleman. It is computed that half a million is yet required for its completion independently of furniture. The Duke of Northumberland is spoken of as the most probable purchaser, it having been refused by Lord Grosvenor.[5]

Unlike his brother George IV, William IV had simple tastes and, according to the diarist, Thomas Creevey,

the King never ceased to impress upon Duncannon that all he and the Queen wish for is to be comfortable.

. . . as for removing to Buckingham House, he will do so if the Government wish it, tho' he thinks it a most ill contrived house; and if he goes there he hopes it may be plain and no gilding for he dislikes it extremely.

He would have been happy to 'live in Marlborough House, which is Crown land and the lease nearly out'. And, added Creevey, 'Billy says if he might have a passage made to unite this house with St James he and the Queen could live there very comfortably indeed.'[6]

The new architect, Edward Blore, wanted to begin straightaway planning his completion of the Palace: but while Parliament was debating its future, work was halted. William IV, determined that he would never have it, still hoped to steer the great white elephant into someone else's patch. In 1831 he suggested the Palace should be a barracks: the 1,500 Footguards at Knightsbridge needed a new home. In 1833 he suggested that 'the present Houses of Parliament and their appendages might be converted into a residence for the Lord Chancellor and into Courts of Law', and then honourable members could take over the Palace. God appeared to be on his side: in 1834 the Houses of Parliament went up in flames. William IV went to inspect the ruins, exulting among the ashes. Sir John Hobhouse and the Speaker watched him: the King was 'gratified as if at a show'. 'Buckingham Palace,' he insisted, 'would as a Parliament building, be the "finest thing in Europe".' As he left the smouldering ruins he called Hobhouse and the Speaker to his carriage: 'Mind, I mean Buckingham Palace as a permanent gift . . . mind that!'

The King's ministers shuddered at the thought of presenting demands for even more expenditure to the newly elected Parliament. Prime Minister Lord Melbourne, master of delaying tactics, in the time-honoured way, asked for a report: Blore would have none of it: such a conversion was impossible. 'But,' shouted the King, 'it was the King's prerogative to appoint the place at which Parliament should meet.' Then Melbourne, with all the tact that in later years he would use on Queen Victoria, suavely suggested to His Majesty that if the Palace were rebuilt as Parliament, 'it will be very difficult to avoid providing much larger accommodation for spectators as well as for members, and Lord Melbourne need not recall to your Majesty's mind the fatal effects which large galleries filled with the multitude have had upon the deliberations of public assemblies'.[7] That clinched it. William IV accepted the inevitable, but he was deeply offended that the press had misunderstood his offer of a gift and attacked him for wanting to shift the expenditure on to the public.

One thing, however, he was determined to shift on to his government's shoulders: the responsibility for supervising the completion of the Palace. Unlike his brother, George IV, he had no intention of turning architect or interior decorator. The Prime Minister accordingly appointed two ministers to supervise the work – Lord Althorp and Lord Duncannon, the new Whig minister who had been appointed in 1834 as the First Commissioner of Woods and Forests. It was the latter who supervised the furnishing of the Palace. This was a fortunate choice. Lord and Lady Duncannon had run their estates in Ireland with great competence.

The work on the Palace was completed with remarkable speed, in spite of strikes on the site. For this the credit must go mainly to Edward Blore and to Duncannon. His department was responsible for Crown lands and the First Commissioner was a political appointment, which changed with the government. The other department concerned with the care of public and government buildings was the Board of Works under a Surveyor-General, responsible to the Treasury. It was to this department that the three architects, Nash, Soane and Smirke had been attached. An enquiry of 1828 had revealed much waste and confusion, with which, in his brief Tory ministry, Wellington had tried to deal. In 1830, however, the new Whig government under the premiership of Lord Grey, and with Duncannon at Woods and Forests, undertook a major reorganization of the departments responsible for expenditure on palaces and public works.

The new Whig Chancellor of the Exchequer, Lord Althorp, asked for detailed accounts from the Surveyor General, Benjamin Stephenson, and he wanted to know who and how many were accommodated in the royal palaces, and what was the cost of their upkeep. The days of unlimited and unquestioned royal expenditure were numbered.

Duncannon inherited from his predecessor, Agar Ellis, a plan for reorganization which Duncannon proceeded rapidly to put into practice: he brought in a bill to amalgamate Woods and Forests with the Board of Works. Later he was to supervise the initial planning stages of the new Houses of Parliament, the building of the new National Gallery and the replanning of the streets of Westminster. That such a major reorganization was carried through with less fuss than might have been expected was due to Duncannon's particular skills not only as an efficient administrator but also as a friendly and charming conciliator. Yet, indispensable though he was to Grey and his government, he never made much impact in Parliament, since he was acutely conscious of an embarrassing stammer.

Duncannon, born John William Ponsonby, had been made an Irish peer in 1793 and in 1834 became 4th Earl of Bessborough. He was one of the great Whig 'Cousinage' that dominated the government of the day, yet another of those aristocrats who, to the confusion of the reader, changes his name with each step up the noble ladder: Cavendish became Duke of Devonshire; Viscount Althorp became Earl Spencer; William Lamb became Viscount Melbourne (later to be Prime Minister).

The network of the 'Cousinage' was formidable. Duncannon's mother was the sister of the ravishing Georgiana, Duchess of Devonshire. His sister was the scandalous Caroline who married William Lamb. Lord Althorp, the Chancellor of the Exchequer when Duncannon took office, was his first cousin. Agar Ellis, his predecessor, was also his cousin by marriage. All these were Whigs, but he also had links with the Tories. His wife, the sweet and gentle Maria, was the younger sister of the formidable Sarah, Lady Jersey, once the 'companion' of George IV and the queen bee of contemporary society. Refurbishing a palace was no great problem for Duncannon, who had stayed, *en famille*, in the great country houses – Chatsworth (Derbyshire), Brocket Hall (Hertford-shire) and Althorp (Northamptonshire). And although he had two other Commissioners working with him, he did not need to waste time consulting them. Decisions could be swiftly taken in the libraries or while riding around the estates of the great Whig houses. So he had the confidence to deal with the problems of the Palace and with the royal family. He could forbid the Duke of Sussex to cut down trees in Green Park and when William IV was difficult, knew how to manage him. It was Duncannon who encouraged the appointment of Blore, having seen his work in the houses of members of his family. He knew he would keep to time and cost.

Edward Blore was born in Derby on 13 September 1787. Encouraged by his historian father, he showed early a talent for careful drawings. He worked on his father's *History of Rutland*, which was published in 1811. He also made a particular study of county histories, sketched York and Peterborough for Britton's *Cathedrals* and developed a special interest in Gothic architecture. His chance came in 1816 when Sir Walter Scott employed him to build a house in the Gothic style at Abbotsford, Roxburghshire, Scotland.

When Scott published his *Provincial Antiquities and Picturesque*

Scenery of Scotland, Blore assisted, contributing all the architectural drawings and acting as a manager for the work. In this capacity he met Turner, who provided some of the illustrations.

In 1824, Blore published his own work, *The Monumental Remains of Noble and Eminent Persons.* He was valued as a careful and competent draughtsman and gained a number of commissions, among them a palace in the Crimea for Prince Woronzow, a castle in Ireland and the government buildings in Sydney, New South Wales, Australia. Much of his work was in churches and cathedrals, and he had some influence on the Gothic revival of the period.

He is usually criticized, with some reason, as a boring architect and certainly there is not much evidence of original or imaginative creative ability in his work. But he was exact and efficient and kept to time. He was also ruthless in cutting costs. All this endeared him to the government. Duncannon, and independent experts reporting to the Parliamentary commissioners, considered he 'would discharge his duty in a most satisfactory manner'. So on 9 August 1831 the Treasury advised the King that Blore was the man to complete the Palace and on 10 August the King confirmed his appointment. Blore estimated that he would need £75,000 to remedy the defects and complete the building, excluding the additional furnishings needed. At least most of these could come from the Brighton Pavilion and Carlton House, as Nash and George IV had suggested. £100,000 was allotted for the work.

Blore now moved with his accustomed speed. He consulted the King – who was not particularly interested, except to insist that money should not be wasted on 'the Decorations which he considers to form part of the Architectural Estimate, especially as he has never calculated upon the use of Buckingham Palace for any purpose of state'.[8]

Blore studied Nash's plans, which he admired, and almost certainly consulted James Pennethorne, now Nash's manager.

He planned some structural alterations. However the King intended to use the Palace, he and his successors would still need better servant accommodation and the small, damp kitchen improved. These could be achieved by building new offices and a servants' hall on to the Pimlico wing of the Palace and an additional storey to the main block for additional bedrooms. So he could get rid of the much-mocked dome and the irrelevant little turrets.

Blore agreed with the many critics who had justly found 'the want of an Architectural Connexion between the Marble Arch and the wings'. He considered that if the fence had been of stone instead of metal, the Arch would have seemed part of the building, instead of being 'isolated and out of place'. He therefore substituted new piers in white Portland stone.

In the interest of economy, George IV's splendid Marble Arch was simplified. The 'attic' with its planned sculptures was removed: Richard Westmacott had finished his carved reliefs of the Duke of Wellington and Prince Blücher of Prussia at the Battle of Waterloo, but these were now placed almost out of sight on the front of the new attic storey over the entrance.

As for the interior of the Palace, Blore kept as much as possible to Nash's plans. At the entrance, the Grand Hall and Staircase were completed according to Nash's plans and by his craftsmen. Joseph Browne, whom he had sent to Italy for marble, used it on the white Corinthian pillars and floor. The latter was inlaid with a border which echoed the swirling pattern of the plasterwork in the ceiling.

Undoubtedly George IV would have liked the walls to have been of marble too, but, instead, Browne lined them with the substitute, scagliola. Even then the cost was £4,000. Browne's total bill for the work done in the Grand Hall was almost £8,000. In addition, Samuel Parker's superb gilt bronze balustrade of the staircase cost £3,900, and Joseph Theakston was paid £1,000 for his magnificent marble chimneypiece. George IV, whose bust crowns the overmantel, had certainly been prepared to employ the finest craftsmen at whatever cost.

On the ground floor, where George III's rooms had been, William IV set his mark. The new King had little use for books: his father's libraries were dismantled and the contents sent to Windsor. The ground-floor rooms were simplified, but in the Household dining room, under the State Dining Room, Blore added white marble Ionic columns at either end.

Blore made a major alteration on the floor above. On the instructions of William IV the Music Room became the State Dining Room. He kept the two marble chimneypieces, with their carved ladies playing musical instruments, but otherwise recreated the room in his characteristic pedestrian style. One has only to compare his ceiling with that in Nash's Blue Drawing Room to see the difference between great talent and competence.

In the north wing on this floor new apartments were created for the King and Queen, although William IV and Queen Adelaide had little desire to live in the Palace.

By October 1834 most of the structural work had been completed, but there was still much to be done. The Treasury allowed an additional £55,000 for furnishing the Palace, which was at the disposal of Lord Duncannon, who continued to be responsible for the work, even though he was now at the Home Office.

Finally George IV's treasures, packed and stored in the Carlton House Riding School (which had been kept as a store and was now demolished), were brought across the Park. The great chandeliers, which had been supplied by Parker & Perry for Carlton House in 1811, now were cleaned and hung. Sofas and chairs, some of which had belonged to Queen Charlotte, were brought in. The French furniture which George IV had acquired over many years, graced the State Rooms. More furniture and fittings came from Windsor and the Royal Pavilion, Brighton.

In 1835 the King decided that he would like to live in the Palace after all; Queen Adelaide had probably been overwhelmed by its splendour.

The King wanted to take over the Palace as soon as possible. Blore, in desperation, asked for an additional grant, since he could not possibly complete the work in two or three months without employing extra workers. Duncannon therefore told the King's secretary, Sir Herbert Taylor, that he could not hand the building over unfinished. There was a further delay after it was decided to light the forecourt and some of the interior with gas.

It was not until May 1837 that Duncannon was able to hand over the building to the King, requesting the appointment of a Clerk of the Works. In fact, William IV and Queen Adelaide were never to occupy Buckingham Palace.

Duncannon's organizing ability had been exceptional. He kept his eye on every detail of the work at Buckingham Palace, yet never became bogged down. The diarist, Creevey, who stayed with him at Bessborough, his country home in Ireland, gives a revealing description of Lord and Lady Duncannon sitting at home at Bessborough, choosing the chintz for Queen Adelaide's sitting room at Buckingham Palace. Duncannon rejected those chosen by his wife, Mary, and Creevey, preferring the cheapest.

... as ... Duncannon manages all the palaces, so yesterday brought him a collection of patterns *for him* to choose out (such manufacture!) for the furniture of the Queen's apartment at Buckingham House. Lady Duncannon and I were quite agreed about which she should have, but Duncannon would not hear of it as being much too dear; he would not go beyond six shillings a yard.

Queen Adelaide has received the credit for choosing silks woven in Ireland for Buckingham Palace in order to help the deprived population. In fact that decision sounds much more like Duncannon's. His devotion to Ireland was passionate; he even remained on friendly terms with the firebrand, Daniel O'Connell, whereas Queen Adelaide was quite convinced that he and his comrades would soon be bundling her into the tumbrel on the way to guillotine. In spite of Duncannon's cost-cutting exercise, there was still much anger at the expense of the 'Palace at Pimlico'.

When the Palace was almost finished, Creevey visited it and was furious. 'As for our Buckingham Palace,' he spat,

never was there such a specimen of wicked, vulgar profusion. It has cost a million of money, and there is not a fault that has not been committed in it. You may be sure there are rooms enough, and large enough, for the money; but for staircases, passages, etc., I observed that instead of being called Buckingham Palace, it should be the 'Brunswick Hotel'. The costly ornaments of the state rooms exceed all belief in their bad taste and every species of infirmity. Raspberry coloured pillars without end, that quite turn you sick to look at; but the Queen's paper for her own apartments far exceed everything else in their ugliness and vulgarity . . . the marble single arch in front of the Palace cost £100,000 and the gateway in Piccadilly cost £40,000. Can one be surprised at people becoming Radical with such specimens of royal prodigality before their eyes? to say nothing of the characters of such royalties themselves.[9]

William, Duke of Clarence, and Mrs Jordan

If William IV is remembered, it is usually either as a bluff and somewhat stupid seadog, strolling along the seafront at Brighton, chatting affably to the passers-by, or as one who heartlessly deserted Mrs Jordan, his companion for more than twenty years and the mother of his ten children, and allowed her to die, exiled in poverty. But he was neither stupid nor heartless. He was an affectionate father and took responsibility for all his children; and he never ceased to feel the deepest sense of guilt at his treatment of Dora Jordan.

Dorothea Jordan (known as Dora), born in 1761, was four years older than William, Duke of Clarence. When the Duke fell in love with her she was one of the greatest actresses on the London stage. The essayist William Hazlitt remembered her: 'Her face, her tears, her manners were irresistible. Her smile had the effect of sunshine and her laugh did one good to hear it . . . She was all gaiety, openness and good nature.'[10] She brought the Duke much happiness; and their steady relationship and her obviously good effect on him persuaded George III to give them Bushey House on the Hampton Court estate. Here they lived happily with their ten children. Although Mrs Jordan was almost continually pregnant she still enchanted her audiences and often paid the Duke's debts with her considerable earnings from the stage. Their children were to marry into the aristocracy: their daughter Mary, for instance, married the natural son of Lord Holland.

When the Duke's brother became Regent, the Duke was in such debt that he considered he must marry an heiress or make a royal marriage and beget an heir: then Parliament would provide him with an additional allowance. The death of Princess Charlotte, George IV's only daughter, made him heir to the throne, and therefore he made haste to take a royal bride. In 1818 he married a German princess, Adelaide of Saxe-Meinengen, who was half his age.

In October 1811 he had parted from Mrs Jordan, making an allowance for her and her children, stipulating that it would be reduced if she went back on the stage. He took care of the children, but she kept in close touch with them all. Swindled by a son-in-law, harassed by creditors, she finally fled to France. She went back on the stage. On 5 July 1816 she died alone and in poverty, in cold, bleak rented rooms in the village of St Cloud.

After his marriage he still kept her portraits. He showed them to friends saying, 'she was a good woman'. Queen Adelaide had two children by William IV, both of whom died. Surprisingly, she accepted the King's past with good grace and was fond of his grandchildren.

When he became King, William IV commissioned Sir Francis Chantrey to make a marble statue of Mrs Jordan with two of their children, which he intended to be placed with the wives of kings in Westminster Abbey. However, the Dean of Westminster refused to have the actress in the Abbey, so the statue remained unclaimed. Queen Victoria was interested in the story but did not want this reminder of her uncle's irregular life. It remained in Chantrey's studio until after his death in 1841.

The statue's subsequent history is a curious tale. One of the sons of William IV and Mrs Jordan, Lord Augustus Fitzclarence, became the vicar of St Margaret's, a little church in Mapledurham. He took the statue and placed it in his church, where it remained for sixty years, unexplained and possibly considered to be a representation of the Madonna with child. The village church was more tolerant than Westminster Abbey. In 1956 and 1972 Mrs Jordan's statue appeared at exhibitions at the Royal Academy. The 5th Earl of Munster, a descendant of William IV and Mrs Jordan, built a garden pavilion for her at Sandhills, Surrey, where the 'child of nature' would have been happy. He was childless and decided to bequeath the statue to Queen Elizabeth II. So finally in

May 1980 Mrs Jordan was brought to Buckingham Palace and given a place in the Picture Gallery beneath paintings of kings and queens.

Queen Victoria Takes the Stage

Queen Adelaide and the King were fond of his niece Princess Victoria, now the accepted successor to the throne, but hated her mother. William IV had been furious when, in 1830, the Duchess of Kent had been made by Parliament 'sole regent' until Princess Victoria should come of age in May 1837. The King was determined to thwart the Duchess and live until then. Soon after his accession, in a fit of xenophobic prejudice, he decided that his successor should change her names, Alexandrina Victoria. 'The two . . . names she bears are unsuitable to our national feeling,' he declared. The name Victoria 'is not even German, but of French origin'. In this battle the Duchess won: Princess Victoria kept her name. He had, however, defeated the Duchess at his Coronation. He insisted that Princess Victoria should walk in the Coronation procession behind his brothers, so the Duchess refused to allow the Princess to attend.

The pressure of this hostility on an adolescent girl was intense. It was increased by her own hatred of her mother's financial adviser, Sir John Conroy. The late Duke of Kent's equerry had taken control of the Duchess, her purse and, some said, her person. In the last years of the King's life, Conroy tried to secure Princess Victoria's promise to make him her Private Secretary when she became Queen. This she adamantly refused to do.

Not surprisingly the general strain made her ill, giving the Duchess the excuse to appropriate better rooms in Kensington Palace (where a number of apartments were used by the royal family), in spite of the King's express command. The Duchess had been allocated 'dreadfully dull and gloomy lower rooms'. She now took over 'lofty and handsome rooms two flights upstairs with a sitting room nicely furnished' for

Princess Victoria, and a large airy bedroom where she slept with her mother until the day she became Queen.

The Duchess could now celebrate Princess Victoria's seventeenth birthday in style. Encouraged by Leopold, her brother (now King of the Belgians), and her friend Stockmar, who had plans for the future, she invited her brother, the Duke of Coburg, and his sons, Princes Ernest and Albert, to stay for the festivities.

The King gave a birthday ball for Princess Victoria at St James's Palace, for Buckingham Palace was not yet ready. Neither the King nor Queen Adelaide attended the magnificent ball given by the Duchess in the State Rooms at Kensington Palace. The two German princes and their father were present, but the succession of late-night parties exhausted Prince Albert, who took to his bed for most of the time. King Leopold had chosen Prince Albert as a possible consort; but the cousins parted as friends but without a firm commitment. Prince Albert's time would come.

The battle between King and Duchess raged on, culminating in a public scene at the King's birthday dinner at Windsor, when the King accused the Duchess of 'disrespectful' behaviour and of 'attempting to keep Victoria away from my drawing room'.

In May 1837 the King gave a gala ball at St James's Palace for Princess Victoria's eighteenth birthday, when cheering crowds filled the Mall and the courtyard. She was now of age to succeed to the throne, but, since she was a minor, Conroy and her mother still attempted to take control. The King had been taken ill in May. As soon as it was clear that William IV was dying Leopold sent Stockmar, now a Baron, to London. His mission was to heal the breach between the Queen-to-be and her mother and to give Princess Victoria constitutional advice. The Duchess had become dominated by the ruthless and sinister Conroy and hoped, even now, to compel Princess Victoria to promise to give her the powers of a regent; Conroy the control of her money; and Conroy's daughter a privileged place in her household. The shrewd Baron quietly summed up the situation. When he heard the whole story from Princess Victoria of her personal observation of Conroy's influence and his relationship with her mother, Stockmar accepted the inevitable.

1. The Duke of Buckingham's Levée by Marcellus Laroon the Younger (1679–1722). The preparation of a grandee for the day was often conducted in his bedroom with an audience of officials, suitors and servants. The Duke of Buckingham, wearing the Garter Ribbon, is combing his wig.

2. (Above left) *George III* (*c.* 1761) by Allan Ramsay (1713–84).

3. (Above) *Queen Charlotte* (1782) by Benjamin West (1738–1820). At Windsor with fourteen of her and George III's children in the background.

4. (Left) *Princesses Louisa and Caroline Matilda* (1767) by Francis Cotes (1726–70). George III's much-loved sisters with their musical instruments.

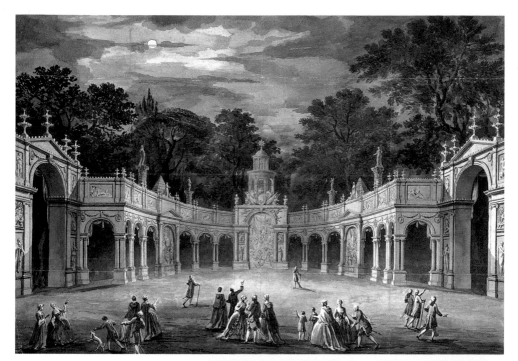

5. (Above) The illuminations at the Queen's House for George III's birthday, 4 June 1763, by Robert Adam (1728–92). One of Robert Adam's designs for the Queen's surprise celebration. The illuminated transparency shows Peace and the Nation's Victories.

6. (Right) *The Great Staircase at Buckingham House* (1818) by James Stephanoff (*c.* 1786–1874). Before the Nash alterations. The wall paintings by Laguerre were as the Duke of Buckingham had left them. Watercolour painted for W. H. Pyne's *History of the Royal Residences*.

7. *The Apotheosis of Prince Octavius* (1783) by Benjamin West. George III was heartbroken at the death of his son Prince Octavius on 3 May 1783. Here the child is welcomed to heaven by his brother, Prince Alfred, who died on 26 August 1782. West captures the charm of the little boy of whom the King said, 'There will be no heaven if Octavius is not there.'

8. *The Queen's Breakfast Room* (1817) by James Stephanoff. It is decorated with lacquer panels in black and gold removed from the Duke of Buckingham's drawing room in 1763. Queen Charlotte's organ can be seen on the fireplace wall, surmounted by a bust of George Frederick Handel.

9. *The Octagon Library* (1818) by James Stephanoff. It was built in 1766–7 under the direction of Sir William Chambers.

10. Breakfronted mahogany bookcase by William Vile, one of George III's favourite cabinetmakers. It was made for Buckingham House in 1762.

11. Ivory chair (*c.* 1770), made in India from an English design. Part of a large set purchased by George III for Queen Charlotte at a country auction, it is now in Buckingham Palace.

12. Chelsea porcelain service, made in 1763 as a present from Queen Charlotte to her brother, the Duke of Mecklenburg-Strelitz. It is displayed in the cabinets around the Bow Room, the room through which guests to HM The Queen's garden parties pass on the way to the garden. It was presented to Queen Elizabeth, now the Queen Mother, in 1947.

13. (Above) *Fanny Burney* (Madame d'Arblay)
(*c.* 1784–5) by Edward Frances Burney
(1760–1848). The novelist, author of *Evelina*,
much admired by Dr Johnson. She was
appointed reader and Lady-in-Waiting to
Queen Charlotte.

14. (Top right) *Queen Charlotte* (1797) by Sir
William Beechey (1753–1839). At the age of
fifty-three. Here she shows clearly the stress
caused by the King's illness.

15. (Right) *Mrs Jordan and Two Children* (1834)
by Sir Francis Chantrey. This idealised
sculpture of the actress and two of her children
by William IV was commissioned by him after
her death. It was presented to HM The Queen
by her descendant, the Earl of Munster, in
1975.

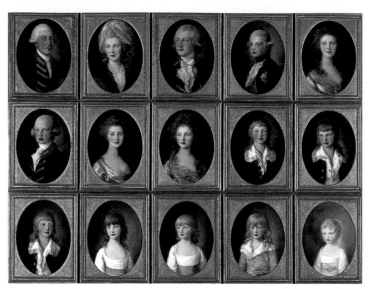

16. *The Family of George III* (1783) by Thomas Gainsborough RA (1727–88). A set of fifteen portraits of the royal family, formerly in Queen Charlotte's Green Closet.

17. *George IV* (1791) by George Stubbs (1724–1806). Shown on horseback when a dashing young Prince of Wales.

In the past she had accepted guidance, if unwillingly; now she was adamant. She must have decided well in advance that one of her first acts as Queen would be to remove her mother's bed from her room and from then on to sleep and act alone. On the evening of 19 June 1837, Princess Victoria was warned that the King was dying. He died at Windsor early the next day.

William IV had been a better king than anyone expected. The diarist Charles Greville had thought him a 'mountebank bidding fair to be a maniac'. Certainly the King's after-dinner speeches were often alarmingly wild. But Lord Holland, whose son Charles was at the King's bedside when he died, praised his absence of guile, kindness and sense of duty. The King's character had been so, Lord Holland added, 'since his accession to the Crown and he was on the whole the best King of his race and perhaps of any race we have ever had, and the one who has left the greatest name as a Constitutional sovereign and the first magistrate of a free and improving people'.[11] A surprising obituary, but considering its author, one that must be taken seriously.

Certainly he had shown sense and judgement, and had sailed through the high seas of the Reform Bill storm without falling overboard or wrecking the ship of state; above all, in his reign the Palace improvements were at last completed.

At six o'clock on the morning of 20 June 1837 Princess Victoria was awakened in her bedroom at Kensington Palace. The Lord Chamberlain, Lord Conyngham, the Archbishop of Canterbury and the King's doctor had travelled directly from William IV's death bed at Windsor and wished to see the Queen. At the door of her sitting room, Victoria, wearing a dressing gown over her night dress, put aside her mother's hand and went in alone, as Queen.

CHAPTER FIVE

Queen Victoria

'They think I am still a girl, but
I will show them that I am Queen of England.'[1]

QUEEN VICTORIA

Queen and Empress

The young Queen Victoria's first appearance at her Privy Council moved even old cynics almost to tears. She seemed so small, so young and vulnerable, yet she was amazingly composed, reading her speech 'in a clear, distinct, and audible voice without any appearance of fear or embarrassment'. The only sign of emotion was when her two old uncles, the Dukes of Cumberland and Sussex, knelt before her, swearing allegiance. Then, wrote Greville, 'I saw her blush up to her eyes, as if she felt the contrast between their civil and their natural relations.' Even the Duke of Wellington was moved – his tribute was typically simple and direct: 'She filled the room.' The old men, who remembered the bloated, self-indulgent George IV and bumbling old William IV rambling through his incoherent after-dinner speeches, listened to the clear young voice and saw a new dawn. It was an impressive performance which has been often described, and the Privy Councillors and the public were understandably overwhelmed.

But the picture of this scene as recorded by Sir David Wilkie was misleading. Queen Victoria was not, as he painted her, floating in a drift of white: in fact, she wore a simple black dress. Nor had she risen, a queen from the foam, at the touch of a wand. She had been prepared for this moment from her birth, and she had readied herself ever since that morning on 11 March 1830 when her governess, Lehzen, had slipped into the pages of her history book Howlett's 'Tables of the Kings and Queens of England' and for the first time she realized her destiny, uttering the famous pledge, 'I will be good.'[2]

In those first days Queen Victoria repeated again and again, with some triumph, that she was facing her new life 'alone, quite quite alone'. But in fact there were advisers behind her who were to give her support for many years to come. Her uncle, King Leopold (who became King of the Belgians in 1830 and was now married again, this time to Louise, daughter of Louis-Philippe, King of France), had a major part to play in the shaping of the Queen. His friend Baron Stockmar was to be her *éminence grise* from the time of her father's death for almost half a century.

Queen Louise became a much loved friend, who gave Queen Victoria the royal companionship she lacked. Queen Louise taught her to play chess, they chatted about clothes, and Queen Victoria tried on the Belgian Queen's Paris dresses. She widened Queen Victoria's horizons and gave her a personal knowledge of France that was to stand her in good stead. Unlike her uncle, William IV, who hated all things French, Queen Victoria was to build new links with France. She later remembered with amusement how William IV had told the boys at Eton College, 'Always remember to hate the French.'

Although Baron Stockmar had earlier been unsuccessful in his attempt to mend the Queen's relationship with her mother, she was perfectly prepared to accept his advice on constitutional and protocol matters. Some days before the death of the old King she had seen Lord Liverpool, who also hoped to conciliate mother and daughter. She saw him alone and surprised him by the authoritative way she produced a memorandum – with headings – for their discussion. Undoubtedly here was the skilful hand of Baron Stockmar. All his life he had a passion for memoranda with headings. It is significant that on the morning of her succession she saw Stockmar before making her famous statement to her Privy Council, and she saw him twice after dinner on the same day. There would be other *éminences grises* in her life, and some, like Conroy, would be distinctly '*noire*'; but the influence of Baron Stockmar, almost until his death, was to be crucial.

Baron Stockmar's secure, loving home background with a shrewd and sensible mother had given him stability and he was always to be grateful for the medical training he had received at Würzburg, Erlangen and Jena. To this he always attributed a gift for assessing people and an understanding of psychology. There is a steadiness, an openness and humour in his early portrait that is still there in his face in old age. That steadiness was to see him through many difficulties to a serene old age. From his early days he had a passionate love of liberty, which inspired him to consider joining in a plot to assassinate the Emperor Napoleon, but common sense had dissuaded him. Kind, competent and reassuring, he sometimes suffered moods of black depression, but to his friends he seemed always equable. Remarkably his passion for producing detailed memoranda and advice, which might have been infuriating in another, rarely offended. Just before Stockmar died he wrote that if he were asked by a young man beginning his career,

What is the chief good for which it behoves a man to strive my only answer would be, 'Love and Friendship'. Were he to ask me, 'What is man's most priceless possession' I must answer, 'The consciousness of having loved and sought the Truth for its own sake.' All else is mere vanity or a sick man's dream.[3]

At this crucial time, as in earlier years, the influence of her beloved Uncle Leopold cannot be overestimated: she was to follow much of his counsel throughout her reign.

Leopold advised her never to give an immediate answer to Ministers; Greville heard that she always said, 'I will think it over', even to Melbourne. Leopold advocated strict business habits such as seeing Ministers between 11am and 1.30 each day; the Queen always saw Lord Melbourne between those hours. Leopold urged her to form her own opinions on all questions and stick to them . . . people soon noticed that she had a will of her own. Leopold insisted that if people spoke to her uninvited on personal matters she should change the subject 'and make the individual feel he has made a mistake'.[4]

When, in the future, Queen Victoria was 'not amused', strong men wilted.

Stockmar and Uncle Leopold were not only to direct her future: they also gave her the knowledge of her links with family history – about which she was intensely curious. They had known well her grandmother, Queen Charlotte; Stockmar had studied the medical case of her grandfather, George III, from his contemporaries – Queen Victoria was always sensitive to the possibility of hereditary madness. The two men had watched the careers of her uncles, George IV and William IV, and above all they had known her father the Duke of Kent – that invisible influence in her life – whom she fondly imagined was 'the best of the lot'. Stockmar had known her mother in Coburg and was with them when her father, the Duke of Kent, died; and Uncle Leopold had known him for many years. Throughout her life she would look for his substitute. For all her independence and powerful will, Queen Victoria always longed for a strong right arm.

No one knew better than King Leopold that other influence in her early life, his sister Victoire, Duchess of Kent. The Duchess was impressionable, easily led, and many thought her 'the most mediocre person it would be possible to meet'.[5] She needed the support of a husband, which is why King Leopold had encouraged her to marry the Duke of Kent after the death of her first husband. Unfortunately her brother had lately been too absorbed in his own affairs as King of the Belgians, so he had not noticed the growing malignant influence of John Conroy.

In bringing up Queen Victoria her mother followed a system recommended by Stockmar. She was excessively strict, as weak people often are, and over-protective, refusing to allow Queen Victoria to meet the family of William IV and Mrs Jordan, since, as she said, her daughter must be taught the difference between right and wrong. Did the Duchess ever attempt to explain Queen Victoria's father's 'wrong relationship' with Madame de St Laurent, his mistress for twenty-seven years?

Although her mother's influence had been constricting, Queen Victoria owed something to her. In the years before her accession she had been prepared for the throne. The Duchess had taken her on royal progresses throughout the country, giving her some glimpse at least of life in the north and west country. She had taught her how to behave royally, to receive municipal addresses with dignity and to accept salutes of guns as her right. This had infuriated William IV, who hated the Duchess and her presumption; he publicly upbraided her and forbade the 'damned popping' of guns. Queen Victoria's self-possession, which so astonished her ministers, was partly the result of her mother's training.

There was one more formative influence on the young Queen. If Uncle Leopold was a substitute for the father she never knew, her governess, Lehzen, took the place of the mother from whom she had become estranged. During the difficult years before her accession, Princess Victoria would have been lonely indeed had it not been for Baroness Louise Lehzen, who should take an honoured place among the unsung teachers of the great. She came from a simple home, the daughter of a German Lutheran pastor in Hanover. Just as Bute had been mocked as an alien Scot, so Lehzen had to endure much anti-German prejudice. But if her own manners were uncourtly, as critics claimed, she certainly taught Queen Victoria grace and poise, and she gave her the warmth and affection that her mother found difficult to show.

In the early days of her reign, when the Queen was learning to stand on her own feet, Lehzen was indispensable. After the ordeals of councils and audiences she could return to the comfort of Lehzen – 'Daisy' as she called her. In the past she had learned her history from the stories Lehzen had told her while she brushed her hair, and Lehzen was still there to brief her. All those who had to deal with the Queen in these early days were astonished that this diminutive young woman was so well informed. Some of the credit for her education must go to Uncle Leopold, Stockmar and her mother, the Duchess of Kent, but it was Lehzen who made history palatable. She gave her a lifelong love of history, teaching it in the way she would always learn best, as an enthralling study of people.

History has not dealt too kindly with Lehzen but she won the admiration of that cultured old politician, Lord Holland, who was a guest at Windsor Castle on 14–16 September 1837 and was able to observe her at leisure. The Queen had said, he wrote in his journal,

she was never alone in a room with any person, her mother excepted, till within three days of her accession. I think she should also have excepted Mdme Letzen

[sic] to whom I suspect She, and the country are chiefly indebted for the admirable education she has received and the happy fruits that it is likely to produce. Mdme de Letzen [sic] is a woman of sense and information, great judgement and yet greater strength of mind. She had been employed in superintending the education of another daughter* of the Duchess of Kent, half sister of Victoria, and she contrived without éclat and without too much subserviency with the Countenance of Leopold to maintain her post at Kensington against the wishes, as it is supposed of both the Duchess of Kent and Sir John Conroy and without furnishing either with any just cause of complaint. I was much struck with the frankness and sagacity of her conversation.[6]

High praise indeed from a man at whose table learned and witty conversationalists such as Macaulay and Sidney Smith regularly dined.

Where Lehzen and everyone else failed was in curbing the self-will that was Queen Victoria's lifelong failing. It was, however, the other side of that independence of spirit that was her greatest strength.

Lord Holland, however, watching the Queen during the same Windsor visit, found her 'a pattern of propriety without impairing the least the charm of youthful and lighthearted manners'. The only fault he could find was

the inconsiderate habit of keeping her Ladies standing too long. When the Ladies retire from dinner, she seldom sits down till the Gentlemen follow them, and I hear the Duchess of Kent first remonstrated and has since retired from the drawing room for half an hour every evening to repose herself in her own room, till she can return and *sit* by her daughter or at the Whist table in the Evening. It was droll enough to see the Ladies, young and old, married or unmarried, with all their *rumps* to the wall when we came from the dining to the drawing room and eagerly availing themselves of their release when the Queen took her seat on the Sofa.[7]

Royal attendants throughout the ages have had to bear with stoicism interminable periods of standing and waiting. Queen Victoria became even stricter as she grew older.

---

*This was Princess Feodore of Leiningen, daughter of the Duchess by her first husband Prince Emich Charles of Leiningen.

There were many who had helped in the shaping of the young Queen, but none of them, and not even Melbourne and Prince Albert in the future, could fundamentally change her. There is no doubt that Queen Victoria was, from childhood, directed by influences that were mainly German. She was, however, no soft clay in the hands of the Coburg potters. The set of the head and the firm little mouth in the early portraits were the outward signs of a uniquely strong personality. Queen Victoria shaped herself.

For William IV Buckingham Palace had been a burden: for Queen Victoria it was a fitting setting for the Great Queen she hoped to be. She could not wait to take up residence, to make a break with her mother and the past. On 13 July she moved from Kensington Palace, even before Buckingham Palace was ready for her. When, on the next day, Sir John Hobhouse, President of the Board of Control, had his first audience, he found the Palace 'in great disorder: the apartments were full of housemaids on their knees scrubbing the floors, and attendants putting down the carpets'. But Queen Victoria, already at ease, 'placed herself on a sofa and desired him to take a chair on the opposite side of the room'.[8] Later she would allow no such freedom: subjects stood in her presence.

In the magical early days in the Palace, the Queen suddenly realized that she had only to wave her wand and the magnificent State Rooms would echo to the sound of the most exquisite music. Immediately she sent for Sigismund Thalberg, who was said to be the finest pianist in the world, and within days a concert was organized. *'J'étais en extase,'* she said. Johann Strauss the Elder composed waltzes for her state balls and on a May evening before her Coronation she danced until four in the morning, finishing with Strauss's specially composed waltz, which began with 'Rule Britannia' and ended with 'God Save The Queen'.

In the whole history of Buckingham Palace only George III and Queen Charlotte moved in with such pleasure and excitement. Queen Victoria and George III had much else in common: both were young, idealistic, determined, in Queen Victoria's words, to be 'good'. Both had tremendous, almost manic, energy with corresponding black troughs. Both were to have huge families – Queen Charlotte had fifteen children, Queen Victoria was to have nine; both families, after a while, outgrew Buckingham Palace.

Queen Victoria was enchanted with her new home – with its high ceilings, huge mirrors and immense, brilliant chandeliers. Others might mock the bright colours of the mock marble pillars, the brashness of the décor, but for her it was all space and light and colour.

'I am pleased with my rooms,' she wrote to her half-sister, Princess Feodora, in October. 'They are high, pleasant and cheerful.' It was not so much the pictures she admired in the long gallery: unlike George IV and her grandfather she had no plans to become a great art collector. But the portraits of her ancestors fascinated her. Most of all the Palace gave her space. 'There are no less than five fine large rooms, *besides* the Gallery and dining room,' she wrote to Louise, Queen of the Belgians, 'and they are so high, the doors so large and they lie so well near one another that it makes an ensemble rarely seen in this country.'[9] She could not wait to show it all to her and Uncle Leopold. One of her earliest concerns was to have a suite prepared for them on the ground floor. Even today those rooms are still called the 'Belgian Suite'.

For the first time in her life she was free. She banished her mother, the Duchess of Kent, to a suite a long way away, to her fury. In her Palace bedroom Queen Victoria slept alone. But one of her first demands was that a door should be made between her room and that of Lehzen. Independent and free as she was, she still needed the support of her old governess.

Best of all she hoped she had got rid of her mother's evil genius, Sir John Conroy. Perhaps she suspected that her mother was his mistress; certainly the Duke of Wellington, when questioned, had said, 'I suppose so.' Whether it was rumour or truth, she hated him, and was delighted when Wellington had offered him a 'golden bridge' to the Continent. Now she could ride in freedom: for the previous two years she had refused the gallops she loved because her mother had insisted that Conroy accompanied her. Now she could even ride on parade beside the Duke of Wellington. He had disapproved, but Queen Victoria had looked the victor of Waterloo in the eye and had won her battle.

In the excitement of the first months, Queen Victoria had no time to consider the running of the Palace. Unlike George III and her uncle George IV, Queen Victoria was never particularly interested in furnishings. She enjoyed comfort and convenience, but she was perfectly happy to accept Duncannon's elegant taste. If the kitchens were damp and smelt, if the windows were not cleaned, if the footmen misbehaved – those were problems for her Master of the Household and Lehzen, who also acted as her secretary. Unaccustomed to dealing with a large income, she soon began to wonder how she was running up such bills.

But the Queen rapidly realized how much she had to learn in her brave new world. Fortunately she found in her Whig Prime Minister not only an excellent tutor, but also a man she could love like a father. To her mother she was still a girl; Lord Melbourne made her feel like a woman and a queen. Even at fifty-eight he was still charming and handsome enough to win the love and admiration of an impressionable young woman.

William, 2nd Lord Melbourne, was immensely experienced both in politics and in life. Born William Lamb, he had been spoilt by his remarkable but somewhat scandalous mother Elizabeth, Lady Melbourne. At his father's houses, Brocket Hall in Hertfordshire and Melbourne House in Piccadilly, leaders of the Whig party were frequent visitors. At Eton College and Trinity College, Cambridge, Lamb was a brilliant student. He was called to the Bar in 1804 but gave up the law for politics. In 1805 he married the notorious Caroline Ponsonby, the only daughter of the 3rd Earl of Bessborough and the sister of Duncannon. After years of patient kindness and tolerance, Lamb finally left her in 1825. She died three years later, a sad wreck.

At this time, although Queen Victoria had been protected from acquaintance with William IV's 'bastards', she was a child of the Regency and had been brought up among the older generation, and Melbourne taught her tolerance. However, he taught her no such tolerance in the world of politics. Although he himself could be relaxed and balanced in his judgement of his political opponents, the Queen was violently partisan. She had been brought up in the Whig world, had visited the grandees in their country houses and had absorbed their attitudes.

William IV had been surrounded by Tories: to Queen Adelaide Whigs, radicals and revolutionaries were all the same, all out to destroy the monarchy. William IV had genuinely tried to maintain some balance. But Queen Victoria hated the Tories with a blind passion. She would have no Tories to her first banquet in Buckingham Palace, nor to her Coronation nor later to her wedding. When Melbourne insisted that she at least invite the Duke of Wellington to the banquet, she grudgingly agreed. But his place card read 'The Chancellor of the University of Oxford'. Wellington was amused and preserved the card.

During the first years of her reign, she was completely besotted with her Prime Minister. As far as she was concerned, Melbourne was the fount of all wisdom: even her beloved Uncle Leopold took second place. But she became more and more imperious and wilful. Just as Melbourne had been unable to contain the extravagances of his wife, Caro Lamb, so he was unable to supply Queen Victoria with the discipline she needed. In private life and in politics he worked on the principle that fires would burn themselves out provided one did not poke them.

Melbourne was a Whig because of his upbringing, but he was more in sympathy with moderate Tories than with reforming Whigs such as Grey and Russell. Had he exerted himself he could have given some balance to Queen Victoria's political judgement. But in fact the young Queen was always to be more interested in people than in politics.

In the organization and running of the Palace, Queen Victoria had surprisingly little help. In the first years Lehzen acted as her Private Secretary and was in part responsible for running the Household. Apparently Lehzen kept the Queen's Ladies-in-Waiting happy and comfortable, but there were many clashes with Lord Conyngham, the Lord Chamberlain, who was a difficult man, unaccustomed to interference in the running of the Palace. There was a Lord Steward whose functions were largely nominal but who looked after the kitchens; and the head of the Office of Woods took care of the outside of the Palace. But these officials did not live in the Palace and for the last twenty years had been happy to take their perks and the salaries without taking much trouble. Consequently – as will be seen – the organization of the Palace was appalling.

The Queen was too inexperienced and too full of the excitement of her new Palace to notice; Melbourne, who should have seen, was blind to such things. His own homes were badly organized and he was the last person to advise Queen Victoria when she found her household expenses inexplicably enormous.

Early in her reign Queen Victoria was to face two crises: the case of Lady Flora Hastings, a Lady-in-Waiting to the Duchess of Kent, which was to bring Queen Victoria and the Court into ill-repute; and the problem of the Ladies of the Bedchamber. In both cases the Queen was too inexperienced and too headstrong to cope. If only Conroy had not been such a villain and her mother so ineffectual: she could have done with a competent major-domo and a wise older woman to advise her. In the following years the Queen was to learn that indeed 'uneasy lies the head that wears a crown'! That perennial plague of palaces – jealousy and intrigue among family, courtiers and advisers – was to infect her Court.

Sir John Conroy was still fomenting bitterness between the Queen and her mother, for though he knew he had been beaten he was demanding too high a bribe for his departure, and was deeply involved in the first of the two great dramas that devastated the Queen in 1839.

The case of Lady Flora Hastings was a complicated one that is not clear even today. Briefly, in January 1839 it seemed from her physical appearance that Lady Flora might be pregnant. The Queen, Lehzen and her ladies noticed; even Sir James Clark, who had been consulted by Lady Flora for 'protuberance of the stomach', told someone that she might indeed be with child. The fact that she was a close friend of Conroy's – who, the Queen told Melbourne, was 'capable of every villainy' – was enough to convince his enemies that he might be the father. The doctor, who had only examined her fully dressed, now asked for a proper examination, which at first Lady Flora refused, then agreed but demanded a second opinion. Sir Charles Clarke – a specialist – was called in. He examined her and gave Lady Flora a certificate, signed also by the first doctor, which stated that 'there are no grounds for believing pregnancy does exist or ever has existed'. Meanwhile Lady Flora, whom the Queen refused to see until her innocence could be proved, was becoming increasingly ill. The Queen attempted to make amends by receiving Lady Flora; later she visited her as she lay dying and Lady Flora thanked her for all she had done for her. In July she died: the post-mortem showed that she had suffered from cancer of the liver. For months the Queen was subjected to fierce attacks from the press and political opponents.

Barely had the Hastings scandal died when the Queen faced a new trial. Throughout history courtiers have had a considerable, though often concealed, influence on the monarch. In this case it was fear of the political influence of the Ladies of the Bedchamber, wives of prominent Whigs, that caused the crisis.

Queen Victoria must have known that her cosy relationship with Lord Melbourne and the Whigs could not last for ever, but in her view the Queen's government should always be Whig, the party that had ridden into power in 1830 and achieved the triumph of the Parliamentary Reform Act of 1832. But the coalition of Whigs and radicals that had driven the successful campaign was now disintegrating. Some great radical reformers, such as Sir Francis Burdett, had joined the Tory party; others were pulling in the opposite direction and Melbourne was too easy-going and indolent to hold them together. The collapse came on 7 May 1839 when the government was brought down over a comparatively minor crisis – a revolt of Jamaican settlers.

Now a weeping Queen said goodbye to her Prime Minister: 'All my happiness gone! that happy peaceful life destroyed,' she sobbed in her journal, 'that dearest kind Lord Melbourne no more my Minister.'[10] She saw Wellington, significantly not in that little Blue Closet where she had always sat at ease with Lord Melbourne, but in the formal Yellow Drawing Room. She had not lost her hostility to and fear of the Iron Duke.

On his recommendation she sent for Sir Robert Peel. The contrast between the urbane and relaxed Melbourne and the shy and awkward Peel appalled her: she made the interview as difficult as possible. She was to tell Melbourne that she was 'very much collected, civil and high'. But when she realized that Peel expected her to change her Ladies of the Bedchamber – who were all Whig supporters – she was not just 'high': she was outraged. She wrote in her Journal: 'I said I could *not* give up *any* of my ladies, and never had imagined such a thing. He asked if I meant to retain all. "All," I said. "The Mistress of the Robes and the ladies of the Bedchamber?" I replied, "All." '¹¹

In fact Peel probably had not meant to be so sweeping, but the Queen managed to manoeuvre him into resigning over the issue. Melbourne, to the Queen's rapture, but to his embarrassment, was back. Peel was told that the changes proposed in the Queen's Household were 'contrary to usage and repugnant to her feelings' and the Whigs returned to power.¹²

Queen Victoria was triumphant. 'The Queen of England,' she had written to Melbourne, 'will not submit to such trickery.' Her repeated use of the phrase 'Queen of England' is significant. Queen Victoria already saw herself performing on the world stage. Melbourne and the Whigs might belong to their own powerful 'cousinry'; Queen Victoria's 'cousinry' crossed national boundaries.

The next night, 10 May 1839, she could bask in the glory of her triumph at a magnificent ball she gave at the Palace in honour of her guest, the Tsarevich Alexander, a relation of her Uncle Leopold. The Queen of England was a match for the Imperial might of Russia – in more senses than one. Now that she could put behind her the unpleasant business of being a Queen, she could enjoy the excitement of being young, and of being whirled round the ballroom night after night by the handsome Tsarevich. He taught her the mazurka: he was 'so very strong, that in running round, you must follow quickly, and after that you are whisked round like in a Valse, which is very pleasant'. He also taught her a German country dance in which the tiny Queen and the tall Tsarevich had to creep under a pocket handkerchief arch and the Tsarevich caught his hair in her wreath. 'I never enjoyed myself more. We were all so merry.'¹³

For Melbourne all this gaiety in the Palace was so much more wearing than his relaxed chats in the little Blue Closet. It was with some relief that he saw the Tsarevich's departure. But Queen Victoria confided in her Journal, 'I felt so sad to take leave of this dear amiable young man whom I really think (talking jokingly) I was a little in love with.'¹⁴ That May week Queen Victoria's fancy was beginning to turn, if only lightly, to 'thoughts of love'.

Uncle Leopold and Baron Stockmar heard with some apprehension of Queen Victoria's political triumphs and May revels. The affair of the Ladies of the Bedchamber and her increasingly imperious behaviour were making her unpopular. The Tories, furious at being deprived of office, whipped up press and public hostility.

The innocent young Queen who had so enchanted all parties had become not only domineering and violently partisan: she and her Court were now tainted with a sleazy scandal and she herself appeared to be cruel and insensitive. The Queen was hissed at Ascot, where there were even cries of 'Mrs Melbourne'. Baron Stockmar wrote, 'The late events in England distress me. How could they let the Queen make such mistakes, to the injury of the monarchy?' He shrewdly realized that she had become her own worst enemy. 'She was', he wrote, 'as passionate as a spoilt child, if she feels offended she throws everything overboard without exception.' And the adoring Lehzen made things worse, 'Just like the nurse who hits the stone that tripped the child up'.[15] The only person she would listen to was Melbourne, but he was growing weary and had been little help to her in the double crisis. Queen Victoria was so exhausting, able to ride at a gallop all day and dance till four in the morning, whereas Melbourne was arthritic and no longer young.

It was a pity Stockmar was not in England; his sound advice was much needed. 'You are too clever not to know', he had once written, 'that it is not the being called King or Queen which can be of the least consequence . . . All trades must be learned, and nowadays the trade of a constitutional Sovereign to do it well, is a very difficult one.'[16]

Her Coburg advisers were also alarmed at reports of the Queen's flirtation with Tsarevich Alexander. This was not the marriage they had planned for her. It was time to produce their candidate for her hand, her cousin, Prince Albert of Saxe-Coburg and Gotha. It was now quite clear to Stockmar, Uncle Leopold and indeed to Queen Victoria herself that she needed a consort. The trade of a consort, like that of a queen, as Uncle Leopold knew only too well, had also to be learned.

In 1836 Uncle Leopold, and her adviser, Stockmar, believed they had found the right apprentice, over whose education they had already watched. In Coburg, Prince Albert, the second son of Ernest, the reigning Duke of the small duchy of Saxe-Coburg and Gotha, had already won high praise not only from the Coburg family but also from his tutors. Uncle Leopold, brother of Duke Ernest and uncle to the young Prince Albert, sent Stockmar to assess the character of the young prince. His judgement was favourable but not uncritical. As for Victoire, widow of the Duke of Kent and aunt of Prince Albert, she and Prince Albert's grandmothers had always hoped for the union of the Duchess of Kent's 'little Mayflower', Queen Victoria, and Prince Albert.

So, while Princess Victoria prepared to be Queen, Uncle Leopold and Stockmar were guiding Prince Albert, giving him the foundation of the skills he would need as consort. Later, in 1861, when Stockmar heard of the early death of Prince Albert, he wrote, 'Here do I see crumble before my eyes that edifice which I have devoted twenty years to construct, prompted by a desire to accomplish something great and good.' But Prince Albert was not so much an edifice to be constructed as an oak that Stockmar had tended with loving care ever since it was a delicate seedling. Prince Albert's success as consort, the happiness of his marriage and the consequent transformation of the image of the British monarchy were all to a great extent due to the influence of Baron Stockmar. He was indeed to create 'something great and good'.[17]

One of the puzzles of nineteenth-century European history is why a small German Duchy, the House of Saxe-Coburg and Gotha, should have produced so many occupants of European thrones. Prince Albert's grandfather, Franz, Duke of Coburg, had seven remarkable children including Prince Ernest, the father of Prince Albert; Prince Ferdinand, father of the King-Consort of Portugal; Prince Leopold, who became King of the Belgians. Of his daughters Princess Julie married the Grand Duke Constantine of Russia and Princess Victoire was the mother of Queen Victoria.

So it was not surprising that the Coburgs hoped to provide one of the family as a husband for Queen Victoria. Whether or not, as it was said, Prince Albert was selected at birth as husband for the 'little Mayflower' in England, he certainly was chosen by Uncle Leopold at an early age.

Prince Albert was born on 26 August 1819 at the Rosenau, some miles out of Coburg. His elder brother, Prince Ernest, was a year older and his constant companion. His mother, Louise, Duchess of Coburg, had married her husband, twice her age, when she was sixteen. She was, her mother-in-law wrote, 'a charming, tiny being, not beautiful but very pretty, through grace and vivacity ... Her big blue eyes often look so sad under her black lashes, and then again she becomes a happy, wild child.'[18] After the birth of her sons she fell in love with Lieutenant von Hanstein, was divorced and was sent away when Prince Albert was five years old. She was not allowed to see her children again, and died of cancer in 1831.

Prince Albert never forgot his lovely, lost mother, from whom he inherited his love of music – and his great blue eyes. After the death of his father in 1844 he had her body brought back to Coburg to be buried beside him. His was not, however, an unhappy childhood; his father was devoted to the boys and they were lucky to have loving grandparents and a kind and wise tutor, Christoph Florschütz – chosen by Stockmar. In the lovely hills round their castle at Coburg, Prince Albert absorbed an abiding love of the country.

In his earliest years Albert was surrounded by love and admiration. All remarked on his beauty. When he was ten months old, his mother wrote, *'Albert est superbe ... d'une beauté superbe; a des grands yeux bleus, une toute petite bouche – un joli nez – et des fossettes à chaque joue ... il est ... toujours gai ... n'est-ce pas un petit prodigue pour dix mois?'*[19] So would Queen Victoria describe him in the first enthusiasm of her love. His grandmothers were equally besotted. 'Albert', wrote his grandmother Gotha, 'is lovely as a little angel with his fair curls.'[20]

As he grew up, his tutor Florschütz found him an earnest and eager pupil, but with rather too strong a will of his own. He had an exceptionally thorough grounding in languages, history, mathematics, Latin and Greek. But though he spent long years of study, he also became proficient in outdoor sports. In later life English courtiers would be surprised that this studious Prince could ride, fence and skate with the best of them. Stockmar and Uncle Leopold kept a close eye on his development. The Princes Albert and Ernest visited Uncle Leopold in his Belgian kingdom and in 1836 Stockmar had been to Coburg to assess the prospective bridegroom. Stockmar described him as 'a handsome youth . . . He is said to be prudent, cautious and already well informed. All this however, is not enough. He must not only have great capacity but true ambition and strength of will.'[21] He needed these qualities if he were to be the husband of the imperious Princess Victoria. Stockmar worried about what he considered a certain indolence in Prince Albert, a reluctance to take an interest in newspapers and politics.

Their next step was to urge the Duchess of Kent to invite the brothers to England, suggesting that the purpose of the visit should be kept from Princess Victoria so that she might be more at ease. This first visit, on the occasion of the ball celebrating the Princess's seventeenth birthday, was not, as we have seen, particularly successful, although she described her first impression warmly enough.

Albert . . . is extremely handsome; his hair is about the same colour as mine; his eyes are large and blue, and he has a beautiful nose, and a very sweet mouth with fine teeth; but the charm of his countenance is his expression, which is most delightful; c'est à la fois full of goodness and sweetness, and very clever and intelligent.[22]

But though Princess Victoria enjoyed the fun of having princes of her own age to dance with, and though Prince Albert was most amusing, he was also too often unwell and tired, with a tendency to fall asleep after dinner. ('Quite right,' Melbourne said.) He was, too, not over-enthusiastic, and he found the Princess too self-willed and imperious. So they left after the visit with feelings of cousinly friendship but neither was in a hurry for marriage. During the next three years, Princess Victoria was at pains to point out to Uncle Leopold that she had not actually promised to marry Prince Albert. They did not meet again for three years: Duke Ernest was invited to Queen Victoria's coronation but not his sons.

Meanwhile Prince Albert was finishing his education, first under the eye of King Leopold in Brussels, and then at the University of Bonn, studying natural sciences, political economy and philosophy, enjoying music, singing and composing, and proving himself a jolly companion and the 'life and soul of the dramatic society'. It was a happy period of his life. It also laid the foundations for his later success as Prince Consort when he became Chancellor of the University of Cambridge. Prince Albert would always be happier in the company of academics rather than among courtiers.

In 1838 Stockmar took him on a long tour of Italy, a grand tour that was to be of prime importance not only to him but to the future of Buckingham Palace. He had already explored the Alps and northern Italy with Prince Ernest. Now Prince Albert was separated from his brother for the first time in his life. As the heir to the Duchy, Prince Ernest had to undergo military training in Dresden. But Prince Albert had two companions who were to be closely involved in his later life. One was Francis Seymour, later General Seymour, who was to become a close friend; his brother was to be in his household for twenty-one years when he was Prince Consort. And it was possibly on this tour that Prince Albert met his other companion, a man who gave him a lifelong interest in fifteenth-century art: Ludwig Gruner, a German from Dresden, who had lived some time in Milan and Rome, working as an engraver and practising fresco work. He was an art connoisseur with a great love of early Renaissance paintings, which were not then popular. Little did the two young men imagine that one day they would work together to bring Italianate style to Buckingham Palace.

The domes of Florence enthralled Prince Albert. 'Oh! Florence, where I have been for two months', he wrote to a friend, 'has gathered to herself noble treasures of art. I am often intoxicated with delight when I come out of the galleries.' He was enchanted by the countryside but had no joy in the whirl of society: 'you know my *passion* for such things, and must admire my strength of character that I have never excused myself – never returned home till five in the morning – that I have emptied the carnival cup to the dregs'.[23]

On Prince Albert's return Uncle Leopold wrote to Stockmar, 'Albert is much improved. One might easily take him to be twenty-two or twenty-three.'[24] It was time that he should meet Queen Victoria again. But in advance neither Prince Albert nor Queen Victoria were particularly enthusiastic. The Queen was not sure whether she had more than cousinly feelings for him, and gave no hope of an early engagement. Prince Albert was sufficiently sure of himself to make it plain that he would not hang around indefinitely waiting for Queen Victoria to make up her mind.

But from the first moment of their meeting all Queen Victoria's doubts disappeared. She wrote in her journal on 11 October:

Albert really is quite charming, and so extremely handsome, such beautiful blue eyes, an exquisite nose and such a pretty mouth with delicate moustachios and slight but very slight whiskers: a beautiful figure, broad in the shoulders and a fine waist; my heart is quite going.[25]

In four days her heart was quite and for ever gone. On 15 October, in her Blue Boudoir at Windsor, she proposed to him. 'I said to him,' she recorded in her journal, '. . . it would make me *too happy* if he would consent to what I wished (to marry me) we embraced each other over and over again and he was so kind and affectionate.'[26] The next day Prince Albert wrote to Stockmar of 'One of the happiest days of my life . . . yesterday in a Private Audience V. declared her love for me and offered me her hand, which I seized in both mine and pressed tenderly to my lips.'[27]

Their engagement was to remain secret for a month – not even her mother was told. As Prince Albert told Stockmar, 'Everyone says she cannot keep her mouth shut and might even make bad use of the secret if it were entrusted to her.'[28]

Her Privy Council was told at a special audience in the Throne Room at Buckingham Palace on 23 November 1839. As on the morning of her accession, so now the eighty-three Councillors were moved and touched by the simplicity of her performance as she sat on her crimson throne surrounded by all the gilded splendour of the Throne Room.

The Queen read the declaration in a clear, firm voice.

It is my intention to ally myself in marriage with the Prince Albert of Saxe-Coburg and Gotha. Deeply impressed with the solemnity of the engagement which I am about to contract I have not come to this decision without mature consideration, nor without feeling a strong assurance that, with the blessing of

Almighty God, it will at once secure me domestic felicity and serve the interests of my country.[29]

The wedding was fixed for 10 February 1840. But there were difficult times ahead.

The Tories quickly seized on what they considered to be a vital omission in the marriage declaration. Melbourne had not mentioned that Prince Albert was a Protestant. Immediately the rumour spread that he was a Catholic and this had to be denied forcibly. Stockmar arrived from Coburg to arrange the marriage contract. In the next seven months in England, he was to need all his tact and diplomacy. He suffered a defeat on the subject of Prince Albert's annuity. In after years he regretted that he himself had not initiated all-party talks in which he could have insisted that it was only fair that Prince Albert should receive the same amount as the preceding consorts. Queen Caroline, wife of George II; Queen Charlotte, wife of George III; Queen Adelaide, wife of William IV – all had received £50,000 per annum. So, too, had Prince Leopold as consort to the heir presumptive, Princess Charlotte. But this time the Tories had the support of the radicals, who argued that at a time of heavy taxation and general distress such an annuity would be excessive. An amendment proposing an allowance of £30,000 a year was passed.

Prince Albert had returned to Coburg to arrange his affairs and say farewell to his old home, the Rosenau. Unwillingly Stockmar agreed that Prince Albert should take Melbourne's secretary George Anson as his own. The Prince, he believed, should be above party politics. In fact Prince Albert came to respect and like Anson.

The wedding took place in the Chapel Royal, St James's Palace. Queen Victoria dressed simply in white satin, with no crown, no coronet – simply a wreath of orange blossom in her hair. They left for a short and blissful honeymoon at Windsor. Prince Albert had hoped for longer, but Queen Victoria had written firmly, 'You forget my dearest love, that I am the sovereign and that business can stop and wait for nothing.'[30]

In those first years of their marriage, Prince Albert was not allowed to forget that she was Queen. He had his desk beside hers in her room overlooking the garden in the north wing of Buckingham Palace, but at first he felt his sole function was to pass his wife the blotting paper. Melbourne still advised her – even when she had a Tory government. He should have firmly made a break, but he was reluctant to lose their unique friendship. Both Prince Albert and Stockmar chafed at this unconstitutional behaviour, and Stockmar tactfully and effectively protested to Melbourne, who saw the justice of the criticism.

Gradually Melbourne's influence faded. He was frequently ill and suffered a severe heart attack. Sadly driving in his carriage past the Palace, he saw a light in the room where he had sat so often with her. Now she no longer needed him. He consoled himself with his mistress, Mrs Norton, who remained his friend until his death.

In their early days the Queen and her consort were deeply happy. Queen Victoria had not only a lover but a most congenial companion, who could ride with her on her furious gallops – her Ladies-in-Waiting found it hard to keep up with her. Prince Albert was full of admiration for her energy, and in the frozen February of 1841 had reason to be grateful for her common sense and courage. The Queen and her Ladies-in-Waiting were watching Prince Albert skating on the frozen lake in the Palace gardens, Queen Victoria glowing with love and pride as Prince Albert gracefully pirouetted before them. Then he fell in. Prince Albert told the story in a letter to the Duchess Caroline of Saxe-Gotha-Altenberg on 12 February 1841.

The cold has been intense . . . Nevertheless, I managed, in skating, three days ago, to break through the ice in Buckingham Palace Gardens. I was making my way to Victoria, who was standing on the bank with one of her ladies, and when within some few yards of the bank I fell plump into the water, and had to swim for two or three minutes in order to get out. Victoria was the only person who had the presence of mind to lend me assistance, her lady being more occupied in screaming for help. The shock from the cold was extremely painful, and I cannot thank Heaven enough, that I escaped with nothing more than a severe cold.[31]

Above all she had someone to share what Melbourne had called her 'inordinate fondness for music'. Just as George III and Queen Charlotte had filled the Palace with music, had encouraged musicians of all kinds and had themselves been no mean performers, so Prince Albert and Queen Victoria played and sang together. The Queen now had a partner to join her in performing at her concerts in Buckingham Palace.

The printed programme of one such concert shows how talented they were.

QUARTETTE	'Nobile Signora' (Comte Ory)	*Rossini*

Prince Albert, Signori Rubini, Signor B. Costa,
and Signor Lablache.

DUO	'Non funestar crudele' (Il Disertora)	*Ricci*

Her Majesty and Prince Albert

CORO PASTORALE	'Felice Eta'	*Costa*

Her Majesty, Lady Sandwich, Lady Williamson,
Lady Normanby, Lady Norreys, Misses Liddell and Anson.
Signor Rubini and Signor Costa. Prince Albert,
Lord C. Paget, and Signor Lablache.

QUARTETTO CON CORO	'Tue di grazia'	*Haydn*

Her Majesty, Lady Williamson, Lady Sandwich,
Lady Norreys, Lady Normanby, Misses Liddell and Anson.
Signor Rubini and Signor Costa. Prince Albert,
Lord C. Paget and Signor Lablache.

CORO	'Oh! Come lieto giunge' (St. Paul)	*Felix Mendelssohn*

Her Majesty, Lady Sandwich, Lady Williamson,
Lady Normanby, Lady Norreys, Misses Liddell and Anson.
Signor Rubini and Signor Costa. Prince Albert,
Lord C. Paget and Signor Lablache.[32]

How delighted Nash would have been, could he have seen his beautiful Music Room put to such good use.

In June 1842 Prince Albert invited the composer Felix Mendelssohn to the Palace to play his organ. Nothing better brings to life his and Queen Victoria's genuine pleasure in music than the account Mendelssohn gave in a letter to his mother of his visit. The composer wrote, 'Queen

Victoria looks so youthful and is so friendly and courteous and . . . speaks such good German and knows all my music so well . . . She seated herself near the piano and made me play to her . . . first seven "Songs without Words".' He drank tea with them in the 'splendid grand gallery in Buckingham Palace . . . where two boars by Paul Potter are hanging'.

On 9 July Mendelssohn returned to the Palace. He described the occasion to his mother:

Prince Albert had asked me to go to him on Saturday at two o'clock, so that I might try his organ before I left England: I found him alone, and as we were talking away the Queen came in, also alone, in a simple morning dress. She said she was obliged to leave for Claremont in an hour, and then, suddenly interrupting herself, exclaimed, 'But goodness, what a confusion!' for the wind had littered the whole room, and even the pedals of the organ (which, by the way, made a very pretty feature of the room), with leaves of music from a large portfolio that lay open. As she spoke she knelt down and began picking up the music; Prince Albert helped, and I too was not idle . . . Prince Albert played me a chorale by heart, with pedals, so charmingly and correctly.

Mendelssohn asked the Queen to sing his 'Schöner und schöner', 'which she sang beautifully in tune, in strict time and with very nice expression . . . The last long C I have never heard purer or more natural by any amateur.'

Before leaving, Mendelssohn played the organ for them, and 'they followed me with so much intelligence . . . that I felt more at ease than ever before.' He remembered that before the Queen sang for him she said,

'But first we must get rid of the parrot, or he will scream louder than I can sing.' Prince Albert rang the bell and the Prince of Gotha said 'I'll take him out'; so I came forward and said, 'Please allow me!' and lifted up the big cage and carried it out to the astonished servants.[33]

Queen Victoria and Prince Albert shared not only a love of music but also a deep interest in art. Queen Victoria was herself a competent artist, and Prince Albert had always loved art and had a particular interest in Italian paintings. Throughout Prince Albert's lifetime, both were to be concerned with the care of the Royal Collection. They added to the collection and commissioned new works.

Queen Victoria was too busy in the first years of her reign to spend much time investigating the immense collection of paintings bequeathed by George IV. Many of the most valuable were still in store at Windsor Castle or elsewhere and until the arrival of Prince Albert the Royal Collection was in a state of utter confusion.

Now, under her husband's influence, the Queen began to take an interest in her inheritance. However, when, in December 1843, she went to St George's Hall, Windsor, 'to look at some more old pictures', as she wrote in her Journal, she was

thunderstruck and shocked . . . in the way in which pictures, many fine ones amongst them and of interesting value, have been thrown about and left in lumber rooms at Hampton Court, while this castle and Buckingham Palace are literally without pictures. George III took the greatest care of them, George IV grew too ill to settle many things and William IV who was not famed for his good taste sent all the pictures away.

My care, or rather my dearest Albert's, for he delights in these things will be to have them restored, find places for them and to prevent, as much as it is in our power, pictures of the family and others of interest and value, from being thrown about again.[34]

Not only did Prince Albert supervise the restoration of the Royal Collection; he was to decide how the paintings should be hung, and his arrangement of pictures in the Picture Gallery at Buckingham Palace was to be sacred, never to be changed in Queen Victoria's lifetime.

Although Prince Albert's influence was profound and lasting, Queen Victoria had been interested in paintings even as a little girl. She had been well taught and drew quite well; her sketches of people and Scottish landscapes have a certain charm. She had, however, strong prejudices. Wilkie was condemned because he had wrongly portrayed her in a white dress at her first council and because the other portraits were not 'like' – they were 'too atrocious'. Sir Edwin Landseer was a firm favourite because he painted the animals she loved so exactly and with such a gloss. His *Free Kirk* was to give her great pleasure because of its Scottish and Jacobite connections – Queen Victoria, like George III and George IV, was always conscious of what she called 'the Stuart blood in my veins'. So the Prince of Wales pleased her with his birthday gift in 1860 of *Flora MacDonald*, painted by Alexander Johnston. Sir George Hayter's state portraits were much admired. But of all her artists the German painter, Franz Xaver Winterhalter, best represented all she admired in art – his clear, bright colours and his ability to catch the character of his subjects delighted her for many years. The portrait of the elderly Duke of Wellington on 1 May presenting a casket to his godson, the baby Prince Arthur, who offers the old Duke a spray of flowers, is a typical and famous example.

Late in life she praised the Austrian painter, Heinrich von Angeli, for his 'wonderfully like portraits, his clear colours and correct drawing'. At the end of her life she chose the Danish painter, Laurits Regner Tuxen, to paint her with her vast crowd of descendants on the occasion of her Golden Jubilee. She insisted that they were 'prettily arranged', not stiff and formal, and that the bust of her dead Albert should be represented.

As a collector of family portraits, Queen Victoria cannot be matched by any other British monarch. It was Prince Albert, however, who was the real connoisseur. As a young man in Italy, the Prince had become interested in early Italian art and after his marriage he collected the works of artists hitherto unfamiliar in England. After his death the Queen was lost, 'always lacking his advice and working in the dark without his unerring and great taste'.[35]

Throughout their marriage Queen Victoria and Prince Albert delighted in giving each other paintings as birthday presents. The Queen allowed herself an annual sum, ranging from £2,000 in 1841 to £3,300 in 1855. From this account she bought Prince Albert many pictures, including Italian landscapes by James Roberts to remind him of the country which she herself had never visited and romantic studies such as W. E. Frost's *Una Among the Fauns and Wood Nymphs*.

Contrary to popular belief, neither she nor Prince Albert were prudes and they obviously enjoyed Frost's lightly veiled, lovely damsels. She commissioned from Daniel Maclise the illustration of the German romantic tale of *Undine*. Their favourite paintings often had lyrical or poetic subjects taken from the words of John Milton, William Shakespeare or Edmund Spenser.

The collection which Queen Victoria bequeathed to Buckingham Palace is not as important as those left by Charles I, George III or George IV. Critics have attacked, as George Moore did, 'the limitation of the Queen's patronage'; he saw in them a sameness, 'a staid Germanic, bourgeois quality, a lack of humour, a liking for the second rate'. In this there is some truth. However, as Sir Oliver Millar has written, 'of all the motives that urged her to buy or commission pictures, the most powerful and pervasive was, simply, love'.[36] As she wrote to her daughter, 'how wrong it is not to paint things as they really are'.[37]

More daunting, however, than the organization of the Royal Collection were problems in the royal Household. One of these was the fact that the Queen had no official secretarial help. It seems incredible to modern observers that Queen Victoria, young and inexperienced as she was, did not have a private office. In addition to Lehzen taking care of some of her private correspondence, Melbourne, as Stockmar's son recorded, 'gave himself up in a far greater degree than a Premier is wont to do',[38] to work which today would be done by a Private Secretary; and if it had not been for Stockmar, who, for her first fifteen months of office acted as an unofficial Private Secretary, the chaos at the Palace would have been even greater than it was.

In fact, Queen Victoria had had less help than any of her predecessors. George III had worn himself out working without a Private Secretary until, when he became blind, he appointed Colonel Herbert Taylor to the post, paying him out of his private purse. This appointment was much criticized: it was considered dangerous for an outsider to have access to state secrets. The Prince Regent, too, was much attacked for making Colonel MacMahon his Private Secretary, especially as he paid him out of public funds. His ministers defended him on the grounds that he needed help to 'get through the mass of mechanical labour which devolved on the crown'. William IV took on his father's former Secretary, Taylor, an appointment which went unchallenged since he had proved to be wise and discreet.

Queen Victoria was considered 'both by the ministry and King Leopold, too young and inexperienced to be entrusted to the hands of any single man . . . whose influence might have become all the more extensive the more he was exempt from all control'.[39]

So Stockmar had been sent to help her at the beginning of her reign. It says much for his tact and discretion that a foreigner should have caused such comparatively little hostility. There was some: there were times when Queen Victoria was irritated by his lengthy memoranda. But he was widely respected. Melbourne considered him not only an excellent man, but also one of the most sensible he had ever met.

Stockmar's undoubted success as an invaluable counsellor throughout the first twenty years of Queen Victoria's reign was due to his guiding principles. These should be engraved in letters of gold over every courtier's desk:

If you are consulted by Princes to whom you are attached give your opinion truthfully, boldly, without reserve or reticence. Should your opinion not be palatable, do not, to please or conciliate them deviate for a moment from what you think the truth . . . never try to make them own how right you were, and how wrong they have been. It must be enough for you that you should, for their good and the good of the country, act upon the principles, the soundness of which is thus acknowledged.[40]

It was Stockmar's firm hand that steered the Queen and Prince Albert through the stormy waters in their first years, past the two great rocks on which their marriage could have foundered – the presence of the increasingly difficult Lehzen, and the management of the royal Household. Stockmar had his own rooms, was allowed special dispensation, could dress as simply as he liked and was allowed to retire before the Queen. He padded quietly round the Palace, observing the incompetence and confusion.

He was also needed to deal with Lehzen, who, now supplanted and jealous, had become a great stumbling block to the happiness of their marriage. Prince Albert knew she must somehow be removed. Although Prince Albert and Queen Victoria were deeply and genuinely in love, they had some spectacular rows – not surprising where two strong-willed

people were concerned. The birth of their first two children clipped
Queen Victoria's wings; she chafed at the loss of freedom and hated the
trauma of childbirth – which she said made her feel like an animal. She
was overstressed and subject to severe headaches, and often exploded
with irrational outbursts of anger, which she desperately tried to control.

In the following years she was so often pregnant. From November
1840, when their first child, Princess Victoria Adelaide Mary Louisa –
'Vicky' – was born, to the birth of Princess Beatrice in 1857, the Queen
had nine children. It was not until the birth of Prince Leopold on 7 April
1853 that the Queen's frequent trials were eased by the use of chloroform.
John Snow, the famous anaesthetist, reported to Dr Simpson that the
Queen was 'greatly pleased with the effect'. It is not surprising that there
were times when Queen Victoria was tetchy. It was difficult enough
being a Queen, but to be the mother of nine children as well was
sometimes an impossible strain. She can be excused her frequent
tantrums.

As for Prince Albert, he became increasingly resentful that he was
not the master in his own house. The jealous, possessive Lehzen drove
him to unaccustomed bitter fury. He soon realized that the Palace would
never be home until he had got rid of her. The governess who had so
impressed Lord Holland in 1837 had now become a 'yellow dragon',
spitting fire and venom; the Queen was her child and the household
was her territory. She was always there, coming between husband and
wife. More dangerous still, as a passionate Whig she encouraged the
Queen's prejudices. There was even a rumour that she was funnelling
income from the estate of the Duchy of Cornwall into Whig party
funds.

The Tories saw her as an enemy: if the Whig government fell, her
position would be threatened. So she was not only insecure, she was
also overstretched. She controlled the Queen's Privy Purse, acted as her
Private Secretary, was in charge of the Queen's domestic affairs and,
above all, was responsible for the care of the children. This last was the
final straw for the Prince.

In January 1842 Stockmar was concerned to receive hysterical letters
from both Queen Victoria and the Prince. There had been an appalling

row in the nursery at the Palace: their child, Vicky, was ill, and Prince Albert blamed the doctor and, indirectly, Lehzen. Clearly he completely lost control, accusing Dr Clark of poisoning 'the child with calomel' and Queen Victoria of starving her. 'Take the child away and do as you like, and if she dies you will have it on your conscience,' he wrote to her in a furious letter. Queen Victoria wrote to Stockmar, appealing for his help. Prince Albert had become paranoid about Lehzen: she was, he wrote to Stockmar, 'a crazy common stupid intriguer, obsessed with lust of power, who regards herself as a demi-god and any one who refuses to recognise her as such, as a criminal'.[41]

Queen Victoria, he wrote, must choose between him and Lehzen. It was time for Stockmar to intervene. With his usual quiet frankness and wisdom, he wrote to the Queen, who realized at last that Lehzen must go. Prince Albert followed Stockmar's advice and tactfully and gradually eased Lehzen out. On 30 September 1842 Lehzen quietly left, early in the morning, not wishing to upset Queen Victoria with a farewell scene.

The other problem which was infuriating the orderly Prince Albert was the mismanagement of Buckingham Palace. The Prince was appalled to find the Palace accounts in such disorder. Queen Victoria, unaccustomed to dealing with money, had entertained vast numbers of people without thought of expense, and even Melbourne was amazed to hear that in addition she had spent £34,000 on pensions and charities in 1839 alone.

In addition, Queen Victoria was nobly paying off her mother's debts. It is not surprising that she had secretly turned for help to Miss Coutts, the heiress, whose grandfather, the banker Thomas Coutts, in his time had bailed out many royal debtors including George III, the Prince Regent, the royal Dukes and her own father.

As for the organization of the royal Household, as Stockmar's son noted in his memoirs,

On the Queen's Accession to the throne, the existing arrangements were in the highest degree impractical and confused, and resulted in disorder and discomfort. Many obsolete customs were kept simply because it lies in the

English character . . . to feel the greatest dread of anything like a systematic and comprehensive reconstruction of things.[42]

To reform the management of the Palace was a task which would take more time than the Prince could spare now that he was taking on more and more of the Queen's work. 'Whenever you need me,' Stockmar had written, 'send for me.' Prince Albert needed him now. He came, and with his help Prince Albert undertook a complete reorganization. Stockmar spent some months at the Palace and on his return to Coburg produced a detailed memorandum.

Stockmar's son claimed in 1872 that at the time he was writing, 'The English court . . . is one of the best ordered courts in Europe; the organization is practical, the service is done with exemplary regularity and punctuality.'[43] He considered that this transformation from a Court still tainted by Regency corruption and inefficiency was mainly due to the work of Prince Albert, under the guidance of Baron Stockmar.

Stockmar described his report as:

Observations on the present state of the Royal Household; written with a view to amend the present scheme, and to unite the security and comfort of the sovereign with the greater regularity and better discipline of the Royal Household.[44]

His first comment was that Court appointments were

great officers of state, who are always noblemen of high rank and political consideration and change with every Government. Since the year 1830 we find five changes in the office of the Lord Chamberlain, and six in that of the Lord Steward.

Then there is another great inconvenience. It is, that none of the great officers can reside in the palace, and that most frequently they cannot even reside in the same place with the Court. Hence, an uninterrupted and effective personal inspection and superintendence of the daily details of their respective departments are made impracticable. Hence follows another bad consequence. Most frequently the great officers of State find themselves so situated, as to be forced to delegate, *pro tempore*, part of their authority to others. From want of proper regulations, they must delegate it, as it were, *ex-tempore*, and to servants very inferior in rank in the Royal Household; a fact which, almost daily, is productive of consequences injurious to the dignity, order, discipline, and security of the Court.[45]

So Edmund Burke had complained in the reign of George III.

Then there was no co-operation between departments responsible for the running of the Palace. At that time the government departments responsible were the Treasury, which provided most of the income, and the Department of Woods and Forests, which took care of the outside. The Lord Chamberlain, the Lord Steward and the Master of the Horse shared responsibility for the interior, but at the beginning of Queen Victoria's reign, no one was quite sure where the demarcation lines were.

As Stockmar's memorandum revealed,

In the time of George III, the Lord Steward had the custody and charge of the whole palace, excepting the Royal apartments, drawing rooms, &c., &c. In George IV.'s and William IV.'s reign, it was held that the whole of the ground-floor, including halls, dining-rooms, &c., were in his charge. In the present reign, the Lord Steward has surrendered to the Lord Chamberlain the grand hall and other rooms on the ground-floor; but whether the kitchen, sculleries, pantries, remain under his charge ... is a question which no one could perhaps at this moment reply to. The outside of the palace is, however, considered to belong to the Woods and Forests; so that as the inside cleaning of the windows belongs to the Lord Chamberlain's department, the degree of light to be admitted into the palace depends proportionably on the well-timed and good understanding between the Lord Chamberlain's Office and that of the Woods and Forests.[46]

There was no general directing officer and the departments were in a ridiculous muddle. Stockmar gave examples.

The housekeepers, pages, housemaids, &c., are under the authority of the Lord Chamberlain; all the footmen, livery-porters, and under-butlers, by the strangest anomaly, under that of the Master of the Horse, at whose office they are clothed and paid, and the rest of the servants, such as the clerk of the kitchen, the cooks, the porters, &c., are under the jurisdiction of the Lord Steward. Yet these ludicrous divisions not only extend to persons, but they extend likewise to things and actions. The Lord Steward, for example, finds the fuel and lays the fire, and the Lord Chamberlain lights it. It was upon this state of things that the writer of this paper, having been sent one day by Her present Majesty to Sir Frederick Watson, then the Master of the Household, to complain that the dining-room was always cold, was gravely answered, 'You see, properly speaking, it is not our fault; for the Lord Steward lays the fire only, and the Lord Chamberlain lights it.' In the same manner the Lord Chamberlain provides all the lamps, and the Lord Steward must clean, trim, and light them. If a pane of glass, or the door of a cupboard in the scullery, requires mending, it cannot now be done without the following process: A requisition is prepared and signed by the chief cook, it is then counter-signed by the clerk of the kitchen, then it is taken to be signed by the Master of the Household, thence it is taken to the Lord Chamberlain's Office, where it is authorised, and then laid before the Clerk of the Works, under the office of Woods and Forests; and consequently many a window and cupboard have remained broken for months.[47]

The Palace also urgently needed improved sanitation. The Queen herself had a flushing lavatory, but even she suffered from the overflow of the room above her dressing room. Stockmar's delicacy prevents us from hearing the full horror of the lack of sanitation in the royal Palaces. We are grateful to John Pudney for enlightening us.

It took more than royal attacks of wherry-go-nimbles and the employment of 'Artists' [plumbers] . . . to improve conditions in Britain's royal palaces. It took that enlightened and persistent reformer, Albert, Prince Consort. There was room for improvement. In 1844, no less than fifty-three overflowing cesspools were discovered under Windsor Castle. The Prince Consort with characteristic energy attacked the sorry state of affairs, replacing Hanoverian commodes with up-to-date water closets.[48]

Perhaps it was as a result of his thorough investigation of the conditions in the royal palaces that Prince Albert included in the Great Exhibition of 1851 a wide variety of the latest water closets. But, alas,

with his death there was a tendency to accept the status quo in sanitation as in everything else, so that all might remain as it had been in his lifetime, all in some degree part of one great Albert memorial.

It was not until ten years after his death that the typhoid of the heir to the throne awakened the national conscience to the perils of its smallest rooms and its noisome drains, the reform of which had for years been strenuously urged by such sanitary pioneers as Edwin Chadwick.[49]

Because the great nobles who held the high offices in the royal Household lived elsewhere, often out of London, there was no supervision, except by the one resident officer, the Master of the Household, who belonged to the Lord Steward's department. But he had no authority over the housekeepers, pages and housemaids, who worked in the Lord Chamberlain's department. Consequently,

As neither the Lord Chamberlain, nor the Master of the Horse, have a regular deputy residing in the palace, more than two thirds of all the male and female servants are left without a master in the house. They can come on and go off duty as they choose, they can remain absent for hours and hours on their days of waiting, or they may commit any excess or irregularity: there is nobody to observe, to correct, or to reprimand them. The various details of internal arrangement, whereon depends the well-being and comfort of the whole establishment, no one is cognisant of or responsible for. There is no officer responsible for the cleanliness, order and security of the rooms and offices throughout the palace. These things are left to providence; and if smoking, drinking, and other irregularities occur in the dormitories, where footmen, &c., sleep ten and twelve in each room, no one can help it.[50]

Most dangerous of all, there was no one authority responsible for the security of the Palace. The Lord Chamberlain did not control the porters, the Lord Steward had 'nothing to do with the disposition of pages', etc. Nor was security in the care of the Master of the Household. Security at the Palaces had always been notoriously lax, though for generations espionage and counter-espionage had been flourishing trades. In the time of Charles II, Pepys had wandered round the old Palace of Whitehall for hours unchallenged. In the reign of George III, biographer James Boswell had chatted easily to 'the old soldiers on guard outside Buckingham Palace, listened to their tales of the battle of Dettingen, "Where," said one he saw, "our cannon make a lane through the French army as broad as that,"' pointing to the Mall. Then Boswell treated them to a pint of beer and they 'talked on the sad mischief of war and on the frequency of poverty'.[51] It was comparatively easy for intruders to get into a building which for two decades had been unoccupied by the royal family, and where for most of that time hundreds

QUEEN VICTORIA

of workmen and officials had been working constantly. It was, too, astonishingly easy to attack the Queen, even immediately outside the Palace.

One such attempted assassination was described by Prince Albert in a letter to his father. On 29 May 1842 he and the Queen were driving along the Mall back to Buckingham Palace when he 'saw a man step out from the crowd and present a pistol full at me'. The Prince heard the trigger snap but there was no shot. However, the next morning a boy came to report to him that he had seen the man presenting the pistol. Nevertheless, although 'we were much agitated and Victoria nervous and unwell' they resolved not to allow their 'miscreant' to deprive them of their necessary exercise. They felt sure he would come skulking about the Palace again, as indeed he did. The next day, when the 'weather was superb and hosts of people on foot', they drove out to Hampstead. On returning, they were just approaching the Palace when 'a shot was fired at us about five paces off. It was the same fellow with the pistol – a little swarthy ill-looking rascal.' The shot passed under the carriage and 'we thanked the Almighty for having preserved us a second time from so great a danger.' The man – John Francis – 'was not out of his mind, but a thorough scamp'. On 3 July 1842, there was another attack, again in the Mall, when a hunchback named Bean tried to shoot at 'the carriage in which Victoria, myself and Uncle Leopold were sitting'.[52] Both John Francis and Bean were tried and sent to jail.

The most notorious intruder was 'the boy Jones'. In December 1838 Edward Jones, then a lad of fourteen, small for his age and inconspicuous, slipped into the Palace and wandered round until he was caught. He was tried and acquitted by a jury. He was back again in December 1840, and was in the Palace for a whole day. He got into the kitchens, as *The Times* reported, 'leaving his finger marks on a cauldron of stock for soup'. He claimed that he sat on the throne, saw the Queen and heard a baby 'squall'. He said at first that he

got in by scaling the garden wall from Constitution Hill and then through the French Windows opening on to the lawn. Whenever he saw someone he hid behind a pillar or furniture. Later he changed his story and said he 'came over the roof and down a chimney'. But since there was no evidence of soot this was not believed. Finally he was found under a sofa in the centre-room in which the Princess Royal and Mrs Lilley her nurse sleep.[53]

This time he was imprisoned in Tothill gaol for three months. When he was asked, after a morning on the treadmill, how he liked his punishment, he answered that he 'had got into a scrape and must do as he could'. There was no evidence that he was insane.

He was released from prison on 2 March 1841 and on 17 March *The Times* reported 'that the urchin Edward Jones was found again in the palace on Tuesday between 1.00 and 2.00 a.m. This time when caught he said curiosity was his motive; he had always been a great reader and he wanted to listen to the Queen and Prince Albert talking – then he could write a book about it and it would sell well.'[54] He was now seventeen years of age, very small for his age and of a sullen countenance. Once again he had visited the kitchen and claimed that he could get into the Palace at any time he wanted.

Again he was sent to Tothill for three months as a 'rogue and a vagabond'. On 23 March 1841 his father, obviously a respectable Methodist, wrote to *The Times* complaining that he had not been allowed to communicate with his son. He was clearly worried because the last time his son was released he was 'very thin and worn out'.[55]

Charles Dickens visited him in prison, anxious to interview the boy 'because he strongly doubted the popular belief in his sharpness of intellect'.[56] The boy is now immortalized in the quip of Lady Sandwich, who thought his 'name must be "In-I-Go" Jones'. 'Supposing he had come into the bedroom,' the Queen remarked. 'How frightened I should have been.'[57] And how impressed she would have been could she have known how composed her great-great-granddaughter Queen Elizabeth II was to be in similar circumstances.

Eventually, as Stockmar's son recorded,

The reform of the royal household was undertaken according to these principles by the Prince Consort and carried out with firmness and prudence. The Master of the Household, who, as we have seen, had been until then a subordinate official of the Lord Chamberlain and possessed of very undefined power, was named delegate of the three departments.

Stockmar proposed to keep the three great officers of Court

in their connection with the political system, but to induce them . . . to delegate as much of his authority as was necessary to the maintenance of the order, discipline and security of the Palace, to one official, who should always reside at court and be responsible to the three departmental chiefs, but . . . be able to secure unity of action.[58]

On 24 June 1842 *The Times* reported that 'strictest precautions' had now been taken 'to guard against intrusions of improper persons into the palace'.[59] At 10.00 p.m., when livery porters went off duty at the lodges, night porters were to relieve them and stay until morning. A strong party of 'A' Division of Police was to be on duty always in the interior during the night, patrolling the corridors; and at the tradesmen's entrance there would be one police constable in plain clothes. But, as later history was to show, there is little defence against madmen.

It needed all Stockmar's tactful advice to get the reforms accepted. Melbourne's Whig Government had finally collapsed in 1841 and he was replaced as Prime Minister by the Tory, Sir Robert Peel, whom Queen Victoria disliked at first. He was shy and therefore cold in manner – so unlike Queen Victoria's 'dear Lord M'. But Peel's intelligence and honesty appealed to the Prince, who eventually persuaded the Queen to share his respect for a politician who was always prepared to put principle above party. Peel was most reluctant to 'decrease the value of the appointments held by the three great officers of State'. It would make them 'less an object of ambition than they are at present to very distinguished members of the House of Peers'.[60] Then the recipient of 35s. a week for 'Red Room Wine' was offended when his perquisite was removed. The 'Red Room' had been closed since the death of George III. The footmen who lost their daily gift of the candles from the public rooms, whether they had been used or not, were incensed. Eighty housemaids who worked only six months of the year had their wages cut from £45 to a minimum of £18 a year and were disgruntled.

On the advice of Stockmar and Prince Albert, Court etiquette was tightened. No one was allowed to sit in the presence of the Queen except in very special circumstances; Lady John Russell, the next Prime Minister's wife, was allowed to sit when she visited the Palace soon after her confinement, 'but the Queen took care when the Prince joined the company to have a very fat lady standing in front of Lady John Russell'.[61] Ministers still had to learn the art of walking backwards in the Queen's presence. It was all part of the transformation of the image of the monarchy from the lax incompetence of her predecessors to Queen Victoria's famously moral court. But there were many who muttered with Melbourne 'this damned morality will ruin us all'.

In June 1843 a wedding was celebrated in the Palace that would link the past and the future. Princess Augusta, elder daughter of the Duke of Cambridge and the Queen's first cousin, married the Grand Duke of Mecklenburg-Strelitz, Queen Charlotte's great-nephew. Princess Augusta's niece Mary, who later became Queen Mary, was to spend many happy months in Mecklenburg-Strelitz and so developed a great sense of empathy with George III's Queen.

In April 1841 *The Times* reported that Her Majesty 'wishes a path laid up the mound and a small pavilion built there'.[62] The 'mound' at the end of the garden, thrown up in Nash's time from the excavation for the lake, helped to screen the garden from the houses in Grosvenor Place. A 'small Swiss looking edifice' was built. Planned by Prince Albert and Professor Gruner, it was decorated by eight leading Royal Academicians, commissioned 1842–3.*

However, by the time it was finished the royal family had found other and greater retreats from the increasing fog and dirt of London, where the Palace and gardens were blackened with soot which fell in black flakes. In 1844 they bought an estate at Osborne, on the Isle of Wight, on which a house was built by the combined talents of Prince Albert, Gruner and the competent builder Thomas Cubitt (who was later to work on Buckingham Palace).

Four years later they found an even wilder remote retreat: they leased the Scottish castle and estate of Balmoral, which later became their

* The pavilion was demolished in 1928.

own. It was the beginning of a love affair with Scotland which lasted all their lives. Osborne and Balmoral were their own properties, where Prince Albert did not have the frustration of asking Parliament for money for necessary repairs, as he did at Buckingham Palace.

By the mid 1840s it became clear that Buckingham Palace needed major alterations. But each time Prince Albert tackled Sir Robert Peel, the Prime Minister, on the subject he looked away and muttered that now was not the time for more expenditure on a Palace that had only been finished in 1837.

There had been minor modifications in the building in the first years of Queen Victoria's reign. She did not like the octagonal chapel on the south side of the Palace (originally one of George III's Libraries). Blore was commissioned to convert one of Nash's conservatories on the west garden front into a chapel. The roof had to be raised and considerable alteration was needed, but in 1843 it was consecrated by the Archbishop of Canterbury.

As far as expenditure on Buckingham Palace was concerned, Peel finally agreed that rebuilding was necessary and, though it was unpopular with his party, he asked Blore to present a report. Meanwhile the Queen wrote urgently and firmly from the Royal Pavilion, Brighton, on 10 February 1845:

Though the Queen knows that Sir Robert Peel has already turned his attention to the urgent necessity of doing something to Buckingham Palace, the Queen thinks it right to recommend this subject herself to his serious consideration. Sir Robert is acquainted with the state of the Palace and the total want of accommodation for our little family, which is fast growing up. Any building must necessarily take some years before it can be safely inhabited. If it were to be begun this autumn, it could hardly be occupied before the spring of 1848, when the Prince of Wales would be nearly seven, and the Princess Royal nearly eight years old, and they cannot possibly be kept in the nursery any longer. A provision for this purpose ought, therefore, to be made this year. Independent of this most parts of the Palace are in a sad state, and will ere long require a further outlay to render them *decent* for the occupation of the Royal Family or any visitors the Queen may have to receive. A room, capable of containing a larger number of those persons whom the Queen has to invite in the course of the season to balls, concerts, etc., than any of the present apartments can at once hold, is much wanted. Equally so, improved offices and servants' rooms, the want of which puts the departments of the household to great expense yearly. It will be for Sir Robert to consider whether it would not be best to remedy all these deficiencies at once, and to make use of this opportunity to render the exterior of the Palace such as no longer to be a *disgrace* to the country, which it certainly now is. The Queen thinks the country would be better pleased to have the question of the Sovereign's residence in London so finally disposed of, than to have it so repeatedly brought before it.[63]

Peel replied, however, that since he had to propose the renewal of income tax he must postpone any decision on the Palace.

It was probably on this visit to Brighton that the Queen and Prince Albert found a possible solution to the problem of the expense involved. They would sell the Royal Pavilion and use the proceeds for Buckingham Palace. The truth was that Queen Victoria disliked the jostling crowds at Brighton.

Queen Victoria wanted these alterations and improvements not because of personal vanity. As she pointed out to Peel, unlike her predecessors she had never asked for knick-knacks and extravagances. She wanted Buckingham Palace to be recognized at home and abroad as the seat of British Majesty. Her famous costume balls were designed to remind the world of the continuity of the history of the British monarchy.

For one of these balls, on 12 May 1842, the medieval period was chosen as the theme, the Queen and Prince Albert appearing as Queen Philippa and Edward III. Sir Edwin Landseer painted them in all their splendour, Queen Victoria glittering in £60,000 worth of jewels. The Duchess of Cambridge, not to be eclipsed, came as Anne of Brittany with a hundred courtiers. This ball was proclaimed to be for the benefit of the Spitalfield silk weavers, though there was little profit made after expenses had been paid.

The next ball, on 6 June 1845, celebrated the centenary of the defeat of the Stuart rebellion. Did Queen Victoria realize that it was on this day in 1763 that Queen Charlotte had given George III his surprise housewarming party? Certainly, on this occasion she wore a splendid brocaded dress cloaked in old lace that had belonged to Queen Charlotte. Uncle Leopold and Stockmar would have been touched that the old Queen they had known so well had been remembered. This time the ladies were allowed to wear only clothes of British manufacture – an attempt to forestall the inevitable criticisms of extravagance at the Palace.

The crowds in the Mall cheered the show, but, according to Hobhouse, Her Majesty's ministers were distinctly uncomfortable, perspiring in wigs that refused to sit straight. The *Annual Register* recorded that the Duke of Wellington, who appeared as 'Butcher Cumberland', was recognizable only by his nose. Lord Cardigan, as an officer of the 11th Dragoons at Culloden, had 'the true jackboot stride'.[64]

There were cheers outside the Palace, but there were hostile faces in the crowds. Ballad mongers wrote with their sharp pens:

> Some curious costumes graced the scene,
>   Of which just one or two I'll name,
> That to the masque of England's Queen,
>   To pay their loyal homage came.
>
> Melbourne, in saucy garb arrayed,
>   Dressed as a Roman *parasite*;
> Who earned the meals his patron paid
>   By 'glozing' jokes and flattery light.
>
> Think, ye aristocrats, whose gold,
>   Squandered in fashion's brittle toys,
> Is like yourselves, so bright and cold,
>   Of this dark contrast to your joys.
>
> Think, what a little part bestowed
>   On those lone huts where misery scowls,
> Would turn from Satan's fearful road
>   Your Brother Men's despairing souls.
>
> Think, did I say! no, heartless crew,
>   Self to your thoughts is all in all,
> Let *them* curse God, and die, while you
>   Dance at Victoria's Fancy Ball![65]

Six years later at a 'Restoration Ball', Prince Albert appeared improbably in over-bright orange satin over crimson velvet breeches and lavender stockings. The United States Minister, who normally refused to dress up for Court, this time wore blue velvet, trimmed with gold lace and a scarlet velvet mantle, which he claimed was the costume of a New England governor of the period.

A particularly splendid banquet was given on the occasion of the christening of Queen Victoria's son Prince Leopold on 28 June 1853. A watercolour by Louis Haghe shows the Picture Gallery glowing with gold plate displayed on the buffet at the end of the Gallery. On the table, surrounded by gilded candelabra, is a monumental christening cake.

These balls and banquets had a political significance and Queen Victoria wanted a larger palace to accommodate her wide network of foreign friends and relations. Over the years this network would spread to France, Belgium, Spain, Portugal and the dukedoms and kingdoms of Germany, Romania, Russia and Denmark. In the end, Queen Victoria was to become the grandmother of Europe. Visits were exchanged with Louis-Philippe, King of France. When Emperor Napoleon III and Empress Eugenie and Tsar Nicholas I of Russia visited Windsor, Queen Victoria and Prince Albert were particularly anxious to impress.

Prince Albert had his own sources of information in Europe and Queen Victoria would establish lasting and useful personal relationships. This was important when Lord Palmerston was Foreign Secretary, since he had an infuriating habit of conducting foreign policy without informing the Queen – or anyone else. When he congratulated the future Emperor Napoleon III on his *coup d'état* he did so entirely on his own responsibility. To everyone's relief he left the Foreign Office but came back later as Prime Minister, when the Queen found him easier to deal with. Foreign Affairs, the Queen considered, were her concern.

Palace Improvements

At last in 1846 Peel agreed to the partial rebuilding of the Palace: since the sale of the Royal Pavilion, Brighton, was to provide a large part of the funds, he could no longer resist Queen Victoria's demands.

In May 1846, Blore produced his plans for the 'Palace Improvements'. He proposed providing more rooms by building a fourth side on the courtyard, enclosing and, incidentally, darkening the entrance to the Palace and obscuring Nash's elegant portico.

However, he found himself hedged in by advisers, some of whom were less than helpful. In addition, when he produced his plans, a committee of architects and medical experts insisted that the new quadrangle be enlarged to permit health-giving currents of air. At this time adequate ventilation was a fetish, since diseases were believed to be caused by 'effluvia'.

Then Blore had to suffer the Prince's enthusiastic co-operation. Blore had had unhappy memories of royal interference in the reign of William IV, and now was often irritated by Prince Albert's involvement, especially when he was not told until October 1846 that he had appointed Thomas Cubitt as the contractor. Even worse, however, for poor Blore was the constant interference of the 'six Commissioners for the enlargement of Buckingham Palace', appointed by the government in May 1846 to co-ordinate the work of the various ministries involved. The Prime Minister, Chancellor of the Exchequer and Chief Commissioner for Woods and Forests were ex-officio members and were joined by the first President of the RIBA, Earl de Grey, who also considered himself the expert on taste, the Earl of Lincoln and Francis Egerton, later 1st Earl of Ellesmere and the owner of a fine art collection.

Then in July 1846 there was a change of government. Peel's Tory government was replaced by the Whigs, with Lord John Russell as Prime Minister, who wanted an even tighter control on expenditure on the Palace. The House of Commons voted an estimate of £150,000 for the enlargement of the Palace, of which £20,000 was to be spent on preliminary work in 1846. Lord Morpeth, later 7th Earl of Carlisle, and one of the old Whig 'cousinry', related to Lord Duncannon, now became an important and active member of the commission.

It was now necessary to convince the public that the expenditure was warranted, so on 13 August 1846 *The Times* announced:

It is proposed that £20,000 be voted in the present year for enlarging and improving Buckingham Palace. The whole cost of the improvements were estimated to cost £150,000. They include building a new east front, clearing out and re-arranging rooms in the south wing, alterations in the north wing, new kitchens and other offices with a ballroom over, decorations and painting, taking down the arch, alterations to drains etc. Her Majesty has agreed to sell the Pavilion at Brighton and the money will go towards the cost of above alterations.

There then followed extracts from a letter from Blore of 4 August: 'I have long been aware of the extreme inconvenience to which HM personally, the juvenile members of the royal family and the whole of the royal establishment have been subjected.' He pointed out that 'the private apartments in the north wing . . . [were] not calculated originally for a married sovereign, the head of a family'. The Lord Chamberlain's department for storerooms, workshops, etc. were in the basement of the same wing and 'the noise and smell from these . . . are at times positively offensive'.

There was also the risk of fire and the Palace was so overcrowded that nothing 'short of an extension of the palace can adequately provide for these services . . . The rooms for the children are very inadequate and inconvenient, this will become worse as they grow up.' The servants' rooms were dark and ill-ventilated, the kitchens not only inconvenient but a downright nuisance and the 'Sanitary condition of the palace has not always been sufficiently considered, in thus overcrowding a great number of persons into small rooms, not always well ventilated'. He might have added that the Palace smells were notorious. Blore also made the point that the 'accommodation for the reception of distinguished foreign visitors within the palace was very inadequate and inconvenient'.[66]

This last point was important: it was not merely that the Queen and the Prince needed more space for their family and for the entertainments, balls and concerts. It was necessary that Buckingham Palace should enhance the dignity and the influence of the British monarchy in the eyes of the world.

Then as now, the correspondence columns of *The Times* provided a venue for lively discussion of current topics. On 24 August 1846, a letter signed 'Sphinx' complained that:

the present structure is so radically, inherently and thoroughly trumpery . . . that not even the plaintive Mr Blore can make it a fit residence for a Sovereign. The situation is not healthy, the neighbourhood is poor . . . be sure some future Sovereign, with more horror of malaria, or more regard to taste, will depute some future Mr Blore to condemn and discard it entirely.[67]

The writer suggested that a new palace should be built in Kensington Gardens.

Plans to enclose the courtyard with a fourth wing to provide more rooms were sharply criticized. If it had to be built it was suggested that Mr Blore might take 'a few lessons in the grandiose and scenic from Greenwich Hospital'.[68] Instead, according to *The Builder*, the façade of the Palace presented 'little more than street architecture in stone, instead of stucco'.[69] *Punch* compared it to a line of shops. The Caen stone used was a mistake, as Cubitt had always claimed. It weathered badly, and later had to be painted and finally, in 1913, rebuilt.

Nash's façade was to suffer one more change. The classical open colonnades along the sides of the courtyard wings were to be filled in, to give sheltered access to the entrance to the Palace.

But however much Blore might be criticized, it had to be admitted that he was quick and cheap. He had been allowed £150,000 for the alterations; he completed the front on time at a cost of £106,000. For this, the builder, Cubitt, was partly responsible. His costings for bricklayers and carpenters were less than expected. Queen Victoria now had rooms for nurseries and for private accommodation and new rooms for visitors.

The front was finished in 1847. The Commissioners now asked Blore to choose handsome articles of furniture or decoration which could be conveniently transferred from the Royal Pavilion, Brighton. So Cubitt was instructed to remove marble fireplaces from the Pavilion and bring them to the Palace by railway and cart, and to take out stains, repolish and refix them in the rooms in the new wing; unfortunately Blore had not measured the size of the grates so some did not fit. Neither had he made provision for 'warming apparatus' for the new wing. This Cubitt now undertook, providing two large 'wrot iron' boilers with four-inch cast-iron pipes circulating the hot water, which he guaranteed would keep two staircases and two galleries of the first floor at a constant temperature of fifty-five degrees.

Cubitt did not install the steel grate and the 'pair of massive Ormolu Firedogs representing Dragons and Chimera' in the Chinese Dining Room. This was executed by a famous London smith, W. M. Feetham – it was the kind of 'fancy' work for which Cubitt was not equipped. This room and two other major rooms in the new wing were furnished with chinoiserie from the Pavilion, the Yellow Drawing Room receiving a fantastic marble chimneypiece designed by Robert Jones.

The exotic Pavilion furnishings and fittings were not out of keeping in the old Nash rooms; but they were somewhat incongruous in the pedestrian architecture of the new Blore east wing. Queen Victoria, however, was pleased with the 'airy new rooms'. On 10 June 1849 she recorded with delight in her journal,

We breakfasted as we already dined last night in the new room . . . very handsomely fitted up with furniture etc from the Pavilion at Brighton; including the Chinese pictures that were on the wall there, the doors with the serpents etc . . . A dragon has been painted on the ceiling and harmonises with the rest. The small sitting room is also furnished with things from the Pavilion – all arranged according to my dearest Albert's taste.[70]

Surprisingly, Prince Albert could accept the exotic Brighton furnishings.

The Palace improvements were not yet completed. It would be six more years before the ballroom was built. But by the spring of 1850, Blore considered his work was finished and retired. He had suffered much in the last years and he finished his career at Buckingham Palace without much praise and with a disagreeable court case. Blore and Cubitt were sued in the spring of 1851 by a Pimlico builder, William

Denley, who claimed that they had infringed his patent for flue lining in the east wing of Buckingham Palace. Apparently he had patented a series of earthenware tubes to line the brickwork of chimneys, which superseded the traditional method of lining them with mortar mixed with fresh cow dung. The case dragged on until Cubitt settled out of court. The government paid their costs, but it was a squalid end to a respectable, if undistinguished career.

Decimus Burton agreed to take over from Blore, but as a successful architect he did not enjoy working under Parliamentary instruction. He did not stay long but did provide designs for the gates to the courtyard.

In 1850 the immediate problem was the Marble Arch, sitting there amongst the builders' rubble in the forecourt like a great stranded whale. Suddenly the members of the Commission realized that the Great Exhibition was due to be opened in May 1851 and the removal of the Arch became urgent. The Queen and Prince Albert intended to make a ceremonial appearance on the new balcony to the crowds expected to throng the Mall: the Palace must look its best.

By September 1850 Burton's plans for the Palace forecourt had been approved, with some alterations, by Lord Seymour, who had replaced Lord Carlisle at the Office of Woods and Forests, but he could not proceed until the Marble Arch was moved. Cubitt's tender for its demolition and removal being accepted, his men began dismantling the Arch behind the great hoarding. Each marble block was numbered and, as *The Builder* recorded, 'a drawing was made of each course, with corresponding numbers on the blocks'.[71] According to Cubitt's biographer, 'all that now remained was the marble itself, the original York landings and stone steps, the iron girders and wooden joists, and copper skylights for the roof'.[72] The dismantled Arch was taken into St James's Park and lay there all autumn behind hoardings while the government made up its mind where to put it. Finally, it was decided to rebuild it at Cumberland Gate at the end of Oxford Street.

The exterior of the Arch was finished before the Great Exhibition in May.

Meanwhile the interior was completed. Inside, the brick-lined Arch steps led up to a 'suite of rooms' at the top, which were fitted with fireplaces and ventilators. The Department of Woods and Forests let these out to the police, who doubtless found it a convenient place to keep watch on the crowds thronging to the Exhibition in Hyde Park.

While Buckingham Palace was being improved and enlarged, Europe was in ferment. In 1848 there had been revolutions in almost every capital and it was the relations of Queen Victoria and Prince Albert who sat on the rickety thrones. Uncle Leopold was safe in Belgium, though in his kingdom seeds of discord were planted that would spread across the world. In a smoke-filled room in Brussels in that February of 1848, Karl Marx, Friedrich Engels and their comrades were producing the *Communist Manifesto*, urging workers to 'arise ye starvelings from your slumbers' and throw off their chains. Prince Albert, who had studied political economy in Germany, was possibly the only one in Her Majesty's Court who read anything of Karl Marx.

On 24 February Louis-Philippe, King of the French, the father of Uncle Leopold's wife Louise, abdicated, escaping on 3 March in disguise to Newhaven. Prince Albert's cousin, Princess Victoire, Duchesse de Nemours, who had danced so gaily in Buckingham Palace with her Coburg brothers, escaped from Paris, leaving her clothes and possessions to be worn by the Paris mob. Three days later excited workers shouted *'Vive la République'* outside Buckingham Palace, and there was news of a monster demonstration planned by the Chartists for 10 April. The six points of their charter were in fact modest enough and most of the Chartists were serious, respectable working men. But accounts of the wild men among them were horrifying. Queen Victoria, still recovering from her sixth confinement, was evacuated to Osborne and she insisted Prince Albert should accompany her.

The Duke of Wellington prepared his plan of action, troops were concealed in the Palace and other critical places, and volunteer special constables were enrolled – among them, Louis Napoleon, the man who was so soon to become Emperor Napoleon III of France.

In the event the demonstration fizzled out. Only half the men expected gathered on Kennington Common for the march on the House of Commons. The Chartist leader, Feargus O'Connor, realizing that the march would not be allowed, took the petition and his lieutenants to Westminster in three cabs.

No one who attended the splendid ball in July 1848 would have guessed that in April the Queen had feared that red-capped revolutionaries would by now be dancing in Buckingham Palace, and that their leaders would appear in triumph on the new balcony.

Of the improvements that were being carried out during these political troubles, the balcony which Prince Albert suggested has become important today. Royal appearances on the balcony are now considered the essential climax for victory celebrations, weddings and every great ceremonial occasion. Buckingham Palace has become the focal point for national celebration.

After the opening of the Great Exhibition in 1851, the Queen stood there with Prince Albert to be cheered by the milling crowds in the Mall. It was a proud moment, the recognition of the Prince's greatest triumph. Three years later in February 1854 they stood there again and were cheered on a more poignant occasion as they saw their soldiers off to the Crimean War.

In the years between these two balcony appearances the prestige of the monarchy had dipped alarmingly. The Great Exhibition saw the high peak of Prince Albert's career, and never had the Queen loved and admired him so much. He had shown immense courage and imagination in conceiving an enormous glass palace to display and encourage the art and industry of the world. It was built at a time when Europe was still reeling from the 1848 year of revolutions and counter-revolutions, when London was filled with dangerous political refugees.

Unfortunately Prince Albert's fame was all too fickle. In the following years leading up to the Crimean War he was subjected to an hysterical campaign against imaginary intrigues of the 'Austrian–Belgian–Coburg–Orleans clique, the avowed enemies of England, and the subservient tools of Russian ambition'.[73] Prince Albert was deeply hurt; Queen Victoria was enraged. On 4 January 1854 she informed the Prime Minister, Lord Aberdeen, that she intended to make Albert Prince Consort: she would have made him King had she been able. If she thought the people really believed the slanders she 'would retire to private life . . . leaving the country to choose another ruler after their own HEART'S CONTENT'.[74] The Prince's enemies had gone too far: the government came to his support, and even Palmerston, who had whipped up the anti-Russian fever, now backtracked. Queen and Consort threw themselves into the war effort and were rewarded with enthusiastic cheers when the soldiers marched before the Palace on their way to Armageddon.

On 28 February 1854 they rose before dawn to see 'the last battalion of the Scots Fusiliers march past Buckingham Palace on the way to embarkation' to the Crimean War. As the Queen wrote in her Journal,

The morning was fine and calm, the sun rising red over the time-honoured towers of Westminster . . . the gradual, steady but slow approach of the Band, almost drowned by the tremendous cheering of the dense crowd following. The soldiers gave three hearty cheers which went straight to my heart. Carriages with ladies, sorrowing wives, mothers and sisters were there, and some women in the crowd were crying. The men were quite sober, in excellent order and none absent. Formerly they would have been all drunk! May God protect these fine men, may they be preserved and victorious! I shall never forget the touching, beautiful sight I witnessed this morning.[75]

So many of those 'fine men' were never to return.

On 27 February 1855 Queen Victoria wrote to Uncle Leopold that she had received at Buckingham Palace

on Thursday twenty-six of the wounded Coldstream Guards and on Friday thirty-four of the Scotch fusiliers . . . Among the Grenadiers there is one sad object, shot dreadfully, a ball having gone through the cheek and behind the nose and eye and through the other side! He is shockingly disfigured but is recovered. I feel so much for them and am *so fond* of my dear soldiers – so proud of them! We could not have avoided sending the Guards; it would have been their ruin if they had not gone.[76]

After the end of the Crimean War, in July 1856, Queen Victoria was able to ride out in all her military glory on her horse, Alma, wearing a gold-braided scarlet military uniform, to review 'the largest force of

Britishers assembled in England since the battle of Worcester'. Now she was royal indeed – the Queen of battles.

The Queen and the Prince Consort were away from London for long periods during the early 1850s, but they still used the Palace from time to time for ceremonial occasions. Frieda Arnold, an intelligent German dresser to the Queen from 1854 to 1859, describes in her letters the penetrating cold of the Palace and the fog and filth of London winters. In the winter of 1855 she wrote:

I have never been so cold in my whole life as I was for two days at the Palace. We arrived in bitter weather at this huge building that had stood empty for a long time; in spite of all the heating, the tomb-like atmosphere only disappeared after several days occupation ... Although the palace is surrounded by parks every time I come into my room my table is quite black, my armchair is speckled with little black particles and my lovely shining candlesticks are quite tarnished in two days. One can never leave any article lying about, and even in the cupboards everything gets dirty.[77]

The building of the new ballroom was delayed but Cubitt still kept an office in the Palace with a manager in charge of the minor works he was still undertaking. He was also working for the Queen at Osborne and was able there to discuss quietly with Prince Albert the plans for the next stage of Palace improvements. Prince Albert would have been perfectly prepared to proceed with work on the ballroom with the help of Cubitt and Gruner and without a professional architect. However, in April 1852 the Office for Woods and Forests in the Derby government appointed James Pennethorne as architect for the new wing.

When the new ballroom suite was being planned, James Pennethorne was concerned with slum clearance in the Pimlico and Westminster area. He was working to improve sanitation there and to prepare the ground for the extension of the Palace. He was the obvious choice as successor to Blore for many reasons. It will be remembered that he was related to John Nash, had been trained by Nash himself and had then been at his expense set to work as a pupil of A. C. Pugin. For many years he had lived at Nash's splendid house 14 Regent Street, and in

1824 Nash paid for him to study for two years on the Continent. A six-month course in draughtsmanship with Lafitte, Pugin's brother-in-law, in Paris gave him not only excellent training as an architect but also an enduring interest in Roman triumphal arches, since Lafitte was at this time designing sculptural panels for the Arc de Triomphe. During his months in Rome, Pennethorne worked on a conjectural restoration of the Roman forum, which was much praised, and in April 1826 he was elected a member of the Academy of St Luke in Rome. So, at the time when Nash was designing the Marble Arch, he was receiving regular letters from James Pennethorne with careful drawings of his work in Rome. These must have had some influence on the impressionable Nash. Imagine Pennethorne's pain now, therefore, as he drove to his work in Pimlico, to see the Marble Arch, their dream of Imperial Rome, demolished and removed. It must have been with particular pleasure that he agreed to continue Nash's work in the Palace. He submitted designs, which were accepted, with his tender, in June 1852.

It is difficult to know how much Pennethorne was responsible for the final success of the Ballroom. But he must have shown great tact and patience, since he was working under the shadow of the Prince Consort and Ludwig Gruner, not to mention Cubitt and the Office of Woods and Forests. After his death in 1871, James Pennethorne was remembered as a man of 'retired and studious habits, admired for his kindness, spotless integrity and universal courtesy'.[78]

In the decade between the mid 1840s and mid 1850s the appearance of Buckingham Palace had been transformed and took on the shape we recognize today.

The 'Palace Improvements' were the creation of many hands and minds, and many voices were raised to counsel or to criticize. During that period the government had changed, as had the architects. But Prince Albert remained throughout the period deeply involved in all concerns. Had it not been for his drive and persistence the improvements would never have taken place. His busy mind could swing from the great international issues of war and peace, to modern devices for the Palace kitchens, from the Great Sanitation problem, public health and sewers, to fifteenth-century frescoes and the decoration of ballroom walls. He was particularly interested, at this period, in building work of all kinds: not only was he concerned with the enlargement of Buckingham Palace – he was also rebuilding Osborne House and, in complete contrast, was planning model dwellings for workers, to be displayed at the Great Exhibition of 1851.*

Throughout the decade of rebuilding there was, however, one more important director of the improvement of the Palace – the great master-builder, Thomas Cubitt. A man of quiet authority, his opinion counted for more with the Prince Consort than almost anyone else's. Throughout this period, Cubitt was the constant element in the decade of change. When in October 1846 he was appointed as the contractor he did so on his own, clearly stated terms. His firm alone was to carry out the work:

I must however have it explicitly understood that I cannot enter into competition with other Tradesmen as to prices at any stage of the progress of the building, but that I must have assurance that I shall be allowed to carry out the whole Building to its completion.[79]

He also insisted that he should be paid 'as the work proceeds' and that he should have 'timely notice on all occasions of your intention to proceed with successive portions of the fabric'. A master-builder could dictate the conditions.

Thomas Cubitt, born in 1788, was the son of a Norfolk carpenter. He was brought up in London in his father's trade, and after his father's death went on board ship to India as a captain's joiner. On his return he started a business with his brothers, William and Lewis, as carpenters and builders. By hard work and sheer ability he built up a highly successful organization, mostly dealing in speculative building. By the 1840s Cubitt had transformed London – new squares and streets of pillars and porticoes rose at his bidding where before there had been marsh and squalor.

* Two of these were moved to Kennington, where they can still be seen.

Thine be the praise, O Cubitt
. . . thine the hand . . .
That caused Belgravia from the dust to rise . . .
A fairer wreath than Wren's should crown thy brow
He raised a dome – a town unrivalled thou.

So wrote a Mrs Gascoigne, one of Cubitt's tenants.

His success was due to his efficient method of contracting, a genius for organization, foresight and an insistence on work of the highest quality. He was a perfectionist and something of an autocrat, notable in committees for never speaking unless he had something to say. This was the man who for a decade, until his death, was an invaluable adviser to the Prince Consort at Osborne and Buckingham Palace and whom Queen Victoria always called affectionately 'our good Mr Cubitt'. Tactful and courteous, he was never subservient, insistent that his Clerk of the Works 'co-operate in the most cordial manner with the other officers of Her Majesty's establishment, giving and receiving willingly friendly hints'.

So during his work at Buckingham Palace he avoided friction with courtiers and architects alike. They sometimes murmured about his influence with the Prince Consort, but they knew his value. What impressed Prince Albert most was the clarity and firmness of his instructions: Stockmar himself could not have produced better memoranda.

In June 1852, in his tender for the work on the Ballroom, he promised 'that the work proposed shall not exceed the estimate of £45,000. That every care shall be taken to carry out the works in the most economical manner consistent with its purpose and an accurate account to be kept of all costs.' He agreed to be satisfied with a profit of seven per cent, taking all the risks and responsibilities. The work was carried out under the direction of his Clerk of the Works, Peter Hogg, who also obtained permission to supply fixtures and fittings for the kitchens.

In the end extra funds had to be provided to pay for the decorations, which were 'so very elaborate, so highly decorated and so different from those of almost every other Building upon which the Builders are employed'.[80] In fact Cubitt made very little profit out of this, his last work for Prince Albert.

Blore had left no adequate plans for the new wing. In any case, Prince Albert had never admired his pedestrian work. Pennethorne submitted his own plans, but they appear to have been based on those drawn up by Cubitt and the Prince. The Prince himself, assisted by Gruner, intended to supervise the interior decoration of the new wing; Cubitt was to be responsible for the carcass. His workmen lined the walls of some of the rooms ready for painting, but he would have nothing to do with what he called 'fancy painting'.

Pennethorne had absorbed much of the spirit of Nash in his years of apprenticeship and later collaboration with him. So the exterior of the Ballroom at the south-west corner of the Palace follows Nash's elegant lines. New kitchens and domestic offices were added below to serve the State Dining Room and supper room.

Inside all was splendour. The vast Ballroom, 123 feet long, 60 feet wide and 45 feet high, was one of the largest in England. At the west end, the throne dais was designed as a magnificent setting for Queen and Consort. Their crimson thrones stood before a dramatic recess, the gilded Corinthian pillars supporting an arch embellished with sculptured figures and ornaments and surmounted by a crowned medallion showing Queen Victoria and Prince Albert in profile. On either side, seated figures represented History and Fame and before the arch two marble statues stood with musical instruments, symbolizing the cultural interests of Queen and Consort. Here they received their subjects in an elegant grandeur guaranteed to outshine emperor, tsar or shah.

Facing them at the other end of the Ballroom a great organ with gilded pipes was set in another recess. Between them, suspended from the ceiling, shone twenty-one gas burners in glass chandeliers. On either side were ten tall bronze candelabra, each fitted with forty-three branches for wax candles. When they were all lit the heat was overwhelming.

The structure of the room, strong but elegant, was designed by James Pennethorne, but the walls were decorated by Gruner under the direction of Prince Albert himself. This was the opportunity Prince Albert and Gruner had longed for – a chance to demonstrate the beauty of fresco painting and encourage its reintroduction. According to *The Builder*, in May 1856, the ceiling rested on a wide richly-decorated cove below which was an elaborate frieze. The upper part of each side wall was divided into thirteen compartments, seven of which were windows and the others filled with wall paintings representing the Twelve Hours. The lower part of the walls was covered with crimson silk brocade, and above the doors were sculptured groups by Theed.

At night the effect was stunning. The seven windows, *The Builder* described,

are the windows which at night are filled with gaslights from behind . . . six are surrounded by large borders and represent figures of the Hours, taken from sketches by Raffaele [sic] and executed about life-size by Professor Consoni at Rome.

There were also 'four cupids from Raffaelle's [sic] frescoes at Farnese Palace'.[81] Prince Albert's passion for the Italian Renaissance at last could be fully expressed. When the room was lit for a ball, filled with flowers, sparkling with the jewels of hundreds of ladies, the effect was brilliant, as the memoirs of the period show.

On 8 May 1856 the Queen held her first state ball in the new room. As she recorded in her Journal, it was a tremendous success, 'the elegant toilettes of the ladies and numerous uniforms' adding even more colour to the glowing room. Many of the officers were her heroes, returned from the Crimean War, resplendent in scarlet, medals flashing. The diplomatic corps was well represented, taking up the whole of one side of the Ballroom. For the first time at a ball in the Palace there was comfort. Three tiers of seats on each side allowed 'everyone to see and be seen'. The Queen herself danced six quadrilles, and Prince Albert, still graceful, though now a little stiff, partnered his Queen as he had done twenty years before. 'It was truly', the Queen wrote, 'a most successful Fete and everyone was in great admiration of the rooms.'[82]

Buckingham Palace, rebuilt and refurbished, was now ready to dazzle even the most splendid of foreign monarchs. On 25 January 1858 Queen Victoria had the chance to display the Queen of England in a worthy setting. On that day, her eldest daughter, Vicky, was married to Prince Frederick William of Prussia, who was to become Emperor of Germany.

Princess Victoria had become engaged in September 1855. It was a marriage arranged by her parents, but the young pair were genuinely in love.

The wedding took place in the Chapel Royal. They returned to Buckingham Palace, then, as the Queen wrote in her Journal, 'we went with the young couple to the celebrated window at which they stepped out and showed themselves, we and the Prince and Princess [of Prussia] standing with them'. The banquet which followed was one of the most splendid ever given in the Palace, for, as the Queen wrote to the British Ambassador in Berlin, apropos of the German desire to have the wedding in Germany, 'It is not *every* day that one marries the eldest daughter of the Queen of England.'[83]

The Palace was decorated as never before. Chandeliers sparkled above the long table, heavy with crystal and gold plate. The immense mirrors reflected the thousand guests, brilliant in diamonds and pearls. The Queen, as her biographer Lady Longford describes, 'smothered herself with diamonds and then with a contrariness which was so much a part of her, decorated her dress and hair with rustic flowers and grass'.[84]

After four days of honeymoon at Windsor, the newly married couple left for Germany, leaving Queen Victoria somewhat relieved to have Prince Albert to herself again. Prince Albert missed the daughter who had been, of all their children, the most like him.

In 1857 Prince Albert also lost the companionship of Stockmar, who finally retired to Germany. He was now old and frail and wanted to spend his last years in his own country. He bequeathed his son to Vicky, now Princess Frederick William of Prussia, to act as her secretary in her German court. For more than twenty years Baron Stockmar had devoted his life to the creation of a stable British monarchy. It is difficult to know what drove him, besides a deep admiration for Britain and its constitution. But his influence on the transformation of the Court from the sleazy corruption of the Regency period should never be underestimated. As a doctor with an interest in psychology he had observed closely all the players in the royal game, from George III onwards. In the young Prince of Wales he could see the family face. When Bertie, as he was known to his family, threw the crockery or was brutal to his equerries, he remembered how the uncles had loved to smash and hurt. When he saw how charming he could be, he recalled how the handsome young Prince Regent had been transformed into a gross and self-indulgent King. When he saw the Prince of Wales wild with irrational rage he recognized the face of Queen Victoria herself; she herself confessed that her son was a caricature of herself.* For the previous ten years Stockmar had helped to prepare the Prince of Wales for kingship. But not even Stockmar could create character, and Bertie was quite unlike his father. Stockmar and Prince Albert had planned his education in numerous memoranda. If Edward VII did not turn out to be the complete Renaissance man, it was not for want of their trying. *Punch* saw the dangers:

> Thou dear little Wales – sure the saddest of tales
>   In the tale of the studies with which they are cramming thee;
> In thy tuckers and bibs, handed over to Gibbs,
>   Who for eight years with solid instruction was ramming thee.
>
> Then, to fill any nook Gibbs had chanced to o'erlook,
>   In those poor little brains, sick of learned palaver,
> When thou'dst fain rolled in clover, they handed thee over,
>   To the prim pedagogic protection of Tarver . . .
>
> Where next the boy *may* go to swell the farrago,
>   We haven't yet heard: but the Palace they're plotting in,
> To Berlin, Jena, Bonn, he'll no doubt be passed on to,
>   And drop in, for a finishing touch, p'raps, at Gottingen.
>
> 'Gainst indulging the passion for the high pressure fashion
>   Of Prince-training, Punch would uplift a loyal warning;
> Locomotives we see, over-stoked soon may be,
>   Till the supersteamed boiler blows up some fine morning.[85]

Stockmar and Prince Albert had striven to train the wayward young man. In April 1849 Bertie had been given a suite of his own in Buckingham Palace and a kind young tutor, Henry Birch, replaced in 1851 by a

---

*Had he been able to look into the future, he would have seen those outbursts repeated in Edward VIII; even the mild King George VI had what the family called his 'gnashes'.

pedantic classical scholar. He was given short spells at Oxford and Cambridge Universities, but always under the strictest control.

Oxford improved him and when, on a visit to Germany, Bertie visited Baron Stockmar in his retirement the old man was delighted with him. Prince Albert was overjoyed that Stockmar had seen such improvement in him. During the long vacation of 1860, Bertie made an official visit to Canada and America, where he was fêted and for the first time developed a confidence in himself. His boyish charm captivated the New World, as it would do all his life. He spent a short spell at Cambridge University. In 1861 during a vacation he spent in infantry training at the Curragh Camp near Dublin, his fellow officers decided to carry on the education of the Prince by smuggling an actress, Nellie Clifden, into his room. It was at Curragh that Bertie learned that delight in women that would mark him throughout his life as Edward VII.

The Prince Consort's health had begun to cause concern in the late 1850s. He was seriously over-stressed: he had, in fact, shouldered much of the responsibility of the Queen, and indeed had worked harder than any cabinet minister for many years. Foreign affairs, which he well understood, concerned him deeply. The Crimean War and the Indian Mutiny had worn him down; and there had been a sudden flurry of French hostility roused by a plot, planned in England, to assassinate the Emperor Napoleon III – no throne was safe.

Prince Albert had been completely drained by his work for the Great Exhibition of 1851 and throughout the decade had continued to take an active part in the encouragement of science, industry and the arts.

So in the autumn of 1860, when he and Queen Victoria paid their last visit to his old home in Coburg, Prince Albert was tired and dispirited. He was seriously shaken by a carriage accident there and Stockmar, who was now in retirement there, visited him immediately afterwards and was deeply concerned. The old man, as he said, had never till now realized how much he loved the Prince and shrewdly foresaw that 'here was a man incapable of fighting an illness'.[86]

Walking around his beloved home, Prince Albert seemed to realize that it would be the last time and wept uncontrollably.

The year 1861 brought tragedy. In March the Duchess of Kent died, leaving the Queen heartbroken. Reading through her mother's papers she realized for the first time how much her mother had loved her.

In spite of the tender love of the Prince, Queen Victoria was in such low spirits all that summer that there were rumours that she might be inheriting the mental instability of her grandfather, George III.

So, when Prince Albert fell ill in November 1861 with what he thought was a chill, they were both at a low ebb. The Prince was, in fact, in the early stages of typhoid fever. Nevertheless he worked on ceaselessly.

On 11 November a devastating blow fell: news reached the ears of the Queen and Prince of the scandal of the Prince of Wales's affair with the actress at the Curragh. The news was deeply shocking, especially as they hoped to arrange a marriage with the lovely Princess Alexandra of Denmark.

Prince Albert travelled in the cold November to Cambridge, where he talked long into the night with his son, urging him to marry soon, for 'you must not, you dare not be lost. The consequences for this country and for the world would be too dreadful.'[87] Father and son were reconciled; but Queen Victoria always believed that it was the stress of this journey that killed Prince Albert. Certainly it must have been one of the factors that weakened his resistance to the typhoid fever which took hold in early December.

He worked to the end. He made his last important political contribution when he was almost too weak to hold a pen, redrafting a terse memorandum that the Foreign Secretary, Lord John Russell, was proposing to send to America which might well have dragged Britain into the American Civil War. His tactful draft turned away the wrath of the Federal government, but it was his last memorandum.

He was obsessed by the fear of typhoid, which had recently killed his favourite cousin, the King of Portugal, and the onset of fever convinced him that death was near.

Again and again in his delirium he called for Stockmar, just as the dying Princess Charlotte had done so long ago. But Stockmar, who had given him so much, could not give him what he needed now: the will to live.

On 14 December 1861 at 10.45 p.m. Prince Albert died. It was not until 1874 that the distraught Queen could bring herself to record his last moments in her Journal. She had asked for '*ein kuss*' and 'he moved his lips, then two or three perfectly gentle breaths were drawn, the hand clasping mine . . .'[88]

Prince Albert's was the simplest of private funerals, held at St George's Chapel, Windsor, on a chill day, under a leaden sky. There was none of the paraphernalia of mourning, but his coffin was followed by his brother, Ernest, Duke of Saxe-Coburg, the Prince of Wales and little Prince Arthur, all three racked by uncontrollable grief. Prince Albert had been a demanding perfectionist, but their tear-stained faces witnessed deep love and a profound sense of loss.

The Queen was not there. She had been taken to Osborne, from where she sent a simple wreath of violets round a white camellia. Leopold, King of the Belgians, immediately offered to come to her. On 20 December she replied like a broken child:

My *own* DEAREST KINDEST *Father* – For as such have I ever loved you! The poor fatherless baby of eight months is now the utterly broken-hearted and crushed widow of forty-two. My life as a happy one is *ended*! The world is gone for me . . . it is henceforth for our poor fatherless children – for my unhappy country, which has lost *all* in losing him . . . and in *only* doing what I know and feel – he would wish, for he is near me – his spirit will guide and inspire me . . .[89]

Before he came, on 26 December, she wrote again, this time to emphasize that 'no human power will make me swerve from what he decided'. And she was determined that 'no person, may he be ever so good . . . is to lead or guide me'[90] – a hint perhaps that her beloved uncle should not try to dominate again.

She was much soothed by Alfred, Lord Tennyson's dedication to his new edition of his *Idylls of the King*:

> . . . we see him as he moved,
> How modest, kindly, all-accomplish'd wise,
> With what sublime suppression of himself . . .
> . . . but thro' all this tract of years
> Wearing the white flower of a blameless life,
> Before a thousand peering littlenesses,
> In that fierce light that beats upon a throne . . .
> Hereafter, thro' all times, Albert the Good.

Baron Stockmar, heartbroken, wrote honest words that she would remember all her life. 'You will grow accustomed to it, but you will never get over it.'[91] And she never did.

Albert, Prince of Saxe-Coburg and Gotha, with the help of Baron Stockmar of Coburg, had transformed Buckingham Palace and in so doing had contributed stability and prestige to the monarchy, which it had lacked during the reigns of Queen Victoria's uncles.

The Widow of Windsor

In the following year, however, the invisible 'widow of Windsor' threatened to destroy their work. Stockmar would have told her that an unseen monarch diminishes the monarchy and that an expensive but unused palace rouses republicans.

For two years she remained in seclusion at Osborne and for twenty years she was seen little in public. Buckingham Palace was deserted and shuttered, the state rooms shrouded in dust sheets, although she allowed her sons, Princes Alfred and Leopold, to have apartments on the second floor. She spent long periods in Balmoral and received her ministers at Windsor. She obstinately refused to delegate work to her eldest son. When on 5 March 1863 the Prince of Wales married Princess Alexandra, the longed-for wedding took place at St George's Chapel, Windsor, but the Queen watched from a dark closet, high above the altar, and did not attend the breakfast. Even after his marriage she refused to allow him to take over Buckingham Palace.

When Queen Victoria's beloved Uncle Leopold died on 10 December 1865, she lost a surrogate father and a lifelong pillar of support. Now she was truly alone. For a while, in her isolation she thought she would go mad; she longed for death.

Gradually, however, that tough spirit that had saved her before she knew Prince Albert reawakened and with it her own intelligence, so long subordinated to that of the Prince. Driven by that royal sense of duty which had impelled even her predecessors, she gradually took up again the work of a queen. Queen Victoria emerged Queen in her own right, standing on her own feet. But she desperately missed a strong right arm, which she found, surprisingly, in her Scottish ghillie John Brown, who combined 'the offices of groom, footman, page and *maid* I almost might say, as he is so handy about cloaks and shawls'. In February 1865 she decided that he should 'remain permanently and make himself useful in other ways besides leading my pony as he is so very dependable'.[92] He began with a wage of £120 a year; later it was raised to £310.

So John Brown became an essential part of the Court, to the displeasure of the rest of the Household. John Brown was always there – behind her chair, on the box of her carriage, handing the Queen her shawl. Honest and outspoken, he was what she needed, but he infuriated ministers and courtiers with his presumption. Her relationship with him is a constant theme for gossip-mongers, but anyone who has studied the character of the Queen or her times can have no doubt that Queen Victoria would never have allowed the relationship to have overstepped the boundary between mistress and servant. It was the kind of friendship that kings and queens often have with devoted servants with whom they are totally at ease and who give them constant support.

Queen Victoria had, too, the help of her equerry, Henry Ponsonby, who became her Private Secretary in 1870. He gave her years of loyal service until January 1895, when a severe stroke released him. He was wise, dedicated and honourable, with the great gift of humour. He was succeeded by Colonel Arthur Bigge, who stayed with her until her death.

To the annoyance of the public, she shunned public appearances. It was not until 6 February 1866 that she consented to open Parliament, but then she drove from Buckingham Palace in her carriage, not the state coach, and took her place on the throne, silent, veiled in black, wearing not a crown but her black widow's cap, leaving the Lord Chancellor to read her speech.

Two years later she consented to open Parliament again. She drove once again from Buckingham Palace in her ordinary carriage – with the windows lowered so that she could be seen; but she was angered by the shouts of demonstrators and the fury in their 'nasty faces'. This time her speech from the throne announced her government's intention to pass the Second Reform Bill. Once again she could not wait to leave the Palace and London. Prince Albert's rooms in Buckingham Palace were kept exactly as he left them, but his spirit was not there.

From 1864, she began holding afternoon receptions at the Palace, and in 1868, gave her first 'breakfast' – as garden parties at the Palace were called – since she was becoming aware that her critics were growing. Why, they asked, should the taxpayers pay for a Palace that was so underused? Again and again successive Prime Ministers urged her to use Buckingham Palace – or at least to let the Prince and Princess of Wales live there. But the Queen was adamant. Bertie could not take her place: she remembered too vividly the stories of the Prince Regent's behaviour during her grandfather's illness and Bertie showed alarming signs of the family inheritance.

Prime Minister Gladstone managed to persuade her to receive the Shah of Persia at Windsor in 1873 and to invite him to stay at Buckingham Palace. She wore her Koh-i-noor diamond to impress him at the Windsor banquet, but it was just as well that she did not receive him personally at Buckingham Palace. She heard, without amusement, of his entourage of lovely ladies, of his feasts of roasted lamb spread on her priceless carpets and how he watched a boxing match in the Palace garden.

In spite of her dislike of public appearances, the Queen was determined to maintain the prestige of the British monarchy. When her son, Prince Alfred, became engaged to Marie, the only daughter of the Tsar of Russia, she was infuriated at the Tsar's suggestion that she should go to Cologne to meet Marie. To the Queen's daughter Princess Alice, who encouraged her to go, she raged,

I do not think dear child that *you* should tell *me* who have been nearly 20 years longer on the throne than the Emperor of Russia, and am the doyenne of Sovereigns and who am a reigning Sovereign which the Empress is not – *what I ought to do.* The proposal received on Wednesday for me to be at Cologne . . . *Tomorrow* was one of the coolest things I ever heard.[93]

Victoria Regina et Imperatrix

It was Disraeli who brought the Queen back into the public eye. She had been fascinated by him ever since 1852 when, as Chancellor of the Exchequer, he sent her Parliamentary reports that were 'just like his novels'. Queen Victoria had no racial prejudice and rebuffed the anti-Semitic gibes directed at the brilliant young Jew.

When, in February 1868, at the age of sixty-four, Disraeli succeeded Lord Derby as Prime Minister, the Queen applauded. 'A proud thing', she wrote to Vicky, 'for a man risen from the people to have attained.'[94]

With consummate skill Disraeli wooed the Queen back to life, encouraged her to take her ladies for a holiday to Switzerland and explained politics to her, making her feel once again in the centre of affairs. In return she sent him primroses from Osborne.

When he was replaced by Gladstone, she was as distressed as she had been when Melbourne had lost power. Her antipathy to the Grand Old Man has been often described. It was Disraeli who was her favourite. On 10 February 1874 he was back again as her Prime Minister.

When in 1876 the Queen decided she wished to be Empress of India, Disraeli encouraged her even though there was fierce opposition in Parliament.

Prosaic and sensible though the Queen was, there was also in her a latent love of the exotic. Though she had disliked Brighton, she was surrounded by oriental fantasies brought from the Pavilion; and she never forgot her wild ride as a girl of seven when the old George IV had scooped her up in his carriage and whirled her to his magical Chinese pagoda on the shores of Virginia Water.

Her immediate desire was to outdo the Tsar of Russia and to secure the place of the Queen of England in the precedence charts of the world. On New Year's Day 1877 Queen Victoria signed herself 'Victoria Regina et Imperatrix'. She had taken her place in the world again, and this time without the help of Uncle Leopold, Stockmar or Prince Albert. Disraeli next laid at the imperial feet the high road to India: the Suez Canal, which on 25 November 1877 he snapped up from the bankrupt Khedive of Egypt for a bargain £4 million. Skilfully he fed Queen Victoria's renewed enthusiasm for the great world destiny of Britain. The imperial triumph had begun.

In the last forty years of her reign Queen Victoria established the morals and manners of her Court in the pattern that Prince Albert – and Stockmar – had set down. In 1854 the Baron had written that he had watched the Court for twenty-eight years and had learned the value of the moral purity of the sovereign 'as moral oil for the driving wheels of the constitutional machine'.[95]

The 'moral oil' could often become a sickening syrup and there was undoubtedly much hypocrisy in Queen Victoria's Court, but certainly in the stability of her last years the magic of monarchy shone as never before. That stability contributed to the fact that at the end of her reign Buckingham Palace was established as the seat of majesty and a unifying symbol for the nation.

Her rules were strict, as Prince Albert had demanded. Gouty old ministers stood painfully in her presence; princes smoked their cigars up the chimney in the privacy of their bedrooms, or sucked lozenges to conceal their sinful tobacco. Courtiers still had to learn the difficult art of walking backwards, and froze in their chilly rooms. The first duty of a courtier was to the Queen: wives had to put up with much loneliness – indeed she did not like her courtiers getting married at all. When her physician, Sir James Reid, became engaged to one of her Maids of Honour without asking her permission, she did not speak to him for days. How could a physician devote himself to two ladies? But his polite reply that he would not do it again turned away her wrath in laughter.

Rules of Court protocol and etiquette were strictly observed, and Court life was described *ad nauseam* by the authors of such guides as *Court Etiquette*, and Court circulars. *Manners and Rules of Good Society*, by a member of the aristocracy, was a much thumbed rule book at the end of the reign. In excruciating language the author reported that 'guests were graciously invited to partake of a collation, and . . . the Queen was humbly wished "an auspicious return of her natal day".'[96]

It was a pity that Queen Victoria, who prided herself on being Queen of all her people, should have allowed herself to be so hemmed in by rigid rules. The honour of attending her Court was open only to the nobility and gentry, and to officers of the armed services, clergy, lawyers, doctors and professional men. Those who engaged in trade were excluded – unless they were merchant princes or bankers. As far as trade was concerned a 'line is drawn and very strictly so'.

The Lord Chamberlain, who was responsible for issuing 'royal commands', as invitations to state occasions were called, also expected ladies and gentlemen to conform to certain rules of dress. For ladies 'the regulation respecting low bodices is absolute', unless a doctor's certificate could be produced. Unmarried ladies were expected to wear white and all should have trains not less than three and a half yards in length, and wear a head dress of three white plumes.

Ladies had to learn the difficult art of managing a bouquet, a train and a curtsey with grace. At drawing rooms ladies held their trains out, and dropped them when they approached the Queen. Officers with white wands spread out the trains and scooped them up again after presentation. 'Train teas' after the drawing rooms were popular social occasions, when the Queen's guests could show off their Court finery to friends.

A gentleman was expected to wear either professional or military uniform, or Court dress – claret-coloured coat, knee breeches, buckled shoes, lace shirt-front, ruffles, long white stockings and sword. He was expected to go down on one knee and raise his right arm, on which the Queen would lay her hand. 'If he wishes to be particularly absurd and vulgar, he will kiss the hand with a loud smack.' A real gentleman would however, 'barely touch the back of the Queen's hand with his lips'.[97]

The ladies were happy to conform, but American men felt the breeches rule an affront to their republican principles – if not their manhood. 'Knickers' they called them. The battle between Court officials and American ministers to the Court of St James caused much embarrassment when, in 1854, an American Secretary of State, William Marcy, issued a ruling that Americans should appear at foreign courts in 'the simple dress of an American citizen'. The American Ambassador to Britain, James Buchanan, who later became American President, insisted on following the ruling – to the consternation of the Lord Chamberlain. If he had to choose between attending a Court function in full Court dress and staying at home, he stayed at home. The last straw came when he refused the invitation to the State Opening of Parliament, since the invitation stated that no one would be admitted except in full Court dress. His absence was noted and gave offence. The same rule was also enforced at the strict Russian court, until the Tsar asked a visiting senator what costume he was expected to wear to visit his President, and received him when the senator explained that he would wear ordinary dress on that occasion too. Finally James Buchanan invented a costume which he persuaded his government and the Court was that of a plain American citizen, a black coat and pantaloons, white waistcoat and cravat and a plain sword. The sword was a concession he made reluctantly.

Similarly, when the radical John Bright became a minister in Gladstone's government in 1868 he refused point-blank to wear gold lace and a sword, saying, 'I have never put on livery and I think I never shall.'[98]

Absurd though the rules often were, and though Queen Victoria herself preferred simplicity, they had been established by her beloved husband as part of his plan to raise the little Queen above the crowd and bring dignity to the throne. He remembered only too painfully how the small Coburg court had degenerated under the relaxed rule of his father and brother.

On 20 June 1887, the day of her Golden Jubilee, Queen Victoria wrote at Buckingham Palace: 'The day has come and I am alone though surrounded by so many dear children . . . Fifty years ago today I came to the throne. God has mercifully sustained me through many great trials and sorrows.'[99]

The day began quietly with breakfast under the trees at Frogmore, where she could be in spirit with her beloved Prince Albert. In brilliant sunshine she travelled from Windsor through cheering crowds by train to Paddington and across the parks to Buckingham Palace and a great assembly of royal guests. That night fifty Royal and Serene Highnesses dined off gold plate in the State Dining Room. They were members of an extended royal family whose network crossed continents. On her right sat Christian IX, King of Denmark, father of her much-loved daughter-in-law, Alexandra, Princess of Wales; on her left George I of Greece (Alexandra's brother); and opposite Leopold II, King of the Belgians, son of her late surrogate father.

The next day she drove out of the Palace to Westminster Abbey in an open landau, escorted by Indian cavalry. She was Queen and Empress. Even so she obstinately refused to wear a crown; she and her ladies, she insisted, must wear bonnets and long, high dresses. Lunch at the Palace was followed by an appearance on the famous balcony, at which she was cheered by a vast throng, then a stately progress to her throne in the Ballroom, where she distributed Jubilee brooches to her family. That night, for once, she wore a splendid gown, embroidered with silver roses, thistles and shamrocks, and after the banquet she received a long procession of diplomats and bejewelled Indian princes. Afterwards she was wheeled in her chair to sit amid the exotic chinoiserie brought from her uncle's Pavilion and to watch the fireworks in the garden. George IV would have enjoyed the festivities, perhaps surprised that his diminutive niece should have so woven his oriental fantasies with her imperial dream. Now she was an old lady, and half dead with fatigue, seeing it all through the mists of the past.

With her taste for the exotic, so long subdued by cool Germanic influences and now awakened by Disraeli, Queen Victoria had developed a passion for India, and that June she had acquired a clever young Indian servant, learned some Hindustani and longed to go to India. Abdul Karim – known as the Munshi (Hindustani for 'teacher') – became a great favourite with the Queen, but was even more disliked than John

Brown had been; in fact the Queen's ladies threatened to resign *en masse* if she took him to the south of France with the Court. But with the Munshi behind her chair, Victoria was secure as the great white Queen.

In the last years of the Queen's life Buckingham Palace awoke again. The Golden Jubilee and, ten years later, the Diamond Jubilee made the Queen realize that she was loved and that it was important that she should be seen. The years of unpopularity and isolation were over; Queen and Empress, she had become a figurehead of myth and majesty.

There were drawing rooms (which had continued during the Queen's seclusion although she herself did not attend them), diplomatic receptions and balls. Lady Monkswell, wife of a Liberal minister, went to a drawing room in February 1889. She started at 12.45 p.m. and had a

miserable long wait in the Brougham in Buckingham Palace Road. It was an immense Drawing Room – to see the Queen and the poor Empress Frederick [Vicky], who, however were gone before I got into the Throne Room – there must have been 500 women there and all in these gorgeous clothes, jewels and such bouquets. The flowers were beyond everything, orchids, lilies of the valley, azaleas, roses, enough to make you scream. When I got up to the Throne Room at last I made three curtsies – to the Princess of Wales, Princess Christian and another for the young Princesses to divide between them. I then backed out . . .[100]

On 29 June 1893 Lady Monkswell was again at the Palace for the Queen's ball; and the next week she watched the royal procession on the occasion of the marriage of Princess Victoria Mary (known in the family as May), daughter of the Queen's cousin, the Duchess of Teck, to George, Duke of York, son of the Prince of Wales.

The pavement was choked with people . . . a dozen state carriages with footmen in gorgeous gold liveries hanging on like bees behind . . . Far away the most enthusiastic welcome was given to the old Queen. The Duchess of Teck was sitting backwards in the carriage with her . . . Before her came fourteen or sixteen of the [horse] soldiers from Australia, in pith helmets, then eight or ten of the Indian cavalry with their brown handsome faces, turbans, curious uniforms and swords.

Lady Monkswell 'felt quite proud of my country that we could do the thing so well'.[101]

The country, with some help from Fate, had indeed 'done well'. George, Duke of York, and Princess May, when they became King George V and Queen Mary, were to bring back stability and respect to the throne; and Queen Mary was to make a significant contribution to the improvement of Buckingham Palace. But it might not have been like that at all.

The Duke and Duchess of York drove out of the Palace under a 'shower of slippers and . . . round the quadrangle amid cheers',[102] through the great gates where the Prince of Wales and all the Princes pelted them with rice, and down the Mall to their honeymoon at Sandringham. They left behind them Queen Victoria, satisfied that at last the future of the monarchy was secure, and the bride's mother, the Duchess of Teck, radiant with joy at the fulfilment of all her hopes. But for Alexandra, Princess of Wales, watching from the balcony, joy was mixed with sadness; the bridegroom should have been her first-born, and she was losing the son she adored.

Events leading to this crucial marriage began in November 1891, when Queen Victoria had invited Princess May of Teck to stay at Balmoral, accompanied by her brother Adolphus. The Queen had firmly insisted they come without their mother, the ebullient Duchess of Teck: Princess May was to be assessed as the future consort for her grandson, and the shy girl must be drawn out of her mother's shadow. At this time the Prince of Wales was next in line to the throne, and after him his eldest son, Prince Albert Victor, Duke of Clarence and Avondale, known to the family as 'Eddy'. Like his father, Eddy was what was called 'emotionally unstable', but lacked his father's charisma. He was lethargic but generally said to be kind, gentle and considerate. What he needed, the shrewd old Queen decided, was a firm, sensible wife; and after watching Princess May carefully for ten days at Balmoral, she decided that she had found the perfect candidate. Her long experience in arranging royal marriages was called on, and the occasion and setting fixed.

In December 1891, Princess May and Eddy were both staying at a friend's country house, Luton Hoo. On 3 December the county ball was held at Luton Hoo. There Eddy and Princess May danced together; then, in her own words, 'To my great surprise Eddy proposed to me during the evening in Mdme de Falbe's boudoir – of course I said yes – we are both very happy – kept it secret from everybody but Mama and Papa.'[103]

May's immediate acceptance of a surprise proposal needs some explanation. First, Eddy was her cousin: she had known him all her life, was fond of him and at ease with him. Also at twenty-six her chances of making a good marriage were slim: she was not a beauty; she had no fortune – her mother was forever in what she called 'short street'; worse, as far as royal suitors were concerned, there was a blot on the family escutcheon which mattered in the protocol-bound German kingdoms, but for which the old Queen cared not a jot. Her mother, Mary Adelaide, the Duchess of Teck, was the daughter of Adolphus, Duke of Cambridge, son of George III. But her paternal grandfather, Duke Alexander of Württemberg, had made a morganatic marriage to a beautiful Hungarian, Countess Rhedey of Kis-Redé, who bore him three children.

Complicated though these family histories are, they are relevant, since Princess May was to bring a deep historical sense to the arrangement of Buckingham Palace. She always felt an empathy with old Queen Charlotte, but also she kept a portrait of her beautiful Hungarian grandmother always in her room. She accepted Eddy's proposal so readily because she needed to escape from the burden of responsibility of an increasingly neurotic father and a mother who had all the charm in the world but obviously no sense of the value of money.

All her life Princess May had felt more in tune with her mother's sister, Augusta, who married the Grand Duke of Mecklenburg-Strelitz, Queen Charlotte's home state. The Princess visited the Grand Duchess in Germany and at her house in London. To her 'mother aunt' Princess May wrote with an ease which she could never achieve in conversation; and the shrewd, intelligent Grand Duchess stimulated a mind that was hungry for knowledge, encouraged her interest in the arts and, above all, developed her love of the history of the royal family. Her aunt had known George IV and she was at William IV's Coronation, which she remembered clearly.

The old lady followed with passionate interest the wedding preparations and the vast trousseau described with such enthusiasm in the
press. 'But who will pay?' she wanted to know. She was devastated by
the shocking news that came from Sandringham in the bitter January
of 1892. On 7 January Eddy, who was there with May and his family to
celebrate his twenty-eighth birthday, was seriously ill with influenza,
which had turned to pneumonia. On the morning of 14 January the
Princess of Wales, Princess May and his family watched his death agony
for six interminable hours.

Eddy had escaped the burden of the Crown: Princess May had not.
Queen Victoria had chosen her as the wife of the heir apparent. Now,
that Eddy was dead, the heir apparent was George Duke of York,
twenty-six and unmarried. Princess May took a tour of France and
Germany and recovered her spirits. Soon the Queen and the Duchess
of Teck once again were ready to set the wedding bells ringing.

The idea that Prince George should marry his dead brother's fiancée
was not strange to the Queen or his mother, Princess Alexandra. Princess
Alexandra's sister had similarly married Prince Alexander, the heir to
the Russian throne, after the death of his older brother. But Alexandra
did not want to share her beloved son with a wife. Princess Alexandra's
suffocating mother-love had cramped George's emotional development.
When he was twenty-five his mother still wrote to him, as though to a
child, of 'his dear tear-stained little face'. After Eddy's death, she had
written of the 'bond of love between us – that of mother and child . . .
and nothing and nobody can or ever shall come between me and my
darling Georgie Boy'.[104] So it was with some sadness that Princess
Alexandra watched George and May drive off from Buckingham Palace
to their honeymoon.

In fact this arranged marriage proved to be deeply happy. Stiff and
cold as Princess May often appeared, abrupt and unfeeling as Prince
George often seemed, they understood each other, writing with an
emotion they found difficult to express in words. 'I love you with all my
heart,' Princess May wrote to him on the morning of her marriage.[105]
And Prince George was to write to her soon after their marriage, 'I love
you darling child, with my whole heart and soul and thank God every

day that I have such a wife as you, who is such a great help and support to me and I believe loves me too.'[106]

It would be seventeen more years before they came back to the Buckingham Palace balcony as King and Queen. In those years they settled in modest quiet at York Cottage, Sandringham, where the Duchess of York bore six children.

The Duke and Duchess of York now slipped quietly into the background, obscured by the dazzle of the Prince and Princess of Wales, and in the shadow of the Queen, imperial in the glow of her last years. But Queen Victoria watched with growing satisfaction the serious young woman she had chosen, preparing herself to be a worthy consort of a future King. She had chosen well.

There was one more grand celebration at Buckingham Palace during Queen Victoria's reign: the Diamond Jubilee of 1897. On 21 June the Queen travelled from Windsor by royal train to Paddington, having first paid a sacred visit to Prince Albert in the Mausoleum. Tumultuous crowds greeted her on her way to the Palace and the next day as she made her royal progress to St Paul's.

The Jubilee was the climax of her long career. In the journal which she had kept all her life, she recorded:

No one ever, I believe, has met with such an ovation as was given to me, passing through those six miles of streets . . . the crowds were quite indescribable and their enthusiasm truly marvellous and deeply touching. The cheering was quite deafening and every face seemed to be filled with joy.[107]

All round the country beacons were lit as towns and villages celebrated with extraordinary enthusiasm.

On Jubilee Day she made history – by pressing an electric button – which sent her message by telegraph round the Empire. 'From my heart I thank all my beloved people. May God bless them.'[108]

There were still tragedies to be faced – the Boer War broke out on 11 October 1899 – but there were two more triumphant progresses to and from Buckingham Palace: after the relief of Ladysmith, and then of Mafeking, when people went 'quite mad with delight'.

In 1900 Queen Victoria left Buckingham Palace for the last time.

Her stamina was extraordinary, although her sight failed in her last years. She worked almost until the end. She died at Osborne House at 6.30 p.m. on Monday 22 January 1901. The Prince of Wales was at her bedside and so was her grandson, Emperor William II of Germany, who upheld the dying Queen on her pillow for the last two and a half hours.

But the Queen's last word was for 'Bertie', now Edward VII.

CHAPTER SIX

Edward VII

'The most kingly of them all.'[1]

LORD ESHER

Edwardian Interlude

When Edward VII succeeded to the throne, he was almost sixty and Queen Alexandra was fifty-six. He had a life of his own, which involved long absences abroad and many affairs with charming ladies; she was still very beautiful but severely deaf and a little lame. They had five children who were now grown up – the last, Princess Maud, was born in 1869. Kingship had come almost too late: they were set in their ways, comfortably established at Marlborough House, and at first had no wish to move to Buckingham Palace.

The Queen was especially unwilling to move from her home, which she loved. She felt that leaving Marlborough House would 'finish' her. 'All my happiness and sorrow were here,' she wrote to her son, George; 'Very nearly all of you were born here, all the reminiscences of my whole life are here and I feel as if by taking me away a cord will be taken out of my heart which can never be mended again.'[2] It took the combined efforts of the King and the Grand Duchess Augusta (who kept a house in London) finally to persuade her.

The Queen had learned to accept Edward VII's failings and compens-ated by enfolding her children with an almost suffocating love. The nation adored her, admiring her serene beauty. The King, in turn, gave her affection and consideration and insisted that she was always shown the greatest respect; in fact, he gave her almost everything – except fidelity. This she accepted with a grace and dignity that silenced or at least diminished scandal. But by the time he came to the throne, though he was still the centre of society life in London and the fashionable spas of Europe, and still attracted to the ladies, his wilder gambling and womanizing days were over. In February 1898 he had met the charming and discreet Mrs Keppel, who was to be his mistress for the rest of his life. The liaisons with ladies such as Lady Brooke (later Countess of Warwick) and the actress Lillie Langtry faded. Even the King's advisers accepted Mrs Keppel, an intelligent liberal, as a useful link with the Liberal Party, especially when it came into power in 1905.

Edward VII inspired devotion and love, mixed with a certain terrified awe. *The Times*, while admitting that he had been 'led astray by temptation in its most seductive forms', claimed that 'in public life . . . he has never failed in his duty to the Throne and the nation'.[3]

Queen Alexandra was loved and admired not only by the people, but also by the King's friends. Her remarkable tolerance may perhaps be explained. After the birth of her sixth baby in 1871 (a boy who lived only twenty-four hours) she may have been content that her husband's Hanoverian energy should be directed elsewhere. In the end she accepted the wise Mrs Keppel as preferable to the undiscriminating affairs in which the King had previously indulged. In the Palace she reigned supreme, and the King had to accept her total absence of a sense of time with unaccustomed patience.

Their children grew up with loving, indulgent parents, with a freedom denied to Edward VII in his own constricted childhood. He treated his second son, the Duke of York (later King George V), more like a brother than a son.

Edward VII took seriously his duties as King and he was determined to bring the Palace into the twentieth century. During the six months' traditional period of mourning, when he was not expected to make many public appearances, he turned his formidable energy into clearing the royal palaces. Queen Victoria had left a vast accumulation of possessions of every kind. Every room in Buckingham Palace, Windsor, Balmoral and Osborne was cluttered with mementoes, portraits, busts and photographs of the Queen's enormous family, and above all of

Prince Albert, whose rooms had been left sacred and unchanged since the day he died.

Buckingham Palace, the King complained, was like a mausoleum. He set to with gusto: as the Duke of Windsor later remembered, 'like a Viennese hussar bursting suddenly in an English vicarage'.[4] This was a little unjust. The King employed careful and highly qualified assistants to make detailed reports and showed great tact when dealing with Osborne House, which had been the Queen's own property. His sisters had houses on the estate and when he decided to give part of the house to the nation as a convalescent home for naval officers and as a training school for naval cadets, he was careful to get their co-operation.

Although he was no lover of desk work and never allowed it to interfere with his pleasures, he went to it with all the energy of a man starved for so long of real work. At first he insisted on opening all his letters himself, signing by hand the vast backlog of service commissions waiting for his signature: there were 6,000 still to be signed after the death of Queen Victoria. In the end he had to resort to a rubber stamp, but at least made sure that he signed by hand all those dealing with people he had known personally. He took a close interest in everything to do with the armed services and foreign affairs. The royal network, stretching from Russia to Spain and Portugal, from Norway and Denmark to Greece and throughout Germany, gave him a personal knowledge of that world. He loved travel, was fluent in several foreign languages and, when he wished, could charm in all of them. Like Queen Victoria, he would always learn from people rather than official reports, and like her, had good judgement.

This personal experience of foreign countries hardly compensated for the fact that he came to the throne knowing little of the business of being a monarch. Queen Victoria had allowed him limited access to government papers; and she had not encouraged him to prepare for kingship by direct experience, any more than she would allow him to live with Princess Alexandra in Buckingham Palace. Neither Liberals nor Tories expected Edward VII to make a good King; he was considered frivolous and headstrong. As Edward's biographer, Sir Philip Magnus, writes, 'The art of constitutional government had to be learnt by King Edward, who found it increasingly convenient to meet and talk to individual ministers upon purely social occasions.'⁵ It was reminiscent of the bypassing of government by the great Whig families in the time of Melbourne.

At the beginning of the new reign the new members of the royal Household were appointed. The Earl of Clarendon became Lord Chamberlain; the Earl of Pembroke, Lord Steward; the Duke of Portland, Master of the Horse; and Sir Arthur Ellis, Comptroller of the Lord Chamberlain's department. Lord Farquhar became Master of the Household; Sir Francis (later Lord) Knollys, the King's Private Secretary; and Sir Dighton Probyn, Keeper of the King's Privy Purse.

Edward VII had no Lord Melbourne to guide him, no Prince Consort to educate him, no Baron Stockmar at his elbow. Instead, like Charles II, he had his 'Cabal', his circle of friends. These were his financial adviser, Sir Ernest Cassel; Sir John (later Lord) Fisher, 2nd Sea Lord from 1902 and 1st Sea Lord from 1904 until 1910; Sir Charles (later Lord) Hardinge of the Foreign Office; and Sir Francis Knollys, who had been Edward's Private Secretary since 1870 and probably understood the new King's character more than anyone and accepted his frailties.

His most influential adviser was Lord Esher, who not only advised the King on military affairs, but has been called the *éminence grise* behind Edward VII. He had been Private Secretary to the Duke of Devonshire, had 'an intimate knowledge of politics' and had sat as a Liberal MP in the House of Commons. Esher had also been Permanent Secretary at the Office of Works (formerly Woods and Forests), an experience which was most useful to the King in his dealings with the royal palaces. It was he who persuaded the King to open some of the royal palaces to the public. He had organized the Diamond Jubilee of 1897 – and could advise the King on precedent and protocol. Sensitive and cultured, he was also a man of great drive and competence. He was the editor of Queen Victoria's letters and he had an unrivalled knowledge of the past, but he also looked to the future, accepting change. He was to be the man responsible for organizing the memorial to Queen Victoria. The

King once said, 'I always think you are the most valuable public servant I have.' In reporting this to his son Maurice, Esher added, 'and then I kissed his hand, as I sometimes do'.[6]

The King inspired this 'dog-like devotion', as his biographer Sir Philip Magnus calls it, in other members of the Cabal – men who knew all his faults, his irrational outbursts, his gambling, his excessive eating and drinking, his love of women, and loved him just the same. Esher's eulogy after the death of the King was typical. After writing that the King 'had one supreme gift, and this was his unerring judgement of men – and women', Esher wrote: 'I can only write of him as a master and friend – and the kindest and most considerate a man could have. If he gave his confidence, it was given absolutely . . . I have known all the great men of my time in this land of ours, and many beyond it. He was the most kingly of them all.'[7]

Outside this group, but equally trusted by the King, was Sir Lionel Cust, the man responsible in the early days for the survey and reorganization of the Palace, which had been so long neglected in the last years of Queen Victoria's life. His memoirs give an invaluable insight into the King's character and his work for Buckingham Palace, as Fanny Burney's did in the reign of George III.

Lionel Cust belonged to a family with long associations with the Crown. One ancestor had fought at the Battle of the Boyne with the Duke of Grafton. Because his grandfather, the Reverend the Honourable Henry Cust, was for thirty years Canon of Windsor, Cust was baptized at St George's Chapel, Windsor. Lionel Cust's wife, Sybil, was the great-niece of Lady Lyttelton, Queen Victoria's wise Lady-in-Waiting, whom the King remembered as 'Laddles', his governess when he was a boy.

But it was not because of these connections that the King was persuaded by Esher to appoint Lionel Cust as Surveyor of the King's Pictures. In 1897, when Prince of Wales, he had been impressed by Cust, who was then Director of the National Portrait Gallery, and who had shown him round, explaining the pictures simply and sensitively. He was at ease with him and when he became King took him into his confidence and trusted him completely. Edward VII, Cust wrote, 'supervised all the arrangements in the private apartments himself, and placed the actual work in my hands. For this reason I was admitted to a peculiar intimacy, which few, if any, of his Household were privileged to enjoy.'

The King was always in a rush when at the Palace but would send for Cust 'while he was changing his coat before going out . . . and give me instructions in his bedroom or dressing room, never wasting time'. This gave Cust the chance to see the King 'divested of regal splendour, just a human being like myself'. As far as Cust was concerned, the saying 'no man is a hero to his valet' was reversed. Not that the King ever treated him like a valet: 'he never failed to apologise to me if I had been kept waiting . . . From being my King and my master, King Edward came to be my hero.' Cust was not blind to the King's faults, such as his explosions of temper, but he, like Esher, grew to love 'a great personality who radiated something special and indescribable from the Throne'.[8]

The King's aim was to modernize the Palace, which had scarcely been touched for thirty years, and to bring some glamour to the throne. Although he was reluctant to move from Marlborough House, which he and the Queen loved and considered home, he was determined to take possession of the Palace as soon as possible.

Cust took up his new position as Surveyor of the King's Pictures on 5 March 1901, keeping his directorship of the National Portrait Gallery. Then he began to make a careful survey of all the royal palaces. Together with Sir Arthur Ellis, Lord Farquhar and Lord Esher as Secretary of the Office of Works, he accompanied the King and Queen on an exhausting tour of each Palace 'from end to end'. Like George III, the new King liked to be personally involved in the work. Queen Alexandra confined her attention to the private rooms, but gamely limped after the ebullient King for most of the tours. Strangely, she had never been in Queen Victoria's private rooms in Buckingham Palace, although the old Queen had been very fond of her lovely daughter-in-law.

At the start of their tour of Buckingham Palace the great entrance hall struck chill and gloomy. The scagliola was peeling, the painted walls were shabby and the lighting dim with dirt. Cust wrote, 'The great entrance Hall had originally been decorated with painted imitations of marble which had darkened with age and the atmosphere of London so that Edward VII spoke of it as the "sepulchre".'

Upstairs in the Picture Gallery the gas-lit chandeliers had to be taken down and cleaned. Not only were they thick with dust, but 'the pictures which had been hanging for years on a level with, or even above, the chandeliers . . . were found in parts to be coated with a thin dark film of dirt, in some places amounting to opaque black'. Fortunately Cust knew a restorer, F. H. Baines, who was now commissioned to clean the pictures.

Cust found Buckingham Palace the most neglected of all the royal palaces. The State Rooms were 'in fair working order', but had been untouched since Prince Albert's death in 1861. The Queen's suite needed modernizing; Cust noted that 'the apartments on the North Side, destined for the occupation of their Majesties, had to be gutted, in some places altered in actual structure, provided with new bathrooms, electric light, and all the innovations for modern comfort'.

Since he was responsible for the care of all the 'Pictures, China, Sculptures, Bronzes, Tapestry, and ornamental furniture', and since the workmen were already creating havoc, he began with the greatest urgency.

The King trusted Cust's discretion completely, knowing that he would handle his responsibilities with infinite care and sensibility. But otherwise, as Cust remembered,

King Edward liked to supervise everything himself, enjoying nothing so much in the intervals of leisure as sitting in a roomful of workmen and giving directions in person. 'Offer it up,' he would say, 'and I will come to see,' and when he came he said Yes or No at once. It was no use asking him to suggest this or that, as he had little imagination, though a quick trained eye and instinct for what was right and what pleased him.

The efforts of Prince Albert and Stockmar had not been in vain: he had absorbed much of the cultural heritage which they had considered so important. 'I do not know much about Art,' he would say with a characteristic rolling of his r's, 'but I think I know something about Arrangement.'[9]

It took all Cust's tact and sensitivity to deal not only with the King but also with his sisters, to whom the break-up of the familiar scenes at Buckingham Palace must have been painful at times in view of the almost sacred memory of Queen Victoria. His task was eased by their 'uniform courtesy'.

Cust's most delicate task was to collect carefully all the 'personal objects' belonging to Queen Victoria which were not specifically mentioned in her will. There were rows of marble busts and statues, including a collection of statuettes of John Brown. At Windsor, Cust heard the King's booming reply to his deaf wife when she asked the identity of a marble baby: 'If that child had lived, you and I would not have been here.' It was Princess Elizabeth, the baby daughter of William IV and Queen Adelaide who, in 1820, had lived only a few months. There were hundreds of gifts from foreign visitors and jubilees, stored away at Windsor – elephant tusks and oriental boxes: even, unidentified, in a box of assorted relics, a codpiece from the armour of Henry VII.

But Cust's most moving experience at Buckingham Palace was to find himself 'alone in the rooms once occupied by Prince Albert, still apparently much the same as when he last used them, one of them containing his private library, another, the organ, on which he had played himself and on which Mendelssohn had performed'.[10] There were family letters in a desk, which he handed over to Princess Beatrice as her mother's executrix. To Esher's profound irritation, Princess Beatrice rewrote and expurgated her mother's journal, and then had the original burnt, in accordance with the old Queen's instructions. Biographers and historians have gnashed their teeth at this piece of literary vandalism ever since.

Cust remembered that 'it was a long business to get Buckingham Palace into working order so much being needed in the way of structural alterations, bathrooms and general decoration . . .' There was

a constant and vigilant warfare with the myrmidons of H.M. Office of Works, especially electricians who all too frequently when a nice spot was available . . .

for hanging pictures in a good light, selected that spot for an electric light fitting which could quite as well be placed elsewhere.[11]

Unfortunately he never quite defeated them; nor could he always prevent radiators being placed next to priceless furniture. Cust does not mention the decorators who, in 1902, were busy covering Prince Albert's polychrome walls of the Grand Hall with gallons of white paint, but they must have been disturbing.

The King had commissioned the interior decorator C. H. Bessant of the firm of Bertram & Son to transform the entrance to the Palace. So the Grand Hall, the walls of the Grand Staircase and the Marble Hall now gleamed – an expanse of white and gold.

Besides Bessant, the King also commissioned the architect Frank T. Verity to modernize the Palace. The son of Thomas Verity, who designed the Criterion restaurant in London, he was at this time a favourite of the King's fashionable Mayfair friends. Trained in Paris, he appealed to the King's love of all things French, and his experience in theatre design was to be useful in dealing with the dramatic State Rooms. It may have been Lillie Langtry who drew the King's attention to Verity: he had designed the improvements of the Imperial Theatre, Westminster, for her. Verity's main challenge was to transform the Ballroom, but his work there was not undertaken until 1907. With the help of these professionals, Edward VII brought the Palace up to date and created the 'Edwardian' style, suitable for his kind of life.

On 20 February 1902 Cust took his wife on a tour of the Palace, now almost finished, except for the Ballroom. He had done his duty with great sensitivity and was rightly proud. His experience at the National Portrait Gallery had been invaluable in the restoration and rehanging of the pictures. The King wanted them where he could see them, so Cust had placed the superb paintings of the Dutch School back in the Picture Gallery, but he considered them still too high. At least the substitution of electric light for gas made them less liable to damage by heat and dirt. He rearranged the pictures in the Belgian Suite on the ground floor (this was the suite that Leopold, King of the Belgians, had always occupied in Queen Victoria's reign). Here he hung the collection of French and Spanish portraits bought by the Queen at the sale of King Leopold's pictures.

Cust was particularly proud of his suggestion for the improvement of the background to the throne. 'By utilizing some of the rich crimson damask curtains which abounded in the state rooms, it might be possible to produce a suitable canopy and curtained background.' It was a dramatic setting for ceremonial occasions for years to come.

With customary generosity, Cust gave most of the credit for the reorganization to Sir Arthur Ellis, whose long experience as

Equerry and Comptroller to the King before his accession, his acquaintance with the palaces in foreign countries and his natural gifts of culture and artistic temperament made him wonderfully fit for the post. . . . If at times he rather over-rated the virtues of economy, he kept prices down in a ruthless fashion, and few of the pleasant and time-honoured abuses in the royal household survived his accession to office.[12]

On 14 March 1902, the King gave his first Court – before he and the Queen had actually moved in. On 27 March he and Queen Alexandra left Marlborough House for ever and took a tour on the royal yacht, *Victoria and Albert*. On 12 April they took up permanent residence in Buckingham Palace, now made ready for the brilliant celebrations planned for the Coronation on 26 June.

In early June preparations for the Coronation were well in hand, thanks to the tireless work and efficient organization of Lord Esher and his colleagues. By mid June London was filled with foreign dignitaries and their followers. Every member of the Household was on duty; Cust described the excitement and traumatic experiences of the time. The King held his first reception for a foreign delegation, that of the Sultan of Morocco, in St James's Palace, but after that these too were held in the newly decorated Buckingham Palace.

Cust had now been made a gentleman usher, in addition to his position as Surveyor of the King's Pictures. All the patience of the royal Household was needed in those crowded days. There were times when all their careful arrangements were thrown into confusion. On one such occasion, the King had been particularly anxious to welcome a distinguished delegation from Japan with extra courtesy. Unfortunately the delegation's visit coincided with that of one from Korea, a separate country but under the suzerainty of Japan. It was essential that the Japanese should be given special treatment, so the delegation from Japan was to be received in state at the Grand Entrance to the Palace, while the Koreans were to enter by the Buckingham Palace Road door. At the same time the King, enthroned in the Ballroom, was receiving addresses from the Lord Mayor of London and a delegation of civic dignitaries. It was all carefully planned; but, as Cust recorded, he was on duty as a gentleman usher upstairs when he was called down to the Grand Entrance, which seemed to be full of 'little men in gold uniforms': the Koreans, who had been directed to the wrong door and were now buried in 'a seething mass of furred and cloaked civic officials'. It was essential to get them out of sight before the Japanese arrived.

It was, however, too late. There was a sound of horses' hoofs, a banging of doors, and of salutes and the Japanese Prince and his suite were shot into the Hall to be swamped in their turn in the ever-increasing crowd of civic dignitaries. Then they had to be extricated, identified, and classified, the Japanese on one side, the Koreans on the other, looking as if they would like to cut each other's throats.[13]

It was finally sorted out; the Japanese Prince was taken directly to be received by the King. But it had been, Cust wrote, 'enough to turn the hair white of any Lord Chamberlain'.[13]

There was worse to come. In mid June it seemed as though there might be no King to be crowned. On 14 June Edward VII was taken ill with what was described as a severe chill. It proved to be appendicitis. During the preceding months the King had not spared himself. Like George III, he rushed at his duties with a frenetic energy, refusing to delegate, insisting on overseeing all the preparations for the Coronation. There were interminable receptions, military reviews and rehearsals in the Abbey, as well as the reorganization of the Palaces and the move from Marlborough House to Buckingham Palace. At the same time he was eating too much: like George IV he was both gourmet and gourmand. As his biographer, Philip Magnus, records 'he had put on so much weight that his abdominal measurement – 48 inches – measured that of his chest'.[14]

By 16 June his doctors were seriously concerned: it was clear to them that the Coronation, due for 26 June, would have to be postponed. But though the King was in agony, he insisted that he would soldier on: he would get to the Abbey if it killed him. At least he agreed not to attend the Ascot races: Queen Alexandra went alone, escorted by the Prince of Wales. They returned to London and drove through cheering crowds to Buckingham Palace, where the King was huddled and grey with pain. It took all the efforts of his doctor, Sir Francis Laking, to persuade him that he was suffering from peritonitis and unless he had an operation immediately he would surely die.

The rooms of Buckingham Palace had, in the past, been put to many uses – there had been births, christenings and weddings – but never before had a king undergone a major operation there. A room overlooking the garden had been converted, ready for the unavoidable event. Queen Alexandra, game as always, stood by the King while an anaesthetic was given, and would have held the King's hand throughout if the doctor had not quietly urged her out of the room. Sir Frederick Treves performed a successful operation. The King 'fell into a healthy sleep, while the Empire was convulsed by a transport of emotional loyalty and of human affection for King Edward which commanded the awed sympathy of the world'.[15]

The postponement of the Coronation, now fixed for 9 August, caused the Lord Chamberlain and Lord Esher many headaches. Some royal visitors left, some stayed on and had to be cared for. The King recovered remarkably quickly and before long was back to his old habits, enjoying enormous meals again. He convalesced with Queen Alexandra in the Mediterranean on the royal yacht and returned for his Coronation bronzed, fit and a great deal slimmer.

Coronation day itself was less spectacular than it would have been, but both the King and Queen were profoundly moved by the magic and mystery of the moment of crowning.*

Unlike Queen Victoria, Edward VII was anxious to prepare his son, George, Prince of Wales, for kingship. He allowed him to see his official papers and encouraged his visits abroad. In April 1904 the Prince and Princess of Wales paid a visit to Emperor Franz Joseph at his court in Vienna. The old-fashioned etiquette and protocol there confirmed the Princess's often repeated belief in the importance of accepting change. Her biographer records that forty years later Queen Mary remarked that

the collapse of the Imperial systems in Austria and in Russia had come as no surprise to her, since she had never conceived how an order so stiff and hierarchical and so totally detached from the people of these countries, could possibly survive in a free and modern world.[16]

In October 1905 the Prince and Princess of Wales set out for a tour of India, which was, for the Princess in particular, a sunburst in the mind. The vibrant colours, the ancient civilizations and the mirrored palaces awakened an intelligent mind that was hungry for new experiences. They were able to wander round the back streets incognito to see 'the mud dwellings of the poor'. She took trouble to read up about India and the religions. '"Hindu, Mohammedan and Buddhism, all this knowledge", she wrote to her Aunt Augusta, ". . . helps one to take a keen interest in all one sees and therefore to enjoy to the utmost every detail of the wonderful sights." Their Chief of Staff was impressed: "You have", he told her, "a very good grasp of Indian affairs, quite remarkable in a woman." '[17]

In their years as Prince and Princess of Wales they were both building up a store of experience and knowledge that was to be invaluable when the Prince became King. Princess Mary was not only to introduce an

* Queen Alexandra instructed the Archbishop to make sure that the holy oil should reach her head through her hair piece. He did so, so thoroughly that it dripped through, running down her nose.

Indian note into the decoration of Buckingham Palace: she also would bequeath to her granddaughter, Queen Elizabeth II, an understanding of the importance of the future Commonwealth.

More and more the Prince realized the quality of his wife's mind, recognizing how indispensable she was to him. Her linguistic ability – she spoke French, German and Italian – her knowledge of history and her understanding of the world were all qualities that would make her an invaluable Queen Consort.

It was also at this time that she developed her 'one great hobby' – a passion for collecting, stimulated and encouraged by Lady Mount-Stephen, the wife of a Canadian railway millionaire. In the quiet, flat countryside of the Sandringham estate the Prince could exercise his skill as a crack shot or painstakingly build up his collection of stamps, while Princess Mary, like the museum curator *manquée* she was, would arrange her 'finds', cataloguing and carefully recording their provenance.

In 1904 the King planned the transformation of the Ballroom. Verity was called in as architect, and White Allom, the Mayfair decorators, as contractors. Verity's assistant remembered 'making his way through piles of discarded furniture that had belonged to Queen Victoria that the King was anxious to throw out'.[18]

Verity and White Allom completely obliterated the work of Professor Gruner and Prince Albert. Gone was the peeling scagliola: the pillars were now white, fluted, classical Ionic, and the polychrome walls were covered with cream paint and hung with framed tapestries. Gilded swags adorned *œil-de-bœuf* windows. All was grand and dramatic in the Parisian style Edward VII loved.

The King was now in the pattern of life that he was to follow throughout his reign. He always spent from Christmas to the end of January at Sandringham, where he held great family parties. He occasionally left for an odd night at Buckingham Palace or for the shooting at the Duke of Devonshire's country house, Chatsworth. February was his London month, when he was engaged in public occasions, the State Opening of Parliament, and diplomatic and other receptions. He hated to be bored and, restless as always, he entertained at the Palace or went out to dinners and theatres almost every evening.

March and April were spent holidaying abroad: first a week in Paris, which he loved and where he was a well-known and popular figure, and then three weeks at Biarritz and a month cruising in the royal yacht. In May he returned to England for the Season, when every night he dined out or gave dinners at restaurants or at the Palace. Every weekend was spent either at Sandringham or at the country houses of friends.

He moved to Windsor Castle for Ascot in mid June, and to the Duke of Richmond's for the Goodwood races at the end of the month. In August he was once more on the royal yacht for the Regatta at Cowes. After all that he needed a rest and health cure, which he took at a favourite hotel in Marienbad in Bohemia.

He returned to Buckingham Palace for a few days in September, then was off again to Doncaster for the races and Balmoral for shooting in October. Back at Buckingham Palace in November, he spent a week on affairs of state, and the last two weeks he was at Windsor. The first week of December was spent at Sandringham; then until Christmas he was back at Buckingham Palace.

This was his regular annual routine, much of it a round of pleasure, but he crowded a great deal of state business into his weeks at Buckingham Palace and Windsor, and he spent some days of every year visiting provincial cities, receiving and listening to local citizens. His energy was formidable: his restlessness, like that of George III, almost pathological. As the years passed, the Queen spent more and more of her time with her sister, the Dowager Empress of Russia, either at the house they bought in Denmark or at Sandringham.

The reign was not, however, all one of self-indulgence. When Edward VII came to the throne, the Boer War, which had broken out in 1899, was still in progress. According to the King's biographer, 'The Secretary of State for War, St John Brodrick, appeared to be closeted almost daily in London.' He was, in fact, at the Palace with the King, who was resolved to 'brush aside all obstacles to speedy victory in the Boer War'. Brodrick, while complaining about 'the active intervention of a constitutional monarch in the work of government', nevertheless considered 'that the impetus which King Edward gave to all military progress was of abiding service to this Country'.[19]

Edward VII had no intention of making Buckingham Palace the centre of political intrigue. Like William IV he endeavoured to be impartial. But, wrote Cust,

Not only did he mean to be king, but also to have a share in the government of his people. If he displayed any political leanings at all, he was inclined to a liberal rather than a conservative view of politics, even on occasion to radical changes. In this he was encouraged by Lord Knollys, himself an advanced radical.

Cust considered that none of the ministers tried to understand the King. Prime Minister Lord Salisbury was too old and ill to make the effort; Arthur Balfour could not 'bring his intellect down to what . . . he considered the low level of the King's'; Henry, Marquess of Lansdowne, the Secretary of State for Foreign Affairs, worried about the King's interest in foreign affairs; and later, Herbert Asquith was 'too much of the don and lawyer' to have any human sympathy for the King.[20]

Although much of the business of government was delegated to his ministers, as Magnus writes, 'Throughout his reign and despite failing health, he performed all his diverse duties with exemplary conscientiousness to the perfect satisfaction of his subjects.'[21]

Often, however, the King found it more agreeable and as efficient to discuss foreign affairs while on his trips abroad. For example, his Secretary of State for War, Viscount Haldane, stayed with him for three days in August at his hotel in Marienbad, and 'during picnics in the surrounding woods explained in outline to him his entire plan of army reform'. This method suited the King, who would have yawned over Stockmar's interminable memoranda.

Towards the end of his life the King began giving a series of dinners at Buckingham Palace for men of distinction. In March of his last year he invited senior civil servants, who were encouraged to speak openly. On this occasion he not only listened but ate a 'huge meal of turtle soup, salmon steak, grilled chicken, saddle of mutton, several snipe stuffed with foie gras, asparagus, a fruit dish, an enormous concoction and a savoury'.[22]

The King and Queen continued the garden parties that Queen Victoria had initiated. There were formal ones, when Queen Alexandra appeared exquisitely dressed and the King maintained his eagle-eyed watch on sartorial correctness. But there were also riotous children's parties in the garden, when, as Cust remembered, balloons were sent up, which, on exploding, scattered little toys among the delighted children. The elegant Queen Alexandra could be skittish on these occasions.

The King did everything with enormous gusto: work and pleasure were attacked with a *joie de vivre* that electrified – and exhausted – his companions. But the pace was too fast even for his tireless energy.

On the evening of 27 April 1910 Edward VII returned to Buckingham Palace from Biarritz. Although exhausted, he insisted on working on his boxes before dressing for a visit to the opera. On 28 April he received Asquith and his ministers. He spent the weekend at Sandringham, where he inspected his estate in an icy wind. On Monday he was back working in Buckingham Palace, with bronchitis. The last entry in the diary he had kept all his life reads sadly: 'The King dines alone.' The Queen was recalled from Corfu and arrived on 5 May. For once the King failed to meet her at the station. Fighting all the way, he insisted on dressing to receive Lord Knollys. Even after a succession of heart attacks, he insisted on remaining hunched in his armchair. The Queen, knowing that the end was not far away, with characteristic generosity sent for Mrs Keppel, quietly left her to say goodbye, and then firmly dismissed her.

At five o'clock the Prince of Wales told the King his horse, Witch of the Air, had won at Kempton Park. For that moment the King was conscious. 'I am very glad,' he said, before sinking again. At 11.45 p.m. on Friday 6 May Edward VII died.

From 17 to 19 May, a quarter of a million people came to Westminster Abbey to pay their last respects, filing silently past the coffin on the catafalque. Edward VII's nephew, the German Emperor, came with suitable solemnity, always anxious to shine, even in the candlelit hall of death.

On 20 May Lionel Cust drove into the Quadrangle of Buckingham Palace,

where the members of the royal procession began to assemble, and horses were waiting in rows ... There were eight crowned heads, King George V, the German Emperor, the Kings of Norway, Greece and Spain, of Bulgaria, Denmark and Portugal, with in addition to our own royal Princes, about thirty others, including the Arch Duke Franz Ferdinand of Austria. There was a babel of tongues and a clashing of hooves all round me. At last at a given signal they were all mounted and the royal cortège passed slowly before me out into the Forecourt. Then came the carriage procession with Queen Alexandra, Queen Mary, the Queen of Norway, and their suites, until at last the quadrangle was empty except for myself, and two or three officials in uniform.

Cust followed the procession to Paddington in a royal carriage 'through a sea of faces, especially in Hyde Park, where there were many rows deep on either side'.[23]

The crowds lining the streets to Paddington watched as the gun carriage carried the King. He was much loved, because with all his faults he was like them, but larger than them. Caesar, his favourite fox terrier, followed the coffin, in the charge of a Highland servant. Behind them came the German Emperor and the eight Kings. It was the first time, noted the Emperor, that a dog had taken precedence before him. The royal train took them to Windsor, where 'Bertie' was buried in St George's Chapel.

Lionel Cust, remembering those days, was haunted by the words of Rudyard Kipling:

> The tumult and the shouting dies;
> The captains and the Kings depart ...
> Lest we forget, lest we forget.

Never again would so great an assembly of monarchs meet to mourn the passing of one of their number.

CHAPTER SEVEN

King George V and Queen Mary

'The finest example in modern
times of the supremely difficult art of
constitutional kingship.'[1]

J. R. CLYNES

The Palace Reborn

For Edward VII Buckingham Palace had been not so much a home as
another grand hotel into which he could comfortably move for short
set periods in his peripatetic life. For King George V it was a ship, to
be run with discipline and authority, and his place of work. For Queen
Mary it was an enormous challenge, a confusion and profusion of
furniture and furnishings and priceless objects which it was her duty
and pleasure to identify and arrange. Here was her chance to use all her
knowledge of history and the arts and make the Palace the showcase of
the nation's history. But in the beginning, as she wrote to Aunt Augusta,
'everything at this moment seems to me to be chaos and with my
methodical mind I suffer in proportion, no doubt some day all will be
right again.'[2]

As for their family, now they would have to move from their London
home, Marlborough House, to the forbidding Buckingham Palace. They
loved Sandringham, which was to remain a refuge during the difficult years
of adolescence and was to be important in the shaping of the monarchy.

Here we should pause to look back at the childhood of the two boys
who walked in their naval cadet uniforms behind their grandfather's coffin
up the Windsor hill to his burial. Both were to become kings: Prince
Edward, known as 'David', for a brief spell as King Edward VIII and
Prince Albert, known as 'Bertie', who succeeded him, as King George VI.

At the beginning of the new reign in 1910, David was fifteen and Bertie fourteen. Their siblings were Princess Mary, thirteen, and Princes Harry, ten, George, seven, and John, the youngest, four. It has often been said that their childhood was not happy: in the words of Mabell, Countess of Airlie, Queen Mary's devoted Lady of the Bedchamber, the King and Queen 'have often been depicted as stern unloving parents, but this they most certainly were not . . . I believe that they were more conscientious and more truly devoted to their children than the majority of parents in that era.'[3]

No one can read the memoirs of Edward VIII, as Duke of Windsor, without seeing that there was truth in her judgement, but certainly the King and Queen found it difficult to express their feelings to their children. That they were undemonstrative, even withdrawn, might be because both had, in their early days, trailed in the wake of exuberant parents, Edward VII and Mary Adelaide, Duchess of Teck. It is a familiar pattern. Their children led restricted lives. 'I never saw them run along the corridors; they walked sedately, generally shepherded by nurses and tutors,' wrote Lady Airlie.[4] It is also true that when very young they were left a great deal in the charge of their nannies, one of whom was extremely cruel. The Duke of Windsor described in his memoirs how, when he was brought down to join his parents in the drawing room at teatime, 'this dreadful nanny would pinch and twist my arm to make me yell'; causing him to be removed peremptorily from the room. But eventually she was removed and replaced by Frederick Finch, a stalwart footman who was first

a sort of nanny; then a valet who travelled with me . . . concocted the pitiless remedy of my first hangover, never hesitated to address unsolicited advice when, in his opinion, the developing interests of his young master required it. Later still he became my butler.[5]

Finch was a splendid example of those devoted and indispensable servants who throughout history have made bearable the loneliness that so often is the lot of royalty.

Another of the unsung characters who had such an important influence on the young lives was the Sandringham village schoolmaster, Walter

Jones. 'Something of a philosopher and sage, he was a self-taught naturalist with an unsurpassed knowledge of the botany and animal lore of Norfolk,' remembered the Duke of Windsor. He filled 'an important if unobtrusive place in the closed world of Sandringham'. King George V respected and was fond of him, and took him with him when he went on his Empire tour in 1901. Jones even tried, not very successfully, to introduce his royal charges to the children of the village school for football matches. Looking back, the exiled Duke remembered with nostalgia that 'there were older and lovelier places in the country, but for my grandfather [Sandringham] summed up his idea of the good life . . . a uniquely English way of life centred around the great estates: an elegant, undoubtedly paternalistic, and self-contained existence'.[6]

The King and Queen were often absent or occupied. Nevertheless they spent time with the children. There was, too, a bond between Prince Edward and his mother that was to survive all the traumatic later events when he was the errant King Edward VIII. Looking back in later life, he would remember her resting on the sofa in her negligée and the family gathered around her on little chairs.

She would read and talk to us . . . I am sure that my cultural interests began at my mother's knee. The years she had lived abroad had mellowed her outlook and reading and observation had equipped her with a prodigious knowledge of Royal history. Her soft voice, her cultivated mind, the cosy room overflowing with personal treasures were all inseparable ingredients of the happiness associated with this last hour of a child's day.[7]

Later the exiled Duke of Windsor remembered with a sense of loss the security and love of his Edwardian childhood.

Sandringham, the Duke of Windsor remembered, 'possessed most of the ingredients for a boyhood idyll'. There, 'free hours were spent mostly on our bicycles when we would face downhill, crouched over the handlebars with Finch bringing up the rear shouting hoarse warnings that I could not hear'. The 'woodland trails of the great estate became . . . an enchanted forest . . . The lake was in our imaginations infested with pirates.' It was said that you could not understand King George V unless you understood what Sandringham meant to him. It is also true,

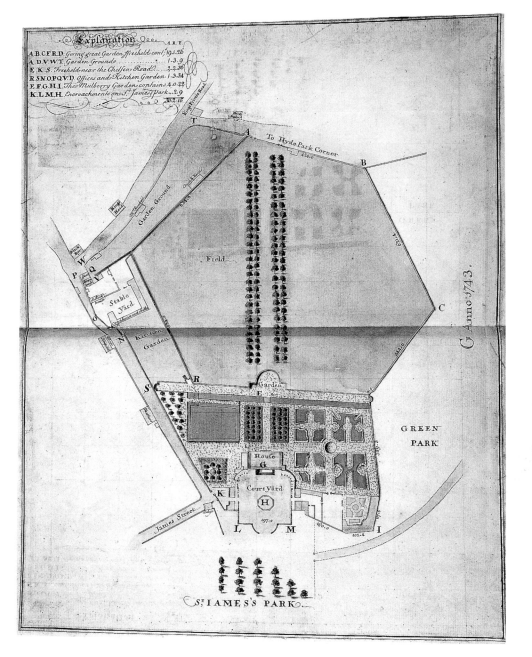

1. Plan of Buckingham House in 1743. The Duke's encroachment into St James's Park and over the site of part of the Mulberry Garden is clearly marked. The gardens at the rear were designed in the formal French manner.

2. Arlington House. The road from Kensington to Chelsea runs close in front of it.

3. Mrs Papendiek and child, from a sketch by her friend Sir Thomas Lawrence (1769–1830). Daughter of Frederick Albert, Queen Charlotte's page, and married to King George III's page. Her memoirs are a valuable source for the period.

4. George III at Windsor in his last illness, c. 1820 after John Jackson.

5. Leopold, King of the Belgians, c. 1857, uncle of both Queen Victoria and Prince Albert. (Photograph)

6. Prince Albert plays the organ for Queen Victoria, with Felix Mendelssohn standing behind, at Buckingham Palace, 1842.

7. (Above) A group of grooms and other servants with the little pony, Webster, taken at the Royal Mews, Buckingham Palace, in 1842.

8. (Left) Queen Victoria with the Prince and Princess of Wales (later King Edward VII and Queen Alexandra) after their marriage in 1863.

9. (Right) Alexandra, Princess of Wales, and her youngest brother, Prince Valdemar of Denmark, c. 1870.

10. (Below) The Prince and Princess of Wales at the time of their Silver Wedding in 1888, with their children (left to right) Prince Albert Victor, Princess Maud, Prince George and Princess Victoria (both seated) and Princess Louise (standing between her parents).

11. In 1942 President Roosevelt sent his wife Eleanor to Britain to report on war conditions
here. In this photograph by Cecil Beaton, Mrs Roosevelt is shown with King George VI,
Queen Elizabeth, Princess Elizabeth and Princess Margaret, in the Bow Room in
Buckingham Palace. During the war many works of art were stored, leaving cabinets
empty, as in this picture.

12. In September 1940 a time bomb dropped during a night raid and exploded, demolishing the swimming pool and part of the north colonnade.

13. King George VI, Queen Elizabeth and Princesses Elizabeth and Margaret on VE Day, 8 May 1945. Princess Elizabeth wears the uniform of an ATS officer.

14. The family group in the White Drawing Room, Buckingham Palace, on 21 October, 1950, on the occasion of the christening of Princess Anne Elizabeth Alice Louise.

though perhaps not so often realized, that to understand the sad end of King Edward VIII, one should remember, as he did, this childhood idyll. When Edward VII and his Court descended on Sandringham 'the great house on the hill would spring into life with a bonfire blaze of lights . . . In my gallery of childhood memories, the portrait of my grandfather seems bathed in perpetual sunlight . . .'[8] Edward VII was his role model. When he became King, David would choose to be called Edward VIII.

But there was a dark corner in that idyllic scene, which the Duke of Windsor had completely pushed out of his mind. There is only the briefest mention in his autobiography of his youngest brother, Prince John, the poor little epileptic boy who lived separately with his nurse on the estate and died on 18 January 1919 at the age of fourteen. Throughout his life, as Prince of Wales, King and Duke of Windsor, David would always be able to blot the unpleasant out of his mind.

But shades of the prison house were closing in. When their parents, the Prince and Princess of Wales, returned from their tour of India in 1906, a new tutor, Hansell, was appointed to prepare the two eldest boys for the Navy, to which their father determined to send them. The Navy, he believed, would teach the heir to the throne all he needed to know.

In May 1909 Prince Edward was transferred from the naval college at Osborne to that at Dartmouth, where he completed his two years' naval training. His brother followed him through the same rough waters. Bertie, unlike the Prince of Wales, was to remain with the Navy. On his grandfather's death, Prince Edward became Duke of Cornwall, a fourteenth-century title given to the King's eldest son. The income from the Duchy, as he explained,

serves to make him financially independent. Its holdings include valuable London property and thousands of acres in the West Country. The greater part of the not inconsiderable income is reinvested in the estate and the rest passes to the Duke of Cornwall . . . for the maintenance of his household and establishment.[9]

If, in her first days there, Buckingham Palace seemed unfriendly to Queen Mary, it was doubly so to the family. From the beginning, to the young Prince Edward, it smelt of death.

My grandfather's body lay in the Throne Room at Buckingham Palace, with the massive bejewelled crown upon the coffin. Four tall Grenadier guardsmen of the King's Company stood rigidly at each corner, resting on their arms reversed, their bearskin-capped heads inclined in respect. My grandmother could not stay out of the Throne Room: she returned there constantly to rearrange the flowers or to show a foreign relative or old friend the scene.[10]

In 2 June 1910, three weeks before his sixteenth birthday, Prince Edward was created Prince of Wales (a title which is not automatically conferred but is bestowed at the monarch's discretion).

In December 1910 the Prince of Wales moved with his parents into Buckingham Palace.

My room was on the 3rd floor overlooking the Mall. The Palace seemed enormous, with its stately rooms and endless corridors and passages. It was something of a walk to reach my mother's room; we used to say we visited her only by appointment. And the vast building seemed pervaded by a curious musty smell that still assails me whenever I enter its portals. I was never happy there.[11]

It had been difficult to persuade Queen Alexandra to move into Buckingham Palace; now it was even more difficult to get her to move out. Cocooned in her deafness, spoilt by universal respect and affection, she seemed blissfully unaware that she was making life difficult for the new King and Queen. Her sister, Marie, now the widow of the Russian Tsar Alexander III, was with her in England and insisted that she should follow rigid Russian rules of protocol, which gave her precedence over Queen Mary, who showed exemplary patience. Finally, however, in December 1910 Queen Alexandra's rooms at the Palace were dismantled and wagonloads of her possessions transferred to Marlborough House or Sandringham. She continued to live in the big house at Sandringham for the rest of her life, while the King, Queen and family remained in the cramped York Cottage. This suited the King, who loved it, and Queen Mary suffered it for his sake. Here he could relax and indulge his two passions, stamp collecting and shooting. His skill with a gun was legendary: on one day it was reported that he 'fired 1,700 cartridges and killed 1,000 pheasants'. He needed relaxation and banging away at pheasants seems to have given him what he needed.

In those first months Queen Mary often felt lonely. She had always been so close to King George V but now he was continually preoccupied. She moved into the Palace a few days before her husband, and in the dark February days, when the wind whistled through the windows, she felt bleak and alone. The Palace at first seemed cold and unfriendly, not as *gemütlich* as Marlborough House. She wrote to her husband:

without you and the children I feel rather lost . . . Oh! how I regret our dear belov'd Marl. Hse, the most perfect of houses and so compact. Here everything is so straggly, such distances to go and so fatiguing. But I ought not to grumble for they have been very anxious to make me as comfortable as possible.[12]

King George V replied briskly, 'The distances are great, but it is good exercise for you as you never walk a yard in London.'[13] But even he had to admit to Esher that he would be happy to pull down Buckingham Palace, sell off its thirty-nine-acre garden and use the money to rebuild Kensington Palace.

But by February 1911 the 'great eruption' was at an end and Queen Mary could begin to think of other things, though, as she wrote, there was still much to be done:

so much has been removed and must be replaced – I am trying to rehang the pictures in the various rooms according to family, date etc – not an easy task when one has miles of corridors to cover to find anything – however I hope to do it in time if my legs hold out.[14]

Queen Mary was not one to wallow in self-pity. She called in Ministry of Works officials and the decorators, White Allom, with whose advice she transferred from Marlborough House her furniture and furnishings and even the green silk wall coverings. Soon, with her great satinwood bookcase filled with her books and papers, her precious ornaments and photographs arranged on her tables and shelves, and the rooms full of the scent of her favourite carnations, Queen Mary was almost as at home as she had been at Marlborough House.

Queen Mary had inherited from her father, the Duke of Teck, a real delight in interior decoration, so rearranging the private rooms was a pleasure. She brought with her full-length portraits of her maternal grandparents, the Duke and Duchess of Cambridge. In the spring of 1911 she still found the sitting room with its pretty bow windows very cold and draughty, but soon she could report that she had dinner 'in my green room which looks charming'.[15]

It is not surprising that at the Coronation on 22 June 1911 both King and Queen looked strained. As one observer noted, the Queen

was almost shrinking as she walked up the aisle . . . the contrast, on her return, crowned, was magnetic as if she had undergone some marvellous transformation. Instead of the shy creature for whom one had felt pity one saw her emerge . . . with a bearing of dignity, and a quiet confidence, signifying that she really felt that she was Queen of this great Empire, and that she derived strength and legitimate pride from the knowledge of it.[16]

The profound effect of the Coronation ceremony on Queen Mary, as on the King and most of England's monarchs, must never be underestimated. Even the Prince of Wales was deeply impressed. As the Duke of Windsor he later wrote, 'There is no occasion that rivals the solemn magnificence of a Coronation, when Church and State unite in the glorification of Kingship.' His diary for that 'auspicious day', as he wrote,

hardly does justice to the impressive, colourful scene . . . We arrived in the Abby [sic] at 10.30 and then walked up the Nave and Choir to my seat in front of the peers. All the relatives and people were most civil and bowed to me as they passed. Then Mama and Papa came in and the ceremony commenced. There was the recognition, the anointing and then the crowning of Papa and then I put on my coronet with the peers. Then I had to go and do hommage [sic] to Papa at his throne and I was very nervous: kneeling at my father's feet, I swore 'I, Edward, Prince of Wales, do become your liegeman of life and limb, and of earthly worship; and faith and truth I will bear unto you, to live and die, against all manner of folks. So help me God.' When my father kissed my cheeks his emotion was great, as was mine.

The entry finished, 'Then Mama was crowned . . . We got into our carriage and had a long drive back. My coronet felt very heavy, as we had to bow to the people as we went along.'[17]

When King George V came to the throne he inherited two immediate problems: the front of the Palace, which needed urgent attention, and the stormy passage of the Liberal government's Parliament Bill, aimed at curbing the power of the Lords. The first was to be quickly and competently dealt with; the second was to give the King sleepless nights for years to come and still has not been resolved. The King must have wished that his political problems could be solved as smartly as the architectural.

The news of the vote which passed the Parliament Bill* reached the

---

* King George V had inherited a constitutional quagmire in which he was to struggle. He was not, as he admitted, a clever man, but he was conscientious, with a deep sense of his duty to hold on to such rights as the monarchy still had. When he came to the throne the Commons could pass a bill after three readings, but the Lords could throw it out. The Liberal government had introduced the Parliament Bill, which aimed to ensure that the peers could not amend or reject any money bill, and that any other bill could be delayed only for two years, after which it would automatically go to the King for his signature. The Commons had passed the Parliament Bill; the Lords rejected it. In November 1910 the Liberal Prime Minister Asquith asked the King to promise to create enough peers to allow the 'will of the people as expressed in the Commons to be carried out'.[18]

The King's Secretaries, to whom he turned for advice, gave him contrary opinions. Knollys – whose sympathies were liberal – advised him to create more peers; Lord Stamfordham – a traditionalist – advised him to use his veto. The King, badgered and bullied by Liberals and Conservatives in turn, finally agreed to Asquith's proposal to call a new election, to be fought on the issue of Lords against Parliament. If the Liberals won, the King secretly promised, if necessary, to create enough peers to carry the Bill through the Lords. It was not in fact necessary. The Liberals were returned with an increased majority of 126 seats. The Lords realized that further blocking would be in vain: after a great deal of backstage wheeling and dealing, at 10.40 p.m. on 10 August 1911 they finally passed the Bill.

King after an absurd delay. His Private Secretary immediately telephoned the news to the Palace, but the message, handed from footman to footman, finally landed with an equerry who, thinking the King already knew, carried on with his work. When he went to report to the King for the night he said, '"I am so thankful, sir." He said, "What for?" and I told him . . . I was the first to bring the news. The Queen jumped off the sofa and the King made a few just remarks.'[19]

This was only the beginning of the King's constitutional worries. The Parliament Bill was crucial to the Liberal government's campaign to introduce Home Rule for Ireland – and this complicated argument, in which the King was deeply involved, was to carry on right until the outbreak of the First World War.

The other problem, of the attention needed to the exterior of the Palace, was more swiftly solved. After the death of Queen Victoria, a committee had been set up, directed by Esher, to decide on a memorial. Architects were invited to submit proposals and Sir Aston Webb, whose design for Admiralty Arch had already been accepted, was chosen. He planned the siting of the statue of Queen Victoria by Thomas Brock in front of the Palace. Attention was now drawn to the shabby east front of the Palace, which, the First Commissioner of Works told Parliament, needed refacing. There had been many complaints that, as one contemporary put it, 'for fifty years the existing front has been a reproach to London and the Empire'. Now the new, sparkling white marble memorial made the Palace look even more dingy. The Caen stonework was crumbling, since, as Cubitt had earlier warned, it was unsuitable for sooty London, and was now quite dangerous. Fortunately there had been a magnificent response to the appeal for funds for the Queen Victoria Memorial and there was now a surplus of £60,000, which the committee for the fund decided to use for the rebuilding of the east façade.

Parliament was told that Blore's Caen stonework had perished so badly that it needed replacing. Therefore it was decided to bring the façade more into keeping with the surroundings created by the memorial, and with the rest of the building. It was also resolved to use Portland stone, the material which had come once more to be recognised as ideal for London, as it had been during the era of Wren.

Webb was at this time a successful architect, much esteemed for his public buildings. The son of an engineer, he had worked himself up from humble beginnings. He had trained as an architect in the firm of Banks & Barry, where he won an RIBA travelling studentship. By 1891 he was undertaking a number of commissions in Kensington, including the completion of the Victoria & Albert Museum.

Webb's aim to simplify the outline of the building was achieved by raising the parapet to hide ugly roofs and chimneys; the centre and wings were emphasized with pediments and the whole front was designed on simple, severe lines.

There was little disturbance at the Palace during the work, since the stone was prepared a year in advance at the yards of the contractors, Leslie & Co.* The actual refacing took only three months, but there were difficulties and tragedies. On 12 September 1913 *The Times* reported that the workmen, 250 on day shift, and 150 on night shift, were threatening to go on strike. That was resolved, but twelve days later 'a number of men lifting a roll of roofing lead weighing 30 cwt . . . when one Charles Clark slipped, the lead fell on his head and killed him. On 14 October a painter, Morris Woodhouse, fell 20–30 ft to his death from the scaffolding in front of the Palace.'[20]

By the end of October, in under thirteen weeks the work was finished, to the delight of the King, whose insistence on punctuality was legendary – and not a pane of glass was broken. It had been efficiently planned, and competently and quickly executed, at no cost to him or Parliament. He made little attempt to interfere, except that he insisted that there

---

* Many of the rough blocks were of great size, some of them, after being shaped and moulded ready for fixing in the building, weighing as much as five tons. For working and preparing the stonework in the yards, an average of about 270 men were employed. Two weeks were spent in erecting the scaffold, six weeks in fixing the main portion of the stone, and the remainder of the time in pointing and cleaning down. Six large Scots derricks were erected, five electric hoists, and two electric passenger lifts. The scaffolding was of unusual strength: 5,000 new scaffold poles and from 10,000 to 12,000 boards were used in its construction.

should be no unnecessary ornament, and that the balcony should be kept. Undemonstrative though he was, King George V realized the importance of royal appearances on the balcony as a focus for the demonstration of national unity.

On Friday 31 October 500 workmen in their Sunday best filled the King's Hall Holborn restaurant for a dinner given by the King. According to *The Times* a letter from him was read out, congratulating them 'on an achievement remarkable both in handicraft and in rapidity of execution and he had words of sympathy for the families of workmen killed during the work'. Apparently the menu was 'Scotch Broth, Boiled Turbot with Hollandaise Sauce, Roast Saddle of Mutton, Roast Beef, baked potatoes, Brussels sprouts and Cauliflower; followed by Saxon pudding and dessert'. There was 'an abundant supply of good ale' but, *The Times* noted with surprise, 'quite a considerable number of men drank water or mineral water',[21] after which the men sang lustily 'For he's a jolly good fellow'. A year later many of those men were in khaki, singing 'Goodbye Piccadilly, Farewell Leicester Square', as they marched to the mud and blood of the trenches of the First World War.

In 1913 and 1914 there was much cause for worry: the perennial problem of Ireland; the constitutional argument over the power of the Lords; the reports of growing German aggression; and the domestic disturbances caused by the suffragettes and their campaign for votes for women. Frustrated by the refusal of their opponents to listen to their reasonable arguments, and maddened by the deafening silence of some of their male supporters in Parliament, the suffragettes had become increasingly violent. Their last hope was to take their campaign to Buckingham Palace.

In March 1913 Queen Mary reported that 'tiresome suffragettes rushed out in the Mall and tried to present petitions, of course the police caught them, but it caused a scene and looked undignified'.[22] The Queen was at the sensational Derby in 1913, when Miss Emily Wilding had thrown herself in front of the King's horse and was killed. Sympathetic though Queen Mary was to many women's causes, she had little patience with uncontrolled behaviour. She found it difficult to understand the women who threw bricks through windows and set fire to houses, especially since they were well-dressed, well-bred ladies, not revolutionary mobs.

In the spring of 1914 police patrolled the Palace grounds day and night; even so two ladies evaded them and chained themselves to the railings. On 22 May 1914 the suffragettes marched up the Mall, attempting to storm the Palace to deliver their 'Votes for Women' petition. The police were ready for them. That day fifty-seven were arrested including their leader, Mrs Pankhurst, newly released from gaol. In prison they went on hunger strike and were subjected to the pain and humiliation of force-feeding.

On 4 June 1914 one young woman managed to take her protest to the steps of the throne itself. Miss Mary Blomfield, the 26-year-old daughter of a distinguished architect who had worked at Sandringham, managed to get an invitation to an evening court. Elegantly dressed, she demurely proceeded in her turn in the prescribed manner to the King and Queen on their dais. As the newspapers reported, she curtsied, but did not rise, lifting her arms and crying, 'Your majesty, won't you stop torturing women!' With her customary restraint the Queen reported in her diary,

George and I received three Maori Chiefs at 11. Sat out in the garden most of the day. We held our 3rd court in the evening and a tiresome suffragette came and fell on her knees before G and held out her arms in a supplicating way, saying 'Oh! your majesty stop'. Then she was gently escorted out by Douglas Dawson and John Hamilton. Very unpleasant.[23]

The Queen was not completely unsympathetic; she and the King disapproved of force-feeding, but she disliked disorderly conduct and was embarrassed by passionate appeals to the emotions.

Now that the exterior was completed, Queen Mary persuaded the King that there were repairs and redecoration needed within the Palace. He recognized that there could be no better supervisor for such work than Queen Mary herself. So, for the rest of his reign, the care and reorganization of the Palace was her major concern.

*

It was fortunate that, during their reign, Queen Mary had her own work and her own inner resources; for King George V was preoccupied by affairs of state: the interminable flow of red boxes, the long meetings with ministers. He was more than happy to leave Queen Mary to sort out the confusion within the Palace. She welcomed a task for which she was uniquely qualified; besides, she was lonely now that the King was so busy. They rarely entertained, and hardly ever dined out – much to the surprise of the Prince of Wales, who could not imagine them enjoying a life that seemed to him to be of such stupefying boredom. In fact, the regular rhythm at Buckingham Palace suited them both.

As Kenneth Rose has described: the King followed 'the clockwork routine of a ship's captain. First thing in the morning and last thing at night he consulted the barometer.'[24] He did two hours work before breakfast, tackled his red boxes and business all morning, and took a brisk walk round the Palace garden; then came luncheon and afterwards exactly fifteen minutes sleep, before tackling the red boxes again. Dinner was almost always quietly *en famille*, but even so the King always dressed formally.

Their sons, the Prince of Wales and Prince Albert, froze in this rigid pattern of life, and in their father's insistence on punctuality and on exact correctness in dress and behaviour. They were terrified of the fusillade of questions he would rap at them during dinner. It was not surprising that, given the opportunity, the Prince of Wales would break out into loud check suits and a rackety lifestyle; or that Bertie would find it difficult to control his stammer.

Queen Mary might have been intimidated too were it not that she knew how much the King loved her and how important she was to him. Nonetheless, she was glad to escape into the congenial work of researching, cataloguing and rearranging.

In these years, visiting museums, art galleries and antique shops became a major interest for the Queen, although she would never allow it to interfere with the King's routine. She would always hurry back from such expeditions to be in time to join him for tea; and she would never neglect any royal duties for the sake of her own interests. King George V was on the whole complaisant – after all, he had his own obsession with stamp collecting – although occasionally he became impatient. 'There you go again, May,' he once said. 'Furniture, furniture!'

It must be remembered that not only had Queen Mary studied history from books and observed with a keen eye life in the countries she had visited as Duchess of York, she had learned a great deal from her mother's sister, her beloved Aunt Augusta, Grand Duchess of Mecklenburg-Strelitz. The Grand Duchess had a prodigious memory going back to the Coronation of William IV, and had known every prime minister and almost every European and Russian monarch. She never forgot that as the daughter of the Duke of Cambridge she was the granddaughter of George III. And as Grand Duchess of Mecklenburg-Strelitz she was especially conscious that Queen Mary reigned in the home of Queen Charlotte, also from Mecklenburg-Strelitz; consequently she strengthened Queen Mary's own deep awareness of the continuity of the monarchy. Her aunt's sympathies were high Tory and she was terrified of change, but her sharp mind always stimulated Queen Mary, and right up to her death in 1916 she was a living source of historical information. She kept a home in London and on her frequent visits could bring to life the portraits on the Palace walls, encouraging Queen Mary's own passionate interest in history.

Now visits to Windsor were a joy: Queen Mary could browse in the archives and search the storerooms for old furnishings, neglected furniture and forgotten precious objects. She took advice from Sir Lionel Cust on the hanging of the paintings in the Picture Gallery. A perfectionist, she was remembered, as an old lady, insisting on the correct hang of pictures. When, in later years, she sent one as a present to Miss Crawford, the present Queen's governess when she was Princess Elizabeth, she sent first the picture, then a workman to hang it, and then she came herself to see that it was properly done.

In her reorganization of the Palace Queen Mary worked as no one in the royal family, not even the Prince Consort, had done before. All her love of history, her passion for collecting, her eye for quality and her meticulous care in labelling and cataloguing were brought into action.

There is a record in the Royal Archives of the work done from 1911 to 1935, year by year, 'under the personal supervision of Queen Mary' and signed by an Inspector from the Ministry of Works. All the King's and Queen's own possessions were firmly marked as 'their Majesties' own property' – even the wall hangings.[25]

As she toured the palaces, her keen eye spotted details. She found an eighteenth-century cabinet and its matching cupboards, which were being used as wardrobes in different parts of the palaces. Antique chairs were rescued from upper rooms, repaired, re-covered and rearranged in rooms of their right period. She found one magnificent council chair, carved and gilded and solid as a Roman chariot, in Kensington Palace, and brought it to join its partner in Buckingham Palace. In the Household corridor she found a handsome piece of furniture, which was later identified as 'a neat mahogany press of linen with four wooden doors made in 1770 . . . the whole inside grooved like a bookcase and mahogany sliding shelves'.[26]

She furnished rooms in different styles and periods. In what she called her Chippendale Room she placed Queen Charlotte's mahogany table with chairs of the same period. There were two satinwood tables made originally for George IV's rooms in Buckingham Palace when he was Prince of Wales, which she placed with other satinwood furniture in one of the smaller, more restrained rooms.

Her work at the Palace continued until the King's death, but her interest lasted until the end of her life. She and her friends searched the sale-rooms for the Royal Collection but she also had her own personal treasures. Much prized was the jewel cabinet that had been made for Queen Charlotte in her first year as Queen. Delicately inlaid with ivory, it had held George III's first gift of jewels to his new bride, and had been passed to Queen Mary by her brother, Prince Adolphus, also a passionate collector. Prince 'Dolly', after 1917 Marquess of Cambridge, had married a wealthy wife, so could indulge his love of fine things. In February 1925 she was to write to him,

what do you want to see, The Wallace Collection, or Victoria & Albert or National Portrait Gallery . . . should any of these smile on you and wd you like me to let the Director know as it is nice . . . to have a knowledgeable person with you . . . There are 2 or 3 things in the Palace I should like to show you, small alterations which I think you will approve of . . .[27]

As her biographer, James Pope-Hennessy, described,

She was forever matching up, cataloguing, reorganising and adding to the historical parts of the royal collection. . . . In conversation at this time she would always attribute her love of fine objects to her father, the Duke of Teck: 'only he was poor', she would add, 'and could not afford to buy.'[28]

It was perhaps the memory of her own youth when funds were so often low that encouraged a certain acquisitive obsession. There are many stories of her skill in persuading friends and acquaintances to part with precious *objets d'art*. Some of them are undoubtedly apocryphal, but there is no doubt that she considered it her mission to release beautiful things from their obscure homes and give them their proper place in her Palace.

She consulted experts in every field and was particularly flattered when the Director of the Victoria & Albert Museum wanted to see her Chinese Chippendale Room because he was arranging 'little rooms of various styles at the V. & A. and he said seeing my rooms would help him very much indeed'.[29]

In 1913 she was to encourage Clifford Smith to edit the first major history of the Royal Collection: his *Buckingham Palace* has been ever since the definitive work. The account books and records of the Commission set up to monitor the Prince Regent's debts and expenditure at the turn of the century were found by a descendant among the papers of the Secretary to the Commission and were sent to the Queen, to her joy. Clifford Smith was thus able to identify and catalogue the makers of many items in the Royal Collection.

But in July 1914 all domestic and political concerns were overshadowed as Britain was drawn irrevocably into the First World War. In the summer of 1914 few people had foreseen that the bloodiest of wars was about to begin. That it should have started in far away Sarajevo, in the words of Queen Mary, 'beggared belief'.

In June the heir to the Austrian throne, Archduke Franz Ferdinand, and his morganatic wife were assassinated in Sarajevo. On 23 July 1914 Austria, affronted by this, the latest and greatest attack on them by their hostile Slav neighbours, sent an ultimatum with terms that Serbia refused to accept completely. On 28 July Austria declared war on Serbia, which brought in Germany; Russia now mobilized in support of its traditional ally, Serbia. Desperately the British government tried a last-minute appeal to the Russian Tsar: a telegram to him was brought to the King in the early hours of 1 August. This the King signed with slight alterations: he addressed it to his cousin, 'Dear Nicky', and signed it 'Georgy'. It had no effect: before the day was out Russia was at war with Germany. France now came to Russia's support, Germany declared war on France, and by 2 August Europe was in flames. Britain still tried to remain outside the battle, but the old Treaty of London 1839, which had guaranteed British support for Belgium, now had to be confirmed. France begged Britain to come to its defence and, as the King reluctantly conceded, 'we cannot allow France to be smashed'. The King's diary for 4 August 1914 began as always with the sailor's look at the weather.

Warm, showers and windy . . . I held a Council at 10.45 to declare war on Germany, it is a terrible catastrophe but it is not our fault. An enormous crowd collected outside the Palace: we went on the balcony before and after dinner. When they declared that war had been declared, the excitement increased and May and I with David went on to the balcony: the cheering was terrific.[30]

The dogs of war had been unleashed with a vengeance.

For the King and Queen it was not only a national disaster but also a personal tragedy. In the international royal family it was civil war – cousin against cousin. The Emperor William II was the son of Edward VII's sister and the grandson of Queen Victoria. It is true that there was not much love lost between them, but they had stood together at the funeral of Edward VII and there had once been a rumour that the Prince of Wales might marry the German Emperor's daughter. But King George V had been much influenced by his Danish mother Queen Alexandra, whose hatred of Germany, roused by the Prussian attack on Schleswig-Holstein in northern Germany, was incandescent, burning throughout her life. Then the German Emperor's treatment of his mother, Queen Victoria's daughter, Vicky, in her last years had enraged King George V. The mistrust of the cousins was mutual: the Emperor was convinced that the King had his spies throughout Germany. Although he came to England in 1911 for the unveiling of Queen Victoria's Memorial outside Buckingham Palace, he startled Admiral Prince Louis of Battenberg with a sudden outburst of violent threats against England.

The Austrian Ambassador in London, Count Mensdorff, was also the King's cousin – and a close friend. The Ambassador was, like King George V, descended from the remarkable Coburg Duke who had sired Prince Albert's father, Queen Victoria's mother and Leopold, King of the Belgians. When Britain and France declared war on Austria, King George V wrote immediately to Mensdorff, who recorded in his journal that the King spoke kindly of their old friendship and hoped later to welcome him back to London.

King George V was also closely connected with the Russian imperial family. The Tsar, Nicholas II, was the son of the King's aunt, Marie. The Tsarina, born Princess Alix of Hesse, was another first cousin. Both were to meet a tragic end in 1918 at the hands of the Bolsheviks. His uncle Alfred, Duke of Edinburgh, had married the daughter of the Tsar Alexander II. His first cousin Marie was Queen of Romania, and Queen Alexandra's brother was King of Greece.

So the network of the royal family stretched across countries and the explosion in Sarajevo ricocheted throughout Europe, dislodging many of their relations from their palaces.

The family ties of the King and Queen with Germany caused great difficulties during the war. There arose in Britain a xenophobic anti-German frenzy, threatening the monarchy itself. Such attacks deeply hurt the King, whose patriotism was deeply felt. When the novelist H. G. Wells attacked the royal family as 'an alien and uninspiring court', the King barked, 'I may be uninspiring but I'll be damned if I am an alien.'[31]

The hostility to all things German finished the career of Admiral Prince Louis of Battenberg, who was born a German and still retained his thick German accent. It did not matter that he had been a British citizen since he was fourteen, nor that he had served with distinction all his adult life in the British Navy, nor that he had married a granddaughter of Queen Victoria. The dogs of war snapped at his heels until he felt he had to resign.

So virulent did the attacks on anything German become that in the end the King had to renounce all 'German degrees, styles, dignities, titles, honours and appellations'. In 1917 a proclamation was issued: henceforward the House of Saxe-Coburg and Gotha was to become the House of Windsor. His Serene Highness, Prince Louis of Battenberg, was created Marquess of Milford Haven and his younger son became Lord Louis Mountbatten. Similarly the Duke of Teck, Queen Mary's brother, took the family name of his grandmother and became Marquess of Cambridge, and his younger brother was made the Earl of Athlone.

It was necessary for the King to stress that if there was any conflict between his loyalty to his country and the members of his foreign family, his country would always win. Fortunately the new name, George of Windsor, had a fine ring. But there was to be an agonizing conflict of loyalties in 1917, when the Tsar of Russia was deposed by the Russian revolutionaries. The Tsar and his family wanted to take refuge in England: after all, Louis Philippe, King of France, and Emperor Napoleon III had retired and died here. But King George V had to make a cruel decision: the Tsar and his family were not welcome in Britain. They remained in Russia and, as is well known, were assassinated.

The King has often been condemned for this rejection of his own cousins. But it must be remembered that when the King made the decision, the Tsar and his family were not in any immediate danger: the Bolsheviks had not yet taken power. It must also be borne in mind that the British throne itself had been much under attack in recent years. Strong and articulate republican voices had been heard in Parliament; virulent articles appeared in the press. The King could not now give support to what was seen as a corrupt, reactionary regime. With a vision of certain demonstrations and turbulence before him, the King felt he had no option. He had to make it clear that the stability of his own country was of paramount importance to him.

*

Throughout the war, and the tumults and stress of the coming years, Queen Mary's work for the preservation of the nation's heritage was not only a labour of love but also an escape to order and beauty in a world that was increasingly dangerous and unstable.

Even during the war some major alterations were made in the Palace. On 8 September 1914 *The Times* reported that

the beginning of extensive interior decoration work at the palace has been hastened by the Queen's desire . . . to give employment to a class of workmen who will be the first to feel the pinch of retrenchment owing to the war. Alterations include a large quantity of parquet flooring specially made by Messrs. Howard of Berners St., a class of work hitherto much in the hands of German makers.[32]

In 1913 Charles Allom, director of the family firm of White Allom, 'Decorative artists to the King and Queen', wrote a long memorandum on their work in Buckingham Palace under the personal direction of Queen Mary. He describes in detail the Queen's years of careful work at the Palace.

It may be well at once to record that Her Majesty takes unusual care in requiring her orders to be carried out as far as possible by British workpeople, and this has helped immensely in the development and discovery of quite unexpected ability in many branches of industrial art.

To mention a few such industries, one at once thinks of goldsmiths, metal workers, enamellers, frame-makers, cabinet-makers, decorators, fan-makers, pottery and china makers, painters, carpet and silk weavers, and others.

On small tables or in cabinets about her apartments, may be seen innumerable examples of the Queen's patronage.

Wherever and whenever an industry has been known to need help by reason of slackness of trade or other causes, Her Majesty has spent much of her time and private money to assist the unemployed, and develop the draughtsmen and craftsmen in the studios, not only by placing orders and taking great personal interest in the work of design, but by lending old works from which to copy or obtain inspiration and knowledge.

He praised the Queen's

very exceptional sense of order, and though years may elapse from the time a thing is neatly put away for possible future use, she remembers exactly where to find it when occasion requires its production. This is the result of a wonderful memory and quite exceptional powers of orderliness and accuracy. Once her attention and interest is given to an art or craft, she rapidly acquires a detailed knowledge of it, in consequence of the ease with which she follows and understands its technical side, and the rapidity with which she acquires knowledge, either by inspection during process of making, or through her reference Library.

He admired her reorganization of rooms according to their period and her search for valuable old furniture in the 'darkness of the Palace stores'.

He described her rooms in detail, including, for example, 'Her Majesty's Bed and Dressing Rooms':

These rooms are in general colour remarkably similar to Her Majesty's Marlborough House suite, and her choice of colour and power of grouping and arranging her furniture, and the very large numbers of personal miniatures, photographs, objets d'art and flowers, with which one associates her surroundings, gives them an unusually bright and cheerful appearance.

The ceilings and cornices of these apartments, as well as the doors, remain exactly as they were left by Queen Alexandra, though the rooms have now been papered with a moiré paper of grey white bordered by an ornamental design of roses and a gilt moulding, which brings the walls into harmony with the rose coloured curtains and pale green grey carpet. The walls are mainly hung with interesting family portraits in water colour.

He was particularly impressed by her structural alteration of her Bedroom.

The room has been structurally altered by throwing the private service corridor into it, and this has led to the occurrence of an unusual feature. The fireplace is left in the centre of the wall, (the openings in which are supported by columns) which was pierced to open up the corridor now utilised for a long range of wardrobes.

Queen Mary needed space for her great collection of exquisite gowns.

To her Boudoir she had brought her light blue silk wall coverings from Marlborough House and the

soft colour that enables it to blend charmingly with the furniture and many cabinets, which contain hundreds of small objets d'art, interesting souvenirs and mementos of many journeys and visits. Collections and purchases of works, representing all phases of the industrial arts in which Her Majesty takes so great an interest are here assembled, yet the colouring of the room, with its curtains of blue silk like the walls and a carpet of soft brown bordered with camel colour on which is a pale blue rose and green design, brings the floor into harmony with the walls and furniture.

Her Boudoir, like all her rooms, was filled with 'beautiful flowers – frequently carnations'.

Next to the Boudoir, the Green Room contained her collection of jade, caskets, jewels, miniatures, 'a very fine collection of biscuit china in an ormolu cabinet . . . and two copies of an old Louis XVI commode'. She had brought the green silk curtains and carpet from Marlborough House.

Queen Mary must have been delighted to find a souvenir of the forgotten, beautiful Hungarian countess, her grandfather's morganatic wife. She discovered

some old lengths of very beautiful brocaded silk of European Chinese design, dating from the early part of the 18th century. The silk came from St. Georgy in Transylvania, the home of the Queen's paternal Grandmother, Countess Claudine Rhedey, wife of Duke Alexander of Württemberg.

The walls have been panelled to frame this brocade, and lacquer mouldings and stiles as well as doors and mantelpiece were made in keeping.

The carpet, specially designed and woven in grey wool, is in keeping with the brocaded wall panels, the ground colour of which has been copied for the curtains, the design of which is reproduced from an old key pattern damask. The curtain valance and architraves are of special interest.

For this room the Queen collected 'very choice old pieces of lacquer work' found in the Palace and elsewhere.

There is a beautiful Chinese lantern in the room, of 18th century enamel work; in its enamelled metal frame some most picturesque panels of painted glass are displayed; from it hang some beautiful pendants of silk linked together with enamelled panels; the prevailing colour of the silk is celadon green. This harmonises perfectly with the room, and adds to its Chinese atmosphere.

In the Chinese Chippendale Room

The panels of the walls are filled with wallpaper of very fine design, the blocks for which were specially cut by Her Majesty's wish, from an old piece of silk in the Chinese taste, which was itself reproduced to form the curtains of the room, and to cover some of the furniture.

Some of the chairs came from the Pavilion at Brighton, designed for the Pavilion when Nash restored and added to it in 1820 and 1821 . . .

Two prominent features of this room are the organ case which has been turned into a bookcase, and the beautiful bookcases, which originally held the barrels for the organ, the design for which may be seen in Pyne's book . . .

The furniture has been covered in some instances with pieces of Chinese silk from some old Mandarin's robes formerly in the Pavilion, and in other cases in the same Chinese Chippendale design silk as has been used for the walls and curtains . . .

At each side of the fireplace are exceptionally fine examples of the Chinese style of painting on glass, which were found in the Palace store room; these have been reframed simply by the Queen's order, and will always remain extremely interesting examples of this work, in which the Brighton Pavilion collection was once so strong . . .

The chandelier hanging from the centre of the ceiling was designed for Her Majesty by her decorative artist, and is quite unique as an example of modern work designed in the feeling of Chinese Chippendale; the centre lights are screened with old Chinese paintings, and in the niches at the bases of the branches, stand small old Chinese porcelain figures.

This room may be said to have received its interest from the fact that its main features are old fragments which Her Majesty has had restored and developed.[33]

It may seem surprising to those who remember the Blitz in the Second World War that in 1914 a new glass roof should have been made for the Picture Gallery. But in 1914 the action was across the Channel, and the threat came in the trenches, not from the air. Only at the end of the war did the Zeppelin bring a foretaste of the future.

In 1914 the problem of the Picture Gallery was regarded as most urgent. Just as Nash's roof of the Royal Pavilion, Brighton had leaked, so did his glass roof of the Buckingham Palace Gallery. The delicately engraved glass was beautiful and 'the hammer beams with pendant arches and seventeen little saucer domes' were graceful, but, once again, Nash had put beauty before practicality. The pictures had not even been properly lit. So in 1914 a new glass roof was built, with a deep frieze decorated with elegant plaster swags, which were echoed in the carved wooden doorcases in the style of Grinling Gibbons, which replaced Nash's white scagliola. Did Queen Mary know that Gibbons, the supreme master of the art of carving, had been introduced to Lord Arlington by John Evelyn in the reign of Charles II and had worked in the house on the site of Buckingham Palace? It is possible: the Queen, who loved history, would have been delighted to salute the old craftsman, but she must have regretted the loss of Nash's elegant engraved glass.

The Gallery walls were hung with new sober green damask chosen by the Queen. She and the King both disliked gold: she had complained to Lady Airlie that there had been a surfeit of 'gilt and orchids' at the Palace in the time of Edward VII. She had admired the old design of a damask at Welbeck Abbey, the Duke of Portland's country seat, and copied it. It was an excellent foil for the superb paintings, now rehung with the advice of Sir Lionel Cust. The new arrangement created 'a perfectly symmetrical hang'[34] in the tradition of Palace rooms since the sixteenth century.

The Queen paid special attention to the room behind the Balcony known as the Centre Room. It was one of the first rooms she rearranged in 1911. It was described in detail at this time.

The furniture and fittings of this room were formerly in Brighton Pavilion or Carlton House . . .

The two finely carved Carrara marble mantels, richly mounted with ormolu, & Chinese figures mounted in niches in the jambs, with the grates & richly mounted fenders and dogs were formerly in Brighton Pavilion.

231

On these mantels are two rare clocks by Vulliamy and candelabra, the one on the right on entering is a striking clock in an ormolu case carried on the back of a beautiful model of a bull in bronze, with a female figure on each side & surmounted by an ormolu figure with sprays of flowers, the whole mounted on a green base containing a bird organ. Vulliamy 1817. This clock formerly stood in the Library at Brighton Pavilion . . .

In 1923 the Queen supervised its redecoration, and as the memorandum notes,

This Room was re-decorated by Messrs White Allom & Co.

Three pairs of new green silk Curtains, the applied Chinese design embroidered panels were made from old silk found in the Stores.

Three new pelmets & three pair of rope holders.

Six panels of yellow Chinese embroidered silk, found in Stores.

Three new giltwood cornice poles with carved dragon ends.

Six giltwood banner poles with carved dragon ends.

Five panels of white lacquer as fitted in doors & overdoor, found in Stores.

Three new, native wood oblong tables, one fitted with a panel of white lacquer, found in Stores.

Four new, reeded wood pedestals.

A bamboo tray top Table was placed here.

The furniture was cleaned and re-upholstered in Chinese silk, from old silk found in Stores.

Two Chinese State junks, were transferred from the Principal Corridor.

The China was re-arranged.

The Carpet was cleaned.[35]

But, after the charismatic Edward VII and the magical beauty of Queen Alexandra, King George V and Queen Mary seemed a dull pair indeed. The King, gruff and unsmiling, moved stiffly through his noble duties. To his critics he would rap, 'a sailor does not smile on duty'.[36]

Queen Mary was equally unbending, a formidable figure in her singularly outdated clothes. Talking to her, the diarist Chips Channon remarked, was 'like addressing a cathedral'. In fact, Queen Mary would have liked to follow the fashion suitable for wartime and shorten her skirts, but the King frowned on such a sartorial revolution. Mabell, Countess of Airlie, remembered,

Having been gifted with perfect legs, she [Queen Mary] once tentatively suggested to me in the nineteen-twenties that we might both shorten our skirts by a modest two or three inches but we lacked the courage to do it until eventually I volunteered to be the guinea pig. I appeared at Windsor one day in a slightly shorter dress than usual, the plan being that if His Majesty made no unfavourable comment the Queen would follow my example.

The next morning she had to report failure. The King on being asked whether he had liked Lady Airlie's new dress had replied decisively, 'No I didn't. It was too short.' So I had my hem let down with all speed and the Queen remained faithful to her long full skirts.[37]

Had it not been for the First World War they might well have remained remote, unbending figures, frozen in outmoded costume and ceremonial in a somewhat forbidding Palace. But the war drew them out, giving them the chance to meet their people at work and at home, and to show their genuine concern and humanity. The Queen's unchanging style, with her toques and long skirts, became reassuring – a symbol of stability in a shaken world. Ordinary women, visited by the Queen in their kitchens, were surprised and warmed by her understanding of their problems. As she toured the hospitals, her eagle eye missed no detail and her advice was always common-sense and practical. It was not enough to bring sympathy to the limbless; the Queen realized how important it was to give wounded men their independence. So she encouraged research into rehabilitation and took particular interest in the workshops at Roehampton and Brighton where artificial limbs were made.

During the war the sheer hard work and dedication to duty of the King and Queen became appreciated. When the King went to the battlefront in France, the soldiers who met him in the trenches were glad of his undemonstrative sympathy. His courage was tested when, on 28 October 1915, he was thrown from his horse while visiting men of the Royal Flying Corps near the village of Hesdigneul. His horse had been trained to accept the gunfire and drumbeats, but not cheering men. It reared up like a rocket and came over on top of the King. He was taken back to England in great pain and was later discovered to have broken a bone in his pelvis, from which he never completely recovered. The accident did not improve his notoriously short temper.

As for the Queen, there were times when even her phenomenal energy flagged, for her programme was punishing. During the King's convalescence she took his place at many of his engagements as well. On 8 November 1915, for example, she inspected the troops on Salisbury Plain.

When the King recovered and began again his tours of workshops, factories and shipyards throughout the country, Queen Mary went too, and the King valued her support. He wrote to her after a particularly gruelling tour of the north – Newcastle, Liverpool and Barrow-in-Furness:

I can't ever express my deep gratitude to you my darling May, for the splendid way in which you are helping me during these terrible, strenuous and anxious times. Very often I feel in despair and if it wasn't for you I should break down.[38]

These tours together brought them close to the people. While other European thrones were rocking, King George V and Queen Mary took the Palace to the country and mutual understanding brought a new stability to the throne.

From the beginning of the war, the Queen was determined that women's voluntary work should be properly organized. She had learned much from her mother Mary Adelaide, Duchess of Teck, who had worked tirelessly for many charitable organizations.

The war stretched the Queen to the limit, but it also widened her horizons, bringing her into contact with people she would otherwise never have met.

During the war Queen Mary was to entertain Labour and trade union women at Buckingham Palace. This caused some surprise, but in the past she had accompanied her mother on expeditions to the East End of London, where the enormous figure of 'Fat Mary' was greeted with affection. As a girl the Queen had helped her mother in her charitable projects and had been much influenced by their friend the wealthy philanthropist Baroness Burdett-Coutts, who had always come to their aid when they were 'in short street'. Her kind of charity, practical and productive, had made a lasting impression on Princess May.

At the beginning of the war, as she recorded in her diary, the Queen 'set to work to make plans to help existing organisations with offers of clothing, money, etc'.[39] The Red Cross had its headquarters at Devonshire House; the National Relief Fund – backed by the Prince of Wales – was based at York House; and the King allowed the Queen to use the State Apartments at St James's Palace for her 'Relief Clothing Guild'. She could now call on her own organization, the Needlework Guild – now called 'Queen Mary's Needlework Guild' – which her mother had run from White Lodge in the old days, and which was now well organized in Surrey and London.

In the first years of the reign the Queen had been mainly concerned with the preservation and conservation of all that was interesting and beautiful in the past. Influenced by Aunt Augusta, she had little patience with, or understanding of, the radical politics that, as she saw it, produced disorder and threatened the throne, although she had also seen the result of blind reaction in other countries and accepted the need for change.

Queen Mary had, however, always been exceedingly brisk in her condemnation of those who would change society by revolutionary or violent means. Her own dedication to the monarchy was total: its protection and preservation came before any personal considerations. Therefore the fiercely republican attacks by some of the early socialists and trade union leaders were deeply offensive. She had not given much thought to political theory, and had been unaware of distinctions between Fabians, Christian Socialists, Marxists – all were equally dangerous.

But Queen Mary was always ready to learn, and on 17 August 1914 an announcement came from Buckingham Palace that a new committee was to be set up of industrial experts and representatives of working-class women unemployed on account of the war. Out of this grew the 'Queen's Work for Women Fund', which was to be a subsidiary of the National Relief Fund. To administer this fund a new committee was set up called the 'Central Committee for Women's Training and Employment', under the Chairmanship of the bright young Lady Crewe. To this the Queen gave her enthusiastic support, and through the work with this committee her horizons were widened, again introducing her to women she would never otherwise have met.

Many unexpected friendships were forged in the war, crossing the boundaries of class and political persuasions, and such was the surprising partnership of Queen Mary and the Scottish trade unionist Mary Mac-Arthur, who was the Honorary Secretary of the new committee. In 1914 the Queen asked Lady Crewe to bring Mary MacArthur to the Palace. Eyebrows were lifted; royal advisers murmured disapproval. Mary Mac-Arthur was the wife of Will Anderson, who, in 1914, was Chairman of the Labour Party: but she was also, as Pope-Hennessy writes, 'the recognised champion, indeed the saviour of the exploited working women of Britain, the Florence Nightingale of women and children in the Sweated Industries. She had organised the Sweated Industries Exhibition of 1906.'⁴⁰ Queen Mary would certainly have heard of her work, for, when Princess of Wales, she had toured this exhibition on her return from India. She had surprised her entourage then by her compassionate interest in and knowledge of that world, to them as foreign as the villages of India.

Mary MacArthur came from a well-to-do middle-class Ayrshire family, but she had taken up the cause of overworked and underpaid women. She was only twenty-six when she organized the Sweated Industries Exhibition, but her drive and energy, combined with an irresistible charm, had already made her a leader of the women's trade union movement. She was the champion of women who stitched night and day to make blouses for 6d. that were sold in Bond Street for 25s., or who sweated over forges in their own backyards to make chains for 7s. a week; and she was the leader of a strike of women jam-makers in Bermondsey. She made the government listen and persuaded it to set up an enquiry into women's working conditions.

Now she came to meet Queen Mary in her elegant room in Bucking-ham Palace. Here, surrounded by the Queen's priceless possessions, unintimidated, the young Scots woman spoke directly, with clarity and common sense. The Queen listened and was deeply impressed. It was indeed a meeting of minds, the beginning of a working partnership that lasted until Mary MacArthur's early death in 1921.

The trade union leader spoke of the devastating effect of the war on working women, and how voluntary work by well-intentioned ladies was taking the bread from those who depended on piecework in their homes. 'Do everything in your power,' Mary MacArthur had told an influential friend, 'to stop these women knitting.'[41] The Queen immediately understood the problem, and that the solution was to provide work not charity.

Mary MacArthur was astonished and delighted at the Queen's understanding. She returned to the offices of the Women's Trade Union League in Gray's Inn Road excitedly, telling her colleagues, 'Here is someone who *can* help and who *means* to help.' This was the first of many meetings in Buckingham Palace which became known in the Labour movement as the 'strange case of Mary M. and Mary R.'. Though they kept their differing political attitudes, each recognized the humanitarian aims and practical ability of the other.

'The Queen does understand and grasp the whole situation from a Trade Union point of view,' Mary MacArthur told her colleagues. Indeed Queen Mary's ever-enquiring mind positively welcomed this new chance to expand. She asked for a list of books on social issues and listened patiently while Mary MacArthur, as she said, 'positively lectured the Queen on the inequality of the classes, the injustice of it, – I fear I talked too much'.[42]

One of Queen Mary's friends was asked once what were her chief qualities: 'humanity and breadth of mind' came the answer.[43] Her friendship with the remarkable trade union leader is a good example of this. Had she not been Queen undoubtedly she would have served on the Committee for Women's Training and Employment; as it was she gave her patronage, studied all the reports of its meetings and where possible gave her help. Her friendship with Mary MacArthur continued after the war, and helped both King and Queen to understand a little better the Labour politicians who came into power in 1924. Queen Mary would have liked Mary MacArthur to have been given an honour in the post-war lists, but since Mary MacArthur's husband had been making fiery, radical speeches, this was not thought suitable. As Pope-Hennessy wrote, it was probably on the advice of 'Lloyd George, who loathed Mary MacArthur and all her work'.*44

During the war Buckingham Palace welcomed other unusual visitors. The gardens were opened to wounded and convalescent officers and for three days in March 1916 the Queen gave a series of entertainments to 2,000 wounded soldiers and sailors in the Riding School. Queen Mary wrote to Aunt Augusta:

They had tea first in the Coach Houses, members of our family presiding at each table and being helped by the ladies and gentlemen of our household and various friends of ours. The entertainment consisted of various artists, acrobats, conjurers etc. an excellent choir singing songs of which men knew the chorus and sung them most lustily. How you would have liked being present, it was all so informal, friendly and nice.45

It is difficult, however, to imagine Aunt Augusta at home among the lusty singers. The Grand Duchess of Mecklenburg-Strelitz belonged to a world that was passing. The war was breaking down the barriers that had protected her all of her life, which was now nearing its end. Her last years had been sad and isolated as she was among the enemies of her native land. On 6 December 1916, Queen Mary wrote in her diary, 'my most beloved Aunt Augusta died yesterday morning after a month's illness . . . A great grief to me, having been devoted to each other.'

But personal grief, however great, had to be endured silently. The King had other problems. '"G. spent a busy day interviewing ministers," [Queen Mary's] diary continues. "Mr. Bonar Law informed G. that he was unable to form a Government & G. sent for Mr Lloyd George & asked him to do so."46

---

*In July 1924, as patroness of the Mary MacArthur Holiday Homes for Working Women, the Queen opened the first Home at Ongar. She described her visit there to Lady Crewe:

I was so glad to be able, in this way, to show my deep appreciation of poor Mary MacArthur's untiring work on behalf of my 'Work for Women' fund during the war. The visit there gave me the opportunity of meeting those workers with whom I do not often come in contact . . . mats for the bedrooms have already been chosen and I am also sending a few pictures to adorn the walls.

The war that in 1914 had been expected to be over by Christmas dragged on painfully. Gradually, in spite of xenophobic suspicion, the King and Queen were becoming accepted and respected. For most of the war they stayed in Buckingham Palace, symbols of stability, courage and self-sacrifice.

The King was determined that the Palace should set a good example. When David Lloyd George, his Prime Minister, told him that munition workers were drinking too much and hindering the war effort, he forbade his Household to drink wine, spirits or beer. The American Ambassador, Walter Page, stayed with the King there for a night and was surprised to be given 'only so much bread, one egg and lemonade'.[47]

Although, unlike in the Second World War, air raids were infrequent, there were occasional Zeppelin attacks. Buckingham Palace had the rudimentary protection of a wire-mesh net over the roof, but otherwise air-raid precautions were not taken seriously. The sinister, slow progress of a Zeppelin overhead was watched with a mixture of fear and interest. 'At 8 we heard that 3 Zeppelins were coming,' the Queen recorded in her diary in October 1915; but at 9.30 p.m. they were still sitting in the Palace

in G.'s room when we heard a distant report (presumably a bomb) so we went on to the balcony when the gun in Green Park began firing and searchlights were turned on . . . We did not see the Zeppelin but Derek saw it quite plainly from his house in Buck. Gate. We then heard some bombs being dropped and were told later that some had fallen in the Strand and elsewhere, killing 8 people and injuring 34. All quiet by 10.15.[48]

The next day they visited the victims of the raid, 'one boy of 17 dying having had his lung pierced by a bit of a bomb. Most sad.'[49]

The Queen had been for some years involved in the work of the voluntary nursing organizations, including the Board of Queen Alexandra's Imperial Military Nursing Service, and also she was a County President of the Red Cross. But it was not enough for her to encourage their work and to visit the wounded in hospitals. She was determined to cross the Channel and share the danger behind the battle lines. So, in the summer of 1917, her devoted Lady of the Bedchamber, Lady Airlie, went with the King and Queen to France. In her memoir *Thatched with Gold*, she described the visit. 'Sitting in the garden of Buckingham Palace while the King worked in the tent erected there, the Queen explained [to Lady Airlie] that she wanted to see for herself the conditions in the hospitals there.' They left Dover on 3 July with an escort of destroyers and seaplanes. 'The ship rolled a great deal, but the Queen walked gracefully about the deck . . . while I staggered on behind being loudly rated by the King – to the delight of the sailors – for not keeping my legs apart.'[50]

While the King toured the battlefields, the Queen and Lady Airlie stayed for ten days at the Château de Beaurepaire, near Montreuil. From this base they toured hospitals, casualty stations, ammunition dumps – 'the Queen's energy never flagged'. They arrived at the headquarters of the Women's Auxiliary Army Corps at the same time as a trainload of men just back from the front, 'covered with mud, bleary-eyed and haggard from fatigue'. There were tremendous cheers as the Queen quietly crossed to speak to them. She and Lady Airlie would have gone to the battle front, twelve miles away, had the King not expressly forbidden it. As it was

The most harrowing sight of our tour was the battlefield . . . once fertile and smiling now a tumbled mass of blackened earth . . . we climbed over a mound composed of German dead . . . Scattered everywhere in the ineffable desolation were the pathetic reminders of human life – rifles fallen from dead hands, old water bottles, iron helmets. . . The Queen's face was ashen and her lips were tightly compressed. I felt that like me she was afraid of breaking down. But she did not: and the men appreciated her strength and silent sympathy. Those who returned did not forget.[51]

When the Queen received wounded soldiers at Buckingham Palace she too remembered. The soldiers who met the King and Queen on the battlefields of France felt the genuine concern and sympathy behind the stiff exteriors. This shared experience was to be remembered in the difficult days ahead.

In 1911, after the Coronation, Prince Edward had undergone the ceremony of investiture as Prince of Wales at Caernarvon. Here, to his embarrassment, dressed in what he described as 'a fantastic costume . . .

of white satin breeches and a mantle and surcoat of purple velvet edged with ermine', he listened while Winston Churchill, as Home Secretary, 'mellifluously' proclaimed his titles; then he 'delivered the Welsh sentences' Lloyd George had taught him. It was at this time that he made a significant discovery about himself: 'while I was prepared to fulfil my rôle in all this pomp and ritual, I recoiled from anything that tended to set me up as a person requiring homage.'[52]

He was 'desperately anxious to be treated exactly like any other boy of my age'. The King understood this, and as part of his training allowed him to go to sea for three months in the battleship *HMS Hindustan* as a midshipman. But after that, the King and Queen decided he must give up the Navy, which was 'too specialised', and take educational trips to France and Germany to 'learn the languages and study their politics'; and then to his dismay the King told him that he must go to Oxford University, though as he himself said he 'had neither the mind nor the will for books'.

In France, thinly disguised as 'Lord Chester', he overcame some of his shyness, thanks to the care of his grandfather's old friend the Marquis de Breteuil, who was a 'bon viveur, a dilettante of the arts and of politics, and as much at home shooting tigers as he was in the exclusive salons of Paris'.

It was with some regret that he left France for Oxford, where he continued to study French and worked to improve his German. But, he wrote, Oxford 'failed to make me studious'[53] – a verdict with which Sir Herbert Warren, President of his college, Magdalen, agreed.

When war was declared he was twenty and he begged to be allowed to serve. He joined the Grenadier Guards, training as an infantry officer. The King and the War Office were most unwilling to allow him to go to France, but he badgered them until they agreed.

He bearded Lord Kitchener himself in his office at Whitehall. '"What does it matter if I am killed?" he asked, "I have four brothers."' The Prince never saw himself, even at this time, as indispensable to the monarchy. It was explained that the threat was not that he would be killed but that he would be taken prisoner. In France the Prince, not satisfied with desk work at Headquarters British Expeditionary Force, frequently walked or cycled up to the front.

On one occasion he was at the front line and, during an attack, he took shelter in the trenches – only to find on his return to his car that it had been shelled and his driver killed. He had seen with his own eyes the horrors of trench warfare, an agony that could never be adequately described to those at home. The first-hand experience of war must be remembered when, as Edward VIII and later as Duke of Windsor, he tried to make peace with the Germans.

Queen Mary was understandably proud of her eldest son, who, in his bright morning, charmed so many other observers. Esher, who saw him at war, described him then: 'his clear skin is tanned and this throws into relief the unusually bright and clear blue eyes.'[54] (Esher, always susceptible to boyish charm and beauty, was more than a little in love with the young Prince of Wales.)

The Queen's second son, Bertie, was also serving, in the Navy. When war was declared, King George V's last thoughts on the fateful evening of 4 August had been, 'Please God it may soon be over . . . and that He will protect dear Bertie's life.'[55]

The mothers Queen Mary met as she toured throughout England with the King knew that, like them, the Queen too feared for her sons' safety and shared the agony of watching and waiting for that telegram.

On 11 November 1918 the end of the Great War was celebrated in a wild frenzy of joy. Once again the balcony at Buckingham Palace was the focus of the nation's enthusiasm as night after night crowds streamed down the Mall calling for the King and Queen.

The Prince of Wales heard the 'shindy' from his rooms overlooking the courtyard. As the King and Queen slipped back into the old formal pattern of life, for him Buckingham Palace once more seemed a prison. After an evening of boredom with his parents, he would frequently climb out of the Palace after they had gone to bed. Eventually he persuaded the King to give him York House, at St James's Palace, as a home of his own. Here Finch, his old friend from childhood, became his major domo, watching over him through his love affairs, and was at his back during his many official visits abroad and at home.

*

It was obvious to King George V and Queen Mary, and to the Prince of Wales himself, that in the post-war world the royal family had to work to keep the monarchy in existence; but they all had differing approaches. The Prince wanted to keep the wartime accessibility of the monarchy; the King, supported by Fritz Ponsonby, thought this dangerous. 'The monarchy', said Ponsonby, 'must always remain on a pedestal,' and though the King agreed that the war made it possible for the Prince to mix with people as never before, he must, he said, never forget his position. Remembering the effect his foreign progresses had had on himself, especially the magnificence of their visit to India, the King wanted the Prince of Wales to tour the Empire, not only because it would be appreciated, but because it would touch the Prince with the magic of the monarchy. As the King's biographer, Harold Nicolson, wrote, Queen Victoria had become a legend throughout the Empire, 'invested with almost divine qualities'. After the tour of India before their accession, King George V and Queen Mary had realized the 'power and symbolism' of this great office. Thenceforth the King

had no doubt about the importance of the monarchy and the heavy responsibilities of a democratic sovereign . . . He saw then the extent to which the whole Empire might stand or fall by the personal example set from the Throne, and to assure the integrity of that example he was to sacrifice much that men hold dear.[56]

The King, knowing how important his own happy marriage had been, hoped that the Prince of Wales would find the same support from a good wife. But the market for foreign royal brides had now closed down. As the Prime Minister told the King, the country would not now accept a German bride for the Prince of Wales. Unfortunately the Prince was showing a tendency to fall in love with married women such as Freda Dudley Ward, the wife of a Liberal MP, and showed no signs of settling down. Whereas on 28 February 1922 Mary, the Princess Royal, made a happy marriage to Henry, Viscount Lascelles, and went to live in Yorkshire.

On 26 April 1923 Bertie, now Duke of York, married a wife who had immediately enchanted the King and Queen, and who for the rest of her life has captured the heart of the nation with her charm and beauty. Lady Elizabeth Bowes-Lyon, youngest daughter of the 14th Earl of Strathmore, was, Chips Channon believed, 'more gentle, lovely and exquisite than any woman alive'.[57] Lady Elizabeth was the first commoner to marry a second-in-line to the throne since James II married Anne Hyde, but she was descended from the ancient kings of Scotland. Brought up in a large and happy family by exceptional parents, she had a strong, enduring spirit behind her delicate beauty. She has never forgotten her Scottish inheritance.

On that chill April morning, as her biographer Dorothy Laird records,

because she was not yet a royal person Lady Elizabeth rode to her wedding in a state landau, modestly escorted by four mounted Metropolitan Policemen and the troops lining the streets did not present arms to the bride on her journey to the Abbey.[58]

The sun came out as the bride entered the Abbey. She wore a simple medieval-style dress gleaming with silver and veiled in old lace. Then, with a gesture so characteristic, she left her father's side and laid her bouquet of white roses upon the Tomb of the Unknown Warrior. It had been planned that she should lay her bouquet at the Cenotaph on her return from the Abbey. Perhaps her spontaneous gesture was in memory of her brother Fergus, killed at Loos.

The Duke and Duchess of York returned to the Palace through cheering crowds and made the expected appearance on the balcony, joined by King George V, Queen Alexandra and the bride's parents, and Queen Mary 'magnificently regal in an aquamarine blue and silver dress and glorious diamonds'.[59]

For this wedding there was no great gathering of German relations – the 'royal mob', as Queen Victoria had called them. A modest 123 guests sat down in the State Dining Room and the Supper Room at round tables decorated with pink tulips and white lilac. The King's toast to the 'health, long life and happiness of the bride and bridegroom' was drunk in silence – according to royal custom. In the Green Drawing Room overlooking the courtyard stood the wedding cake: nine feet high, with four tiers, decorated with coats of arms and topped with symbols of love and peace. The little Duchess could scarcely reach to cut it.

As the open landau left the Palace with its escort of cavalry, the Prince of Wales and his brothers threw rose petals over the bride and groom. One reporter noted that the new Duchess of York wore 'a going away dress of dove grey crêpe romain . . . her going away hat a small affair in tones of brown with upturned brim and a feather mount at the side. She made this choice so that those in the crowd may not have their view impeded by a brim.'[60] A characteristic touch!

The new Duchess of York quickly established a rare empathy with King George V, understanding the kindness under his gruff manner. For her he even made exceptions to his rigid rules. To be a minute late for meals was, in the King's eyes, a mortal sin, to be met by thunderous rebuke; but when the Duchess of York was a few minutes late on one occasion, he apologized, saying they must have sat down earlier that day.

The wedding of the Yorks was for the King, as he said, 'a gleam of sunshine' in a black period. There was another wedding held at Buckingham Palace itself: in 1935 the Duke of Gloucester married Lady Alice Montagu-Douglas-Scott there rather than at the Abbey because of the recent death of her father the Duke of Buccleuch.

But there were graver concerns than weddings. The political disturbances of the period weighed heavily on a King whose health was not sound at the best of times. On the one hand, for well-to-do bright young things it was an age of frivolity; but at the same time there was deep disillusion amongst those who returned from war to find themselves homeless and unemployed. Abroad, the old world was breaking up. Monarchies and dukedoms had disappeared. In Russia the Tsar and his family had been assassinated. The German Emperor was in exile. In Germany dictator Adolf Hitler was gaining power; while in Italy Prime Minister Mussolini swaggered, and in 1935 invaded Abyssinia (now Ethiopia).

For the rest of his life the King continued to wrestle with the problem of Ireland. His Buckingham Palace Conference, convened before the war to try to solve this, had been interrupted by the war, but now he tried again. In June 1921, when he went to Belfast to open the new Northern Ireland Parliament, he made a ringing appeal for peace, concluding, 'the future of Ireland lies in the hands of my Irish people themselves.' Queen Mary accompanied him, knowing there was danger. Their reward was a thunderous welcome from enormous crowds outside the railway station on their return home.

At home pressure on the King mounted. These were days of bitter divisions, strikes and demonstrations.

At a time of international and national unrest he had a quick succession of prime ministers, which increased the weight of responsibility on his shoulders. His relationship with Prime Minister Lloyd George at the end of the war was difficult. As Palmerston had bypassed Queen Victoria, so Lloyd George tended to ignore King George V. He was succeeded briefly by Andrew Bonar Law, who was fighting the cancer that was to destroy him. In May 1923 Bonar Law resigned and Stanley Baldwin, who followed him, called an election in December 1923, which he and his Conservative Party lost.

In the election of January 1924 Baldwin was defeated by James Ramsay MacDonald, who brought in the first Labour administration – a minority government, relying on Liberal support. There were apprehensions on both sides: the Labour ministers were inexperienced; the King, with memories of his assassinated relations, feared revolution. In the event the King found his new Labour ministers friendly and refreshing, and they found the King determined to be above party and to defend their constitutional rights.

Surprisingly, the King and his ministers established a good relationship – the King liked the directness and salty humour of the men in the Cabinet who had come from such different backgrounds. He welcomed the fierce patriotism of the new Colonial Secretary, J. H. Thomas, whose outrageous jokes set off the King in roars of appreciative laughter. In his turn, Thomas thought the King was 'by God a great human creature'.[61]

The ministers were surprised to find the King so human. The new Lord Privy Seal, J. R. Clynes, later recalled,

As we stood waiting for his Majesty, amid the gold and crimson magnificence of the Palace, I could not help marvelling at the strange turn of Fortune's wheel, which had brought MacDonald, the starveling clerk, J. H. Thomas the engine driver, Henderson the foundry labourer and Clynes the mill-hand to this pinnacle beside the man whose forebears had been kings for so many generations. We were perhaps somewhat embarrassed but the quiet little man whom we addressed as your Majesty swiftly put us at our ease. I have no doubt he had read the wild statements of some of our extremists and I think he wondered to what he was committing his people. I had expected to find him unbending, instead he was kindness and sympathy itself.[62]

King George V liked MacDonald and found him 'quite straight': 'he impressed me very much.' On 22 January 1924, the King wrote in his diary 'he wishes to do the right thing. Today 23 years ago dear Grandmama died. I wonder what she would have thought of a Labour Government,' and MacDonald wrote in his diary, 'The King has never seen me as a minister without making me feel that he was also seeing me as a friend.'[63]

Since this first Labour government had no overall majority, the King and his advisers considered that it would not be able to pursue extremist policies. In fact the government did not last long, thanks to the publication of the forged Zinoviev letter which, it was claimed, called on British Communists to persuade members of the Labour Party to work for armed revolution.

MacDonald's government fell, and in November 1924 Baldwin was returned again. But the new ministers caused the King trouble. Winston Churchill at the Home Office handled the miners' strike of 1926 with insensitive vigour, causing lasting resentment.

King George had a heated argument with Lord Durham ... about a week before the strike was called. When the King said he was sorry for the miners, Lord Durham replied that they were a damned lot of revolutionaries. At that his Majesty exploded, 'Try living on their wages before you judge them,' and some high words followed.[64]

It was business as usual at Buckingham Palace during the strike. Only the changed uniform of the sentries at the gates marked the emergency. Khaki and forage caps replaced red coats and bearskins.

The strike ended on 13 May but as Lady Airlie wrote, 'There was no jubilation over the defeat of the strikers . . . As Lord Salisbury said in the House, "it was not a time for triumph." '[65]

But sixteen days later there was cause for celebration. The Duke and Duchess of York brought their first baby to be christened in the Private Chapel at Buckingham Palace. She was named Elizabeth after her mother and

cried so much all through the ceremony that immediately after it her old fashioned nurse dosed her well from a bottle of dill water – to the surprise of the modern young mothers present and the amusement of her uncle the Prince of Wales.[66]

The King, low and depressed, longed for peace. The accumulated stress of this period undoubtedly helped to cause the serious illness which almost killed him in November 1928. On 21 November Lord Dawson of Penn, the King's surgeon, was summoned to the Palace and, realizing that they were in for a serious illness, sent for the young pathologist Dr Lionel Whitby, whose tests showed the King was suffering from a streptococcal infection of the chest.

Just as Buckingham Palace had been turned into a hospital before, when Edward VII had an operation for appendicitis, so now a room in the Belgian Suite was prepared and an X-ray machine was delivered in a lorry and the cable brought through the King's bedroom window.

In the makeshift hospital in Buckingham Palace Queen Mary was a tower of strength: Queen Alexandra had been brave, but Queen Mary was 'as practical as Florence Nightingale'. As the King's biographer Kenneth Rose recorded,

When Dawson asked for moistened muslin to filter the air of the sick room, the Queen knew . . . where to find it. She led Dawson along corridors and up back stairs to a small room at the top of the Palace; made him climb on a chair and hand down a bundle from a cupboard, untied it to reveal some curtains of Queen Victoria's which years ago she had thriftily brought down from Balmoral and stowed away.[67]

The King's chest was X-rayed – it was the first time X-rays had been available to a patient outside the big hospitals – but it failed to show the cause of the trouble. By the afternoon of 12 December, all hope seemed gone. But at the crucial moment, when the King's life was slipping away, Lord Dawson of Penn came into the room. 'Will you give me a syringe,' he said. 'I think I will make one more try to find that fluid.' [68] By intuition he found the abcess, inserted the syringe and drew off the poisonous fluid.

It took months of convalescence – a Mediterranean cruise, three months at Bognor and weeks at Windsor – before the King recovered. Lord Dawson had shown his skill, but 'It had been', said the forthright Labour minister J. H. Thomas, 'his bloody guts that pulled him through.' [69]

In 1931, the King lost his faithful friend and secretary, Lord Stamfordham, who died, still in harness, at the age of eighty-one. Lord Stamfordham had been in royal service since 1880 when, as Colonel Arthur Bigge, he had been appointed Assistant Private Secretary to Queen Victoria. He had been brought to the Queen's notice by the Empress Eugénie, wife of the deposed French Emperor, Napoleon III. She had been much taken by the kindness and sensitivity of the young officer Arthur Bigge, who had accompanied her to South Africa to visit the scene of the death of her son, the Prince Imperial, during the Zulu War. Bigge had been a close friend and fellow officer of the Prince Imperial, though he had been in hospital during the action in which the Prince had been killed. Eugenie had warmly praised Bigge to Queen Victoria, who had therefore brought him on to her staff. From then until her death he had been a great source of strength to her. After her death, Edward VII made him Private Secretary to George, Prince of Wales, whom he continued to serve faithfully when the Prince became King.

As Kenneth Rose points out, 'Most courtiers of the Victorian Age came of aristocratic family; Grey and Ponsonby, Phipps and Knollys. Bigge was the son of a Northumbrian parson.' [70] Slight of stature and unassuming in appearance, he was, nevertheless, physically and morally brave. His comparatively humble origins in no way gave him a sense of inferiority among his aristocratic colleagues. Though charming in his dealings with high and low, he could be extremely firm and outspoken – as he was, for example, to Edward, Prince of Wales. And though his political judgement was by no means always infallible, it was always given honestly and directly, after clear and careful thought. He could always be relied upon to tell the truth, however disagreeable.

To the end he kept the habit, acquired in the reign of Queen Victoria, of writing much of his immense correspondence entirely by hand. Queen Victoria had disliked typewritten communication: even after the late 1880s, when typewriters were introduced into government offices, she insisted on having all communications in handwriting. This was especially difficult in her last years when her eyesight failed. Then Bigge learned to write large in thick black ink.

To King George V, Bigge was invaluable. Many monarchs have been deeply indebted to their Private Secretaries, but perhaps none acknowledged the debt so movingly as gruff King George V. On Christmas Day 1907, when he was still Prince of Wales, he wrote to Bigge:

Fancy, how quickly time flies, it is nearly seven years already since you came to me. You have nothing to thank us for, it is all the other way and we have indeed much to thank you for. As for myself during these seven years you have made my life comparatively an easy one, by your kind help and assistance and entire devotion to work connected with me. What would have happened to me if you had not been there to prepare and help me with my speeches, I can hardly write a letter of any importance without your assistance. I fear sometimes I have lost my temper with you and often been very rude, but I am sure you know me well enough by now to know that I did not mean it . . .

I offer you my thanks from the bottom of my heart. I am a bad hand at saying what I feel, but I thank God that I have a friend like you, in whom I have the fullest confidence and from whom I know on all occasions I shall get the best and soundest advice whenever I seek it.[71]*

While at home and abroad there was 'change and decay', riots and revolution, at Buckingham Palace life had slipped back into the old formal round. The traditional protocol was still observed: above all the King and Queen expected correct formal clothes to be worn to the Palace, and the King's eagle eye spotted immediately any discrepancy,

---

*When Bigge's grandson, Michael Adeane, became Private Secretary to Queen Elizabeth II he brought with him a long family tradition of loyal and distinguished service to the Crown.

such as a medal wrongly placed. 'Have you come in the suite of the American Ambassador?' he would ask if any of his family or household appeared in unfamiliar garb. The King dressed as he had always done: his trousers were always creased at the side. He thought turn-ups were vulgar; 'Is it raining outside?' was his customary query – as though the offender had appeared with his trouser legs rolled up.

There were some relaxations, but the King expected his ministers to wear top hats and morning coats when calling on him in the daytime, and white tie and knee breeches at dinner. Even when he and the Queen dined alone he would wear white tie and his Garter Star, and Queen Mary would always be splendid with jewels and a tiara. Old customs were still kept: forks were always laid with their prongs facing downwards, a relic of the days when gentlemen wore lace cuffs in which the forks might get entangled.

Before the war visitors to the Palace had been happy to conform, but the younger officers who had slept in their clothes in the rain-soaked trenches and drunk out of tin mugs found the formality of the Palace stifling.

Ever since the reign of Queen Victoria much time and diplomatic energy had been expended on questions of protocol and, particularly, what should be worn to Buckingham Palace. Republicans, both American and British, had been unduly exercised about what they considered to be the outward signs of subservience and the same objections to wearing court costume had been made by some British radicals and socialists over the years. When John Bright, in 1868, a minister in Gladstone's government, insisted that as a working man he felt it morally wrong to wear court costume. Queen Victoria accepted his compromise – an old-fashioned black velvet suit. She even permitted him to stand instead of kneeling when he kissed hands.

Correct dress was also excessively important to both King George V and Queen Mary: it was as though they needed the rigid carapace of royalty to protect their vulnerability.

When, in 1924, the first Labour government had taken office, many of the new ministers felt that their clothes were symbols of what they were, and were unwilling to conform. When the new Prime Minister,

Ramsay MacDonald, led his team to the Palace to kiss hands, Court officials were apprehensive. What would these new men wear? Ministers were expected to receive their seals of office from the King wearing frock coats and top hats. Some Labour ministers had such an outfit; Fred Jowett and John Wheatly felt they had to make a gesture and went to the Palace in their best ordinary clothes, wearing a felt cap and a bowler hat respectively. It was said that this shocked Ramsay MacDonald more than the King, who probably sympathized with their obstinate refusal to change or pretend: if that was their uniform, then they should wear it. So, as Lady Airlie wrote,

The King and Queen adapted themselves without difficulty to the new Labour Government, rather to the surprise of members of their entourage who remembered sulphurous speeches on the subject of the monarchy during the General Election . . . but King George was too fair and openminded to harbour personal prejudices.[72]

In fact the King and his new ministers got on surprisingly well. It must be remembered that the King had met a wide variety of his people during the war; and when Queen Mary entertained the ministers' wives to tea in the Palace she could draw on a long experience of those who lived on the other side of the tracks: Mary MacArthur and her friends had given her a new insight into trade union and Labour people. There were many traditionalists in the Labour Party who found the sight of their colleagues in court garb, wearing swords, shocking. On 12 March 1924 photographs appeared in the newspapers of the new Labour ministers at their first levee. MacDonald was shown in a

long cloak beneath which appeared the tip of a sword. He was wearing trousers with a broad stripe. Two future peers, Mr. Sidney Webb and Mr. Noel Buxton, were very obviously wearing breeches. Mr. Tom Griffiths wore the same style of dress as the Prime Minister with a plumed hat.[73]

The Member for Pontypool, who had earned 4d. a day at a tin-plate works, and his colleagues were perfectly prepared to wear fancy dress if they had to – provided it did not cost much, for MPs received no salary at this time. After all, the hats were no funnier than helmets or other working gear. But the photographs created excessive resentment from both sides of the social and political divide.

Nevertheless, although the war had broken down some of the barriers between classes, the King certainly would have had no desire to create a classless society. There were deep, old wounds that would never heal. The miners of South Wales would never forget Churchill's bellicose insensitivity during their strike. Nor did the King forget the Russian Revolution, as Lady Airlie remembered:

Mr Sokolnikov, the first Soviet Ambassador to be appointed to the Court of St James since the Russian Revolution, presented his credentials. The King bitterly resented having to receive him with other ambassadors at a Levée. I was sitting next to his Majesty at dinner in the spring of 1930 when someone rather tactlessly referred to the new appointment. The King burst out with "What do you think it means to me to be forced to shake hands with a man of the party that murdered my cousin?" Neither Ramsay MacDonald, nor Snowden, or even Henderson, would receive him in their houses, but they let me in for it.[74]

The Queen and Lady Airlie treated the new ministers of each government and their wives with unfailing courtesy and genuine kindness. When Elizabeth, Duchess of York, was expecting her second child in the summer of 1930, she decided it should be born at her old home, Glamis Castle in Scotland. The Home Secretary, J. R. Clynes, and the official civil servant, Harry Boyd, by tradition, were expected to be present at the birth. As Clynes told Lady Airlie in some agitation, 'This child is in direct succession to the Throne, and if its birth is not properly witnessed its legal right might be questioned. It has happened before in history.' Then he showed Lady Airlie 'a book which he had brought with him from the Home Office . . . giving an account of the birth of the son of James II and Mary of Modena'.

Rather than allow the two ministers to stay in a cheerless hotel, Lady Airlie invited them to stay with her in her castle near Glamis Castle. A telegraph wire linked the two castles and dispatch riders stood by: but the baby, which was due on 6 August, did not arrive until 21 August. Meanwhile Lady Airlie learned to admire Clynes: 'He was enraptured with the countryside and as his shyness wore off, I discovered under his homely exterior a deeply sensitive mind, touchingly appreciative of beauty.'

Finally the call came – they had only an hour to get there. Boyd was frenetic with agitation.

But Mr. Clynes was calmly waiting at the door in his big coat and Homburg hat . . . a lovely sunset was breaking. He pointed to the sky, 'Just look at that, Boyd, "In such a night did Dido from the walls of Carthage . . ."' He continued the quotation with great feeling till Boyd pushed him into the car. They arrived at Glamis with nearly half an hour to spare.[75]

So Princess Margaret's birth, on a summer night, was witnessed by a Labour minister, preceded by a, somewhat garbled, Shakespearian quotation.

Not all the courtiers had Lady Airlie's intelligent understanding. Many an amusing story – true and apocryphal – went the rounds. They were all the more humorous when told in a Cockney accent, without aitches. One wife was reported to have said at a grand reception at Buckingham Palace: 'Me shoes is tight, me corsets's tight, me 'usband's tight, and I want to go 'ome.' For those who had never met a Labour politician socially before, laughter was a protection: the unfamiliar was disturbing.

Lady Airlie was more discriminating. She had met some of the Labour leaders and their wives at a dinner given for the King and Queen by Lady Astor in 1923 and had been instinctively drawn to Mrs Philip Snowden. Just as Queen Mary had been impressed by the radiant Mary MacArthur, so her Lady-in-Waiting was attracted by the vivid, colourful personality of Ethel Snowden. Like Lady Airlie, she loved music.

Behind her rather dusty untidy appearance and schoolma'am mannerisms was a noble generous nature. I liked her exuberance, her passionate enthusiasms and violent hatreds. I could never forget her bitterness when she described the poverty of the mining village and the scenes of hardship and misery which she had witnessed as a girl in Wales. 'You people, with your marble tiled bathrooms and your soft towels, can you ever imagine what it meant to a man to have nowhere to wash himself when he came up from the pit except in the street or in the kitchen, stripped naked on a winter day.'[76]

So too she recognized in Mrs James Brown, the wife of the Ayrshire miners' leader, a woman of intelligence and natural dignity. When her husband was appointed Lord High Commissioner to the Church of Scotland and 'they exchanged their miner's cottage at Annbank for the royal state of the Palace of Holyrood, Mrs Brown took up her position with a natural dignity that silenced the snide remarks of supercilious courtiers'.[77]

Throughout the years, successive monarchs and their consorts have been influenced, sometimes for ill, but often for good, by their Private Secretaries and Ladies-in-Waiting. Lady Airlie's long and close friendship with Queen Mary was of inestimable value. Not only did she give comfort to the Queen, so isolated in the gilded cage of royalty, but also she listened with understanding and a sympathetic ear to unfamiliar voices in strange accents. Through Queen Mary, who was herself always ready to listen, Lady Airlie's observations reached the King.

Apart from the garb of Labour ministers there were many other unusual costumes seen at Buckingham Palace, particularly during the 'Round Table Empire Conference' in 1931 on the future of India, but none more sensational than that worn by the Mahatma Gandhi. The Indian leader had twice before been His Majesty's guest – but then in British prisons in India. In his non-violent campaign for Indian independence, Gandhi had always insisted on wearing the humble dress of the poorest Indian. Now the man the King called 'this rebel fakir' was his guest in his Palace and still simply dressed. The Duke of Windsor remembered:

The scene was the Picture Gallery at Buckingham Palace. The screen of black morning coats suddenly parted; and I descried an extraordinary figure: a bald wizened Indian clad in a dhoti and sandals advancing towards my father. It was Mahatma Gandhi. Only nine years before, when I was in India, the Viceroy had thrown this man into jail for sedition. Now the King Emperor was shaking his hand. Standing with me . . . were a group of jewelled Indian Princes with whom I had played polo . . . one of them murmured 'This will cost you India.'[78]

The King did not mince his words. At the end of the meeting he said, 'Remember, Mr Gandhi, I won't have any attacks on my Empire.'

To which the Indian leader replied courteously, 'I must not be drawn into a political argument in your majesty's palace, after receiving your majesty's hospitality.'

King George V did not have the breadth of tolerance of Queen Victoria, but he did strongly condemn the colour bar as practised in India. He and Queen Mary had been powerfully moved by their visit to India when they were Prince and Princess of Wales and he felt strongly his duty to India and the Empire, just as George III had felt towards his American colonies. The King considered Gandhi a dangerous if somewhat misguided figure; nevertheless, like other members of his family, he could not help being impressed by the magnetic personality of the Mahatma.

In the election of 1929 the Labour Party had been returned to office. The King sent for MacDonald, who formed the second Labour government – this time with a woman, Miss Margaret Bondfield, as Minister of Labour. When in June the Cabinet ministers went down to Windsor to be sworn in as Privy Councillors, he greeted her with surprising warmth, saying how pleased he was to receive the first woman Privy Councillor.

The new government had scarcely got into its stride before it had to face the world financial crisis of 1931, the subsequent economic crisis in Britain, and a run on the gold and currency reserves. In August 1931 the King called another all-party Buckingham Palace Conference, with MacDonald, with Sir Herbert Samuel representing the Liberal Party, since Lloyd George was ill, and Baldwin for the Conservatives. 'I am determined,' he wrote to the Duke of York, 'to do everything and anything in my power to prevent the old ship running on the rocks.'[79]

The King's own wish was for a national government headed by MacDonald, but the cuts in unemployment benefits demanded by the New York bankers who were funding the rescue were too much for nine of the Labour members of the government to accept. MacDonald was on the verge of resignation, when the King sent for him to come to the Palace late on Sunday night. Somehow, in that meeting with the King,

MacDonald was persuaded that he was the only man to lead the country in its hour of crisis.

The next morning the three party leaders met in the Indian Room at the Palace, among the symbols of imperial glory. The King, as Rose has written, 'in his best quarterdeck manner impressed on the three party leaders that before they left the Palace there should be a communiqué to end speculation at home and abroad. Then he withdrew to his own rooms to let them get on with it.'[80]

So the decision was taken: there would be a national government, led by MacDonald, which would make stringent economies, including the disagreeable 10 per cent cut in the unemployment benefit. Only three of MacDonald's Labour colleagues agreed to join him, and it was a gloomy new Prime Minister who returned from a meeting at 10 Downing Street to 'kiss hands' at the Palace. 'You look as if you were attending your own funeral,' the King joked. In a sense it was, as far as the Labour Party was concerned: MacDonald was branded as a traitor, and remained so in Labour Party mythology.

The political and constitutional rights and wrongs of these events have been much discussed elsewhere. The interesting facts from the point of view of the history of Buckingham Palace are that the King had hosted once again crucial conferences at the Palace; significant decisions had been taken there, rather than at 10 Downing Street; a complete financial bankruptcy had been avoided; and above all the King had made it clear that his deepest desire was to reign over a united kingdom.

The King was no political theorist, but he had sense and could show authority when necessary. Years before he said, about his son, 'The Navy will teach him all he needs to know,' and in his view that had certainly been true for him: the Navy had taught him not only the need for authority and discipline but also the importance of working together. Once again he showed his readiness to share sacrifice: he reduced his own income from the Civil List by £50,000.

But the stress of the crisis and long hours of hard work were beginning to take their toll on the King; as they did on Ramsay MacDonald, who, on 7 June 1935, resigned on the grounds of ill health. Baldwin took his place. The King bade MacDonald a sad and affectionate farewell:

I hoped you might see me through . . . but I do not think it will be very long. I wonder how you have stood it, especially with the loss of your friends and their beastly behaviour . . . You have been the Prime Minister I have liked best . . . you have kept up the dignity of the office without using it to give you dignity.[81]

These last words might have been used to describe King George V himself.

On 6 May that year the King and Queen had celebrated their Silver Jubilee. As they drove from Buckingham Palace to St Paul's Cathedral with the royal family, they were overwhelmed by the immense crowds that cheered them all along the way. Chips Channon watched the procession from St James's Palace.

. . . the Speaker . . . passed at a walking pace in a gorgeous coach. Then came the Prime Ministers of the Dominions, led by Ramsay MacDonald, seated with his daughter, Ishbel. He looked grim and she dowdy. No applause. Then the Lord Chancellor, wig and all; then the minor Royalties – a few cheers. Then masses of troops, magnificent and virile, resplendent in grand uniforms, with the sun glistening on their helmets. Then thunderous applause for the royal carriages. The Yorks in a large landau with the two tiny pink children. The Duchess of York was charming and gracious, the baby princesses much interested in the proceedings, and waving. The next landau carried the Kents, that dazzling pair; Princess Marina wore an enormous platter hat, chic but slightly unsuitable. Finally the Prince of Wales smiling his dentist smile and waving to his friends, but he still has his old spell for the crowd. The Norway aunt who was with him looked comic, and then more troops, and suddenly, the coach with Their Majesties. All eyes were on the Queen in her white and silvery splendour. Never has she looked so serene, so regally majestic, even so attractive. She completely eclipsed the King. Suddenly she has become the best-dressed woman in the world.

'"It was," the King said simply, "the greatest number of people in the streets that I have ever seen in my life." And, later, "I did not realise they felt like this." '[82]

Millions of his subjects had heard his voice on the radio since the BBC first recorded his speeches in 1924. In 1932 he had been persuaded to give the first Christmas broadcast from Sandringham, for which

Kipling had drafted the text: 'I speak now from my home and from my heart to you all . . .' On Jubilee Night he broadcast from Buckingham Palace with even deeper emotion:

I can only say to you, my very very dear people that the Queen and I thank you from the depths of our hearts for all the loyalty and – may I say so – love, with which this day and always you have surrounded us. I dedicate myself anew to your service for all the years that may still be given me.[83]

Throughout these critical years Queen Mary was a tower of strength. On the twentieth anniversary of his accession King George V had written to the Queen, 'I can never sufficiently express my deep gratitude to you, darling May, for the way you have helped and stood by me in these difficult times . . . This is not sentimental rubbish but what I really feel.'[84]

During the last years of his life, King George V was weighed down by a multiplicity of worries. Abroad, war clouds threatened. The Nazis were on the march in Germany, Il Duce and the Fascists in Italy; at home there was industrial unrest. But behind all these worries there was one growing concern: the future of the Prince of Wales.

In the last years of King George V's life the Prince of Wales's home was at Fort Belvedere, 'a castellated conglomeration on Crown Land'[85] bordering Windsor Great Park near Sunningdale, Berkshire. His brother, The Duke of York, and the Duchess (later King George VI and Queen Elizabeth) had a house near by at Royal Lodge in the Great Park. The King was aware that the Prince of Wales had had many love affairs in the past, but since 1934 he had obviously become deeply in love with a chic American, Mrs Wallis Simpson, who was a frequent visitor at the Fort.

Mrs Simpson had divorced her first husband, a lieutenant attached to the US Navy, with whom she had spent some time in China, and was now living in London with her second, Ernest Simpson, a quiet, intelligent Englishman who worked in his father's shipping business. Her elegant dinners at their small flat became famous and gradually she attracted the attention of the Prince of Wales. He noticed her at a Court in Buckingham Palace, being presented to my parents. I was as usual standing behind their gilt thrones as Wallis approached in the slowly moving line of women, brilliant in Court feathers and trains. When her turn came to curtsey first to my father then to my mother, I was struck by the grace of her carriage and the natural dignity of her movements.[86]

Wallis described the event to her Aunt Bessie in Baltimore, who after her mother's death had become her confidante and later her chaperone. That night, Wallis told her, she wore a 'large aquamarine cross' – imitation, she confessed, but effective.

In the summer of 1934, Wallis was firmly established as the Prince's new favourite, accompanying him on a Mediterranean holiday.

Aware that since she was thirty-nine this might well be, as she wrote, her 'last fling', she was determined to enjoy it until she was supplanted by a younger woman. Then she would 'fold her tent and silently slip away'.[87]

Meanwhile her husband Ernest must be kept happy as her security for the future. However, when Wallis returned from holiday, it was, she wrote in her memoirs, 'like being Wallis in Wonderland. Ernest remarked at me quizzically. "It sounds to me", he said thoughtfully, "indeed like a trip behind the Looking Glass, or better yet into the realm of Peter Pan's Never-Never Land." From then on the Prince was always Peter Pan to Ernest.'[88] Wallis too was becoming aware that in losing her husband she would 'lose something noble for a boy who may always remain Peter Pan'.[89]

But the Prince of Wales was hopelessly and for ever infatuated. . . . On Wallis's next appearance at the State Ball at Buckingham Palace, part of the Jubilee celebration of May 1935, Ernest Simpson was with her but she was wearing the Prince's jewels. This was her third visit to Buckingham Palace. On the previous occasions she had been treated with the usual royal courtesy as an ordinary guest. This time was different: she was now a threat to the throne.

In the last year of his life King George V was haunted by the fear that after his death his son would wreck the monarchy that he and the Queen had so striven to uphold. But, though they were perfectly aware that Mrs Simpson was the Prince's constant companion, not only at the Fort but also at York House, where she acted as his hostess, yet neither he nor the Queen had been able to discuss it with him, and the Prince himself could never find the right moment to broach the subject.

At this May ball, although King and Queen behaved with impeccable courtesy, Mrs Simpson was perfectly aware of the King's hostility. The Prince of Wales danced first with the Queen and then led Mrs Simpson on to the floor. She wrote in her memoirs:

As David and I danced past, I thought I felt the King's eyes rest searchingly on me. Something in his look made me feel that all this graciousness and pageantry were but the glittering tip of an iceberg . . . filled with icy menace for such as me.[90]

That summer Ernest chose to take a long business trip to the USA, while Wallis spent the summer with the Prince and other guests, first at his rented villa in Cannes, then cruising round the Greek islands and afterwards touring through Europe to Paris. After this summer the Prince realized that he could not live without Wallis and clearly was prepared to renounce the throne rather than lose her.

King George V watched his son's behaviour with growing horror, contrasting him with his second son, The Duke of York, who he saw would make a better king. A few weeks before his death the King exclaimed with passion to their friend Blanche Lennox, 'I pray to God that my eldest son will never marry and have children, and that nothing will come between Bertie and Lilibet and the Throne.'[91]

The year 1935 ended in sorrow. The loss of his sister, Princess Victoria, on 3 December grieved him deeply. Though somewhat bad-tempered in her lonely old age, Princess Victoria had adored her brother, and they had spoken every day on the telephone. She was one of his last links with his beloved mother, Queen Alexandra, who had died in 1925. Since then he and the Queen had moved into the big house at Sandringham, where Princess Victoria still lived.

The family Christmas at Sandringham was sadder this year. When the King broadcast his last Christmas message, friends noticed the hoarseness in his voice, and the emotion in his words for his family.

He made his last entry in his diary on Friday 17 January 1936. There was the sailor's last record of the weather, then 'Dawson arrived this evening. I saw him and feel rotten.'[92]

He worked, however, to the end. As he lay dying he realized that a Council of State must be appointed to act on his behalf. His Privy Council was sent for and waited in the room next to his bedroom. The Lord President read the order to him: he managed to say, 'Approved'. But it was with infinite difficulty that he struggled to write 'G R' with Dawson's help.

That night Lord Dawson, his surgeon, wrote the final, memorable bulletin. 'The King's life is moving peacefully towards its close.'[93] Death came just before midnight.

The next morning at a little country school the present writer listened while the headmaster announced that the King was dead. Then, to her surprise and embarrassment, a man who normally showed no emotion broke down and sobbed uncontrollably. He wept for a simple, honest man, a King who had become much loved. Even the radical Clynes described his reign as 'the finest example in modern times of the supremely difficult art of constitutional kingship. He took the trouble to understand his people and to progress with them through the age in which they lived.'[94]

After the King's death, Queen Mary wrote in her diary with character-istic simplicity, 'Am heartbroken ... at 5 to 12 my darling husband passed peacefully away, my children were angelic.' And then she wrote, 'The sunset of his death tinged the whole world's sky.'[95]

Only those who knew her well understood the intensity of her grief; she was calm and controlled, sustained by unchanging ritual. As the old King died she was the first to turn to the new King, take his hand and kiss it in reverent homage.

There was some comfort for the Queen in the shared grief of 'our own kind people' at Sandringham and the thousands of mourning Londoners who filed past the great catafalque in Westminster Hall; and above all, at the thought of her sons. 'At midnight,' she wrote, 'my four sons stood guard over their father's coffin for 20 minutes, a very touching thought.'[96]

The new King, Edward VIII, never forgot their vigil: 'I had been to the Hall,' he wrote, 'and was greatly moved by the scene. It occurred to me that here was a way in which my brothers and I might pay our respects to our dead father.'[97] So he arranged that he and his brothers in full dress uniform

without the public being aware of our presence should station ourselves around the catafalque between the officers already in vigil. Even at so late an hour the river of people still flowed past the coffin. But I doubt whether many recognized the King's four sons among the motionless uniformed figures bent over swords reversed. We stood there for twenty minutes in the dim candlelight and great silence. I felt close to my father and all that he had stood for.

From the glowing heights the great clock chimed the half hour its lingering reverberations obliterating . . . the sound of countless shuffling feet.[98]

It was in the silence of Westminster Hall that King Edward VIII must have felt the 'uneasy sensation of being left alone on a vast stage, a stage that was the British Empire, to play a part not yet written'.

So a great partnership ended – one that had been of major importance in the history of Buckingham Palace.

King George V had used Buckingham Palace as no other monarch had done. It was his home and his headquarters; it was the setting for many a magnificent occasion enhancing the prestige of the Crown; and, above all, it was a place for conferences, which he convened with the aim of creating unity in his kingdom. In his private rooms or in the great State Rooms he had repeatedly brought together men of different political views in his intense desire for harmony and stability.

Queen Mary had made a contribution as significant as that of the Prince Consort in the reign of Queen Victoria, by being the first to organize the Royal Collection in a professional way. She awakened an interest in history and brought a sense of continuity and stability in times of great change and disturbance.

For the rest of her long life, until her death in 1953, Queen Mary remained the keeper of the flame.

CHAPTER EIGHT

King Edward VIII

'Into the realm of Peter Pan's Never-Never Land.'[1]

ERNEST SIMPSON TO MRS SIMPSON

Abdication

The reign of King Edward VIII was brief, but crucial in the history of the Palace. It was only eleven months from his accession to the throne on 20 January 1936 to his abdication on 11 December 1936. During that time he kept offices in the Palace but spent little time there and did not take up residence until 1 October. He left the Palace late at night on 3 December and never returned as King. His Coronation, planned for 12 May 1937, never took place. King Edward VIII contributed little to the history of Buckingham Palace itself, but had he not abdicated, the British monarchy, and therefore the Palace, would have been fundamentally changed.

At the beginning of his reign, he set up an office in Buckingham Palace but found it dark and depressing. It was, he wrote, 'on the ground [floor in] a small waiting-room, decorated and furnished in Oriental style. It looked out upon the Great Courtyard through two windows; on all but the brightest days I keep a light burning on my desk.'[2] Now an office in the Lord Chamberlain's department, it is still dark, but only the Chinese decoration of the fireplace remains of the 'Oriental style'.

Queen Mary did not leave the Palace until October. After King George V's death she found comfort in 'filling her mind with trivial things, with the packing of *objets d'art* and the redecoration of Marlborough House, to shut out her loneliness and anxiety'.[3] The 'anxiety' was for the future of the monarchy, now the responsibility of her eldest son.

King George V's papers had to be dealt with, and there were hundreds of letters to be answered. Her own possessions had to be distinguished from those belonging to the Crown. 'It was', King Edward VIII wrote, 'a melancholy task of no mean magnitude, for in the course of her active life she had assembled an immense collection of *objets d'art* and historical souvenirs of the Royal family.'[4] It was with great regret that she locked away the magnificent royal jewels, shuddering at the thought of Mrs Simpson arrayed in them. 'He gives Mrs Simpson the most beautiful jewels,'[5] she sighed. She even suspected that the new King was giving Mrs Simpson jewellery that rightly belonged to the Crown.

For months she worked methodically, and at the same time supervised the redecoration of Marlborough House. Meanwhile she watched her son taking his father's place. On 23 June she drove from the Palace through cheering crowds to the Horse Guards Parade for Trooping the Colour. 'David held the parade,' she wrote, 'which was a lovely sight as usual, but tears were often in my eyes thinking of the past and of him we sorely miss.'[6]

From her window in Buckingham Palace, Queen Mary watched while her son received the guests to garden parties on 21 and 22 July, as she and King George V had done so many times before. However, King Edward VIII did things differently. During the six months of Court mourning the usual courts for the presentation of débutantes were postponed. In order to deal with what the Duke of Windsor called in his memoirs the 'social bottleneck', he decided to hold two garden parties when 600 débutantes could be presented.

When that first afternoon I joined my guests in the garden, I found pitched near the lake the huge silken Durbar canopy with hammered silver poles that my parents had brought back from India. Under it was a large gilt chair for me to sit on. Members of the Royal Family, the Diplomatic Corps, and the Household were seated directly behind; a Guards' band alternating with the pipers of a Highland regiment played under the trees a little distance away. The scene was undeniably charming as the attractively dressed women advanced down the red carpet to make their curtsies to the King.[7]

However, on 21 July a sudden storm blew up:

If only the tempo of the curtsying could have been speeded, the day might have been saved. But these Court presentations, like an assembly line, have a cadence all their own: ten seconds for each debutante to make her curtsy and pass on. Meanwhile the wind came up; and the first big, wet drops began to fall. Then came the downpour. Prudently, the other guests who were not being presented scampered into the protection of the tea tents. But with scarcely a waver the debutantes came on. Their costly hats and dresses, which had taken weeks to make, became progressively more bedraggled; and their expressions increasingly woebegone. From the shelter of the embroidered Durbar canopy . . .

the King decided to stop the presentations.

The Lord Chamberlain agreed that it would be the most dignified and sensible thing to do. Rising from the gilt chair, I made a bow in the direction of the still unpresented young ladies, and with a gesture intended to convey my regret over the inadvertent shower that had necessitated cutting the garden party short, I retired to the Palace.[8]

Although the rain stopped the King did not return. He could never understand why his guests were so offended. This insensitivity and selfishness were typical. King George V and Queen Mary would not have behaved so.

At last the Queen left Buckingham Palace. 'I took leave of my lovely rooms with a sad heart,' she wrote in her diary. 'David kindly came to see me off.'[9] As always, she found it difficult to talk to her son, but she wrote to him: 'I feel sure you realized that I felt very sad at leaving those lovely comfortable rooms which have been my happy home for 25 years and that I was terribly afraid of breaking down.'[10] She had transformed the cold building that she had found so 'ungemütlich', into a gracious friendly home.

Of the many tributes paid to her, one gave her deep pleasure to the end of her life. In May 1924, at the British Empire Exhibition, Wembley, the most popular exhibit had been Queen Mary's Dolls' House. One of Queen Victoria's grandchildren, Princess Marie Louise, had had the brilliant idea of persuading the architect Sir Edwin Lutyens to design a dolls' house for Queen Mary. Lutyens, who was building New Delhi at the time, agreed with enthusiasm – the contrast would be refreshing; and Queen Mary decided it should 'enable future generations to see how a King and Queen of England lived in the twentieth century'.[11] So it became a perfect replica of a Georgian house, with real minute paintings and a library of miniature books contributed by great authors of the day. Bathrooms and kitchens were perfect in all details; the dining table could be laid with gold plate or Royal Doulton. There were costly replicas of the royal Daimlers in the garage and a Pipe Major and five Guardsmen stood at attention in sentry boxes. After the exhibition it was moved to Windsor, where Queen Mary often came to look at it, and to arrange and rearrange the rooms. She kept a key so that she could come alone without her servants. The Dolls' House was her dream palace where all was perfection: where there was no war, no children with problems and the only sound that of the gramophone in the nursery playing 'God Save The King'. Here time stood still while she remembered a marriage of deep, though often unspoken, love and happiness.

While Queen Mary was in residence the new King planned rooms for himself with little enthusiasm. The new King hated Buckingham Palace with an intense loathing. 'The dank musty smell I had always associated with the building assailed me afresh the instant I set foot inside the King's door.' He told friends that he and his brother 'always froze when they entered the gates'.[12]

The Fort was his new home which he loved with an equal intensity. He gave York House at St James's to his younger brother, Prince George, and until October, when he moved into the Palace, he held his official receptions at St James's Palace. The Duke and Duchess of York had their London home at 145 Piccadilly.

King George V had done little to prepare the Prince of Wales for the throne. He had always allowed Queen Mary to see even the most confidential papers; Edward VII had allowed his son to see confidential papers, though it was a privilege he denied Queen Alexandra. But King George V had never trusted the discretion of his eldest son, and certainly not that of his companions.

So until those first months in his dark office at Buckingham Palace, King Edward VIII had never understood the magnitude of the task before him. Though private functions during the period of mourning were cancelled, the world did not stand still while Britain mourned, and minister after minister came to him at the Palace with news of a real world of alarming problems. He recalled,

The international situation was steadily deteriorating. Mr. Anthony Eden, who had succeeded Sir Samuel Hoare as Foreign Secretary four weeks before my father's death, appeared in the little Chinese room to tell me of his hopes of saving the Peace of Europe by strengthening the policy of collective security fostered by the League of Nations [13]

and that

Mr Duff Cooper, Secretary of State for War, described the first feeble beginnings of British rearmament. The Minister of Labour, Mr Ernest Brown, came to report to me on the slow progress made by the Government to combat the demoralisation in the depressed areas.[14]

King Edward VIII began with good intentions, determined to be a 'modern twentieth-century King', but he was to discover early how difficult it was to make the transition. The public was, as always, notoriously inconsistent: they wanted him to be an ordinary fellow and when he behaved like one they were offended. As he wrote, he was expected to drive to the Palace in 'the immense sombre Daimler known to my brothers and me as the Crystal Palace'.[15] On one occasion when he had tried to walk in the rain from York House, carrying an umbrella, there was such an outcry in the press that he never tried it again.

For this new life King Edward VIII wanted a Household and officers of his own choosing, in touch with the modern world. By tradition, the Court officials of the old reign were kept on during the six months' period of mourning; but many of the members of King George V's Household were now elderly and none too anxious to serve a King who was notoriously difficult to manage.

The most important post to be filled was that of Private Secretary. Since Lord Wigram asked to be replaced, the King offered the position to Godfrey Thomas, who had been on his staff when he was Prince of Wales. He had left the Foreign Office to join the Prince and remained in his service for seventeen years, but modestly considered he was not up to the demanding post of Private Secretary. He became deputy to Major Alexander Hardinge, who had been Assistant Private Secretary to King George V for sixteen years. Hardinge, wrongly dismissed by Chips Channon as a 'dreary, narrow minded fogey',[16] was in fact a man of great ability and honesty, who now, as Private Secretary, faced the most difficult year of his life.

Major Ulick Alexander was appointed Keeper of the Privy Purse, a post that was almost as demanding as that of Private Secretary, since the King was passionately interested in his money, but combined a stinginess where his Household expenses were concerned with a stunning extravagance in his gifts to Mrs Simpson.

The King dismissed servants in Buckingham Palace, ignoring the long-established practice of ensuring that they had alternative employment to which to go. At the end of six months, he was so preoccupied with his private life and so dependent on his Household that he made few changes.

The King was capable of hard work, particularly if it involved encouraging trade or business relationships, and he enjoyed visits to the Army and Navy, but he was easily bored and, because he was remarkably insensitive, he often gave deep offence. At first he made an effort to work at his red boxes and received innumerable delegations at the Palace – provincial mayors, Lieutenant-Colonels of the Brigade of Guards, industrialists, Royal Academicians, journalists, scientists, ambassadors, Cabinet ministers, bishops, Maharajahs and colonial governors. But he soon lost patience and, as he recalled, was irritated when he was 'informed out of the blue that I would have to begin to squeeze into my already crowded calendar, delegations from the so called "Privileged bodies" ie leading corporate elements with the traditional right of access to the monarch'.[17] Much to the irritation of his staff and the annoyance of the twenty privileged bodies, he decided to lump them all together and receive them in the Throne Room at the Palace with one response to their scroll of loyal congratulations: 'The Lord Mayor of London was placated only after I agreed to receive him and his aldermen separately in an anteroom before the ceremony.'[18]

Even more worrying for his officials was his negligent treatment of the sacred red boxes. His Private Secretaries and the Palace Household were not welcome at the Fort, except by special invitation. As a result the boxes, often with urgent papers to be signed, though delivered daily, were often allowed to stay unopened for days. Documents were said to be returned sometimes marked with the ring of cocktail glasses.

The King's affair with Mrs Simpson was an important element in the arguments for the abdication, but it was not the only one. There were those who, like Winston Churchill, romanticized the 'greatest love story of all time', and some, like Lord Beaverbrook, who backed King Edward VIII out of a mischievous desire to make trouble for Prime Minister Baldwin. But those in his Household who were closest to the King, even when they remained with him out of loyalty, saw as the months went by that he would be an impossible King. He himself felt the weight of the Crown, and the constant hard work that is the lot of the monarch.

Apart from his political instability, and his reluctance to accept the hard grind of kingship, there was also an insensitivity and a psychological immaturity, the 'Peter Pan mentality' that Ernest Simpson had described. Sir Alan Lascelles, who had served King Edward VIII when Prince of Wales, wrote that it was important to understand that morally and psychologically the King's development had stopped at the age of fifteen. Mrs Simpson saw this only too clearly.

His 'Never-Never Land' was the Fort – his home before he moved into Buckingham Palace and to which he escaped more and more frequently thereafter, to be away from the problems of the real world. Here Mrs Simpson could direct his life as his mother had done in his childhood at Sandringham. His letters to Mrs Simpson are significant and embarrassingly infantile.

Although others in the King's circle managed husbands and lovers quite successfully, the King's attentions to Wallis were now so blatant that even her husband Ernest's tolerance was strained. Totally insensitive to public opinion, the King was now treating another man's wife as his consort. Finally Ernest went to see the King at York House and, like an aggrieved parent, bluntly asked the King what his intentions were. According to this friend, the King replied, 'Do you think that I would be crowned without Wallis at my side?'[19] At this meeting, of which Wallis was unaware, Ernest agreed to give Wallis grounds for divorce.

'I believe that man is seldom master of his own fate,' King Edward VIII wrote. What worried his ministers in those first months was the increasing knowledge that here was a King not only not master of his own fate, but also totally dominated by the woman he wanted to marry. His ministers must have left the little Chinese Room in the Palace with uneasy foreboding.

While the Prime Minister and his Cabinet had wrestled with the problems of the world and the worries about the future of the King, Queen Mary, before she had moved out of Buckingham Palace, had watched and listened with growing apprehension but a feeling of help-lessness. Letters of condolence had poured into the Palace after the death of her husband, moving her to tears, but there were many others that alarmed and angered her. There were cuttings from American papers with sensational headlines and photographs of the lady from Baltimore, and there were scores of letters from well-wishers, begging her to intervene.

After the King's death there was only one of her Household with whom she could discuss the rumours that now reached her from all quarters. Her much loved friend and Lady of the Bedchamber Lady Airlie remembered how one afternoon, when she was reading to the Queen, suddenly she was asked if her sons had ever disappointed her. She replied that in her case she

had always tried not to be possessive, and to remember that their lives were their own and not mine.

'Yes, one can apply that to individuals, but not to a Sovereign,' the Queen said. 'He is not responsible to himself alone.' She picked up her embroidery and stitched in silence for a moment, then added, 'I have not liked to talk to David about this affair with Mrs Simpson, in the first place because I don't want to give the impression that I am interfering with his private life and also because he is the most obstinate of all my sons. To oppose him over doing anything is only to make him more determined to do it. At present he is utterly infatuated, but my great hope is that violent infatuations usually wear off.'[20]

As the Queen walked through the Palace State Rooms before she left, did the portraits on the wall remind her that she was not the first Queen to suffer because of her children? As a historian, Queen Mary would have recognized a pattern and perhaps have been comforted. Children of the great have often reacted against their parents, but that 'fierce light that beats upon the throne' has always been especially remorseless. Perhaps, too, she would have been comforted by the words of Lady Airlie: 'the generations pass but the green shoots live.'[21]

The British newspapers remained astonishingly silent about a royal affair which was now the talk of London society. It was interesting that the King's direct influence on two press moguls – Beaverbrook, who owned the *Daily Express* and *Evening Standard*, and Harmsworth, son of Lord Rothermere, who owned the *Daily Mail* and *Evening News* – was strong enough to achieve this silence.

With the knowledge that divorce proceedings were due to begin on 1 October, the King behaved with even less discretion – as though Mrs Simpson were already free. As he wrote,

Wallis had . . . been my guest at two official dinner parties at York House when I had entertained among others the Prime Minister and Mrs Baldwin and Mr & Mrs Winston Churchill . . . Her presence at my table was duly recorded in the Court Circular. Secrecy and concealment were not in my nature.[22]

Wallis, in fact, was not merely a guest: she was beginning to arrange his official entertaining at York House and at the Fort she openly acted as his hostess.

It was, however, the King's lack of discretion during his summer holiday that alarmed Queen Mary, his ministers and his Household. The King chartered a large yacht, *The Nahlin*, for a Mediterranean cruise.

Along with an Assistant Private Secretary and an equerry, I took with me some friends, among whom were my Minister for War, Mr Duff Cooper and Lady

Diana Duff Cooper. Wallis was also a member of the party, although she and I were both by then well aware that my interest in her had attracted attention and speculation.[23]

The Duff Coopers were there because there was some attempt to give the cruise official cover. The Foreign Office suggested that the King should extend his cruise and pay a call on the Turkish President, Kemal Atatürk, as a 'gesture of friendship since discussions were taking place about commercial credits'. The King expected the Duff Coopers, who led an unconventional life, to be understanding. But, tolerant as they were, even they were surprised when they joined the yacht and saw the King 'scrambling down the gangway naked but for straw sandals, grey flannel shorts and two crosses on a gold chain round his neck. Ominously Mrs Simpson wore duplicates of the crosses on her wrist.'[24]

Not surprisingly, the foreign press was now in full cry. Though the British press still was silent, pictures and reports flooded back to the government and to Buckingham Palace, where Queen Mary quietly read them and filed them away. There were photographs of the King and Wallis sunning together: on one occasion the camera caught them in a small boat, her hand on his arm and he looking lovingly down on her.

King Edward VIII was beginning to realize that his new position brought unwelcome publicity. He returned from the cruise more than ever determined to marry Wallis, even if it meant forgoing the dubious pleasure of kingship. But he still could not bring himself to tell his mother.

Still the British press remained silent. Wallis's divorce petition was heard on 27 October. The decree nisi was granted, but it would take six months before the decree was declared absolute. Once the decree nisi was granted it could be only a matter of time before the voluntary press embargo was lifted.

Wallis was established in great style in a splendid Regency house in Cumberland Terrace, and Aunt Bessie was brought over from Washington to act as chaperone. The King divided his time between her house, the Fort at weekends and Buckingham Palace, where he conducted what he called his 'Kingy business'. When Queen Mary had finally moved out of the Palace, the King, at her suggestion, moved into the Belgian Suite on the ground floor kept for visiting foreign monarchs. He was reluctant to occupy his father's old room on the second floor 'out of respect for my father's memory'. There were other reasons for his preference: 'This five-room suite', he wrote, 'had tall french windows opening on the gardens, and was conveniently adjacent to the private Garden Entrance which is always used, except on State occasions, by the Royal Family.'[25] So Wallis could visit him quietly there, and he could easily avoid unwelcome visitors by slipping out into the gardens.

He made a few alterations.

One never tinkers much with palaces; like museums, they seem to resist change. Besides, a curious presentiment induced me to leave the rooms as they were. Somehow I had a feeling that I might not be there very long. About the only changes I made for my comfort were to add a shower to the bathtub and to replace the ornate four-poster bed with a single one of my own. I installed a small extra switchboard to handle my personal calls, and added a private line to The Fort. During the two months I lived at Buckingham Palace, I never got over the feeling of not quite belonging there. I felt lost in its regal immensity.[26]

In the last months of his reign, the Household became more and more irritated by the King's unprofessional attitude to his work. He called them at all hours, and when they wished to report to him at the end of the day, they would often be told 'The lady is still there'. As she looked at the priceless furniture in the magnificence of the Palace, in the Never-Never Land of her imagination, did she see herself as Queen? Even if she did, she was tough and worldly-wise, and at the back of her mind was always the expectation that the magic would suddenly disappear. In the next weeks, when the press swarmed round her gates, she was often to wish that she could do just that.

In November, Chips Channon picked up hostile gossip in the House of Commons. On 10 November unemployed hunger marchers besieged Parliament, crowding into the Lobby. To them the King and his bejewelled lady were irrelevant, if not offensive. In the chamber for the first time Mrs Simpson's name was called out in a rowdy question time;

the smoking room and lobbies buzzed with rumours. 'The Truth is', Chips wrote, 'that the monarchy has lost ground in a frightening manner. Prince Charming charms his people no more.'[27] A Conservative MP estimated that if a vote had been taken in the Commons, more than 100 MPs would have voted for a republic.

Still Channon and his friends, including Duff Cooper and Churchill, fêted the King in their elegant houses, where Mrs Simpson appeared, 'dripping with jewels'. 'Why', wrote Channon, 'should we forsake our Sovereign?' Yet even he admitted that the King had been foolish, and, as the King continued to seem blind and deaf, he and other loyal friends became alarmed: 'The King is insane about Wallis, insane.'[28]

In mid November the King received a letter from his Private Secretary, Hardinge, which brought him down to earth: it was his duty to advise the King and he did so with bluntness. Hardinge appealed to the King to send Mrs Simpson away 'without further delay'. As the King remembered, 'I was shocked and angry – shocked by the suddenness of the blow, angry because of the way it was launched, with the startling suggestion that I should send from my land, my realm, the woman I intended to marry.'[29]

But the King no longer trusted Hardinge and sent for his old friend, the lawyer, Sir Walter Monckton, who generously gave up his work and until the end of the King's reign acted as his legal adviser and contact with the Prime Minister.

On the weekend of 14–15 November the King tried to explain to Wallis, who was with her aunt at the Fort, the dangers ahead. On 16 November the King returned to the Palace and sent for Baldwin, determined to have it out with him. There have been many meetings in Buckingham Palace between Prime Minister and monarch, but none so strained as that at 6.30 p.m. that Monday. Outwardly both were courteous, but the King could hardly conceal his dislike of Baldwin – his mannerisms, the irritating way he snapped his fingers, even the sound of his little black beetle of a car crunching on the gravel of the Palace courtyard. He told the Prime Minister that he was determined to marry Mrs Simpson and hoped he could do so as King; if not he was prepared to go. Baldwin replied, 'Sir, that is most grievous news.'

Exasperated and worn out, he returned to Downing Street and went straight to bed, telling his Chief Whip, Margesson, 'David, I have heard such things from my King tonight as I never thought to hear.'[30] He could not even bring himself to see the King's Assistant Private Secretary, Alan Lascelles, who was waiting for his report.

That same evening the King went over to Marlborough House to see Queen Mary. He told her of his decision to marry Wallis and if necessary to abdicate. Queen Mary, who had always put duty before anything else, was deeply shaken but remained compassionate. During the next days he told his brothers of his decision.

Still he carried out some royal duties. It was as King that he went on a tour of the South Wales coalfields, meeting the unemployed, during which, in a famous speech, he assured them that 'something must be done'. Yet at the same time he knew he was going to abdicate. On his return he consulted his friends in the government, especially Duff Cooper and Churchill. Both counselled delay: neither could imagine Wallis as Queen, but they hoped that after the Coronation the King would break with her.

At this stage a new way out – a morganatic marriage – was suggested. Baldwin, who now only wanted a speedy abdication, seized the opportunity. He consulted his Cabinet and the Dominion governments and none of them would consent to a morganatic marriage. Abdication was the King's only course.

On 1 December the dam broke. The Right Reverend A. W. F. Blunt, Bishop of Bradford, addressed an audience of clergy of his diocese and, in the course of his speech, criticized the King, not for immorality, but for his failure to attend church. The *Yorkshire Post* picked up the story and the rest of the press scrambled to follow suit. Now the editors, released at last, went into action.

Wallis now decided to escape. She telephoned her old friends Mr and Mrs Rogers at the Villa Lou Viei near Cannes and that night, secretly, she left for Newhaven and Dieppe.

The same night, after Wallis had left, the King returned to Buckingham Palace. Encouraged by Beaverbrook and Churchill, he had been persuaded to try to mobilize popular support, which he believed he had in the country. Deciding to make an appeal over the head of the government, he drafted a broadcast. He sent for Baldwin and gave him the draft to present to the Cabinet the next day and also sent his legal advisers with copies to Beaverbrook and Churchill. Late though it was, while waiting for their replies he drove across to Marlborough House. His mother had written gently asking him to call, since she had not heard from him for ten days. He tried to explain his neglect: that he had to make his own decision and that was irrevocable. He must marry Wallis. 'All that matters is our happiness,' he repeatedly told her. Then he drove back to the Palace. Now it symbolized all that he hated. He wrote in his memoirs:

The immense forbidding bulk of the Palace loomed up as the motor turned into the Mall. Few windows showed any light. My presence in London had evidently become known, for as I approached the gates I perceived, gathered around the foot of Queen Victoria's memorial, a small crowd staring at the edifice, thinking of God knows what. At that moment there came over me, like a wave, a powerful resurgence of the intense dislike for the building I had always felt. Did I really belong there at all? The answer came immediately – certainly not alone.[31]

Desperately tired, the King decided to return to the Fort and wait for the Cabinet's reply to his suggested broadcast. Monckton, who throughout these days had served him with efficiency and kindness, would not allow him to return to the Fort alone. So at 1.00 a.m., accompanied by Monckton, he drove out of the Palace.

Even at that hour, there was still a small cheering crowd outside the Palace. In a revealing passage in his memoirs he wrote:

In this simple, spontaneous demonstration I found consolation for a day of trial. And the episode gave rise to a fleeting and tempting thought – a notion so ephemeral and obviously so impossible that I mention it now merely as an illustration of a how hard-pressed mind will clutch at straws. The people at the gate were for me. Why not turn their undoubted affection to proper account? Manifestly, my Ministers were not going to let me speak to my people. What was there to prevent me from addressing them where they stood? My parents' practice of 'showing' themselves on the balcony of Buckingham Palace provided a precedent. The spotlights playing on the façade, the lonely figure of the King pleading his cause – the scene could have been extremely effective. But no sooner had the image formed in my mind than it vanished. For one thing, it smacked of balcony politics, of which there was already too much in the Europe of that era. What was more important, it would have meant driving a wedge into the nation.[32]

He had never enjoyed the balcony appearances, but he was aware of their power to unite the nation. 'The car sped up Constitution Hill,' he wrote, 'leaving the crowd behind. I never again set foot inside Buckingham Palace as King.'[33]

From now on the Fort became his headquarters. However, he kept his private telephone line through the Palace; it was to serve him in these last days as a link with Wallis in Cannes. Daily they talked for hours, keeping his telephone line constantly engaged, to the annoyance of his Household at the Palace. His loyal telephonist, William Bateman, kept watch over this phone, sleeping by it at night to protect the King's secrecy.

On Friday 4 December, Baldwin motored down, bringing the Cabinet's decision not to permit him to make a broadcast. Churchill, who still hoped for popular support, came to dine that night and tried to persuade him to delay decisions to allow time for 'the battalions to march'. But after he had gone, the King spent a sleepless night facing the reality that there could be no 'King's Party' without national division and possibly civil war.

That night, pacing the bedroom floor, he made his decision. On Saturday morning he sent Monckton to Baldwin to tell him of his decision to abdicate.

Throughout this dramatic weekend when the fate of the monarchy was being decided, the Duke of York, the one man most nearly concerned, was not consulted. It was not until Monday night that the King agreed to see his brother.

When Bertie arrived at the Fort the next evening, he found Baldwin there, righteously determined to make one more effort to persuade the King to give up Wallis. He wanted, he said, to help him 'wrestle with his conscience – all through the night if necessary'.[34] The King begged his aides to get rid of him. But, courteous as ever, he invited him to stay for dinner.

It was a strained dinner party that night. But, as Monckton wrote, it was the King's

tour de force. In that quiet panelled room he sat at the head of the table with his boyish face and smile, with a good fresh colour while the rest of us were pale as sheets, rippling over with bright conversation, and with a careful eye to see that his guests were being looked after. He wore his white kilt. On Mr Baldwin's right was the Duke of York, and I was next to him, and as the dinner went on the Duke turned to me and said: 'Look at him. We simply cannot let him go.' But we both knew there was nothing we could say or do to stop him.[35]

The Duke of York was silent, bowed down under the burden that he now had to take up. Only the King was lively; as Baldwin told the Cabinet, he was 'happy and gay as if he were looking forward to his honeymoon'.[36]

For two days the Duke of Kent, also present, remained at the Fort, still trying by every means 'to persuade the King to stay'. In London his wife, Princess Marina, confessed to her friend Chips Channon that she believed 'if this issue had not arisen something else could have'. Two years ago, she said, the King had told the Duke that he did not know if he 'could stick it'.[37]

In the House of Commons on Monday, MPs cheered Baldwin's statement. Thursday 10 December 1936 was a historic day in the history of Parliament and the monarchy. At 2.00 p.m. members of the House of Commons met, among them Chips Channon:

The House was full for there had not been an Abdication since 1399 . . . Baldwin was greeted with cheers . . . At last he went to the Bar, bowed twice – a message from the King and he presented a paper to the Speaker who proceeded to read it out. At the words 'renounce the throne' his voice broke and there were stifled sobs in the House.[38]

Baldwin's statement that day, outlining the sequence of events leading to the abdication, was rambling and muddled, but he paid tribute to the King, who 'had behaved in a constitutional manner'. Baldwin told how in October he had warned the King 'that the respect grown up in the last three generations for the monarchy . . . might lose that power far more rapidly than it was built up, and once lost, I doubt if anything could restore it'. One sentence revealed Baldwin's irritation at the King's immaturity. 'It is difficult to realise that his Majesty is not a boy, although he looks so young.'[39] Otherwise his references to the King were courteous, even complimentary.

In the House of Lords the next morning, 11 December 1936, the Bill accepting the King's abdication was passed. Chips Channon was there again.

Black Rod was sent to summon the Speaker from the House of Commons. The Clerk read the Royal Commission. The three Lords bowed and doffed their hats. The Bill was read. The King was still King Edward. The Clerk bowed 'Le Roi le veult'* and Edward, the beautiful boy King with his gaiety and honesty, his nervous twitching, his flair and glamour, was part of history. It was 1.52.[40]

* 'Le Roi le veult' is the Norman French command traditionally used on the final passage of Bills in the House of Lords.

CHAPTER NINE

King George VI and Queen Elizabeth

'Elizabeth could make a home anywhere'.[1]

KING GEORGE VI

The Palace under Fire

On 11 December 1936 at 1.52 p.m., in the chamber of the House of Lords, Bertie, the Duke of York, became officially King George VI of Great Britain. Usually a monarch succeeds after the last breath of a dying King or Queen – 'The King is dead, long live the King.' But for the Duke of York the agony had been prolonged. His brother, King Edward VIII, had signed the instrument of abdication at 10.00 a.m. on Thursday 10 December in the Octagonal Drawing Room at Fort Belvedere with his brothers as witnesses. It was not until after Prime Minister Baldwin had presented the document to the House of Commons on the afternoon of the same day, and completion by the House of Lords of 'His Majesty's Declaration of Abdication Bill'. The next morning, that agony was over.

Only then did the new King, at luncheon at 145 Piccadilly with his wife and daughters, received a message brought to him by his secretary, Sir Eric Miéville: 'Will you tell his majesty that he has just been proclaimed King.' According to Queen Elizabeth The Queen Mother's biographer, King George 'looked round the luncheon table and said, "Now if someone comes through on the telephone, *who* shall I say I am?"'[2] It was a characteristic remark of a shy and diffident man who had always been outshone by his older brother. It took some time before he became aware of his own strengths, and only gradually

281

did the public become aware that here was a King with the authority of a naval officer and the dedication and high seriousness of a deeply religious man.

From the time when, on 12 December, he took the oath of succession at St James's Palace to 12 May 1937, the day of his Coronation, he took charge of the preparations with a competence and foresight that King Edward VIII would never have shown. And at the same time he fought with determination to conquer the stammer that made every speech of his life a nightmare. That he did finally succeed was due partly to the skill of his Australian speech therapist, Lionel Logue, but even more to the loving support of his wife, who, with the touch of a hand or an encouraging smile, gave him confidence.

His brother, King Edward VIII, may have been full of his admiration for his grandfather, the flamboyant Edward VII. The Duke of York, however, signalled by his adoption of his father's name, George, that it was in his footsteps he intended to walk. On the same day that he took the oath he created the former King, Edward VIII, HRH The Duke of Windsor. It was typical that King Edward VIII had not given a thought to his future title, and equally typical that King George VI carefully considered the question with its implications for the future. That morning, the Clerk of the Crown, Sir Claud Schuster, came to find out how King Edward VIII should be announced in the broadcast he was due to make that night. Crisply, the new King told him:

I suggest H.R.H. D[uke] of W[indsor]. He cannot be Mr. E. W. as he was born the son of a Duke. That makes him Ld E. W. anyhow. If he ever comes back to this country, he can stand & be elected to the H. of C. Would you like that? S. replied No. As D. of W. he can sit and vote in the H. of L. Would you like that? S. replied No. Well if he becomes a Royal Duke he cannot speak or vote in the H. of L. & he is not being deprived of his rank in the Navy, Army or R. Air Force. This gave Schuster a new lease of life & he went off quite happy.[3]

That same night the new King gave the old King a farewell dinner at Royal Lodge, Windsor, his country home. Queen Elizabeth was not there. Through all these difficult last days she was seriously ill with influenza and stayed at their Piccadilly home. 'I kept right out of it all,' she remembered.[4] The Duke of Windsor later recalled, 'The dinner passed pleasantly enough, I hope I was a good guest.'[5]

Afterwards the Duke of Windsor went across to Windsor Castle to make the broadcast with the memorable words: 'I have found it impossible to carry the heavy burden of responsibility and to discharge my duties as King as I would wish to do without the help and support of the woman I love.'[6]

Queen Mary, who had disliked the idea of so public a declaration, was somewhat relieved by the dignity of the broadcast. She bade her son 'the dreadful goodbye as he was leaving that evening for Austria'.[7] Throughout, she had behaved with magnificent control. There was an unforgettable moment when her four sons stood to see her leave for the drive back to London. She gave one last look from her big black Daimler, there was a final bow from the son who had rejected his kingdom, and Queen Mary swept off into the foggy night.

The brothers talked on until after midnight. 'When D & I said goodbye,' King George VI wrote with characteristic simplicity, 'we kissed, parted as freemasons & he bowed to me as King.'[8] Their old affectionate friendship would never be the same again.

'There was', the Duke later wrote, 'great sadness in my heart at leaving Great Britain and its people.'[9] Yet all who observed him at this time noted his air of euphoria. He was like a prisoner released – Peter Pan did not have to grow up after all. As Queen Mary later wrote to him, he did not seem to comprehend the magnitude of his decision, nor the hurt and humiliation he had caused to those who loved him.

On the first night of his reign, King George VI was with his cousin Lord Louis Mountbatten at Fort Belvedere, while the Duke of Windsor prepared for his final departure. 'Dickie, this is absolutely terrible,' the King said. 'I never wanted this to happen; I'm quite unprepared for it. David has been trained for this all his life. I've never even seen a State Paper. I'm only a naval officer, it's the only thing I know about.'[10] In just these words King George V had complained to Lord Louis' father. To which he had replied, 'There is no more fitting preparation for a King than to have been trained for the Navy.'

King George VI had been too modest; in fact, he had not only learned in the Navy self-discipline, common sense and an ability to command: as a biographer wrote,

living as a member of a ship's company gave him an understanding of humanity . . .

He had learned too that in a ship you work together or sink. He had also qualities that his more charismatic brother had lacked – a determination to succeed, a sense of dedication that kept him going through periods of ill health. His father had understood him. 'Bertie,' he had said, 'has more guts than the rest of his brothers put together.'[11]

Above all, he had the unfailing support of the woman he loved. Queen Elizabeth had then, as now, unique charm and a friendly ease of manner that endeared her to all classes. But she has too a Scottish hardiness and strength of character that were to be proved in the fire of war.

No monarch has succeeded to the throne under such painful circumstances. The last months had been an intolerable strain on a man who had always shunned the limelight. On 12 December, King George VI faced his first ordeal, the first meeting of the Privy Council at St James's Palace, with courage; but his stammer, which he was beginning to overcome, was very pronounced that day. He spoke with obvious difficulty.

On 15 February King George VI and his Queen left 145 Piccadilly and moved into Buckingham Palace: the simplicity of their private life was gone for ever. The cosy house where they had entertained informally, and got their own supper when they came in late from a theatre, had to be exchanged for the cold magnificence of Buckingham Palace.

For the King the Palace was his place of work, his flagship – as it had been for King George V – and in wartime he was to make it the symbol of the unity of the nation, but he was determined that it should also be a home. For the Queen that was a challenge.

Buckingham Palace had chilled many a royal heart over the past years. Queen Elizabeth was the first to bring warmth and the happiness of a young family there. 'Elizabeth could make a home anywhere,' King George VI told Lady Airlie when she first had tea with them in the Queen's Sitting Room at Buckingham Palace a few weeks after his accession. 'I saw that the room was already beginning to show the traces of her own personality – the little feminine touches which I had always associated with her. It looks homelike already.'[12]

For the first time in almost a century Buckingham Palace became alive. The two little girls ran down the long corridors, chased with their dogs around the gardens and rowed on the lake. 'It was rather green and dirty,'[13] Princess Margaret remembered, but the children found the big lake

enchanting ... all kinds of amusing birds came there and it had its own population of ducks. One of them, for reasons best known to herself, always laid her eggs and hatched them out in the smaller lake outside the Palace grounds. She then walked her children back to the Palace, over the courtyard and into the gardens. The Police on duty stopped the traffic for her and opened the gates.[14]

Queen Elizabeth created their own microclimate within the chilly grandeur which gave the shy King the warmth and security he needed so desperately in the first difficult months of his reign.

He regretted most that now he had less time for his beloved daughters, but he made sure that they had bright, cheerful rooms in the north-east corner of the Palace on the second floor. The dark study above the Balcony Room was rejected; he had never forgotten the gloom of the lessons he and his brother had shared there. It became a room for the children's piano practice.

While they were still living at Piccadilly, the Princesses had been enjoying swimming lessons at the Bath Club and no one had taken much notice of the two little girls in their regulation swimming costumes; but now that Princess Elizabeth was heir to the throne they attracted too much attention. So in the summer of 1938 it was decided to build 'a swimming bath and squash court' on the north side of the Palace, in one of Nash's conservatories. According to *The Times* 'the glass roof was left in position'.[15]

The King took a personal interest in every stage of its construction. On 29 August Sir Philip Sassoon wrote from the Ministry of Works asking the King's approval of their plans 'for the lining of the bath and the walking ways around it'. He suggested vitreous mosaic rather than glazed tiles for the lining and walkways because 'it is less harsh in appearance and less slippery'. He sent samples of the vitreous mosaic, 'the black marking the edge of the bath', and suggested that 'we introduce two bands of green, one to show immediately above the level of the water and the other near the bottom, with the idea that they will add a certain amount of sparkle and liveliness to the water'.[16] They had consulted the Ministry of Health and the Bath Club, who both advised that they should alter their plans to give more room for walking round. The pool was finished in 1939 but only a year later one of the first bombs to fall on the Palace shattered the sparkling water.

Princess Elizabeth, who was nearly eleven when her father came to the throne, at first regretted leaving her home at 145 Piccadilly, asking if a tunnel could be built to the Palace so that she could still sleep in her own bedroom. She was a composed, orderly girl in whom Queen Mary saw the hope of the future. She and Lady Airlie agreed that there was something in the set of her head that reminded them of Queen Victoria. However, in the year of the Coronation, as the Queen's mother, Lady Strathmore, remembered, 'the Princess, who had heard from her governess of her position as heir to the throne, was ardently praying for a baby brother'.[17]

Lady Airlie thought her

one of the most unselfish girls I had ever met ... no two sisters could have been less alike ... the elder with her quiet simplicity, the younger with her puckish expression and irrepressible high spirits – often liberated in mimicry. Queen Mary described her as 'espiègle', which was precisely the right word although it has no equivalent in English – adding 'All the same she is so outrageously amusing that one can't help encouraging her.'[18]

Lady Airlie was a wise observer who had known the royal family all her life. Her judgement of their characters is confirmed by the account given by Marion Crawford, the Princesses' governess, in her story of the early years of the Princesses, written and published after she had left the royal service. Although it gives a flattering, even sycophantic, picture of the life of the royal family, she broke her sworn promise not to describe her time at the Palace.

Yet she was a much loved governess who brought her Scottish practical good sense and intelligence to the Palace. She came from a simple home and trained as a teacher at Moray House Training College in Edinburgh, where her studies took her 'into the poorer parts of the city . . . I was at that time very young and I became fired with a crusading spirit.'[19] She devoted many years of her life to the Princesses, and the future Queen's absence of prejudice owes much to the influence of 'Crawfie'. Like many other devoted royal servants throughout history, she sacrificed her own happiness, finding it as difficult to leave as Fanny Burney had done in the time of Queen Charlotte. Like that of Queen Victoria's devoted governess, the sad end to her royal career has obscured the very real contribution she made to the present Queen's education.

Her book gives an excellent picture of Buckingham Palace at that time. 'I still recall with a shudder', she wrote, 'that first night spent in the Palace. The wind moaned in the chimneys like a thousand ghosts.' She describes the 'interminable' corridors, the mice that scuttled through their rooms, her dusty curtains that fell, 'pelmets, brass rod and all', at the first vigorous tug, the chairs that collapsed and the chill of their bedrooms, which all faced north. As Sir Lionel Cust had earlier noted, electric switches were in the most inconvenient places: Crawfie's bedroom light could be switched off only by going out and down the draughty corridor. Queen Mary had kept an eagle eye on the State Rooms and on their own apartments, but there were scores of rooms in the vast Palace that had been unvisited for years. 'Life in a Palace', Crawfie reflected, 'was like camping in a museum.'[20]

We can be grateful to Crawfie for her picture of the underside of Buckingham Palace. Behind the grand façade there was an army of workmen. The 300 elaborate clocks, so admired by Queen Mary, took two men a week to wind. Thousands of electric light bulbs needed regular attention.

Crawfie met the 'vermin man', whose job was to trap the mice that scuttled through the marble halls and nested in unused bedrooms. He used 'the sticky trap', 'a piece of cardboard with a lump of aniseed in the middle'. This was surrounded by a sea of treacle with a dry inch all round to give the victim a footing. Attracted by the smell of a lump of aniseed the mouse would be stuck in the treacle. The vermin man would then come and dispatch the trapped mouse.

Crawfie was uncomfortable in her isolated and chilly room, but the Princesses accepted their new home. The King made sure that their schoolroom was attractive, unlike the forbidding attics in which he and his brothers had been educated. He liked having his daughters near him, and encouraged them to keep their rocking horses outside his study door so that he could hear them at play. Princess Margaret was allowed to ride her tricycle down the long corridors, and they had room outside their door for their collection of beloved toy horses. As Crawfie remembered, they remained there until Princess Elizabeth's wedding morning.

The Palace held no terrors for the Princesses; secure in their happy family they enjoyed exploring.

It was strange to hear the little girls' happy voices, laughing and shouting as usual as they ran downstairs and along the corridors to Mummie and Papa's room.

In a very short time [they] set some of the ghosts to flight. The whole atmosphere lightened. Many people noticed this. 'It was as though the place had been dead and had suddenly come alive,' they told me.[21]

While the suite occupied by King George V and Queen Mary was being redecorated, the King and Queen moved into the Belgian Suite on the ground floor, which had been briefly occupied by Edward VIII. In Queen Mary's rooms the silk hangings on the walls were her own and she had taken them with her to Marlborough House. Queen Elizabeth chose her own light wallpaper and installed new bathrooms. Kenneth Campbell remembered that when, during the Coronation year, his firm, Campbell Smith & Co., was redecorating the Queen's rooms,

She complained, in her delightfully humorous and gentle manner, that she was a little tired of the everlasting cream and gold throughout the Palace and couldn't she have something a little different in her own bedroom? We promptly made up a pleasant peach colour and as our foreman was painting a sample on the wall she asked if she could have a go as she had seldom been allowed to do any painting. My father handed her the brush and she slapped away with great gusto.[22]

The King 'chose to use his father's dressing room as his bedroom . . . because it reminded him so much of his father's evening ritual of dressing for dinner with his family around him'.[23]

The Princesses' rooms were two floors above, but this did not prevent them from racing down the corridors to join their parents. Princess Elizabeth had her own sitting room, though her maid, Margaret Mac-Donald ('Bobo'), slept in her bedroom. Crawfie had her own room. The nurse, Clara Knight ('Alah'), was in charge of the day nursery and the night nursery. It was comfortable enough, but the practical Scots governess saw to it that her charges were not spoilt by luxury.

Crawfie, realizing that the Princesses' life in the Palace was too isolated, asked for permission to set up the 1st Buckingham Palace Company of Girl Guides. Princess Margaret was too young but was allowed to join with a friend as a Brownie. The King was an enthusiastic supporter, for during his years as Duke of York he had set up a boys' camp to which boys from different backgrounds came once a year. Some of his happiest days had been spent with them, joining in their singing round the campfire. Now he delighted to join his daughters at their camp, lustily singing his favourite 'Underneath the Spreading Chestnut Tree'. Crawfie wrote

The King made one stipulation only. 'I'll stand anything,' he said, 'but I won't have those hideous long black stockings. Reminds me too much of my youth.' . . . Just at first some of the children who joined started coming in party frocks, with white gloves, accompanied by fleets of nannies and governesses. We soon put a stop to all that.

When half the children did not recognize their own shoes, taken off for a game, the Princesses were scornful. 'There was never any nonsense of that kind in their nursery.'[24]

When, as often happened in the coming years, the King and Queen were away, Queen Mary watched over them. She took them on instructive trips to museums and brought to life for them the history of their own royal family. Lady Airlie said that she 'was more interested in the education of the two Princesses than she had been in her own children'. She 'was very anxious for Princess Elizabeth to read the best type of children's books'. Nor was she the forbidding figure of legend. To the astonishment of the family, after the Second World War she and Lady Airlie were to outshine the young in country dancing at Sandringham, 'stripping the willow' and weaving through 'Sir Roger de Coverley' until early morning. 'We were foolishly pleased to . . . discover that . . . she at nearly 79 and I at nearly 80, outshone the young Princesses and their guests.'[25]

Queen Mary's influence on Princess Elizabeth was strong and lasting. They had much in common: like Queen Mary, who had lived in the shadow of an outgoing mother, Princess Elizabeth was shy, and throughout her life would always allow her mother to take centre stage.

Princess Elizabeth's love for her maternal grandmother, Lady Strathmore, was even stronger. Visits to her at the family home, Glamis Castle, were pure enchantment. An early photograph shows her arriving at the railway station, descending the steps, one hand in that of the whiskered stationmaster, the other firmly clutching her fishing rod. Queen Elizabeth II has deep roots in the Scottish countryside.

Loving parents, a sensible and devoted governess, and, in the background, those enduring rocks, Queen Mary and Lady Strathmore, gave the two Princesses a secure and happy childhood. So for the family, Buckingham Palace was not a prison, nor a mausoleum, nor an unwanted white elephant, nor an imperial fantasy. Queen Elizabeth and King George VI accepted it and charmed the best out of it, filling the chilly rooms with flowers.

But the King did not have as much time as he would have liked to give to his family or the Palace. He faced urgent problems at home and abroad. There were loud and persuasive voices calling for an end to the monarchy. To many of those without work, the monarchy was at best an irrelevance, at its worst an offence. King Edward VIII had been impressed by the misery of the unemployed steelworkers. King George

VI had a social conscience and unlike his brother could not run away from the problems. In foreign affairs there were difficult decisions to be taken: like his father and all who had seen the devastation and agony of the First World War, King George VI wanted peace, but the growing menace of Fascism in Spain, Germany and Italy, and the rise of the dictators Franco, Hitler and Mussolini had to be faced.

At home there was the immediate problem of the Coronation, which normally took a year to prepare. He decided to keep the date fixed for his brother's crowning, 12 May 1937. Fortunately King Edward VIII had involved his brother in the preliminary planning and King George VI had the trained competence of a naval officer. Queen Mary was ready with advice on the history and protocol of the ceremony.

When the day came, for once she broke with tradition, and though no previous dowager Queen had attended the Coronation of the successor, Queen Mary drove out from Marlborough House in the glass coach to the loudest cheers of the crowd. Magnificently regal in purple and gold, a diamond crown on her white hair, she was all that was enduring to a people whose faith in the monarchy was badly shaken. She wore the Garter Star, which belonged to Edward VIII and which she had firmly borrowed as though to emphasize the continuity of the monarchy. She had picked up her son's fallen baton. She wrote with customary simplicity,

Maud and I processed up the Abbey to the Royal box. I sat between Maud and Lilibet, and Margaret came next, they looked too sweet in their lace dresses and robes, especially when they put on their coronets. Bertie and E. looked so well when they came in and did it all too beautifully. The Service was wonderful and impressive – we were all much moved.[26]

Was it Queen Mary, or Marion Crawford, or her own initiative, that inspired Princess Elizabeth to write her account of the day?

The Coronation 12 May 1937. To Mummy and Papa. In Memory of Their Coronation, From Lilibet By Herself.

At 5 o'clock in the morning I was woken up by the band of the Royal Marines striking up just outside my window. I leapt out of bed and so did Bobo. We put on dressing gowns and shoes and Bobo made me put on an eiderdown as it was so cold, and we crouched in the window looking out onto a cold, misty morning. There were already some people in the stands and all the time people were coming to them in a stream . . . Every now and then we were hopping in and out of bed looking at the bands and the soldiers. At six o'clock Bobo got up and instead of getting up at my usual time I jumped out of bed at half-past seven.[27]

It is a rare glimpse inside the Palace on a great state occasion.

'At first it was very jolly,' Princess Elizabeth remembered, but she was concerned, as she told Crawfie, that Princess Margaret should not disgrace us by falling asleep in the middle. After all she is very young for a Coronation isn't she? In fact she was wonderful, I only had to nudge her once or twice when she played with the prayer books too loudly.'[28]

But Princess Elizabeth found the service 'rather boring as it was all prayers, Grannie and I were looking to see how many more pages to the end, and we turned one more and it said "Finis". We both smiled at each other.' In that sentence the empathy between Queen Mary and Princess Elizabeth is strikingly revealed. 'Grannie' had 'looked too beautiful in a gold dress patterned with gold flowers. I thought it all *very* wonderful,' the Princess wrote, 'and I expect the Abbey did too. The arches and beams at the top were covered with a sort of haze of wonder as Papa was crowned.'[29] It was an unusually romantic touch from a girl noted for her practical good sense.

The age-old ritual of the Coronation profoundly moved the King and Queen, and uplifted them, as it had done Queen Mary and King George V before them. Unlike his brother, King George VI was deeply religious. Later he told Archbishop Lang that he felt throughout that 'Some One Else was with him'. A feeling of exaltation transformed him, making him, as he said, for long periods during the ceremony, unaware of what was happening.

Winston Churchill, watching the Queen, whispered to his wife, 'You were right. I see now that the "other one" wouldn't have done.'[30] Again and again in the coming years it would be realized with chilling force how nearly the country had escaped disaster, and how fortunate they were in a King and Queen whose Coronation vows were of such profound importance to them.

Three weeks later, on 3 June 1937, at the borrowed Château de Candé near Tours, France, another ceremony, simpler and sadder, took place. The Duke of Windsor and Wallis Simpson were finally united in matrimony. Charles and Fern Bedaux had lent their castle fully staffed and free of charge. On the eve of the wedding, Sir Walter Monckton arrived with what the Duke bitterly described as a 'fine wedding present' from his brother. It was a letter which said that 'The Duke, notwithstanding his act of abdication shall be able to enjoy for himself only the title, style or attribute of Royal Highness, so however that his wife and descendants shall not hold the said title.'[31]

The Duke never forgave what he considered to be an insult to his wife. Monckton had warned the Home Secretary that the denial of the title HRH would cause trouble, but he was told that the Dominions would not approve the title for Mrs Simpson. The real reason was that few people expected the marriage to last, and if it broke up, as Wallis's two previous marriages had done, it was unthinkable that she should take her title into some future relationship. And, as Frances Donaldson wrote, 'As King George VI reminded Baldwin . . . once a person has become a Royal Highness there is no means of depriving her of her title.'[32] He was in fact mistaken, as later history was to show.

With the Spanish Civil War in 1936 the curtain had gone up on the tragedy of the Second World War and the first years of King George VI's reign were overshadowed by the growing threat of war with Germany. In March 1936 Hitler had invaded the Rhineland. On 15 March 1939 Hitler occupied Prague and issued the proclamation that 'Czechoslovakia had ceased to exist'.

The Nazi forces still advanced. Poland was the next target. In March Hitler demanded Danzig from Poland; in April Mussolini invaded Albania. On 31 March, in the House of Commons, Chamberlain announced the support of the British and Commonwealth governments for Poland. In April this pledge was extended to Greece, Romania, Denmark, the Netherlands and Switzerland.

Against this background of gathering war clouds the government announced that the visit of the King and Queen to Canada and North America would still take place. It was important to strengthen the British links with the New World.

In the royal tours at home and abroad of 1937, 1938 and 1939 the King impressed all with his thorough mastery of his briefs and Queen Elizabeth charmed the crowds with her easy lack of affectation. Then it was realized indeed that 'the other' would not have done. In July 1937 there was a tumultuous welcome in Edinburgh, where the Queen was invested with Scotland's highest order of chivalry – the Order of the Thistle. In May 1938 their visit to France was delayed by the death of the Queen's mother. The Queen chose to wear white – the alternative mourning – and in Norman Hartnell's white crinoline established her particular style, delighting the Parisian crowds. The visit was not only a personal success; it also strengthened the Anglo-French alliance at a crucial moment in European affairs.

Their six-week tour of Canada and the United States in May and June 1939 was the turning point in the public perception of them, and in the development of the King's self-confidence. With the Queen's help, King George VI, speaking with a new authority, was conquering his crippling stammer, and the Queen captured the crowds with her spontaneous gestures of friendship and affection. Timetables were disrupted while she plunged into the crowds, taking special delight in greeting the many fellow Scots in Canada. In a typically graceful gesture she laid a bunch of wild poppies, given her by a boy, on the grave of the Unknown Warrior. In Quebec she reminded her audience, in fluent French, that as a Scot she too came from a separate background. On their brief visit to the USA they established a lasting friendship with President and Mrs Roosevelt.

In the relaxed atmosphere of the Roosevelts' family home at Hyde Park, the King and President chatted informally about world politics long into the night until Roosevelt patted the King's knee and said, 'It's time for you to go to bed, young man.'[33] King George VI never forgot their conversation, always wishing that his own ministers could talk to him so frankly. Listening to Roosevelt's explanation of his New Deal to cope with the massive unemployment in the USA after the slump, the King realized how much he had to learn.

On 1 September 1939 the German army invaded Poland, ignoring the British and French ultimatum. At eleven o'clock on Sunday 3 September Britain declared war.

The King's diary for 3 September recorded his simple faith in the justice of the cause, and that 'those of us who had been through the Great War never wanted another'.

On 3 September the King broadcast to the nation from Buckingham Palace:

we have been forced into a conflict . . . to meet the challenge of a principle . . . which permits a State, in the selfish pursuit of power, to disregard its treaties and its solemn pledges . . . For the sake of all that we hold ourselves dear, and of the world's order and peace, it is unthinkable that we should refuse to meet the challenge.[34]

There followed a period of 'phoney war' when the King was advised by his War Cabinet under Chamberlain, with Churchill at the Admiralty and Eden at the Dominion Office. He was kept fully informed; with authority grown out of his experience as a naval officer, he was able to fulfil his historic duty to advise. Buckingham Palace became his wartime headquarters. There was no question of sending his wife and daughters to Canada or America, as many did. Queen Elizabeth firmly insisted 'The King will not leave, and I will not leave him and the Princesses will not leave us.'[35] During the Blitz the Princesses were sent to Windsor with Miss Crawford, but throughout the war, even during the worst of the Blitz, the King and Queen worked from Buckingham Palace during the week.

Buckingham Palace was now stripped of its valuable contents. Pictures were taken down and the porcelain taken from the display cases and carefully packed. Chandeliers were dismantled and taken to places of safety in country houses. Dust sheets covered the gilt furniture. The Palace Mews were now empty and silent, the ornate carriages removed to Windsor, where the horses worked on the farm.

The phoney war dragged on and the spirit of high resolve was disappearing as Cabinet ministers quarrelled among themselves. Meanwhile, Queen Wilhelmina of the Netherlands and Leopold, King of the Belgians, warned that Hitler was planning to attack.

The King, in his Christmas message in 1939, broadcast from Sandringham, aimed to inspire unity of purpose. He conquered his stammer with difficulty, hesitating at first. He ended with, 'A new year is at hand, we cannot tell what it will bring.' Then he quoted from Minnie Louise Haskins's 'The Gate of the Year':

> 'Go out into the darkness and put your hand into the hand of God.
> That shall be to you better than a light and safer than a known way.'[36]

The year 1940 was to test his faith. Hitler's armies advanced through Europe: the King's fellow monarchs were in danger. On 9 April the Germans occupied Denmark and after the disastrous allied campaign in Norway King Haakon escaped to a British warship and took refuge in Buckingham Palace. On 10 May Hitler mounted a massive ground and air attack on Holland, Belgium and Luxemburg, and a weary and sick Chamberlain was replaced by Winston Churchill.

The King was at first uneasy with Churchill, remembering his support for King Edward VIII. But in September he started a tradition of intimate private luncheons in his room at Buckingham Palace. The two men met every Tuesday in complete privacy and served themselves from a buffet. Although the King missed his orderly weekly talks with Chamberlain at the Palace, he came to appreciate Winston's qualities, and, as John Colville, Churchill's private secretary, wrote, 'Winston, however cavalierly he may treat his Sovereign, is at least a most vehement royalist.'[37]

Churchill now transferred his loyalty to the anointed King, and supported King George VI in his difficult negotiations with the Duke of Windsor, who, when war broke out, came back and saw the King at Buckingham Palace to discuss what war work he could do. He was given a post at Headquarters of the British Expeditionary Force in Paris, but, dissatisfied, returned to London without the King's permission, and tried in vain to enlist Winston Churchill's support. He now saw himself as a leader of a world peace movement. After the fall of France he and the Duchess fled to Spain, where his relationship with German contacts made him a cause of acute embarrassment to the King and government. Eventually he was appointed Governor and Commander-in-Chief of the Bahamas. Here, from August 1940, he and the Duchess spent the war years in diminished grandeur. The activity of the Duke of Windsor was one of many causes of concern for the King during the black months of the spring and summer of 1940.

On 13 May the King had been awakened at Buckingham Palace by a telephone call from Queen Wilhelmina of the Netherlands: in great distress she begged the King to send aircraft to defend her country. Later that day he heard from her again; this time she was ringing from Harwich. She had escaped with only half an hour to spare before German parachutists had descended on her Palace. Determined to join her forces in south Holland, the courageous sixty-year-old Queen had made her way to the Hook of Holland, boarded a British destroyer and asked to be taken south to Flushing. The Admiralty, however, had ordered the warship back to Harwich, and an unwilling Queen Wilhelmina was obliged to take refuge in England. The King met her at Liverpool Street and brought her back to Buckingham Palace, where Queen Elizabeth, as she remembers, organized a wardrobe for her. She had left Holland with nothing except her handbag, the clothes she stood up in and a tin helmet. As she had done with the other royal refugee, King Haakon of Norway, Queen Elizabeth provided all that was needed, although it was not easy in wartime Britain when even the clothes of the royal family were rationed. Queen Wilhelmina's son-in-law, Prince Bernhard, later brought over from Holland his wife Princess Juliana, the heir to the Dutch throne, and their two children, Princess Beatrix (later Queen of the Netherlands) and Princess Irene. On 15 May the Dutch Army capitulated. Queen Wilhelmina never forgot the spontaneous and thoughtful kindness of King George VI and Queen Elizabeth in those tragic days. Later Princess Irene was baptized in the Chapel of Buckingham Palace on the day that had been appointed for her christening in Amsterdam. It was almost the last ceremony to take place in the Chapel at Buckingham Palace, which was destroyed in the Blitz of 1940.

The two war-hardened refugees in the Palace regarded the Palace preparations with some scepticism: they knew the danger from determined German paratroops. Whereas the King and Queen went reluctantly down to the air-raid shelter, King Haakon took air-raid warnings seriously. Queen Elizabeth still remembers stepping over the sleeping body of the snoring King of Norway stretched out on the floor of their basement shelter.

During the first months of the war, it had been realized that, unlike during the First World War, the danger would come from the air. The Home Secretary, Sir John Anderson, ordered air-raid shelters to be made – but at Buckingham Palace the precautions were somewhat haphazard. Queen Elizabeth The Queen Mother's biographer recorded that the housekeeper's rooms in the basement were taken over,

the ceiling reinforced with some steel girders, and the window which was at ceiling height was protected by steel shutters. It was incongruously furnished with gilt chairs, a regency settee and a large mahogany table, surrealistically surrounded by emergency steps to reach the window, axes on the wall to hack one's way out, oil lamps, electric torches, a bottle of smelling salts and a supply of glossy magazines. Next door the room used by the Household was supplied with a piano, though the attempts of a member of a refugee monarch's Household to enliven the nocturnal hours with a rousing sing song were not appreciated by the King.[38]

What would happen, King Haakon asked King George VI, if parachutists descended on the Palace? To which the King replied that a special guard was prepared day and night to defend them. As the King's biographer records,

The King explained the method of alerting the guard, and King Haakon, somewhat sceptically, asked to see it in operation. Obligingly the King pressed the alarm signal and, together with the Queen, they went into the garden to watch the result. There followed anti-climax; nothing happened at all. Apparently the officer of the guard had been told by the police sergeant on duty that 'no attack was impending as he had heard nothing about it . . .' Then a number of guardsmen rushed to the Palace gardens and to the horror of King Haakon but to the vast amusement of the King and Queen proceeded to thrash the undergrowth in the manner of beaters at a shoot rather than men engaged in the pursuit of a dangerous enemy.[39]

King Haakon's fears were soon to be justified: Buckingham Palace was to be the direct target of Hitler's assault.

The fall of Holland was succeeded by the collapse of the Belgian Army. Now that the threat of invasion was very real, the Princesses were sent to Windsor.

The King had a shooting range laid down in the gardens of Buckingham Palace and another at Windsor, at which he and his equerries practised regularly with rifles, pistols and tommy guns. The Queen too took instruction and became a good shot. 'I shall not go down like the others,' she said. No one doubted the steely resolution behind the Queen's sweet charm.[40]

She had proved her skill with a gun in the early days of their marriage when on safari in Africa.

It was feared that the Allied forces would be wiped out at Dunkirk but a flotilla of little ships came to the rescue. At the end of May, Paris was under German occupation and German troops were massing on the Channel coast preparing to invade. As King Haakon and Queen Wilhelmina had been at pains to impress on the King and Queen, there was now real danger: the children might be taken hostage, paratroopers might descend on Buckingham Palace, or they themselves might be captured. Lord Hailsham recommended that the Princesses should be sent to Canada; the King and Queen firmly refused, but they were kept under close watch. Queen Mary, against her will, was evacuated to Badminton in Gloucestershire, where she spent the rest of the war with her niece the Duchess of Beaufort. Here she employed her formidable energy, clearing the woodlands. 'Bring your very oldest clothes,' she told Lady Airlie. She had an obsessive hatred of ivy, which she had attacked with venom in the gardens of Buckingham Palace. Now she worked off her hatred of Hitler by hacking away at the encroaching ivy at Badminton.

The King and his ministers had learned that Hitler had set August for his invasion date. 'We did not know what the future would bring,' Queen Elizabeth The Queen Mother still remembers. She commissioned John Piper to paint a series of pictures of Windsor Castle, 'so that it would be remembered as it was,' she said, 'if the worst happened'.[41] They hang at Clarence House today. In 1940, also, Augustus John began a portrait of her at Buckingham Palace, but it was never finished. It was taken for safety to the artist's house in the country during the Blitz and not discovered until 1960, when it was found in his cellar. It also now hangs in Clarence House.

In spite of the imminent danger of invasion, the King and Queen determined to stay in Buckingham Palace, although there were other, safer houses in London, less easily distinguished from the air. But King George VI, though he was the least demonstrative of kings, realized the importance of this visible gesture of solidarity with their people.

Hitler's planned invasion was prevented by the courage of the airmen who beat back the German attacking planes. In Churchill's celebrated words, 'Never . . . was so much owed by so many to so few.'[42]

On 7 September the Blitz began. During the first night 200 German planes bombed London, killing 400 and seriously wounding 4,357.

Hitler's plan was to destroy London and to kill or capture the King. During the following years Buckingham Palace was a direct target, suffering nine direct hits, and on more than one occasion the King and Queen narrowly escaped.

On 11 September 1940 the King wrote to his mother, Queen Mary,

My darling Mama,

You will have heard about the time bomb which fell near the Garden Entrance at Buckingham Palace last Sunday night, & which exploded on Monday night. I am sending you photographs taken on Monday & Tuesday before & after the explosion showing the damage done. Except for damaging the swimming pool, the main structure of the Palace is untouched. All the windows on each floor were broken. The blast was all upward & only one ceiling is damaged. We were down here at Windsor luckily, & no one in B.P. felt the worse for the 'thud' as the bomb fell on Sunday night, though all our shelters are on that side. Everybody was evacuated on Monday night to the other side of the Palace, in case it exploded & it did at 1.25 a.m.[43]

The Palace Superintendent reported at 2.03 a.m:

Time bomb has smashed many windows. Some of the ceiling in the Queen's small Chinese room is down. Some damage in Empire Room. The Queen's bedroom and boudoir comparatively undamaged apart from windows. Glass skylight over Minister's staircase is down. Swimming pool extensively damaged at end. Crater 15 ft wide where explosion occurred. No-one hurt. Great quantities of broken glass everywhere on that side of the Palace.[44]

Then on 13 September came a much more dramatic and serious attack. A German bomber drove under low clouds straight up the Mall, dropping a stick of bombs directly on the Palace. It was, as the King wrote to Queen Mary on 14 September,

a ghastly experience yesterday & it was so very unexpected coming as it did out of low clouds & pouring rain at the time. We had just arrived at B.P. from here, & were still in our rooms upstairs. Elizabeth, Alec Hardinge & I were talking in my little room overlooking the quadrangle when it happened. We heard the aircraft, saw the 2 bombs, & then came the resounding crashes in the courtyard. Our windows were open, & nothing in the room moved. We were out of that room & into the passage at once, but we felt none the worse & thanked God that we were still alive . . .

The door opposite the King's Door did not come down. All the windows were broken in the passage & the 2 full length pictures of the Duke & Duchess of Cambridge were perforated. But none of the others of the procession.

The aircraft was seen flying along the Mall before dropping the bombs. The 2 delay action bombs in front of the Palace have exploded & part of the railings & centre gates are damaged. There is no damage to the Palace itself I am glad to say & no windows are broken. What a good thing it is that the Palace is so thin though & that the bombs fell in the open spaces. It was most certainly a direct attack on B.P. to demolish it, & it won't make me like Hitler any better for it.[45]

The Queen gave an even more vivid account of the day when death came close and when the history of Buckingham Palace might well have come to an end. Her letter to Queen Mary, written on 13 September from Windsor Castle, is worth quoting in full.

My darling Mama,
    I hardly know how to begin to tell you of the horrible attack on Buckingham Palace this morning.

Bertie & I arrived there at about ¼ to 11, and he & I went up to our poor windowless rooms to collect a few odds and ends – I must tell you that there was a 'Red' warning on, and I went into the little room opposite B's room, to see if he was coming down to the shelter. He asked me to take an eyelash out of his eye, and while I was battling with this task, Alec [Hardinge] came into the room with a batch of papers in his hand. At this moment we heard the unmistakable whirr-whirr of a German plane. We said 'ah a German', and before anything else could be said, there was the noise of aircraft diving at great speed, and then the scream of a bomb. It all happened so quickly, that we had only time to look foolishly at each other, when the scream hurtled past us, and exploded with a tremendous crash in the quadrangle. I saw a great column of smoke & earth thrown up into the air, and then we all dashed like lightning into the corridor. There was another tremendous explosion, and we & our 2 pages who were outside the door, remained for a moment or two in the corridor away from the staircase, in case of flying glass. It is curious how one's instinct works at those moments of great danger, as quite without thinking, the urge was to get away from the windows. Everybody remained wonderfully calm, and we went down to the shelter. I went along to see if the housemaids were alright, and found them busy in their various shelters. Then came a cry for 'bandages', and the first aid party, who had been training for over a year, rose magnificently to the occasion, and treated 3 poor casualties calmly and correctly.

They, poor men, were working below the Chapel, and how they survived I don't know. Their whole work-shop was a shambles, for the bomb had gone bang through the floor above them. My knees trembled a little bit for a minute or two after the explosions! But we both feel quite well today, tho' just a bit tired. I *was* so pleased with the behaviour of our Servants. They were really magnificent. I went along to the kitchen which, as you will remember, has a glass roof.

I found the chef bustling about, and when I asked him if he was alright, he replied cheerfully that there had been une petit quelque chose dans le coin, un petit bruit, with a broad smile. The petite quelque chose was the bomb on the Chapel just next door! He was perfectly unmoved, and took the opportunity to tell me of his unshakeable conviction that France will rise again!

We lunched down in our shelter, and luckily at about 1.30 the all-clear sounded, so we were able to set out on our tour of East and West Ham. The damage there is ghastly. I really felt as if I was walking in a dead city, when we walked down a little empty street. All the houses evacuated and yet through the broken windows one saw all the poor little possessions, photographs, beds, just as they were left. At the end of the street is a school which was hit, and collapsed on the top of 500 people waiting to be evacuated – about 200 are still under the ruins. It does affect me seeing this terrible and senseless destruction. I think that really I mind it much more than being bombed myself. The people are marvellous, and full of fight. One could not imagine that life *could* become so terrible. We *must* win in the end.

Darling Mama, I do hope that you will let me come & stay a day or two later. It is so sad being parted, as this War has parted families.

> With my love, and prayers
> for your Safety, ever
> darling Mama your
> loving daughter in law
>
> Elizabeth

P.S. Dear old B.P. is still standing and that is the main thing.[46]

The sheer daring of the German pilot evoked the unwilling admiration of a police constable, an old soldier, who immediately after the raid said to the Queen, 'A magnificent piece of bombing, ma'am, if you'll pardon my saying so.'[47]

Princess Margaret was not amused. 'The pilot got a double iron cross, the beast!'[48]

Both King and Queen made light of the attack, as the Lady-in-Waiting reported: 'The King was not in the least upset . . . the Queen was of course marvellous, quite unruffled.'[49] But as the King wrote, he later suffered delayed shock, 'found myself unable to read, always in a hurry and glancing out of the window'.[50]

No one, not even Churchill, was told how near an escape they had had. Perhaps he would have reproved his King for failing to go down to the shelter when a 'red' alert was on. Now, as they continued that afternoon with their planned visit to the shattered East End, the Queen could say, 'I'm glad we've been bombed. It makes me feel I can look the East End in the face.' The Lady-in-Waiting on duty said, 'When we saw the devastation there, we were ashamed even of the glass of sherry we had had after the bang.'[51] The Queen's courage has been often praised, but it must be remembered that her Ladies-in-Waiting were also with her in the thick of the Blitz, often worrying about their own families and homes.

Nothing united the country more than the knowledge that the King and Queen shared their suffering. Lord Louis Mountbatten told the King, 'If Goering could have realised the depths of feeling which his bombing of Buckingham Palace has aroused throughout the Empire and America, he would have been well advised to instruct his assassins to keep off.'[52]

Two of Nash's original conservatories were damaged, but the Palace stood firm. Nash's much criticized construction proved its strength. The Queen asked anxiously after the fate of the altar cloth in the Chapel which was made by disabled soldiers of the last war. An old soldier wrote to assure her that it 'was not on the Altar at the time the Chapel was bombed. It is in very good order and is being well looked after. The altar cloth that was on I had carefully removed from the debris, cleaned and put away. It is only slightly damaged and can be repaired.'[53]

Buckingham Palace suffered four more direct hits. On 16 November 1940 *The Times* reported a small bomb that fell on the Palace Mews. On 8 March 1941 the Northern Lodge of the Palace was wrecked, and a policeman killed by the flying debris.

The full story of this policeman was told only in December 1994 in the *London Police Pensioner*. It is worth recording the death of one otherwise unsung hero. PC Steve Robertson PC629A was doing a 'casual' duty. He was based with other policemen inside the Wellington Arch, which, like Marble Arch, contained a number of rooms. It became a somewhat uncomfortable base for the police on guard in that area. When the King's old home, 145 Piccadilly, was bombed, it was policemen from this section who helped to dig the caretaker and his wife from the rubble. PC Robertson's colleague, PC Douglas Lightwood, later Chief Superintendent, Metropolitan Police, who, like many of PC Robertson's friends, was anxious that he should not be forgotten, wrote:

Most of the Wellington Arch personnel had narrow squeaks at one time or another, but the most serious and most tragic incident was that which befell a close pal of mine, PC 629A Steve Robertson. Steve was doing a 'casual' duty on late turn relief on No 1 Garden Beat at Buckingham Palace on Saturday March 8 1941.

During a short sharp air raid by 123 bombers of Luft Flotte Nr. 3 based in northern France that evening, a bomber dropped a basket of 1 kilo phosphorous incendiary bombs on the area around the North Lodge where Steve was on duty. Shunning the safety afforded by the bell steel shelter nearby and ignoring the orders not to tackle incendiaries unless they were threatening the Palace itself, because some contained high explosives which could kill, Steve began to snuff out the blazing devices.

With his attention totally absorbed in this dangerous undertaking, he failed to hear or chose to ignore the sound of another bomber heading his way. A stick of six bombs was aimed at the Palace, the first falling on the parade ground of Wellington Barracks, another on the lawns of Queens Gardens, three on the forecourt of the Palace, and the last one scoring a direct hit on the North Lodge, completely demolishing it. Steve was buried beneath a pile of masonry.

He should have reported off duty at 10 p.m. but when he failed to do so a Sergeant Parrott and another officer went in search. They came upon the pile of rubble which was once the North Lodge and heard a sound coming from underneath, just like someone tapping one piece of stone on another. By clearing some of the debris away they found Steve who, although he was still alive, was barely conscious and in a bad way. They raised the alarm, a rescue squad arrived, and they dug Steve out and put him in an ambulance but he died before reaching Charing Cross Hospital.

The most cruel thing about Steve's untimely end was he need not have been there at all that evening. He did a colleague a favour by agreeing to do a swap of duties with him.

He added:

Since that tragic night there have been reports of unexplained scratching sounds coming from the exact spot where Steve lay dying, and there has been one report of the ghostly figure of a policeman in wartime uniform which dissolved before the eyes of the onlooker.[54]

Ghost or no ghost, without the courage of PC Robertson and many like him, there would have been no more history of Buckingham Palace to be written.

In June 1941 another bomb caused minor damage in the grounds. In August 1944 there was more serious destruction when a 'flying bomb' landed in the grounds of the Palace, shattering windows and destroying trees. These pilotless missiles, known as the V1, were unnerving. After the sudden silence, when the drone of the engine stopped, came a heart-stopping 'crump'. But they were no more successful in destroying the morale of Londoners than the earlier conventional bombs. The invasion attempt of 1940 had failed. The Blitz had shattered cities, but not determination.

In Hitler's plan the destruction of Buckingham Palace was to be a symbolic prelude to his invasion of Britain. If the King was killed – so much the better.

Day after day the King and Queen toured the blitzed city, Queen Elizabeth deliberately choosing to wear her most cheerful clothes. An admiring woman from Chicago sent her this tribute:

> Be it said to your renown
> That you wore your gayest gown,
> Your bravest smile, and stayed in Town
> When London Bridge was burning down,
>   My fair lady.[55]

Tirelessly the King and Queen toured hospitals and factories – not only in London, they also travelled in their special train to Bristol, Birmingham, Glasgow, Portsmouth and South Wales, and wherever cities were under attack. The King's sudden appearance in Coventry, for instance, after the city had been devastated, lifted morale.

Throughout 1941 the bombing of London continued. In the fierce attack of 10 May the Houses of Parliament were hit. The Chamber of the House of Commons was reduced to ashes and the roof of the twelfth-century Westminster Hall was set on fire.

Even the young Princesses played their part. The fourteen-year-old Princess Elizabeth spoke on 13 October 1940 on the BBC radio's

18. *Queen Victoria and Prince Albert at the Bal Costumé of 12 May 1842* by
Sir Edwin Landseer (1803–73). Prince Albert appears as Edward III and Queen Victoria as
Queen Philippa. They stand under a canopy in the Throne Room. The setting and costumes
were designed by James Planché. Edward III founded the Order of the Garter in 1348,
a period that much interested Prince Albert.

19. *Queen Victoria's Sitting-Room* (1848) by James Roberts (*c.* 1800–1867).
Filled with portraits and mementoes of her family.

20. *The New Ballroom at Buckingham Palace* by Louis Haghe (1806–85). This
clearly shows the mural decorations designed by Professor Gruner, which were later to be
obliterated by Edward VII's changes.

21. *The Family of Queen Victoria* (1887) by Laurits Tuxen (1853–1927). The Queen insisted that her family should be 'prettily arranged' and regarded the portraits as 'very like'.

22. *The Queen's Garden Party 26 June 1897* by Laurits Tuxen. Queen Victoria is accompanied by Princess Alexandra. Many of the guests can be identified.

23. *King Edward VII in Garter Robes* (1907) by Sir Arthur Cope (1857–1940).
'The most kingly of them all.'

24. (Right) *Queen Mary* (1911–13) by Sir William Llewellyn (1858–1941). In Coronation robes.

25. (Below) *George V and Queen Mary Enthroned at the Great Coronation Durbar, Delhi, 12 December 1911* by George Percy Jacomb-Hood (1857–1927). They were acclaimed by a quarter of a million people from all over India. The King thought it 'the most beautiful and wonderful sight I ever saw'.

26. (Below) *George V with Princesses Elizabeth and Margaret* by T. P. Earl (1874–1947).

27. The Duke of Edinburgh marches on the fiftieth anniversary of VJ Day, 15 August 1995, with veterans from the war against Japan. Beside him is the Countess Mountbatten of Burma, daughter of the late Earl Mountbatten.

28. (Top right) HM Queen Elizabeth The Queen Mother (1948), a study by Cecil Beaton (1904–80). An unusual portrait of The Queen Mother.

29. (Above) The Prince and Princess of Wales on the balcony on their wedding day, 29 July 1981.

30. (Left) HM The Queen at a Buckingham Palace Garden Party. The Queen and the royal party progress through lines of guests.

31. HM The Queen with President Nelson Mandela at the banquet at
Buckingham Palace given in his honour on 9 July 1996.

32. (Left) 'The Greate Peece': *Charles I and Henrietta Maria with Their Two Eldest Children, Charles, Prince of Wales and Mary, Princess Royal* (1632) by Sir Anthony Van Dyck (1599–1641) in the old Palace of Whitehall.

33. (Below) The Picture Gallery prepared for the banquet given on 21 March 1996 to celebrate Yehudi Menuhin's eightieth birthday.

Children's Hour. 'We know,' she said, in her high, clear, girlish voice, 'every one of us, that in the end all will be well.'[56] But it was to be long years before all was well.

On 7 December 1941 the Japanese bombed Pearl Harbor. America now declared war on Japan and Germany. Franklin Roosevelt had been sympathetic throughout the war, giving what help he could in spite of the US's official policy of neutrality. The King's friendship with the American President had been maintained throughout the dark days of the Blitz by their informal letters. But in October 1942 it was important to strengthen the alliance and to bring home to the Americans the dangers the British were enduring. It would obviously be impossible for the crippled President to visit Britain himself, but the King had shrewdly judged Eleanor Roosevelt and invited her to visit Britain. She had courage and energy, and was observant, intelligent and articulate. She would report back honestly to the President. Mrs Roosevelt made the perilous flight to Britain. She was invited to spend a weekend at Chequers, and Queen Mary asked her to stay a night with her at Badminton, but nothing gave her a better sense of the danger and misery the King and Queen shared with their people than her visit to Buckingham Palace. The Queen wrote to Queen Mary from Balmoral on 19 October 1942, telling her that 'Mrs R' was going to Chequers for the weekend, but

I am sure that she will be so pleased at being asked to visit you.

We are leaving for London this evening, and I must admit that I do not look forward to London life again.

It is *so* dreary at Buckingham Palace, so dirty & dark and draughty, & I long to see the old house tidy & clean once again, with carpets & curtains & no beastly air raids. I feel so sorry for poor Mrs Ferguson & the housemaids, for it is most depressing having to look after a house that is half ruined!

I am putting Mrs R in my own bedroom upstairs. I have had some small windows put in, and she can use Bertie's own sitting room as mine is dismantled & windowless. It is quite a problem to put up *one* guest nowadays! She is only bringing a Secretary with her, & travels very simply & quietly.[57]

The King intensely disliked going down to the basement air-raid shelter, but with the renewed and intensified bombing the Queen insisted 'that the housemaids & all except the watchers should take shelter, we shall have to as well, and I behave like a governess & drive Bertie down!'

Mrs Roosevelt came to London more concerned, it would seem, about staying in Buckingham Palace than at facing air raids. 'But I finally told myself', she wrote in her autobiography, *This I Remember*, 'that one can live through any strange experience for two days.'

I could not travel in such style but as I worried over the problem I realized that I did not have much experience to draw on in deciding what I would need. Clothes had been of very little importance when I visited England during the war. I was flying then and was permitted to take very little luggage. Furthermore, there was no elaborate entertaining during the war and I did not need many changes. Even so, I had been a bit taken aback when I arrived at Buckingham Palace on that trip and was shown my dressing-room with huge closets all around the walls. The maid who unpacked my luggage was well trained but I could see that she was surprised when all she could find to hang up in the enormous expanse of wardrobes was one evening dress, one afternoon dress, a few blouses and an extra skirt![58]

Mrs Roosevelt remembered the darkness and freezing cold of her rooms at the Palace, and the shattered windows repaired with mica. These, though she did not realize it, were the Queen's own rooms, where the hardy Scot had endured the cold. 'Everything in Great Britain', the President's wife recorded,

was done as one would expect it to be. The restrictions on heat and water and food were observed as carefully in the royal household as in any other home in England. There was a plainly marked black line in my bathtub above which I was not supposed to run the water. We were served on gold and silver plates, but our bread was the same kind of war bread that every other family had to eat, and, except for the fact that occasionally game from one of the royal preserves appeared on the table, nothing was served in the way of food that was not served in any of the war canteens.

The dinner given for her in the Palace was, in her favourite phrase, 'not a hilarious meal'. Churchill was silent and preoccupied, as well he might have been. He was waiting anxiously for news of General Montgomery's progress at El Alamein. Finally he excused himself to make a telephone call and came back singing lustily 'Roll Out the Barrel'. He had good news to tell. Montgomery's victory at El Alamein was to be the turning point of the war.

After dinner they

saw the fine Noël Coward film 'In Which We Serve', based on the story of Lord Mountbatten's ship and partly on the story of Dunkirk. It was a novel experience to watch a movie about a man who was himself present, and a very moving experience to see it in the company of people who must have been deeply stirred by it.

During that visit, as she later described, she drove with the King and Queen to St Paul's Cathedral 'because they wanted to give the faithful watchers who had saved the Cathedral the satisfaction of a visit from them . . . and partly so that I could stand on the steps and see what modern warfare could do to a great city'.[59] She never forgot

how people would gather . . . standing outside the ruins of their houses and waiting until their majesties had tramped through the rubble. Often the King and Queen spoke to them quietly and on other occasions the people would address their monarch, but these exchanges . . . were always in a tone of sympathetic understanding. The people suffered stoically and I never heard them complain or speak bitterly.[60]

Mrs Roosevelt was also able to experience royal protocol old-style when she stayed for a night with Queen Mary at Badminton.

Though it was the Japanese attack on Pearl Harbor in 1941 that had finally brought America into the war, it was these personal ties of affection between the Roosevelts and the royal family that had encouraged the President in his efforts to help Britain during the period of the official neutrality of the USA. On this friendly basis, Churchill had been able to build.

As the war dragged on, Buckingham Palace had become increasingly dilapidated. 'It is so cold now, with howling draughts through the cardboard windows,' Queen Elizabeth wrote to Queen Mary. She was beginning to think of taking refuge in a flat they owned in London 'which we have lent to Harry & Alice [Duke & Duchess of Gloucester]'.[61]

But, as the King realized, it was of great symbolic importance that they should be seen holding firm at Buckingham Palace.

So they continued to receive guests there: Prince Bernhard of the Netherlands and King Peter of Yugoslavia came to stay. Haakon, King of Norway, had removed himself after the bombing of 1940, but still had his mail sent to the Palace.

Although the royal family, like everyone else, had their ration cards for food, furnishings and clothing, they had an extra allowance and in September 1943 the Queen was able to send 150 clothing coupons to Queen Mary; as she said, 'there comes a moment, as I know only too well, when one simply *must* have some clothes for all the work that has to be done, and the coupons don't go very far'.[62]

Meanwhile Princesses Elizabeth and Margaret watched the progress of the war from the safety of Windsor Castle and Balmoral. When war broke out, the Princesses had been staying on the Balmoral estate and then had been sent to the Royal Lodge at Windsor with their Scottish nurse, Clara Knight (Alah), and Miss Crawford. But, as Crawfie remembered, on 12 May 1940 the Queen telephoned her with instructions to move into Windsor Castle 'for the week at least'. In fact they were there for 'five years until the war ended'.[63]

Although their rooms in the Lancaster Tower in Windsor Castle were familiar – Princess Elizabeth had always celebrated her birthday there – the blacked-out Castle was eerie and icy cold. In that enclosed world their household became doubly important. Alah slept in Princess Margaret's room, and Miss MacDonald – 'Bobo' – in Princess Elizabeth's. Bobo was to be an important part of Princess Elizabeth's life. She was, as Crawfie remembered, 'A sensible Scottish lass, who one felt would come calm and imperturbable through innumerable bombardments. She hails from a place in Invernesshire called the Black Isle.'[64] Bobo was to become more than a maid. She was a friend, a companion, an adviser. It is important to remember that during the formative years of the life of Queen Elizabeth II, her most constant companions were sensible Scots young women from ordinary homes.

Crawfie followed a curriculum which Queen Mary had helped to plan, adding, at the old Queen's suggestion, more history and less mathematics. The Princesses, she said, would never have to do their household books, but history was important for Princess Elizabeth's career; so she was given two lessons a week at Eton College with the Vice-Provost, Sir Henry Marten. She and Princess Margaret were exceptionally well tutored in French by Mrs Montaudon Smith and later by the Vicomtesse de Bellaigue – a training that has been of lasting value.

If the Princesses needed artistic encouragement they had the example of Sir Gerald Kelly, who was at this time at the Castle working happily and interminably on the Coronation portraits. So, in spite of the war and their isolation, the Princesses' education was not neglected.

It was during these years that Princess Elizabeth's love of horses became a passion and one of her main interests throughout her life. She and Princess Margaret groomed their horses and galloped in comparative safety round the Windsor estate. 'We were in love with our horses,' Princess Margaret remembered.[65]

In 1942, when she was sixteen, Elizabeth insisted on registering for war service, and appeared at the Windsor office, looking young and vulnerable in her Girl Guide uniform. To her disappointment she was not allowed to join up until the war was nearly over.

To Queen Mary's delight, in 1944, Princess Elizabeth became a Councillor of State, signing her first Acts of Parliament when the King was visiting his forces in Italy, and again playing her part in the Council of State when he was visiting Montgomery's army at Eindhoven. Queen Elizabeth had written to Queen Mary on 25 September 1943: 'I am so glad that you approve about Lilibet being made a councillor of state. When Bertie was away in Africa one felt how silly it would be if she could not take any part until the age of twenty-one.'[66]

Sheltered though she had been, Princess Elizabeth had more under-standing of foreign affairs than most girls of her age, since she had family ties throughout Europe and in Russia. So she watched the progress of the war from the black days of the Blitz, to the fight back and the North African offensive with a personal interest.

When Germany overran Hungary, Romania, Bulgaria, Yugoslavia, Greece and Crete, her own family and friends were involved – for instance, the young King Peter of Yugoslavia was the King's godson, and she herself had fallen in love with Prince Philip of Greece when she was still a girl of thirteen. She had met Prince Philip when she and Princess Margaret went with their parents for a weekend visit to Dartmouth College, where the King had spent uncomfortable years as a young man. Prince Philip was eighteen, and hardly noticed her then; but for Princess Elizabeth he was, and would always be, the chosen one. Marion Crawford went to Dartmouth with the family and remembered Prince Philip that, a

fair-haired boy, rather like a Viking, with a sharp face and piercing blue eyes, came in. He was good-looking, though rather off-hand in his manner. He said, 'How do you do,' to Lilibet, and for a while they knelt side by side playing with the trains. He soon got bored with that. We had ginger crackers and lemonade, in which he joined, and then he said, 'Let's go to the tennis courts and have some real fun jumping the nets.'

Off they went. At the tennis courts I thought he showed off a good deal, but the little girls were much impressed.

Lilibet said, 'How good he is, Crawfie. How high he can jump.' She never took her eyes off him the whole time. He was quite polite to her, but did not pay her any special attention.

They met again during the weekend and Prince Philip impressed the little girls enormously with his appetite when, at tea with the Queen, he 'ate several platefuls of shrimps and a banana split among other trifles'.

As they sailed away, Princess Elizabeth watched him through her glasses until he 'became just a very small speck in the distance'.[67]

Prince Philip's uncle was King Constantine, who succeeded to the throne of Greece on his father's death in 1913. Prince Philip's mother, Princess Alice, was the daughter of Prince Louis of Battenberg and Princess Victoria, the eldest child of Queen Victoria's daughter, Princess Alice. In 1917 the Battenberg family name was changed to Mountbatten. The link with the Mountbatten family was to be of the greatest importance, not only to Prince Philip, but also in later years to his son, Prince Charles.

Prince Philip was brought up in Paris until the age of eight. When his parents separated, his uncle, Lord Louis Mountbatten, became his guardian. After prep school at Cheam, Surrey, he was educated at the progressive school run by Dr Kurt Hahn, first in Germany, then at Gordonstoun. The regime at Gordonstoun was tough and demanding, both physically and mentally, but Prince Philip thrived on it. At Gordonstoun, Prince Philip was, as Dr Hahn wrote in December 1938, 'universally trusted, liked and respected'. An experienced and discriminating judge of men, his assessment of Prince Philip's character is important.

He has the greatest sense of service of all the boys in the school. Prince Philip is a born leader, but will need the exacting demands of a great service to do justice to himself. His best is outstanding – his second best is not good enough. Prince Philip will make his mark in any profession where he will have to prove himself in a full trial of strength. His gifts would run to waste if he was soon condemned to lead a life where neither superior officers, nor the routine of the day forced him to tap his hidden resources.[68]

His hidden resources were in fact to be tested at the naval college at Dartmouth, which he entered in 1939 and where he was in his first year when he first met Princess Elizabeth. At this time neither Dr Hahn, nor his officers at Dartmouth, had any inkling that he would one day become the consort of the Queen, so their praise was untainted by sycophancy.

During the war Princess Elizabeth and Prince Philip wrote to each other and the Prince came to stay at Windsor on his rare leaves. His photograph now appeared on Princess Elizabeth's bedside table, and she followed his progress with intense interest.

The war dragged on but on D-Day, 6 June 1944, the Allied invasion of France began and in August Paris was liberated after four years of Nazi occupation. By September the Germans were retreating throughout Europe, and the Allied advance across the Rhine on 22 March 1945 brought victory in Europe.

Now that the King knew the war was nearly over he allowed Princess Elizabeth to enrol in a vehicle maintenance course at Camberley, Surrey, as a subaltern in the ATS, where she completed the course, passing all the tests. She delighted in showing off her new mechanical expertise when the King and Queen visited her at Camberley.

On 28 April Mussolini was hanged in Milan and on 30 April 1945 Hitler shot himself in his Berlin bunker. On 7 May the German Chief of Staff surrendered unconditionally.

The balcony at Buckingham Palace had seen many royal appearances to cheering crowds, but never had there been so triumphant a day as on 8 May 1945. The King, Queen and Princesses, with Churchill, came out again and again to the roar of a vast crowd. That evening the Princesses Elizabeth and Margaret, escorted by young officers, slipped out to join the exuberant crowds. As the King indulgently said, 'Poor darlings, they have never had any fun yet.'[69]

For the present writer and many others in the crowds outside the Palace, there was a certain flatness after the rejoicing. The King and the royal family felt this too. The war with Japan was not yet over; servicemen and women were still abroad; and Lieutenant Philip Mountbatten RN was still serving in the Far East.

The Palace to which the royal family returned after the war was still battered and dusty: the State Rooms had to be quickly refurbished, pictures rehung and the private apartments redecorated. Princess Elizabeth was now fully occupied in establishing a routine that she would later follow as Queen. Family life was still important: the early-morning visits to her parents' rooms before their nursery breakfast continued right up until the days before her wedding.

Now Princess Elizabeth's days were, Crawfie wrote, 'so full of functions and duties that cannot have been other than oppressive for a girl of nineteen'. In fact, the Princess accepted her new role with remarkable equanimity. She

had her own suite and household at the Palace, which really meant that one of the housemaids and a footman made it their particular duty to look after her.

Her bedroom was pink and fawn, with flowered chintz and plain white furniture. Nothing at all magnificent or ornate. She never took a very personal interest in furnishings or decorations, the way Margaret did. She tended to accept gratefully anything that was done for her, and settle down happily in a sitting-room arranged by someone else.

This has been done so often at the Palace, where there is so much of everything already, though most of it is appallingly out of date. With mounds and mounds of furniture around already, furnishing a room tends to mean adapting things. It would be extravagant to buy more. So it boils down to rearranging a few whatnots and valuable antiques that would be wonderful in a museum but are somewhat depressing in a private apartment. One of the subjects Alah and I agreed on wholeheartedly was one day voiced by her as we moved out of sight some truly amazing candlesticks.

'What we need here, Miss Crawford,' she said grimly, 'is one really good fire.'

At ten o'clock Princess Elizabeth would ring for her Lady-in-Waiting to help with her growing pile of correspondence. 'Most afternoons,' wrote Crawfie, 'she would either open some bazaar or visit factories or hospitals. She always managed to find a little while to go into the garden with the dogs and mostly I joined her.'

Crawfie tried to arrange some light relief: 'We started the madrigal classes again, and now we got together thirty or forty young people. They came into the Bow Room, and after singing we had sherry and biscuits.'[70] Even the Queen's horse-loving friend, Lord Porchester, joined the singers. But, closeted, as she often was, with her father in his study, Princess Elizabeth was learning the heavy responsibility that awaited her.

Princess Margaret, however, was still young and undaunted by the cold, dusty Palace, echoing with the noise and confusion of the rebuilding. Crawfie recalls:

On wet days when we could not get out, Margaret would say, 'Let's explore.' Then we would wander off round the Palace, to the war-scarred and shut-off apartments where the workmen were busy. During the war the glass chandeliers had all been removed for safety, the pictures and ornaments packed away. Now they were back, waiting to be unpacked and returned to their places, and sometimes we took a hand. It was fun undoing the beautiful crystal pieces and china figures. There was no saying what we might find next. We polished with our handkerchiefs the bits we unpacked. Often as she worked, Margaret would sing in what she called her 'village-choir voice'. This caused considerable amazement among the workmen who passed by.

And one day, pottering through the half-dismantled rooms, we came upon a very old piano. Margaret was delighted with this find. She dragged up a packing-case, sat down and proceeded to play Chopin. As she touched the notes, great clouds of dust flew out.[71]

As for the King and Queen, they felt jaded and worn out, finding it 'difficult to rejoice or relax as there is so much hard work ahead'.[72] London and many other cities lay in ruins, food and clothing were scarce, there was still rationing, and demobilization would present many problems. Above all the Japanese had still to be defeated and the King was one of the few who held the heavy secret of the atom bomb.

To add to his worries, the wartime coalition of Conservative, Labour and Liberal parties broke up with the dissolution of Parliament on 15 June. To the surprise of the King, and also of the Labour Party, Churchill lost the election and the Labour Party swept into power with a working majority of 180. Even Clement Attlee, the new Prime Minister, had been surprised by their success. For the King, who disliked change, it meant unexpected readjustment to a new set of ministers; and the King and Queen were conservative by nature, though the King was always scrupulously careful to be seen to be above party politics.

There would be no more intimate Tuesday luncheons at the Palace with Churchill and it would be some time before he got the measure of Clement Attlee. But in fact they had much in common. After Haileybury College and Oxford and a legal career, Attlee had come into politics because of his work among the deprived in London's East End. He became MP for Limehouse in 1922 and held the seat until 1950. The King, when Duke of York, had also had experience of work among underprivileged boys when he was involved in the Industrial Welfare Society. His annual boys' camp, which brought together public school and working boys, was a major interest until his accession. Both were shy men and there were some long silences in their Tuesday meetings at Buckingham Palace – quite unlike the early chats with Churchill. (A Labour MP once said that conversation with most men was like a game of tennis – words flew back and forth. With Attlee it was like throwing biscuits to a dog – 'yup' and they were gone.) Gradually, however, they talked more easily and each learned to respect the integrity of the other.

John Colville, Churchill's Private Secretary, praised Attlee's total honesty, quickness, efficiency and common sense.

The King, however, could never understand Attlee's phlegmatic calm in the face of crisis. To the present writer Attlee once remarked, 'Secret of success for a minister? Don't be a worrier. Eden was a worrier. Made him ill.'[73] And the King was a worrier.

From now on the word 'worried' rang like a refrain through the King's letters. He was now the elder statesman. His government was new, and though Attlee and the senior ministers had some experience of government during the wartime coalition, they were setting off into uncharted waters, powered by the knowledge they had the people's mandate to introduce democratic socialism. The ministers who had been in the coalition Cabinet during the war were exhausted, and the King felt strongly his own responsibility. As Attlee said, 'the old pattern is worn out, it is for us to weave the new'. And the King worried about the rebuilding of Britain, about the shortage of materials and food, and about the economic situation. With the end of America's Lend-Lease programme Attlee had to cut imports of food, cotton, tobacco and petrol, and reintroduce rationing. The King had sympathy with some of his aims but throughout Attlee's period of office he felt that the Labour government was going too fast, and it was his duty 'to be consulted, . . . to encourage, . . . to warn': this meant that he felt he must follow in detail every stage in its progress. The problems were immense: there were one million servicemen and women to be demobbed and employed, and houses had to be built without building materials. Attlee tried to reassure the King – they were giving more permits to build. 'But where are the houses? I asked him. The delay is very worrying . . . As to clothing, the P.M. told me all available stocks go to the demobilised men . . . I said we must all have new clothes and my family are down to the lowest ebb.'[74]

Gradually he learned to understand and value other Labour leaders.

He was interested in the fellow stammerer, Aneurin Bevan, who 'thought modern houses should be built as homes not "just boxes of bricks", and designs must suit environments'.[75] The King showed good judgement in his assessment of Ernest Bevin. He wrote to Queen Mary, 'I was much struck by his knowledge of the foreign affairs subject.'[76] He approved Attlee's choice and regarded the forthright minister with amused affection, observing how his immense bulk overlapped the gilt chairs in the Palace. 'Now look what you've done,' he laughed with tolerance at an official banquet for Mrs Roosevelt at Buckingham Palace when Bevin sent some glasses flying.

On Saturday 28 July 1945, in the Bow Room at Buckingham Palace, the new Prime Minister and some of his colleagues stood to receive their seals of office. That evening Attlee and Bevin, the new Foreign Minister, flew off to take the places of Churchill and Eden at the Potsdam Conference. In August the King was one of the few to know that a decision had been taken that would bring relief to the Allies but a terrible devastation to the Japanese. On 6 and 9 August, two atomic bombs were dropped on Hiroshima and Nagasaki, putting an end to the war with Japan. On 15 August – VJ Day – once again crowds surged down the Mall to cheer the royal family on the balcony of Buckingham Palace. On 2 September the Japanese surrender was finally signed in Tokyo Bay on the USS *Missouri*, in the presence of the Supreme Allied Commander in South East Asia, Lord Louis Mountbatten. His nephew, Lieutenant Philip Mountbatten, was also present on an historic occasion he has never forgotten.

It was clear to the King that, on top of all other disturbing changes, he must now face the possibility of losing his daughter, on whose companionship and help he had come to rely. It would be some time before he gave his consent to Princess Elizabeth's engagement. He liked Prince Philip and respected his competence as a fellow sailor, and his lack of a fortune was not important. But the King's close, happy family life was of supreme importance to him, and he was reluctant to see it broken. Perhaps the difficulty Prince Philip experienced in becoming naturalized was not unwelcome to the King.

Encouraged by Lord Mountbatten, Prince Philip had some time

earlier begun the lengthy proceedure to become naturalized, renouncing his membership of the Greek and Danish royal families, and on 18 March 1947 the naturalization of Lieutenant Philip Mountbatten, RN, was announced in the *London Gazette*. In fact, Prince Philip was already a British citizen because of his royal descent, his mother, Alice, being the granddaughter of Queen Victoria's daughter, Alice.

In the face of national and international crises the King's own domestic problems were minor. Nevertheless Buckingham Palace was in urgent need of repair after nine bomb attacks, and, aware as he was of national shortages, he found it difficult to come to decisions about its rebuilding. Little maintenance work had been done during the war and now the Ministry of Works produced many schemes for improvements, most of which had to be rejected. There had been a proposal in 1943 for a small royal kitchen and coffee room. This proposal was to be dropped in 1947. In 1944, they also abandoned a plan to build a new staff block near the Royal Mews with bedrooms and recreation rooms and a dining room. Instead, it was proposed in 1945 to 'install central heating and h/c water in all bedrooms and to improve staff quarters'.[77]

The repair of the swimming pool was scheduled to begin in September 1946, to be finished early in 1947. This went ahead.

The destroyed east end of the Pavilion is to be reinstated and all necessary repairs carried out to the floor and walls of the swimming pool. The work will entail re-roofing a considerable portion of the Pavilion and renewing engineering services, including infiltration plant and repairs to the squash court.[78]

Careful though he had always been to avoid any personal extravagance, the King authorized this work to be started in the autumn of 1946. This was greatly to the pleasure and surprise of the two Princesses. Perhaps it was not simply paternal indulgence: the King also found swimming a great relaxation in times of stress. The work was done in conjunction with the repairs to the North Colonnade and boundary wall.

The other problem to be solved was that of the other bombed Nash pavilion, that had been turned into a chapel. Various proposals were submitted. At first the King had wanted it designed on the lines of a chapel in Chester, but another plan of 1945 was to keep the

exterior without alteration, removing Pennethorne's defacements and restoring the original work of Nash. Pennethorne introduced height by raising the roof but instead of doing this the nave floor has been lowered so as not to interfere with the roof line as originally designed.

It is understood that the King and Queen desire to sit in the nave and the suggested approach is from the ground floor ante-room down a flight of 12 steps, positioned immediately below those which originally served the Royal Gallery.

The suggested plan was based upon the adoption of nave and side aisles, enabling arcading to be introduced to support the semi-circular or barrel ceiling of the nave. This ceiling treatment is continuous from the gallery to the altar. Solid fillings to the windows on both sides of the Chapel would be removed and glazing provided as a means of natural lighting; roof or clerestory lights are dispensed with. The solid wall behind the altar is retained.

This plan too was rejected, as was a scheme to build a cinema under the Chapel. This would not be possible, it was said, 'without producing a structure incompatible with the existing elevation of the Palace, unless the present Chapel is pulled down and rebuilt. The estimated cost of this would be £50,000.'[79]

In 1945 this was obviously an indefensible expense. The memory of the devastated cathedral the King had seen at Coventry kept the loss of this little-used Chapel in perspective.

The greater problem was the installation of central heating. In 1945 the cost was estimated at £50,000, but it was argued that its installation would effect great economies. The work could be finished in twelve to eighteen months if the Palace were unoccupied, but otherwise, if the work had to be phased, it could be done in four sections so that three-quarters of the Palace 'would be habitable during the whole period of work'. Although this would take three and a half years, the King needed to use the Palace; it was to be his headquarters during the trials of peace as it had been in war – conferences, audiences and investitures were to be held there during the post-war period. But these were years of considerable discomfort in the Palace.

In the bitter February of 1947 a *cri de cœur* from the Marshal of the Diplomatic Corps, Sir John Monck, was sent to Sir Ulick Alexander, Keeper of the Privy Purse. He made a plea for central heating in his offices, where the temperature remains in the low fifties in cold weather, 'a very cheerless welcome to give all the new Ambassadors', who 'mostly come from centrally-heated hotels such as Claridges, the Ritz, the Dorchester etc. and it is not very dignified, after they have experienced the cold entrance passage, to ask them to keep on their overcoats as the temperature is much lower than anything to which they are accustomed'.[80] Sir Ulick Alexander promised that in August 1947 work would begin on the installation of central heating 'as part of the overall modernisation of the Palace'.[81]

So many different projects and costings were envisaged that it is difficult to ascertain exactly what the work at the Palace finally cost. But the news of armies of workmen there set the Parliamentary watch-dogs barking. When thousands were homeless few tears were shed for the chilly ambassadors. And at this period there was the strictest control of building materials.

In Parliament on 31 March 1947 Mr Ernest Davies

asked the Minister of Works the nature of the works now being undertaken at Buckingham Palace, the cost thereof, and the numbers employed thereon.

Mr. Key [replied]: The special work now in hand at Buckingham Palace includes bomb damage repairs, excavation work for a new boiler house and mains in connection with the modernisation of the heating system, and the improvement of the servants' quarters in the attics. There is also some work in connection with redecoration of certain rooms and the re-wiring of part of the State rooms. The total cost of this work is about £54,300, of which about half is on bomb damage repairs. The number of men employed is 178. I am satisfied that this work is necessary. The general programme for modernising engineering services in the Palace will be spread over many years, but the opportunity has been taken of the absence of the Royal Family in South Africa to carry out certain noisy and dirty work connected with the installation of new boilers which will be oil fired.[82]

The King's planned tour of South Africa in February, taking the Queen and Princesses with him, was a relief to his staff, who were anxious to begin the work: and the ministers and Household, concerned about the King's health, hoped that the sea trip would revive him.

Queen Mary had noticed how desperately tired the King was at the family gathering at Sandringham over the New Year in 1946–7. The constant stress of the war years had taken their toll of a man who had never been strong. In the seven years ahead, until his death in 1952, he was to face fundamental changes and crises at home and abroad. Like George III he had a deep sense of his royal responsibilities, and like him he insisted on being involved in every major and most minor decisions. He did not have George III's wide cultural and scientific interests, but he carried a similar burden. George III had to face the loss of America; King George VI had to accept the transformation of the British Empire into the Commonwealth of Nations, with the granting of independence to India and the separation of Eire from the Commonwealth.

The problem of India had weighed heavily on the King. He had been shocked when in July 1942 Churchill told him that his colleagues 'and all three parties were quite prepared to give up India to the Indians after the war'.[83] When Attlee came to power, determined to give India her independence, the King studied the complex problems of the Hindu and Muslim communities, followed closely the progress of the talks held at the London Conference of December 1946, and worried. He invited the leaders of the Muslim and Hindu communities to luncheon at Buckingham Palace and, after sitting between the silent Indian leaders, Jawaharlal Nehru and Mohammed Ali Jinnah, reflected gloomily that they would never agree.

The appointment of his cousin, Lord Mountbatten, as Viceroy of India did much to change the King's attitude. Attlee's choice was a brilliant stroke. Mountbatten was sympathetic to the Labour government, but, at the same time, was in his devotion to royalty more royal than the royals. His charm, energy and ruthless drive, combined with Attlee's determined idealism, were to bring about the change at a remarkable speed. Appointed on 20 February 1947, he left for India in March; meanwhile the King himself had left for South Africa on 1 February, on a tour which, he hoped, would strengthen the ties with that country and keep it in the Commonwealth.

If the Household had hoped the sea voyage would take his mind off his worries they were mistaken. In fact, he followed closely all that was happening at home, consumed with guilt that he was not there to share the misery of frozen England as he had been during the war. Britain was suffering the worst winter on record: fuel stocks were low, transport was bogged down and the whole country was encased in a glittering coat of ice.

There was another change ahead that he dreaded. He now had to accept that Princess Elizabeth had made up her mind to marry Prince Philip. However, to delay the moment of separation, he insisted that she should wait until her twenty-first birthday and that she should go with them on the South African tour.

Her birthday was to be during the tour and the night before they left, Lady Airlie led a deputation to present the Household's birthday present – a silver inkstand. One member from each grade of the Household stood outside the Princess's room in the Palace. Lady Airlie spoke for them all, adding that she 'had played as a child with her grandmother Queen Mary, seen her mother learning her first dancing steps in the nursery at Glamis, and had watched herself grow up from babyhood'.[84] This continuity of service has always been deeply important to Queen Elizabeth II.

Their tour gave Princess Elizabeth an understanding of the vast continent and its problems that would be invaluable to her when she became Queen. It was in South Africa that, on 21 April 1947, she celebrated her coming of age with a moving speech of dedication.

I should like to make that dedication now. It is very simple. I declare before you all that my whole life, whether it be long or short, shall be devoted to your service and the service of our great Commonwealth to which we all belong. But I shall not have strength to carry out this resolution unless you join in it with me, as I now invite you to do; I know that your support will be unfailingly given. God bless all of you who share it.'[85]

The King returned from South Africa desperately tired and alarmingly thin. In fact, he had lost seventeen pounds during the tour. Standing in line with the other members of the Household in the Grand Hall of the Palace to welcome home the royal family, Marion Crawford was shocked to see how ill and tired they all appeared.

It was the beginning of a gradual deterioration in the King's health. However, he could not rest. Attlee and Mountbatten were pressing ahead with their plans for Indian independence. On 10 July 1947 Attlee introduced the Indian Independence Bill in the House of Commons without opposition. It became law on 18 July. None of us who saw Attlee's unaccustomed emotion that July day could fail to be moved. He had realized an ideal. Attlee's determination, and Mountbatten's drive and royal magic, had succeeded.

On 15 August, Lord Mountbatten became Governor General of the Dominion of India, and Jinnah of the Dominion of Pakistan. It was with great sadness that the King ceased to sign himself 'GRI'. On 18 August 1947 Queen Mary received a letter from him. On the back of the envelope she wrote, 'The first time Bertie wrote me a letter with the I for Emperor left out, very sad.'[86] For Queen Mary, more than any other member of the royal family, India had been, indeed, the 'Jewel in the Crown'.

The King accepted the inevitable with good grace, just as he did on 10 July 1947 when he announced the engagement of Princess Elizabeth and Prince Philip. Lady Airlie watched them both at the Buckingham Palace garden party in July. Elizabeth was

flushed and radiant with happiness and I was again reminded of Queen Victoria. Although the Queen had been old, fat and plain when I had seen her and this girl was young, pretty and slim, she had the same air of majesty. Even Queen Mary was not as regal as the 21 year old Princess.[87]

Queen Mary herself saw in Princess Elizabeth 'something very steadfast and determined . . . like her father. She won't give her heart lightly, but when she does it will be for always.'[88]

In July there had been little ease for the King. In that month a new economic crisis made further stringent measures necessary. During his summer break at Balmoral he worried about the world. And he worried that Attlee did not appear to worry. 'I do wish one could see a glimmer of a bright light anywhere in world affairs,' he wrote to Queen Mary. 'Never in the history of mankind have things looked gloomier than they do now and one feels powerless to help.'[89] In fact, the King was 'burned out', and unlike his Prime Minister he could not look forward to the respite of a possible period of opposition.

That autumn the Palace was not a restful place. It was still the King's headquarters, where he received Attlee for their silent Tuesday sessions. But workmen were still hammering, rushing to complete the repairs to the State Rooms in time for the wedding on 20 November.

Princess Elizabeth and Prince Philip would have been perfectly happy with a simple wedding, but it was decided to make this marriage an occasion for national celebration. The royal wedding was to take place in the sanctified setting of Westminster Abbey and it was hoped that the unpleasant affair of King Edward VIII would be forgotten.

Attlee, however, was strongly criticized by some members of his left wing for extravagance in a time of economic crisis, especially since the Chancellor of the Exchequer, Hugh Dalton, was to bring in a stringent emergency budget. Not all critics were silenced by the statement that the King would bear most of the cost out of his Civil List allowance. Most members of the Labour Party were content, however, knowing that the country needed a chance to cheer.

Settling the income of the royal couple was a more difficult problem. By tradition the heir to the throne could expect an increase in his or her Civil List allowance on marriage. Sir Alan Lascelles and Sir Ulick Alexander, the Keeper of the Privy Purse, asked for an increase of £35,000 – bringing Princess Elizabeth's annuity to £50,000. Dalton rejected this proposal. It would be unacceptable when the nation was being asked to tighten its belts. However, in the middle of the negotiations, Dalton resigned. He had accidentally let slip some part of his budget to a journalist just before his speech to the Commons. There was great relief at the Palace, where Dalton was very unpopular. His successor, Stafford Cripps, recommended that Princess Elizabeth should have an annuity of £50,000, with £10,000 for Prince Philip. The King was to provide £100,000 from his own savings from the Civil List. The annuity was approved by the Cabinet – even Aneurin Bevan remarked that 'so long as Britain had a monarchy we ought never to lower [its] standards'.[90]

The marriage became a rare chance to celebrate. 'London was grey, life was grey,' Princess Elizabeth's Private Secretary, John Colville, wrote. It was an 'event which with nationwide rejoicing, splendid decorations and the re-emergence of State Carriages and the Household Cavalry in full-dress uniform, helped to lift the encircling gloom'.[91]

Queen Mary, for all her frugality, firmly believed that majesty should shine on such occasions, and delighted in the 'magnificent evening party'[92] held at Buckingham Palace before the wedding, for which sparkling tiaras and orders emerged from long years of storage. To Lady Airlie it seemed

after the years of austerity like a scene out of a fairy tale . . . Old friends scattered far and wide by the war were reunited . . . most of us were sadly shabby – anyone fortunate enough to have a new dress drew all eyes – but all the famous diamonds came out again, even though most of them had not been cleaned since 1939. Queen Mary looked supremely happy . . . For the first time in many years I saw the old radiance in her smile. When Winston Churchill went up to greet her she held out both hands to him, a thing I had never known her to do before . . . Philip had won . . . her liking and her approbation. When someone complained to her that he had been at a 'crank school where boys were taught to mix with all and sundry and that it remained to be seen whether the objects of this training would be useful or baneful to the King's son-in-law,' she had replied decisively 'useful'.[93]

John Colville remembered:

The guests were as various as half a dozen foreign Kings and Queens on one hand and Beatrice Lillie and Noël Coward on the other. An Indian Rajah got uncontrollably drunk and assaulted the Duke of Devonshire (who was sober) . . . Queen Mary, scintillating as ever in a huge display of jewellery without giving the least impression of vulgarity or ostentation, was somewhat taken aback when Field Marshal Smuts said to her, 'You are the big potato; the other Queens are small potatoes.'[94]

Food at this time was still rationed, so the menu at this party and for the wedding breakfast was simple. In fact the Palace had been 'overwhelmed by food parcels from all over the world. Hundreds of tons of tinned food of every variety arrived, given by British communities abroad.' [95] The official solution, to hand it over to the Ministry of Food, was rejected by Princess Elizabeth as being too 'unimaginative'. At Colville's suggestion Lady Reading brought in her WVS volunteers after the wedding and took over the Palace kitchens during the royal family's Balmoral holiday.

By the end of September 1948 thousands of beautifully packed and well assorted food parcels had been despatched to widows and old age pensioners throughout the Kingdom, each containing a message from Princess Elizabeth personally. These were sent by the Post Office free of charge.[96]

As John Colville remembered, it was a hectic time for all the House-hold. Presents arrived from all over the world to be unpacked and put on display at St James's Palace. There were jewels and 'hundreds of beautiful handkerchiefs, linen, lace and lawn. Hundreds of pairs of nylon stockings . . . gifts of silk and muslin and brocades that came from distant parts of the Empire.'[97] Gandhi sent a tray cloth, woven by himself, which some humourist said was a loin cloth. Queen Mary was deeply shocked.

On his marriage Prince Philip was made Duke of Edinburgh. The night before the wedding, while he enjoyed his stag night with his uncle, Lord Mountbatten, the Princesses were practising a new descant to be sung in the Abbey the next day. Marion Crawford heard 'the most awful sounds coming from the old music room. They were all trying to sing Crimond's setting of the old Scottish paraphrase of "The Lord is my Shepherd" . . . [and] they could not get the descant right.'[98] That descant, as John Colville recorded, had been taught to the Princesses on the moors at Balmoral by one of Princess Elizabeth's Ladies-in-Waiting, Lady Margaret Egerton, 'endowed with a beautiful voice. She had been wont to sing a metrical psalm "The Lord is My Shepherd" (Crimond) in the heather at Balmoral and had taught the Princesses a little known descant.'*

Nobody could find the score of the descant. Lady Margaret tunefully accompanied the two Princesses, and sang it to the Organist and Precentor of Westminster Abbey who took the notes down in musical shorthand and taught it to the Abbey Choir. On the wedding day nobody was more surprised than the composer of the descant who, far away in Stirling, listened to the service on his radio. Since then both the metrical psalm to the tune Crimond and the descant have been consistently popular in churches throughout the British Isles and the Commonwealth.[99]

On the morning of the wedding Marion Crawford went early to Princess Elizabeth's room and found her in her dressing gown watching the crowds outside the Palace. Crawfie was justly proud of Princess Elizabeth that day. She had, for sixteen years, through war and tragedies, given her love and total loyalty. As she later said to the Queen, she felt that 'she too was losing a daughter'.[100] She had not the elegance of style of Fanny Burney but, like her, brought humanity and immediacy to her description of the great occasion. If her usual common sense was on this day touched with sentiment, it can be forgiven. 'I could not help remembering', she wrote, 'that small golden-headed little girl I had first seen sixteen years ago, sitting up in bed, the cord of her dressing gown tied to the bed posts, driving her imaginary team round the Park.'[101]

There were last-minute panics. A lost bouquet was finally found in a cool cupboard. Colville had to rush over to St James's Palace to collect a string of pearls that Princess Elizabeth wanted to wear and only with difficulty persuaded the police to give it to him. He was escorted back to the Palace with a policeman and a couple of detectives.

Only Margaret MacDonald, 'the staunch Bobo remained . . . calm and cool'. She dressed her Princess and then went over to the Abbey to be on hand when she arrived there. 'Throughout the years,' Crawfie wrote, 'I had many reasons for admiring the Queen's self-control but I have never admired her more. And I thought as I watched her enter

---

*John Colville was bewitched by the owner of the lovely voice. He later married 'Meg' Egerton.

the Abbey and kneel for a moment in prayer that the most she could ask for her child was the happiness she herself had found in her marriage.'

From her privileged seat in Poet's Corner, Crawfie watched. 'First the Queen in apricot silk brocade', more becoming Crawfie thought 'than her usual pastel violet, blue or mauve', then at last the bride. 'Her veil was a white cloud about her and the light from the tall windows and from the candelabra caught and reflected the jewelled embroidery of her dress.' She hoped that her younger sister walking alone was noticed too; she 'moved with extraordinary dignity and grace, her head held high'. Crawfie loved and understood Princess Margaret and knew more than anyone else how lonely she would be from now on. The most touching moment of the service, Crawfie thought, was when the couple came out of the 'vestry, paused for a moment before the King and Queen and Elizabeth swept them a beautiful curtsey'. Afterwards Crawfie

was rushed through the crowds in a police car to take my place at the family luncheon party at Buckingham Palace. The tables were decorated with smilax and white carnations and at each of our places there was a little bunch of white heather sent down from Balmoral. The famous gold plate and the scarlet coated footmen gave a fairy-tale atmosphere to it all and I was in a veritable dream. The skirl of the bagpipes warmed the hearts of those of us who came from North of the Tweed. The French gentleman seated next to me, however, winced from time to time, but he bore it with fortitude.[102]

At this royal wedding, unlike earlier ones, the accent was Scottish not German. Many of the Household were from 'North of the Tweed' – recruited in Aberdeen and Edinburgh. There were few of the old German families present – 'the royal mob', as Queen Victoria had called them. Even Prince Philip's sisters, who had married into German families, were not present.

For the devoted governess in her 'cherry red velvet frock and a large black hat with black ostrich feathers held in place with ruby clips', it was a magical day. For the King it had been a day of sadness and joy. As he wrote to Princess Elizabeth afterwards:

I was so proud of you and thrilled to have you close on our long walk in Westminster Abbey, but when I handed your hand to the Archbishop, I felt I had lost something very precious . . . Our family, us Four, the Royal family must remain together, with suitable additions of course at suitable moments.

I have watched you grow up all these years with pride under the skilful direction of Mummy who as you know is the most marvellous person in the world . . .

Your leaving us has left a great blank in our lives but do remember that your old home is still yours and do come back to it as much and as often as possible.[103]

There was some consolation for the King. Clarence House, which was to be the newly-weds' new home, was not ready, so after their honeymoon at Broadlands, Hampshire, the home of Lord Mountbatten, and at Balmoral Princess Elizabeth and Prince Philip returned to live in the Princess's old rooms at Buckingham Palace and were to remain there for another year. While the Prince worked as a naval officer at the Admiralty, the King spent much time with Princess Elizabeth, guiding her in her path to the throne. He would not allow her to be unprepared, as he himself had been.

In 1948 the King's fears about the world seemed realized. Gandhi was assassinated in New Delhi in January, and India was torn by riots. In February came the Russian coup in Czechoslovakia. His spirits were lifted by the enthusiastic crowds that cheered him and the Queen on their Silver Wedding, when they drove through the streets of London and afterwards made the traditional balcony appearance.

By the autumn, however, his doctors were worried. His left foot was numb all day. Nevertheless he soldiered on. There was a dinner for the Commonwealth Prime Ministers at Buckingham Palace on 13 October. On 26 October he opened Parliament for the first time since the war in full state.

He was still hoping to undertake a tour of Australia and New Zealand in the New Year, but a specialist, Professor Learmonth, diagnosed arteriosclerosis. The King was ordered to rest and since he was warned that the blocked artery might cause gangrene and even result in the amputation of the leg, he agreed to do so. Reluctantly he cancelled the tour.

There was one great joy that November. He and the Queen had concealed from Princess Elizabeth the gravity of his illness until after the birth of her first child. Prince Charles was born on 14 November 1948, in her old nursery at Buckingham Palace, as his mother had wished. He was the first baby to be born in the Palace since Queen Victoria had given birth to Princess Beatrice there.

Soon afterwards Princess Elizabeth and Prince Philip took their son to their new home, Clarence House, which after long delays was finally ready. Prince Philip took much pleasure in arranging and equipping his first real home. It was run on the same lines as Buckingham Palace. Prince Philip had his old friend and Navy colleague Michael Parker as his aide, and the staunch John Dean as his valet. Princess Elizabeth had two Scottish nurses, Helen Lightbody and Mabel Anderson, who were to be of immense importance in the lives of Prince Charles and his sister, Princess Anne, who was to be born at Clarence House on 15 August 1950. They were especially important when Prince Philip was allowed to return to active service in the Royal Navy, and Princess Elizabeth joined him in Malta.

Slowly the King recovered and was able to carry out an investiture at the Palace in February 1949, though he remained seated. But his doctors realized that he could not recover fully without an operation. It was suggested that the King, as a Mason, should go into the Royal Masonic Hospital. 'But', said the King, 'I have never heard of a King going into hospital.'[104] So, on 12 February, a room in the Belgian Suite was again turned into an operating theatre. Professor Learmonth performed a lumbar sympathectomy, which cut the nerve to his leg. The Queen, who was his constant support, was deeply concerned and prayed to be 'granted not a lighter load but a stronger back'.[105]

The King's load certainly did not lighten, nor did he have the Queen's physical strength. He continued to watch closely events in India. Independence had come, but not without blood and tears. Mountbatten had retired as Governor General in 1948 but kept a close friendship with Nehru, which helped to create a new relationship between India and Great Britain. Nehru came to London and was received by the King at Buckingham Palace in October 1948. The newly elected Indian Constituent Assembly had voted to become a democratic republic, but both the King and Lord Mountbatten were anxious to keep India within the Commonwealth, even though it was a republic. This time the King was impressed with Nehru's genuine desire to achieve this settlement.

The Commonwealth premiers met in London on 21 April 1949 to discuss India's relationship with the new Commonwealth. On Wednesday 27 April, still convalescent from his operation, the King received Attlee and seven other prime ministers and Lester Pearson, Canadian Minister for External Affairs, in the White Drawing Room at Buckingham Palace. In his speech he praised the 'commonsense and good temper of their conference'.

Their solution, expressed in the Declaration of 27 April 1949, stated that 'the Governments of the United Kingdom, Canada, Australia, New Zealand, South Africa, India, Pakistan and Ceylon . . . have considered the impending constitutional changes in India'.[106] Although India was to become a sovereign independent republic, she still wished to remain a member of the Commonwealth and wished to accept the King as the symbol of the free association of its independent member nations and as such as the Head of the Commonwealth. The King believed that the solution they had found to a 'problem that has given us all very grave concern' was a 'striking example of the elasticity of our system . . . He believed that their association of nations had immense powers of good for humanity generally.' Praising their 'wisdom and tolerance', he hoped the new arrangement would 'redound to the greater happiness of all those millions whose well being is the responsibility of all of us in this room today'.[107]

It was a trust he was to bequeath to his daughter and it has remained her greatest pride. There have been many assemblies in the White Drawing Room at Buckingham Palace but perhaps none more important. Just as his father, King George V, had done, King George VI had made the Palace the symbol of unity.

The year 1950 was a difficult one, with political and economic crises at home and international tension caused by the Korean war.

In the winter of 1950–51 two books were published which caused concern at the Palace. Marion Crawford published her memoirs, *The Little Princesses*, in breach of her solemn promise to the Queen. Poor Crawfie had been badgered by a difficult husband and seduced by her publisher's offer of large sums of money. The Royal family was shocked: she had broken her word and betrayed their trust. She could not be forgiven. Yet in the words of Princess Margaret, 'We loved her, and the irony was she made us loved.'[108] Crawfie finally left her little grace-and-favour house at Kensington Palace, which she had been given for life instead of a pension. She died in 1988. There were no flowers from the Palace.

In March 1951 the Duke of Windsor published his *A King's Story*, which sold 80,000 copies in the first month. It was innocuous enough – in fact, the Duke wrote of Queen Mary with a warmth that is absent from the bitter letters he wrote to Wallis after her death. But such publicity in those days was distasteful – even vulgar.

There was some cheer on 3 May 1951 when the King opened the Festival of Britain on a bomb site on the South Bank, near Waterloo. Masterminded by Herbert Morrison, it celebrated the centenary of the Great Exhibition of 1851 and did something to lighten the period of austerity. It was intended to be a symbol of renewal and hope. Queen Mary, however, considered the architecture 'really extraordinary and very ugly'.[109] Now in her old age she looked more to the past than the future.

The Festival did not cheer the tired King, who wrote, 'The incessant worries and crises through which we have been have got me down properly.'[110] During May his doctors were concerned: after an attack of influenza, an X-ray showed a shadow on his lung. In July 1951, concerned at the King's increasing weakness, Prince Philip, now a Lieutenant-Commander, gave up the career he loved to support his wife in her increasingly heavy duties as heir to the throne.

The King rested as much as he could during the summer but in September caught a chill at Balmoral and returned to Buckingham Palace for a bronchoscopy. Though he was not told, this revealed a cancerous growth. Once again a room in Buckingham Palace became an operating theatre and his left lung was removed on 23 September.

From now on, in the words of Churchill, the King 'walked with death'.[111]

Even in this illness the 'cares of state' did not lighten. Attlee decided the government could carry on no longer and asked for a dissolution.

On 5 October a Privy Council was held at Buckingham Palace in a room adjoining the King's Bedroom to receive the King's command for the dissolution of Parliament. The Councillors, the Queen and Princess Elizabeth stood in the doorway while the King struggled to sign the necessary documents.

The Conservatives won the election on 25 October. In Attlee the King lost a Prime Minister whose total integrity he had learned to trust, but Churchill, who returned as Prime Minister, was a welcome and familiar figure, although at seventy-six he was no longer the vigorous war-leader. More and more the King relied on Princess Elizabeth, who in October, with Prince Philip, represented him on a highly successful tour of Canada and America.

The King's last Christmas at Sandringham was full of peace and happiness. Members of his Household noticed how relaxed and contented he seemed. He returned to Buckingham Palace at the end of January to see his doctors and to say goodbye to Princess Elizabeth and Prince Philip, who were leaving to undertake the tour of East Africa, New Zealand and Australia that he and the Queen had hoped to make.

On the eve of their departure there was a happy family party at the musical *South Pacific*. Then came the leave-taking at London airport and the unforgettable picture of the King standing bareheaded in the chilly wind, his eyes fixed on the disappearing plane. Few who saw him doubted that this was a last farewell. He returned to Sandringham with Princess Margaret and the Queen.

The King's last days were peaceful and he seemed happier and more serene than he had been for a long time. The day of 5 February was the kind of country day he loved best – cold and bright; and he had a happy day shooting on the estate, wearing his electrically heated waistcoat.

That evening he spent quietly with the Queen while Princess Margaret played the piano for him. 'There were jolly jokes – and then he wasn't there any more,' she remembered.[112] At 10.30 p.m. he retired to his room and his servant brought him a cup of cocoa. At midnight, the watchman in the garden saw him shut his bedroom window. It was not until 7.30 the following morning that it was discovered that the King had died in his sleep during the night.

Meanwhile, unaware that she had become Queen, Princess Elizabeth and Prince Philip were at Treetops in Kenya. That morning was etched indelibly on the memory of every member of the royal party. Mike Parker, Prince Philip's friend and equerry, took the Princess to the observation platform at the top of the tree to watch the sunrise. 'While they looked at the iridescent light that preceded the sunrise, they saw an eagle hovering just above their heads.'[113] He guessed that it was at this time that the King died.

Princess Elizabeth and Prince Philip returned to Sagana Lodge, the house given to them as a wedding present, ten miles away. Martin Charteris (now Lord Charteris), who was later to become for many years Private Secretary to Queen Elizabeth II, remembers picking up the news from a reporter. He telephoned Mike Parker, who heard it confirmed on the BBC Overseas Service, and told the Duke of Edinburgh. It was 11.45 a.m. London time before Princess Elizabeth knew that she was now Queen. Parker watched the Duke of Edinburgh take his wife 'up to the garden . . . and they walked slowly up and down the lawn while he talked and talked and talked to her'.[114] Martin Charteris remembers that day. Unashamedly he says, 'I was in love with her.' Now as he saw her at the Lodge, 'sitting, erect, no tears, colour up a little, fully accepting her destiny', his admiration was profound.[115]

The radiant girl in blue jeans was now a sad young Queen in mourning. She sat, as Charteris remembers, still and grave. Below, the vast African landscape unfolded, here and there bush fires flared. She called Charteris to join her. 'What happens next, Martin?' she asked. She had not been unprepared: her father, the King, had been so clearly a sick man. But she had then, as now, the ability to take each time in its season. There had been a time for pleasure; now was the time for duty. When Charteris was asked how the Queen had taken her loss. 'Bravely, like a Queen,' he replied.[116]

Churchill and Attlee were lined up on the tarmac at London airport: two old men who bowed to the slight young woman veiled in black.

The King's limousine took the Queen and the Duke not to Buckingham Palace but to Clarence House. Queen Mary came over from Marlborough House: she must be, she said, the first to offer her duty to the new Queen, and the old lady's deep curtsy was the most moving moment of the homecoming. Queen Mary had lived through five reigns, and now she could go in peace, knowing that the monarchy to which she had dedicated her life was safe with Elizabeth.

Later she joined the widowed Queen Elizabeth The Queen Mother and The Queen for the lying-in-state at Westminster Abbey. Immortalized in an unforgettable photograph, three Queens stood veiled and frozen in grief.

Queen Mary did not go to the burial at Windsor Castle. Instead she watched the funeral procession from her window in Marlborough House. She had sent for Mabell Airlie to be with her.

As the entourage wound slowly along, the Queen whispered in a broken voice, 'Here he is', and I knew that her dry eyes were seeing beyond the coffin a little boy in a sailor suit. She was past weeping . . . My tears choked me. The words I wanted to say would not come. We held each other's hands in silence.'[117]

At Windsor, as the coffin was lowered into the tomb, the Lord Chamberlain broke in two his White Wand of Office as tradition demanded and dropped it into the grave. It was the last act of reverence for a King who against all odds had won the respect and admiration of all who knew him.

The words Churchill inscribed on his wreath were rightly chosen: 'FOR VALOUR'.

On 11 February 1952 the House of Commons met to pay their tributes. Churchill had seen the death of Queen Victoria and had lived through the reigns of Edward VII, King George V, King Edward VIII and now that of King George VI. As he could witness,

No British monarch in living memory had a harder time . . . Never in our long history were we exposed to greater perils of invasion and destruction than in that year when we stood alone and kept the flag of freedom flying . . . The late King lived through every minute of this struggle with a heart that never quavered and a spirit undaunted.[118]

Attlee, for the Labour Party, spoke of the 'noble example that both George V and King George VI had set to the world and showed what true Kingship meant in a democracy'.[119] People had not realized the time and care the King gave to public affairs . . . with this close study went a good judgement and a sure instinct for what was really vital . . . No two people could have done more to strengthen the influence of the crown than King George and Queen Elizabeth. That throne is firmly established in the hearts and homes of the people.

All spoke that day with genuine love and admiration for a man who was, in the words of Attlee, 'a great King and a very good man'.[120]

CHAPTER TEN

Queen Elizabeth II

'The generations pass but the green shoots live.'[1]

LADY AIRLIE

The Age of Change

The Queen and Prince Philip did not move immediately back into Buckingham Palace. Together they had turned the dilapidated Clarence House into a charming family home, which they had been able to enjoy for less than three years; it had been Prince Philip's first real home and The Queen's first symbol of independence; it was with real sadness that they exchanged it for the chilly grandeur of Buckingham Palace. But The Queen accepted the move as part of her royal duty. It was not a showcase, as it had been for George IV, nor a 'mausoleum', as Edward VII had called it, nor a prison, as it had been for King Edward VIII. It became her place of work, the headquarters of her establishment as Head of State and the backdrop for ceremonies.

It would take some time for Queen Elizabeth The Queen Mother to adjust to her new life: she had been in command at Buckingham Palace for fifteen years and now must leave. In May 1952, when the new Queen and consort moved into the Palace, Queen Elizabeth The Queen Mother and Princess Margaret were installed in Clarence House. For both of them the death of the King had been unexpected and a profound shock. Princess Margaret, who adored her doting father, was numbed with grief. Queen Elizabeth The Queen Mother was 'engulfed by great black clouds of unhappiness and misery',[2] as she wrote to Edith Sitwell, thanking her for a consoling book of poetry.

The Queen and Prince Philip moved into the apartments on the first and second floors of the north side of the central courtyard of the Palace. Their children, Prince Charles and Princess Anne, were in the care of their two Scottish nurses in The Queen's old nursery on the second floor. Helen Lightbody was an old-fashioned martinet who ran the nursery like an empress dominating her empire. Mabel Anderson, warm and loving, was to become a major influence on Prince Charles: she made their nursery a bright, welcoming place to which even the grander courtiers came with pleasure, to sit by Mabel Anderson's fire and chat.

The importance of the nurses and governesses who have cared for royal children should not be underestimated. They were often closer to their charges than their parents, sometimes remaining with the family until death. They could do lasting damage – as in the case of the excessively cruel nurse of the Duke of Windsor; but the present royal family has been singularly fortunate in their children's nurses and governesses. Alah Knight, Margaret and her sister Ruby MacDonald, Mabel Anderson, Marion Crawford and many others deserve their places in the history of Buckingham Palace, as do the German nurses and governesses of Queen Charlotte and Queen Victoria.

Margaret MacDonald ('Bobo') was a classic example of the devoted personal servant, totally trusted, with whom kings and queens are perfectly at ease as with no one else. Like Queen Charlotte's ferocious Mrs Schwellenberg or Queen Victoria's Lehzen, Miss MacDonald became possessive and imperious, and in her last years a terror to the rest of the Household, but her complete dedication and love made her an invaluable comfort to The Queen in the inevitable loneliness of royal life. Daughter of a Scottish railway worker, she had come to 145 Piccadilly as a nursery maid, accompanied the Princesses to Windsor during the war, shared Princess Elizabeth's bedroom in the early years and on her accession moved into the Palace as The Queen's dresser and remained with her until death. On the morning of The Queen's own Coronation, she was the one unflappable member of the Household.

Miss MacDonald was in charge of The Queen's clothes – and responsible for her hats and handbags. She attended The Queen at fittings with Sir Norman Hartnell, the royal dressmaker, insisting that while he designed the outfits, she was responsible for the accessories. In spite of her humble origins, like many royal servants of the past she was a firm champion of protocol, precedence and hierarchy, which, as Mrs Roosevelt had noted, was rigidly observed below stairs. Together with Ernest Bennett, The Queen's Page of the Presence, she kept The Queen in touch with Palace news and gossip. Knowing that she had The Queen's ear, even heads of departments were wary of crossing Miss MacDonald.

Although The Queen was now surrounded by courtiers from ancient noble families, their influence was balanced by young Scots women from ordinary backgrounds. This has undoubtedly been an element in the making of Queen Elizabeth II. In the early days, however, it must have been comforting to be able to call on the experience and knowledge of tradition of the old guard. Her adoring courtiers were mostly elderly, and all of them were steeped in Palace tradition, with long years of experience. Her Prime Minister, Churchill, was now seventy-seven, had fought in the Boer War and had lived through the reigns of five monarchs. The Earl of Clarendon, her first Lord Chamberlain, was the son of a Lord-in-Waiting to Queen Victoria. He was seventy-four and had been a Lord-in-Waiting to King George V. He had broken his leg at Eton and was badly crippled all his life. He was too frail to take part in the Coronation and retired after six months.

His successor as Lord Chamberlain, the 4th Earl of Scarbrough, was fifty-six and came from a similar background. His experience in foreign and Commonwealth affairs as a Conservative member of Parliament was useful to the new Queen. In 1952, after the resignation of Lord Clarendon, he worked with the Earl Marshal, the Duke of Norfolk, on the arrangements for the Coronation.

The other key position in the Palace, that of The Queen's Private Secretary, was filled by Sir Alan Lascelles, who, at sixty-five, could have retired, but stayed on until after the Coronation, when his extraordinary memory was of great service. However, his somewhat grim manner hardly endeared him to the Duke of Edinburgh, who now chaired the committee responsible for the arrangements for the Coronation, which was to take place in June 1953. There were long arguments about protocol and the wisdom of televising the proceedings; although The Queen subsequently allowed the ceremony to be shown on television she was unwilling to have the cameras focused on her at the most sacred moments in the ritual.

Prince Philip and the Coronation Committee received valuable advice from Queen Mary, whose memory reached back to the Coronation of King Edward VII. However, in the New Year she had become very frail, and, knowing that she was nearly at the end of her road, she insisted that, should she die before the Coronation, they must carry on as planned.

She died on 24 March 1953 at Marlborough House. The first Queen Consort to be born in England since Henry VIII's wife, Catherine Parr, she had been on the throne for twenty-five years. Chosen by Queen Victoria, she had seen the deaths of four monarchs, and had lived to witness the accession of her granddaughter, Queen Elizabeth II, and the birth of her great-grandson, Prince Charles. In the last years of her life, in all the royal processions her upright and majestic figure had received the loudest cheers. Now crowds lined the streets to pay the last tribute to a unique figure who had become the symbol of the enduring values of the monarchy.

On 25 March 1953 the House of Commons, led by Churchill, paid tribute to a Queen who, in the words of Attlee, 'was so beloved by everybody for her wide sympathy and extraordinary kindness'.[3] The importance of her work for Buckingham Palace and for the stability of the monarchy cannot be underestimated. In her last years she had taken comfort in the words of Lady Airlie: 'The generations pass but the green shoots live.'

It was sad that Queen Mary did not live to see the Coronation. She would have approved the traditional magnificence. The Coronation was a resounding success, watched on television by millions. It was a tribute to the committee's ability to reconcile tradition and modernity. The television pictures, seen all over the world, awakened a new interest in and respect for the British monarchy. There were some who scathingly called it 'tribal magic'. So, in a sense, it was; but to those of us, seated in the magnificence of the Abbey, who watched a dedicated young woman in a simple white shift bending under the weight of the glittering crown, it was deeply moving – almost a ritual sacrifice.

Although the first years of The Queen's reign were not easy, at least, unlike Prince Philip, she was on familiar ground surrounded by friendly faces. The Palace, which her predecessors had first entered with dislike and apprehension, had been her home since she was ten – with only a short period at Clarence House – and her first child had been born there in her old nursery. She took over her father's familiar rooms, where she had so often watched him at work. Unlike King Edward VII, Princess Elizabeth had been prepared for the throne, had watched her father at work and could move smoothly into the rhythm of his life in Buckingham Palace. King George VI, remembering that neither he, nor his father, King George V, had originally expected to succeed to the throne, was determined that his beloved daughter should be well equipped for the hard road ahead. In their private rooms at the north side of the Palace her mother, when Queen, had brought light and flowers to Queen Alexandra's cluttered rooms.

In the years after the Coronation, The Queen has had the difficult task of combining her many different, and sometimes conflicting, roles. At Buckingham Palace she is not only Queen of Great Britain, she is also Head of the Commonwealth; and as Head of the Church of England she is the 'Defender of the Faith', with many duties involved. She is the 'Fount of Honour', conferring distinctions. She is hostess to the nation and the world, receiving ambassadors and heads of state of foreign countries, and thousands of the general public at garden parties and receptions. Above all, she is Head of State, and although her constitutional power is now minimal, the work involved in her duties is unremitting. She has, in trust, palaces and their contents, for which she is responsible. But she is also a wife and mother of four children: Prince Charles, Princess Anne, Prince Andrew and Prince Edward. In the setting of Buckingham Palace The Queen has been able to combine all these roles not only because of her own natural ability and dedication, but because, unlike her father, she is not a 'worrier'.

Eleanor Roosevelt recalled in her autobiography, *On My Own*, how, when she came again to England after the death of President Roosevelt, The Queen invited her to the Palace 'for a chat'. She and Lady Reading were met on the ground floor of the Palace by a Lady-in-Waiting and a secretary. 'We went up', she remembered,

in the old-style cage-type lift and to The Queen's sitting-room overlooking a garden. She was at her desk with a fire crackling in the fireplace, and she greeted me graciously . . .

We talked for a while about the troubles facing our two countries and the difficulties in the relations of the United States and Britain. After half an hour – since it is protocol to wait for The Queen to end a conversation – she smiled and remarked that she knew I had to have time to get dressed for a dinner engagement, and I departed.

She reflected that The Queen's 'loveliness does not change but she seems to me still more serious, as one might expect her to be under the burden of her duties'.

Mrs Roosevelt was escorted to her car by a young secretary and noticed

that The Queen's *entourage* seemed much younger than when I had previously visited the Palace . . .

'It must be terribly hard,' I said to him, 'for anyone as young as The Queen to have so many official responsibilities and also carry on as a wife and mother.' He looked at me with what I thought was a surprised expression and said briskly: 'Oh, no. Not at all. The Queen is very well departmentalized.' How does one departmentalize one's heart, I thought![4]

It is partly this ability to 'departmentalize' that has given The Queen her extraordinary balance and equanimity.

She could not have succeeded without the help of devoted supporting assistants, headed by her husband and her family. Throughout her reign Prince Philip has been a pillar of strength. Although he has no official role in the running of the Palace, The Queen can rely on his advice, and he is beside her at ceremonies in the Palace and Westminster, and on tours at home and abroad.

Throughout history the position of the consorts has never been easy, especially when they have had strong personalities. Queen Charlotte,

Prince Albert, Queen Mary, Queen Elizabeth and Prince Philip have, however, all given their sovereigns invaluable support. Prince Philip now had to accept the end of a career he loved and the beginning of a life hedged in by courtiers, who adored his wife but who regarded him with some suspicion. Mountbatten's radical sympathies, it was feared, might influence his nephew: Prince Philip, with his fast cars, his casual clothes, his breezy bluntness and his unconventional schooling was disturbing. Understandably he was sometimes irascible: it must have been galling for a man of exceptional ability to have no official role.

In the first years of her reign The Queen was too busy to spend time on the organization of the Palace. Prince Philip, however, saw how much needed to be done. In the post-war years King George VI had been too concerned with the state of the nation to deal with the state of the Palace, and for the last years he had been too ill.

Prince Albert had faced a similar situation, but he did not have to deal with an experienced Secretariat and Household. In effect, he had acted as Queen Victoria's Private Secretary himself and was strong enough to be able to overcome her Household's reluctance to change; on the whole, Queen Victoria's prime ministers had welcomed Prince Albert's help and he had been able to use Stockmar to conduct a thorough survey of the Palace.

Prince Philip, however, had no desire to be a second Prince Albert. He does not see official papers as Prince Albert and even Queen Mary did, and Mike Parker, his secretary and friend from Navy days, was certainly no Stockmar. Nevertheless, as this lively Australian told The Queen's biographer, Ben Pimlott, they did make a private study of the whole organization and its methods, in which they included an exploration of the basements:

we were fascinated by the wine cellar, which went on for miles and miles, and there were one or two very ancient wines indeed, plus some very old menus from the early Victorian period, which were utterly fascinating.[5]

In the first year of The Queen's reign, the Household discouraged Prince Philip's involvement in the reorganization of the Palace. It was not until 1962, when he was Chairman of the National Productivity

Year, that he was able to persuade the Treasury to send in a team to produce a survey.

Lord Cobbold, later to be Lord Chamberlain, remembered:

When I first came to the Household in 1963, I discovered that, at the instigation of Prince Philip, the Treasury had been asked to provide an Organisation and Methods Study, which, if I may say so, if that had not been so I should have tried to arrange myself, and they did come and have a very thorough examination of organisation and methods . . . Sir Basil Smallpiece was to come in full-time for a year and half time for another year, and he remains on in an honorary capacity available for consultation for exactly that purpose, to go through the thing with a toothcomb.

Lord Cobbold also remembered that at that time 'many of the staff worked for no salary but expenses only, it was considered that the prestige of work in the Palace compensated for inadequate financial reward'.[6]

As a result of the survey and Lord Cobbold's support, some improvements were made in the organization and salaries, but it was not for another eight years that a fuller investigation was held.

Meanwhile Prince Philip immediately modernized his own department, in his office on the first floor of the Palace; this is a large, high-ceilinged room with a view through the tall windows of Constitution Hill. One of Prince Philip's first innovations was to have a false ceiling made to conserve heat and a number of labour-saving gadgets installed so that, for example, the window curtains could be opened and closed at the touch of a button, and he could be linked by an intercom system to the rest of the Palace.

Prince Philip's remarkable energy has now been channelled into supervising the running of Balmoral, Sandringham and Windsor Great Park. In addition, over the years he has become actively involved in the work of hundreds of organizations. In 1956 he launched the Duke of Edinburgh's Award, encouraging thousands of young people to develop their talents.

In many fields he has been able to give The Queen his own advice to supplement that of her officials. The media are more likely to pick up his more unconventional remarks than to highlight the hard and valuable work he does in support of The Queen and in the service of the country at home and abroad.

The Royal Household

A key figure at Buckingham Palace is the Lord Chamberlain, who is the head of the royal Household and responsible for all appointments of all offices and all ceremonial affairs. He is the permanent link between The Queen and the House of Lords. The Lord Chamberlain should not be confused with the Comptroller, Lord Chamberlain's Office, who is responsible for the administration of state visits, ceremonial engagements, investitures and garden parties.

It was not until 1963, when Lord Cobbold became Lord Chamberlain, that fundamental changes were made in the royal Household. He brought a new expertise to the Palace. He was Governor of the Bank of England from 1949 until two years before his appointment as Lord Chamberlain in 1963. His business experience was invaluable during his period of office and also after his retirement, when in 1971 he gave evidence to the Select Committee on the Civil List.

By the time Queen Elizabeth II came to the throne, wars and successive economic crises had left the Palace in urgent need of repair and reorganization, but for the first decade little was done. Cautious by nature and with a deep respect for tradition, The Queen took time before making changes.

In 1967, however, Lord Cobbold appointed a new Master of the Household, Brigadier Hardy-Roberts (later Sir Geoffrey Hardy-Roberts). A small man with tremendous drive and energy, he had a formidable military reputation. He undertook a major reorganization of the Household, giving greater responsibility to his three principal assistants. One was put in charge of the Palace Steward's Department – the silver, china and glass sections, the Royal Cellars, pages and footmen. The Palace china and porcelain and silver gilt are in frequent use and demand expert care; so Brigadier Hardy-Roberts introduced a training scheme for footmen, just as he had introduced new training for nurses at the Middlesex Hospital. He insisted that the royal cooks should have the highest training; most now have a college background.

Another assistant was given responsibility for the department of the Royal Chef. To provide meals for such a large organization as Buckingham Palace is a major undertaking. Even when The Queen is not in residence, there are hundreds of people of various grades working in the Palace who have to be fed. There are banquets and receptions, dinner and lunch parties when she is there, as well as daily provision for the royal family and Household. When The Queen is in residence, five dining rooms are in use for the various grades of the royal Household. When she is absent the number is reduced to three. The Royal Chef is in charge of the kitchen and, together with the Assistant to the Master of the Household, prepares menus. The Chef submits a choice of menu daily to The Queen and other members of the royal family in residence, and prepares weekly menus for the Household dining rooms.

The kitchens are organized like those in great hotels; the Assistant to the Master of the Household will probably have had hotel experience. There are sous-chefs, senior cooks and assistant cooks working at the Palace, but the Royal Chef himself may accompany The Queen to her other residences or on the Royal Yacht. All menus for banquets are recorded in the menu book, as are also the menus for The Queen's private meals.

The Brigadier's immediate act, within weeks of taking up his appointment, was, for the first time, to give all staff a choice at their meals. His greatest concern was with the personnel of the Palace. 'You deal with things,' he would say to his deputy, 'I'll deal with people.' The Brigadier had a particular gift for seeing the potential in those who worked in the Palace and for encouraging them to develop. He was fortunate that he had an exceptional Deputy Master of the Household.

In 1954 Patrick Plunket, later Lord Plunket, was appointed Deputy Master of the Household. He had been an equerry to King George VI and to The Queen from the time of her accession. He was an old personal friend of The Queen, but he never took advantage of his privileged position. As Deputy Master of the Household he gave advice on refurbishing and decoration. He was generally considered to be a consummate artist in the arrangement of the décor for state and private receptions at the Palace. He was an inspiration to all who worked with him: as one senior courtier has said, 'We learned so much from him, working with him was like a university education.'

He was a discerning art critic, and, as a trustee of the Wallace Collection and member of the committee of the National Art Collection Fund, encouraged The Queen to take more interest in art than she might have done otherwise. When, at Prince Philip's suggestion, the royal Chapel, destroyed in the war, was turned into a picture gallery, The Queen's Gallery, Lord Plunket brought his enthusiasm and expertise to the project (a small section was walled off to be a tiny Chapel). The Gallery opened on 25 July 1962. It was the first part of the Palace to be opened to the public.

His death at the early age of fifty-two left a gap in the lives of The Queen and Princess Margaret which can never be filled. He will also be remembered by many a visitor to the Palace for his kindness and unfailing courtesy.

Brigadier Hardy-Roberts's reforms improved the organization of the Household. They also saved money. Much of the work that had previously been done by expensive interior decorators could now be brought in-house. Buckingham Palace is a national monument and The Queen takes her responsibility for its care and conservation very seriously. According to a senior member of the royal Household, 'Much of what Queen Mary did, The Queen would not allow to be altered ... No State Apartments are decorated without The Queen's involvement at the earliest stage and the final decisions are her Majesty's.'[7] At the end of a long day, she will often call in her adviser from the Master of the Household's Department and concentrate on wallpapers and curtains before turning to her red boxes.

Nowadays much work on curtains and upholstery is done in the Household's own workshops: care is taken to preserve as much as possible of worn or faded old silk curtains and wall coverings. As Queen Mary did, The Queen makes sure that good pieces of old material and wall hangings are used again as curtains or chair covers in offices or corridors. In 1928 Queen Mary had found a roll of the green and gold damask which Lord Duncannon had sent from Ireland in 1834 and used it to re-cover the gilt Regency chairs in the Green Drawing Room. The Queen ordered the same pattern to be used in the same colour when the curtains and upholstery needed renewing.

In the 1844 Room – so named after the visit of the Emperor Nicholas of Russia in that year – the sofa and armchairs are covered with silk embroidered with flowers by the wife of Frederick, Duke of York. Her work has been given an invisible protective cover of fine nylon netting. It is pleasant that something of the work of that eccentric, forgotten duchess has been preserved.

There is a five-year programme of redecoration, funded by moderate yearly increases in line with inflation. Like Queen Mary, The Queen is careful by nature and always conscious of cost. 'How much?' and 'Will it clean?', she frequently asks the Master of the Household's Department.

Buckingham Palace: Headquarters of State

On affairs of state, The Queen's most important adviser is the Private Secretary, who holds a most sensitive position as her link with the Prime Minister and with Parliament. Prime Ministers come and go, but Private Secretaries tend to stay for many years. It is a position that has evolved and changed over the years. George III had no Private Secretary until 1805 when, almost blind, he appointed Sir Herbert Taylor. Queen Victoria at first managed, with the help of Lehzen and clerks, to do without a Private Secretary. '"Are you afraid of hard work?" Melbourne had asked her. "No," said Victoria. "In that case," her Prime Minister advised her, "don't have a Private Secretary."'[8] In fact, the Prince Consort became her Private Secretary. After his death, the Queen took Prince Albert's own secretary, General Grey, as her own. He was succeeded by Colonel Henry Ponsonby, who came from a family with long connections to the Crown and who stayed for twenty-five years. Arthur Bigge, who became Lord Stamfordham, succeeded him and served under three monarchs from 1895 till his death in 1931.

One of the best descriptions of the work of the Private Secretary was written in 1942 by Professor Harold Laski, in a review of Lord Ponsonby's life of his father. Although he was writing of the past, much is relevant to the present.

The royal secretary walks on a tightrope below which he is never unaware that an abyss is yawning. If the Monarch is lazy, like Edward VII, his very presence may almost become an error of judgment. If the Monarch is hard-working, like Queen Victoria, all his tact and discretion are required to keep firmly drawn the possible lines of working relations in a constitutional system ... He must accept its pomps and ceremonies without fatigue; and he must be able to make the elegant minuet he is constantly performing capable of adaptation to a world which is constantly changing. Half of him must be in a real sense a statesman, and the other half must be prepared, if the occasion arise, to be something it is not very easy to distinguish from a lacquey.[9]

Or, as Sir Michael Adeane, a later Private Secretary, once said, 'It is no use thinking you are a mandarin. You must also be a nanny. One moment you are writing to the Prime Minister. The next you are carrying a small boy's mac.'[10]

Laski reminds us that the Private Secretary's influence has been crucial in the great political crises in past reigns – for example, when 'the dynamite might so easily have exploded at the time of Edward VIII's abdication'. 'Because our generation is entering upon a period in which, as in the seventeenth century, we shall be compelled to re-examine the foundations of our society, the post of the King's secretary is likely to be a post of quite outstanding importance.'[11] They serve the Queen for many years, starting as Assistants before becoming Private Secretaries.

It is worth looking briefly at the men who, throughout The Queen's reign, have – to borrow the words of Harold Laski – 'shaped the whisper of the throne'.

Alan Lascelles was a highly intelligent and cultured man. As Assistant

Private Secretary to King George V, and to King Edward VIII when he was Prince of Wales, he had endured the traumas of the abdication year. After The Queen's Coronation, he was succeeded by Michael Adeane, who was to serve The Queen as Private Secretary for the next nineteen years.

Sir Michael Adeane, like many of The Queen's courtiers, was an old Etonian. Adeane was an experienced diplomat, who, as aide-de-camp to the Governor General in Ottawa from 1934–36, brought with him a first-hand knowledge of Canada that was to be of great value to her as Head of the Commonwealth. He was Assistant Private Secretary to King George VI under Hardinge from 1937 to 1952.

Adeane was considered to be in the mould of an ideal Private Secretary. To his courage, proved in the war, was added a high intelligence. He could hold his own with the great intellects in the land, yet he wore his learning lightly and at official receptions at Buckingham Palace listened with patience and every appearance of interest to the most modest guest. Conservative by nature and steeped in tradition, he always behaved with the greatest courtesy to those with whose politics he disagreed. His influence in the first twenty years of The Queen's reign was great.

The Queen could also rely on the support and advice of her father's trusted and devoted Assistant Private Secretary, Edward Ford. He worked well with Her Majesty's ministers, by whom he was highly respected. He had first-hand knowledge of the Middle East, especially of Egypt, where he had worked as tutor to King Farouk's son. His expertise was of great value during the Suez Crisis.

His colleague, Martin Charteris, who had been Private Secretary to Princess Elizabeth, became Assistant Private Secretary in 1952 and succeeded Adeane as The Queen's Private Secretary in 1972, remaining until 1977. In his long years of service to The Queen he brought a lighter touch and a wit that enlivened the Court and The Queen's speeches. Adeane and Charteris between them saw seven successive Prime Ministers come and go.

The successor to Martin Charteris was Sir Philip Moore. He came to Buckingham Palace with a distinguished record in many fields. He was serving as Chief of Public Relations at the Ministry of Defence when the Lord Chamberlain, Lord Cobbold, persuaded him to become an Assistant Private Secretary to Martin Charteris in 1966. After he became Private Secretary in 1977 his wide experience of the Commonwealth made him invaluable to The Queen during the period of constitutional changes made in Canada and Australia in 1982 and 1986, which gave them complete independence. On royal tours to these countries he not only showed sensitivity in dealing with their governments, but also encouraged The Queen and Prince Philip to break through old barriers, to 'go walkabout' and to meet the people.

This informality was encouraged by the other Assistant Private Secretary, William Heseltine, an Australian who had made a great impression on Princess Marina when he accompanied her in 1964 on her tour of Australia and was thereafter appointed Press Secretary at the Palace. He then joined Sir Philip Moore as The Queen's Assistant Private Secretary and when Moore retired became the first Australian to become Private Secretary to The Queen. He retired on his sixtieth birthday in 1990, having played an important part in the Silver Jubilee celebrations of 1977.

He was succeeded by the present Private Secretary, Sir Robert Fellowes. He has had long experience of Court life, since he was brought up at Sandringham, where his father was Land Agent to King George VI. His easy, friendly manner conceals a keen intelligence and understanding.

So in her role as Head of State, The Queen has been guided by a succession of exceptionally qualified Private Secretaries.

Less well understood than the work in the Palace undertaken by The Queen's Private Secretaries is the important role of her private staff, the Mistress of the Robes, and the Ladies and Women of the Bedchamber. The archaic names mislead. These are highly professional personal assistants who, in a comparable business, could command high salaries. In fact, they receive no salaries, only expenses and allowances; and as one courtier has remarked, it is just as well that they have their own private incomes. They themselves do not complain; they count it an honour to serve The Queen for as long as she needs them: there is no retiring age. Whether young women in the future will be so self-sacrificing is another matter.

The Queen herself chooses them, sometimes on the recommendation of friends. The Mistress of the Robes is usually a Duchess: at present it is the Duchess of Grafton, who has been in her position for nearly thirty years. Her husband's title, it will be remembered, was given by Charles II to his natural son – and the 'Fitzroy' in the family name is a reminder of their royal blood.

As Mistress of the Robes she usually appears on great State occasions, standing behind The Queen, and she sometimes accompanies The Queen on important overseas tours; she is also responsible for the organization of the rotas for the Ladies and two Women of the Bedchamber. The former are always wives of peers and, like the Mistress of the Robes, are called upon mostly on great ceremonial occasions. Gone are the days of the power of the Duchess of Marlborough, Mistress of the Robes to Queen Anne. She is, however, a valued assistant to The Queen, with long experience of the Court. She is assisted by a Lady of the Bedchamber, Lady Airlie, who is the wife of the Lord Chamberlain; although usually in the background she is herself an excellent public speaker with long experience in charitable work. She also gives support to the Women of the Bedchamber when they are exceptionally busy.

There are usually two Women of the Bedchamber, one of whom is on duty for a fortnight at a time. When The Queen is at Buckingham Palace they have the use of a small bedroom and sitting room on the second floor. They accompany The Queen on tours at home and abroad and are seen, elegantly dressed, in the background, often buried under The Queen's bouquets. Like Ladies-in-Waiting throughout history, as Fanny Burney and others have recalled, they have to have one essential qualification – the ability to stand for long periods.

The work of the Women of the Bedchamber is not merely social. Lady Susan Hussey and the Hon. Mary Morrison are responsible for answering the letters of thousands of children who write to The Queen. Some years ago the telegrams of congratulations to centenarians were sent from their department; but it is an interesting reflection on the changed expectation of life that now there are so many that it needs a special department to deal with them. During times of celebration and crisis, the Women of the Bedchamber have an enormous pile of correspondence to deal with. In Jubilee year, from midsummer, when they started counting, to the end of the year, they answered more than 4,000 letters on The Queen's behalf.

The Queen usually receives between 200 and 400 letters a day, all of which initially go to her each morning for sifting and opening. They then go to the Private Secretary. Some deal with political matters: they go to the relevant government ministry. Some are marked by a personal symbol: these are from her friends and she opens and answers them herself. Some are directed to the office of the Ladies-in-Waiting.

Reading letters from the public is an important part of The Queen's day; she is intensely interested in the lives of her subjects. During difficult periods with family problems she has derived great consolation from the large number of letters of sympathy from mothers with similar anxieties. It is also important to her that people in trouble feel they can turn to her as a last resort, believing in her as an impartial counsellor.

Palace and Parliament

Every Tuesday when The Queen is in residence at Buckingham Palace she receives the Prime Minister for an entirely private audience when neither her Private Secretary nor the Prime Minister's is present. In this, as in so much, she has followed not only her father's example, but also her own love of tradition. However different the Prime Ministers may be, the pattern is unchanging. There are practical reasons for this, as there is with much ritual. The Prime Minister, accompanied by his or her Private Secretary, is received at the entrance to the Palace by The Queen's Private Secretary – the walk down long corridors gives the latter a chance to exchange a few words with the Prime Minister and judge his or her mood. While the Prime Minister is closeted with The Queen, the two Private Secretaries have an opportunity to talk. The

Queen's Private Secretary is disappointed if, after the audience, the Prime Minister is too busy to stay for further discussions.

The Prime Minister is ushered into The Queen's presence with formality, but then all is relaxed and friendly: unlike Queen Victoria, The Queen does not keep her Prime Ministers standing. Because their conversation is completely confidential, each Prime Minister has found it a great relief to be able to talk to someone impartial and above the fray. According to successive Private Secretaries they come out with a lighter step, like pilgrims relieved from their burdens.

During her reign of more than four decades, The Queen has had only six Private Secretaries, while there have been ten Prime Ministers. During those years she has become more experienced than many of her ministers or her secretaries, but she has been guided by them through wars and constitutional crises. The Queen may not have had to deal with the kind of world wars that were suffered in the time of her parents and grandparents, but during her reign there has been a succession of limited wars and armed conflicts, including Suez; the confrontation in Borneo; the Falklands War, in which her son, Prince Andrew, served as a helicopter pilot; the Gulf War; and the ongoing conflict in Northern Ireland, which brought about personal tragedy when on 27 August 1979 Lord Mountbatten and members of his family were killed by an IRA bomb. A dominant figure in the lives of Prince Philip, Prince Charles and The Queen herself, he was regarded with great affection by all the family.

Each Prime Minister in turn has been impressed by The Queen's steadiness in time of crisis and her knowledge not only of domestic but of world problems. Prime Ministers have come with different worries and found her an intelligent and understanding listener. She has also shown a shrewd judgement in dealing with a succession of very different characters. The Queen's first Prime Minister, Winston Churchill, was old enough to be her grandfather; her latest, Tony Blair, is young enough to be her son. Today she holds in her exceptional memory a wide knowledge of world affairs.

In the early years she was somewhat in awe of Churchill. When his secretary, John Colville, had brought the news of King George VI's death to him, Churchill, stricken, had exclaimed, 'But she is just a child,' and he tended to treat the new Queen as such. Though an ailing man of seventy-seven, he was determined to stay in office to see her crowned. Few people knew that in July 1953 he suffered a near fatal stroke, just at the time when his deputy, Anthony Eden, was undergoing a serious operation.

However, Churchill recovered to enjoy more Tuesday chats until April 1955. 'What do you talk about?' his secretary once asked. 'Oh, racing,' he replied cheerfully. At the farewell dinner he gave for The Queen at Number 10 Downing Street, he drank her health from the same glass 'from which he had drunk as a cavalry subaltern to her great-great-grandmother'.[12] The Queen was touched.

This had been a difficult time for the young Queen; had Churchill died in office she would have had to exercise her prerogative to choose his successor. There was no difficulty in choosing his successor. Anthony Eden had been Prime Minister in waiting for a very long time. His decision to plunge the country into war with Egypt over Nasser's nationalization of the Suez Canal was deeply controversial; even The Queen's closest advisers were divided. Eden's health finally failed and he retired in 1957, to be succeeded by the shrewd and urbane Macmillan. In his period of office, his government was rocked by the Profumo scandal, and ended with constitutional problems for The Queen. Macmillan underwent an operation and resigned while in hospital. The Queen had the constitutional duty to choose his successor. For once, The Queen's meeting with her Prime Minister took place not in Buckingham Palace but at Macmillan's bedside in hospital. He made it clear to The Queen that Sir Alec Douglas-Home, who was regarded on all sides with genuine affection, would be able to form a government.

Self-deprecating as always, Douglas-Home once said that the Tuesday audiences were like visits to the headmaster's study: he always had to be sure he had done his homework. However, his period of office was short. In the election of 1964 Harold Wilson led the Labour Party to victory. He too quickly learned that The Queen always masters her briefs. At his first audience he was confounded when she asked him about the Milton Keynes New Town project, which he had not yet had time to study. She also showed an unexpected interest in and knowledge about back-to-back housing in Leeds, where she had opened a new housing estate. Wilson, who had once been a university don, enjoyed explaining the political situation and The Queen enjoyed learning. There were times, however, when the position was reversed and the mature student became the teacher. Wilson became The Queen's most devoted admirer. He was to be Prime Minister from 1964–1970 and again from 1974 to 1976, after Edward Heath's brief period of office.

Changes of government meant changes of ministerial faces at receptions at Buckingham Palace. Like her father, The Queen always behaves impeccably. She is careful to remain impartial, above the party fray, and all her dealings with Commonwealth and Parliament show her to be tolerant, compassionate and pragmatic. Like her grandmother, Queen Mary, she accepts change yet has a deep sense of the value of tradition.

Harold Wilson made one untraditional appointment. In 1974, for the first time, the Captain of Her Majesty's Body Guard of the Honourable Corps of Gentlemen at Arms was a woman, Baroness Llewelyn-Davies, who was Government Chief Whip in the Lords. The Captain has always been chosen by the government from the House of Lords and is usually the Chief Whip. So Baroness Llewelyn-Davies received the gold stick of office from The Queen, and the right of direct access to The Queen on any matter dealing with the Corps. The Queen decided that she should not be expected to wear a uniform, but a special brooch was designed as her badge of office.

In 1970 the Labour government was defeated and Wilson was succeeded by Ted Heath. He is not an easy conversationalist, so their early talks at the Palace may have been somewhat reminiscent of those between George VI and Clement Attlee. They were certainly businesslike. Heath came with his fixed agenda and they followed it. He too, however, was eventually melted by The Queen's charm. She discovered that he responded to teasing, and he tells, with a shaking of the shoulders, how firmly she rejected a suggestion from The Queen of Spain that she should attend a concert Heath was conducting in Spain. The Queen did not pretend to share his passion for music. 'Are you still at it?' she would ask him, waving an imaginary baton.

Then there was the moment, captured on television, when at a Buckingham Palace party he rebuked an American diplomat because America had not sent a personal envoy to Saddam Hussein of Iraq. He himself went, he said, and hostages were released. 'Ah,' The Queen interjected, 'but you are expendable.' Mr Heath is delighted to repeat the story.

In 1974 Heath's Conservative government was defeated after the miners' strike and Wilson returned to office. This time, concerned about his health, he did not intend to stay the course.

In 1976 Wilson resigned, to the surprise of the public, although he had confided in The Queen and some others before. There was no constitutional problem this time. It was a smooth transition to James Callaghan. Like Wilson, during his term of office he developed a deep respect and affection for The Queen, admiring her pragmatism and good judgement. He remembers the lighter moments. One warm evening, The Queen suggested they should continue the audience in the Palace garden. As they walked and talked, The Queen picked a rosebud and handed it to him for his buttonhole.

The Queen and Prime Minister usually bring to the Tuesday audiences the agenda for their discussions recommended by their respective Private Secretaries. Callaghan's method was relaxed and their agendas were often forgotten while they chatted about other matters: farming and family, for example.

When Margaret Thatcher with her Conservative government succeeded Callaghan, she brought a new challenge to the Tuesday audiences. It is widely believed that Queen and Prime Minister did not always see eye-to-eye, particularly on the question of the Commonwealth and sanctions on South Africa. But The Queen keeps her counsel and no one really knows. However, their relations were cordial and courteous and Mrs Thatcher won praise at Buckingham Palace for her punctuality at the Tuesday audiences and for her crisp competence. She arrived with her agenda clearly set out and they followed it.

John Major, successor to Margaret Thatcher as Conservative Prime Minister, and the Labour Prime Minister Tony Blair, who replaced him in May 1997, were both less experienced in world affairs than The

Queen was herself. The Queen is more than ever before fully qualified for her classic role: to encourage, to warn and to be consulted.

Besides the Prime Minister, there are other political links between Palace and Parliament: members of the royal Household who are appointed on government advice, who change with changing governments, and who also have political duties in Parliament. These are the Treasurer of the Household, the Comptroller of the Household and the Vice-Chamberlain of the Household who are all members of the government Whips' Office in the House of Commons. The Vice-Chamberlain is also responsible for sending a daily report to The Queen on the events in Parliament. There are also officers chosen from among the government and whips in the House of Lords, who represent The Queen at funeral or memorial services, and who meet and greet important visitors to the United Kingdom.

One cabinet minister has a special audience with The Queen: the Chancellor of the Exchequer always sees her on the day before he presents his budget, to tell her of its contents.

The Privy Council

Meetings of the Privy Council are usually held at Buckingham Palace, although when The Queen is in residence at Windsor or Balmoral, the Privy Councillors travel there. When The Queen is absent abroad two or more Councillors of State are appointed to take her place.

The Privy Council has its origin in early medieval times; it is part of the machinery of government. At these meetings The Queen, on the advice of the Council, gives her approval of a vast number of royal proclamations and orders in Council.

Since the reign of Queen Victoria, Privy Councillors have been appointed for life. They now number nearly 400. A Privy Councillor is titled 'the Right Honourable', and may use the initials PC after his name. Privy Councillors are mostly chosen from members of Parliament; all members of Cabinet must be Privy Councillors, as are the leaders of opposition parties in both Houses of Parliament. Some judges, archbishops and members of the royal Household may also be appointed. Privy Councillors take the oath of allegiance to The Queen at a traditional ceremony at Buckingham Palace; at the end they retreat backwards from the Royal presence in what Fanny Burney called 'the retrograde action'.

Nowadays not more than four Privy Councillors are called to a meeting. There are now only two occasions when the whole Council is summoned – on the accession of a new sovereign, when the Council meets in St James's Palace, and when an unmarried sovereign announces his or her proposed marriage. This, it will be remembered, was the occasion which Queen Victoria found so unnerving.

Palace and Commonwealth

The Queen is not only Head of State for Britain, she is also the Head of the Commonwealth and its sixteen member countries. Her Private Secretary is the link between her and the Commonwealth Prime Ministers. From the beginning of her reign The Queen has made it clear that the Commonwealth, as a family of nations, is of major importance to her.

As Head of the Commonwealth she plays no official part in the machinery of its constitutional governments, but she is now a wise and experienced human link between many different peoples, and because of her obvious dedication to the ideal of a family of nations, so sincerely expressed at her coming of age in South Africa, she is greatly respected.

The organization of the Commonwealth, which had been worked out by King George VI, Mountbatten and Attlee, was finally made legal by the Royal Titles Act of 1953. The Indian government had set the pattern: now it is possible for member states to accept The Queen as the symbolic head of their free association, and yet, if they wish, to become republics.

When Heads of Commonwealth countries come to Britain The

Queen does not host their meetings in Buckingham Palace, but she does receive them individually there, and she is available to be consulted. She receives them at banquets at Buckingham Palace and offers them hospitality.

She does not attend their meetings in London: these are now organized by the Commonwealth Secretariat, a body set up in 1965 by the Heads of Governments, to co-ordinate the work of the various departments within the Commonwealth. The Heads of Government meet biannually in different countries in turn.

The Queen preserves the distinction between being Queen of Great Britain, with her headquarters in Buckingham Palace, and Head of the Commonwealth, which has its offices and holds its meetings in Marlborough House – Queen Mary's old home. To mark her separate roles, The Queen flies a different personal standard when acting as Head of the Commonwealth – the initial E within a chaplet of roses.

In the year after her Coronation she began regular visits with Prince Philip to Commonwealth countries, particularly to Africa, India, Canada, Australia and New Zealand, which have continued throughout her reign. In the winter of 1953–4 they spent five months in Australia, New Zealand and the Far East. In 1962, when she opened the new Commonwealth Institute in Holland Park, London, she could justly claim, 'I suppose that between us my husband and I have seen more of the Commonwealth than almost any people alive.'[13]

Throughout the following years The Queen was to develop an exceptional understanding of Commonwealth leaders because she saw them at work in their own countries. In spite of his efforts, her father, King George VI, could never achieve this, because he usually met them in the formal and unreal setting of Buckingham Palace. So when Commonwealth Prime Ministers come to England The Queen can receive them at the Palace as old friends. That friendship has survived growing republicanism in Australia and Canada. Changes in the constitutions of both countries have been made amicably mainly because of The Queen's skill at defusing tension.

She takes great pains to be well briefed. She has known many of the leaders for many years. Sonny Ramphal, who was Secretary General of the Commonwealth Heads of Government, has the greatest respect for her knowledge and understanding of Commonwealth leaders.

As Sonny Ramphal explained, 'She grew up with them, understood them and related to them ... Even at the times when the British Government was at odds with many of these leaders, she was able to understand their point of view without taking sides, and managed to convey to them that she did.'[14]

It was with the greatest pleasure that The Queen welcomed President Nelson Mandela of South Africa on a state visit in July 1996. She had visited South Africa the previous year and had been much moved by the warmth of her welcome. It had been in Africa that she had made her speech of dedication on her twenty-first birthday. In welcoming South Africa back into the Commonwealth she was lighting a beacon of hope in a changing world.

The Palace: Host to the World

Once a year The Queen holds a grand evening reception at Buckingham Palace, to which 1,000 members of the diplomatic corps from 130 countries are invited, together with 350 British guests and the Prime Minister, members of the Cabinet and other public figures. The guests are courteously, but firmly, marshalled through the State Rooms by elegant gentlemen ushers; on the left stand the diplomats and their wives, and on the right, the British contingent. At last comes the resplendent royal party, jewels and decorations glittering under the chandeliers. The Queen stops to talk to foreign diplomats and their wives as she progresses slowly through the rooms. Members of the royal family follow behind and divide their attentions between the ambassadors and diplomats, and political figures. When the royal progress reaches the last State Room, the guests proceed to the supper rooms; there is dancing in the ballroom until the band plays 'God Save The Queen'.

Unlike Queen Victoria's balls, which sometimes went on till four in the morning, this party usually ends at midnight. Seasoned guests wear comfortable shoes to these occasions, for there are prolonged periods when they 'only stand and wait'. The Queen herself is tireless, having long ago mastered the royal art of standing, feet apart, the body's weight evenly distributed. The present writer remembers one distinguished lady standing in blissful ease: she had forgotten to change her shoes and was wearing her bedroom slippers under her elegant gown.

Although foreign diplomats are still officially accredited to the Court of St James, it is to Buckingham Palace that a new ambassador is invited to present his credentials to The Queen, as soon as possible after his arrival. Then the Marshal of the Diplomatic Corps, who is usually a retired officer, is driven in a state landau, drawn by a pair of bay horses, to collect the new ambassador from his residence. Driven by a coachman in full state livery and followed by his suite in other state landaus, the ambassador's coach clatters through the courtyard of Buckingham Palace to halt at the red-carpeted stairs to the Grand Hall, where he is greeted by the Vice-Marshal and the Permanent Under-Secretary of State from the Foreign and Commonwealth Office, and the Lady-in-Waiting if the ambassador's wife is present. The party is led up the steps to the Bow Room overlooking the gardens. The Queen receives the ambassador in the 1844 Room next door; he is ushered in by the Marshal and an equerry, who then withdraw. The ambassador presents his credentials and then introduces his suite as they enter one by one. His wife is presented by the Marshal afterwards. At the end of the audience the ambassador signs The Queen's visitors' book and withdraws.

All such ceremonies are conducted with military precision. The procedure is explained to the ambassador in exact detail by the equerry and nothing is left to chance.

Similarly members of the public who are honoured at investitures are instructed exactly so that the ceremony runs like clockwork. There are twenty investitures a year, of which the Prince of Wales undertakes six. The Queen holds six in February, two in July, and six between October and December.

The recipients, who may bring three guests, are received in the Grand

Hall and guided to the Ballroom by four gentlemen ushers. The guests are seated and those who are to be honoured are taken separately to be instructed. Meanwhile a selection of light music is played by an orchestra from the Household Division. Occasionally the music is selected with particular reference to the recipient.

At this ceremony members of a Gurkha regiment are on duty – two escort The Queen as she enters the Ballroom and two stand behind her with five Yeomen of the Guard. The Lord Chamberlain, standing to the right of The Queen, announces the name and achievements of the recipient. The Queen takes the medal from a cushion held by the Master of the Household or his representative. Those receiving knighthoods kneel on a stool and are dubbed with the investiture sword.

The apparent ease with which these traditional ceremonies are conducted never fails to impress and delight even the most cynical. Much of the credit for this goes to the Comptroller, the Lord Chamberlain's office.

Even grander than the diplomatic receptions are the state banquets, held in the Palace Ballroom on the first evening of the visit of a head of state.

The long tables, arranged in a horseshoe, are set out with the gold plate, glass and porcelain from the Royal Collection. The distinguished guests – Prime Minister, Cabinet ministers, diplomats, politicians, archbishops and others – take their places. Then the royal family, led by The Queen and the head of state, Prince Philip and the consort, progress to the top of the horseshoe. Before them the Lord Chamberlain and the Lord Steward walk backwards, according to the old tradition.

At the beginning of the meal The Queen reads her formal speech of welcome. She is too experienced, and too cautious, to attempt off-the-cuff remarks, although she has been known to inform her guests that she does not normally dine in such state. The visiting head replies, outlining his government's long links with Britain.

Then the tinkle of silver on porcelain dies away as, in startling contrast, the distant wail of bagpipes heralds the entrance of twelve enormous

Highlanders, kilts swinging, bagpipes skirling. They march twice around the tables. 'Terrifying!' a foreign diplomat exclaimed to the present writer on one occasion. 'Not even in the war have I seen anything so barbaric.'[15] This breeze from the Scottish moors shakes the chandeliers, and is a reminder that The Queen is descended, through her mother, from the ancient kings of Scotland. Like George III, George IV and Queen Victoria, she is also proud of her ancestry, which goes back beyond the Hanoverians to the sister of Charles II and the Stuarts.

The Queen also hosts working dinners at the Palace. For example, a large dinner party was given for the G7* Summit in the State Dining Room. It was followed by a firework and laser display in the courtyard, watched by guests through the Green Drawing Room windows. On this occasion James Galway played the flute: did he remember the Gainsborough portrait of George III's miraculous flautist, Johann Christian Fischer, who so enchanted Fanny Burney?

On such occasions it is impossible for The Queen to talk at any length with any of her visitors. But in 1956, encouraged by Prince Philip, she began a series of small luncheon parties to which a cross-section of people, distinguished in their various professions or trades, are invited and with whom The Queen is able to talk freely and informally. Such luncheons are usually limited to eight guests and are held sometimes in the Bow Room overlooking the gardens, but more usually in the neighbouring smaller 1844 Room.

Besides the thousands of distinguished men and women who come annually as guests or to receive their medals at the Palace, almost 30,000 members of a wide cross-section of the public are The Queen's guests at the three garden parties held in July each year, where bishops, ambassadors and foreign potentates mingle with mayors, midwives and voluntary workers. The invitations, or rather commands, are sent out from the Lord Chamberlain's office. In the past, morning dress or uniform was *de rigueur* for men, while ladies wore afternoon or national dress – with hats. In recent years there are fewer top hats and now the

---

* The group of seven major countries.

invitation even indicates that hats need not be worn, to the disappointment of ladies who enjoy this once-in-a-lifetime extravagance. Guests,
in all their finery, begin queuing outside the Palace gates before they
are opened at 3.00 p.m.

The royal garden parties were started by Queen Victoria in 1868 –
and were a rare opportunity for the public to see her in the years after
the death of Prince Albert. There were receptions in the gardens during
the reign of Edward VII and even during the First and Second World
Wars. King Edward VIII, as has been seen, was bored by them.
However, they became a regular feature in the time of King George
VI. Queen Elizabeth The Queen Mother, who has inherited a love of
gardens from her mother, the Countess of Strathmore, was responsible
for clearing the soot-blackened Victorian shrubberies and initiating the
spectacular 175-yard-long herbaceous border, which, in its full high-
summer beauty, is much admired. She is also proud that, during her
time as consort, a shoot of an original mulberry tree was planted and
has become established.

The Queen takes a great interest in the Buckingham Palace Gardens
and in 1961 she planted a curved avenue of Indian horse chestnut
trees. There is a characteristic memento from the reign of George IV
– the massive Waterloo vase that stands on the lawn. The piece of
Carrara marble was presented to King George IV when Prince Regent
by the Duke of Tuscany in gratitude for British aid in the Napoleonic
Wars. It was carved by Richard Westmacott.

In 1958, when The Queen discontinued the tradition, started by Queen
Victoria, of the presentation of débutantes, an additional garden party
was added to the original two. Unlike King Edward VIII, The Queen
has never cut short the party because of the weather, even when, as
happened in July 1996, a thunderbolt struck a tree and injured some
guests. In 1997, the year of their Golden Wedding anniversary, The
Queen and Prince Philip invited to a special garden party couples from
all over Britain who, like them, in this year celebrated fifty years of
marriage.

Guests arrive at the main gates, cross the gravelled courtyard, enter
the Grand Hall and ascend the steps to the Bow Room. Here they can

admire the porcelain Chelsea service in glass-fronted cupboards, sent as a present by Queen Charlotte to her brother the Duke of Mecklenburg-Strelitz. As they move through the open doors, they can pause on the broad terrace and look down over the camomile lawns to the sweeping curves of the four-acre lake. Queen Charlotte would have seen not a lake but a formal tree-lined canal, laid out in the French manner for the Duke of Buckingham. In the reign of King George IV, William Townsend Aiton of Kew Gardens, encouraged by Nash, had remodelled the garden, hollowing out a romantic serpentine lake. The spoil from the excavation was used to make the mound which still exists at the end of the garden. The summer house that Prince Albert had built for Queen Victoria was demolished between the wars.

Guests may pause on the terrace, look down to the north-east and imagine, beyond the herbaceous border, Pepys and Evelyn in the time of Charles II, strolling through the mulberry gardens to feast on mulberry tarts. They may look up and admire the grace of Nash's garden frontage, the delicate carvings in Coade stone above the windows and the elegant urns on the terrace.

Times and fashions have changed, but during Queen Elizabeth II's reign the ritual remains the same as in Queen Victoria's day. The Queen, Prince Philip and members of the royal family emerge on the terrace at exactly 4.00 p.m. and progress through a lane of guests to the tea tent reserved for the privileged at the end of the lawn. Two military bands take it in turn to play while guests take tea or stroll through the grounds and admire the herbaceous border.

At six o'clock the bands play 'God Save The Queen' as the royal family takes its leave. Then gentlemen ushers, in morning dress with a distinguishing flower in their buttonholes, quietly but firmly shepherd the guests towards the exits.

As the kaleidoscope of colour coalesces, shifts and changes, the robes and saris of Commonwealth and overseas guests glow brilliantly among the flowery dresses on the green lawns, a reminder that on this occasion, as on so many others, The Queen and Prince Philip at Buckingham Palace are hosts to the world.

The most spectacular ceremony during The Queen's year is undoubtedly that of Trooping the Colour, which takes place each June on Horse Guards Parade and is enjoyed by thousands of spectators lining the route from the Palace along the Mall. The ceremony had its origin in the early eighteenth century, when in time of war the guards and sentries for the royal palaces were mounted on the parade ground and 'trooped' the colours of their particular battalion, slowly carrying them through the ranks so that soldiers could recognize and rally to them on the battlefield. In 1749 it was ordered that the parade should mark the monarch's official birthday, and from the reign of King George IV it became an annual event – much enjoyed by Queen Victoria, especially when she watched Prince Albert, a skilled horseman, riding with her troops for the first time.

In 1914 King George V placed himself at the head of his guards and rode down the Mall to Buckingham Palace behind the massed bands. The troops who were to provide the King's guard at the Palace rode into the forecourt and the King took up his position in the centre gateway, and took the salute as the rest of the troops marched by and back to their barracks.

King George VI introduced the custom of the RAF fly-past at the end of the Trooping, when he appeared with the rest of the royal family on the balcony.

The Queen first rode on parade in 1947, when, as Princess Elizabeth, she appeared as Colonel of the Grenadier Guards. It was the first birthday parade after the Second World War and the Princess was in the blue uniform of the WRAC. In 1951, when the King was ill, she took the salute in his place and since then has done so every year, except 1955, when the Trooping was cancelled because of the National Strike. Rain or shine, she rode side-saddle at the head of her troops wearing a stunning scarlet tunic and a tricorn hat with a plume, designed by Aage Thaarup. From 1969 The Queen rode her well-trained horse, Burmese, until 1986; she now rides to the saluting base in a phaeton.

There was one occasion when The Queen feared she might have to cancel Trooping the Colour. On 28 May 1972 the Duke of Windsor died of cancer at his home in Paris. Ten days earlier The Queen had visited him, knowing that he was near death. His body was flown back to Britain on 31 May to lie in state at St George's Chapel, Windsor. His funeral was to be held on 5 June at the Frogmore burial ground, a spot he had chosen himself with a space prepared for his wife, the Duchess of Windsor. The Queen invited her to stay at Buckingham Palace before the funeral, though her visit coincided with the Saturday planned for Trooping the Colour. However, The Queen insisted that a ceremony she valued so highly should not be cancelled. Her Private Secretary, Martin Charteris, came up with a solution. The Trooping went ahead but included the playing of the Lament by the pipes and drums of the Scots Guards.

The Duchess of Windsor watched from the Palace window as The Queen rode out. Those watching with her will never forget the strength of the Duchess's grief and regret. It was almost as though she said out loud, 'All this might have been mine.' In a memorable photograph she is seen, a sad-eyed old lady wearing a string of pearls, peering through the window of a room on the first floor of the Palace.

Palace Security

During her reign The Queen has received many thousands of invited guests at Buckingham Palace, and she has also had uninvited visitors.

Security at the Palace is very tight and for obvious reasons is not discussed. But gone are the days when King Charles II could dine in public and Pepys and Evelyn could walk unchallenged in the Privy Gardens at the Palace of Whitehall. The Queen, Prince Philip and their family accept the dangers in their position, yet they know that, however efficient the protection, it is difficult to guard against attacks by madmen.

The most obvious sign of Palace security is the guard outside Buckingham Palace. When 'they're changing guard at Buckingham Palace', not only Christopher Robin and Alice are there to watch. Hundreds of tourists gather every morning at 11.30 a.m. to see the ceremony.

Since 1660 the sovereign has been guarded by troops of the Household Division, first at the old Palace of Whitehall and then, after 1689, at St James's Palace. When Queen Victoria moved into Buckingham Palace in 1837, the Queen's guard remained at St James's Palace, but a detachment was detailed to guard Buckingham Palace.

The Changing of the Guard at Buckingham Palace lasts about forty-five minutes. The new guard forms up in Wellington Barracks on Birdcage Walk and marches with its band to the forecourt of Buckingham Palace, where the handing over of the guard and changing of sentries takes place. So, sometimes, does a confrontation of regimental mascots. The new guard marches to St James's Palace behind its corps of drums, leaving the detachment at Buckingham Palace. The old guard returns to Wellington Barracks with the band.

The public should not be misled by the toy soldier appearance of the men on guard. They may well have just returned from dangerous service in Northern Ireland or overseas and will go back after their spell of duty on guard.

Even though The Queen is guarded, on the morning of 9 July 1982 an unemployed Londoner, Michael Fagan, managed to get into the Palace and reach The Queen's bedroom. She awoke to find her curtains being drawn back and a bare-footed young man standing there. Thinking it was a window-cleaner The Queen called, 'You are in the wrong room.' To which came the chilling reply, 'Oh no, I am in the right room.' He came and sat on the end of her bed, holding a broken glass ashtray. The Queen's repeated attempts to alert her security guards failed. Her page, who normally kept watch outside her door, had taken the corgis into the garden; one of her maids was in the next room and heard nothing. While the man babbled incoherently about family affairs, The Queen got out of bed and crossed the room to pick up her dressing gown. As she later told friends, she drew herself up to her full height and told him to get out. He refused. The Queen then persuaded him to go with her to a nearby pantry in search of the cigarettes he demanded, confronting an astonished maid, who is reported to have said, 'Bloody hell, ma'am, what's he doing here?' At last her security guards arrived and Fagan was overpowered and led away. The Queen was not amused: for once she was very angry indeed.

There are other exits and entrances which are permitted. For many years it has been the custom for mother ducks to lead their young broods from the Palace lake, across the road, to the wider expanse of the lake in St James's Park. On one occasion an unaccustomed sound of hilarity was heard from one of the Private Secretary's rooms. Upon investigation The Queen was discovered catching a flurry of ducklings, gently scooping them up into a waste-paper basket. She had been walking in the gardens, had seen a mother duck and brood who had obviously decided to take a short cut through an open door, and had come to their rescue.

The Palace as Home

Buckingham Palace is not only a splendid setting for The Queen as Head of State: it is also her home for some part of each year.

There she brought up her four children, who now have their own households, apart from Prince Edward, who lives in Buckingham Palace. It has also been the scene of many happy private occasions. The Prince of Wales, for instance, has organized some memorable concerts at Buckingham Palace at his own expense. In 1763 Queen Charlotte had given King George III a surprise birthday party: on 22 October 1992 her descendant, Prince Charles, gave another surprise celebration, this time for the eightieth birthday of the great conductor Sir Georg Solti. Lady Solti, who helped to plan this memorable occasion, remembers:

Solti thought we were going to the Palace for a small dinner party. We were ushered into the first drawing room to find nobody there, but shortly afterwards fourteen members of the royal family appeared and we all stood around having drinks. Then the doors were opened and all was revealed: 300 guests and a concert in the Throne Room. We told Solti it was to be a short concert of military band music. It was in fact an amazing line-up of stars. The two highlights were a performance of Wagner's Siegfried Idyll, by representatives from all over the world of the orchestras that he had conducted during the previous year, and the fugue in the Finale of Verdi's *Falstaff* in which many of his singing friends took part, including Placido Domingo, Kiri Te Kanawa, Birgit Nilsson and Hans Hotter. After which there was dinner in the Picture Gallery, Throne Room, Green Drawing Room and White Drawing Room. A very grand private house had come to life for the occasion. I shall always remember helping myself to chicken salad at the buffet underneath the wonderful van Dycks. The organization was impeccable yet the atmosphere was informal.[16]

On this night excerpts from Mozart's *Marriage of Figaro* were played in the place where the composer himself had performed for Queen Charlotte when he was a little boy of seven; and Handel, whose music had so inspired King George III and Queen Charlotte, would have been delighted to hear his song 'Where E'er you Walk' so beautifully sung.

Throughout the centuries Buckingham Palace has sometimes chilled monarchs and their guests, but again and again music has warmed its marble halls. In 1842 Mendelssohn had written, 'The only friendly English house, one that is really comfortable, and where one feels at ease . . . is Buckingham Palace.' So too, Lady Solti was deeply conscious of 'a feeling of love from the people who live in it'.[17]

Another notable occasion was a particularly splendid dinner and concert for the eightieth birthday of Yehudi Menuhin. That night each of the State Rooms echoed with the music of Lord Menuhin's students and hundreds of guests sat down to a banquet in the Picture Gallery – the first time it had been used in this way since Queen Victoria's day.

The Price of Palaces

Inevitably the recent adverse publicity surrounding the younger members of the royal family has given ammunition to those who would like the monarchy to be drastically reformed or indeed abolished altogether. Complaining voices have been heard throughout the ages, particularly in the last years of George IV and Edward VII. After the abdication of King Edward VIII there were many who seriously considered it was time to draw a line under the institution of the monarchy.

During Queen Elizabeth II's reign, it has not only been that hammer of the royal family, William Hamilton MP, who voiced loud criticisms. In August 1957 the then Lord Altrincham roused royal supporters to fury with an article in the *English and National Review* criticizing The Queen and the composition of the Court. In a television interview he said he hoped to bring about a change. The Queen, he claimed, was surrounded by people of 'the tweedy sort', and he advocated 'a classless and Commonwealth Court'. He was supported in the columns of *The Times* by the nineteen-year-old Lord Londonderry, who could not believe that anyone, 'however moronic', would sit back and have fed to him the idea that the monarchy was a 'sacrosanct head of the family that parades benignly and sedately in front of their loving children whenever they are wanted to, flashing their toothpaste smiles, displaying their latest hairdos and exhibiting their deplorable taste in clothes'.[18] The journalist Malcolm Muggeridge joined in the chorus of disapproval.

But louder voices were raised in defence of The Queen. Lord Altrincham had his face slapped in public: the Archbishop of Canterbury pronounced him 'a very silly man' and the town of Altrincham dissociated itself from the noble lord. In October the BBC withdrew invitations to Lord Altrincham and Malcolm Muggeridge to appear on *Any Questions* and *Panorama*.

Added to the criticisms of the royal lifestyle were a concern with the cost of maintaining the monarchy and its palaces and doubts about the efficiency of their financial organization.

When Lord Cobbold succeeded as Lord Chamberlain in 1963, as well as reorganizing the Household he played a key role in the reform of Palace finances.

The Queen's finances and the cost of running Buckingham Palace have been much discussed – and much misunderstood. The Palace is the headquarters of the Head of State and as such is paid for partly by the Treasury through the Civil List, but as the private home of The Queen and the Duke of Edinburgh, it is paid for by The Queen out of that part of the royal income known as 'the Privy Purse'.

The whole question of The Queen's finances was brought into the limelight in 1969. It had been customary to settle the amount of the Civil List allowance – which included a provision for annuities for certain members of the royal family, including the monarch's children and royal widows – at the beginning of a new reign and to keep it unchanged for that reign. But in 1969 Prince Philip breezily remarked in the course of an interview in America that the royal family was going rapidly into the red and that he would have to sell his polo ponies and their yacht. His point was that though prices and the wages of their employees had increased considerably in the years since the beginning of the reign, the annuities paid to the royal family had remained static.

Prince Philip's remarks caused a stir. It was not the moment for the Labour government, which was at that time trying to bring in prices and incomes legislation, to recommend increases in the royal income. The Labour MP R. H. Crossman said, 'The Queen pays no estate or death duties . . . and this has made her by far the richest person in the country.'[19] There were, however, those on the Labour benches, including Emanuel Shinwell, who said: 'If we want a monarchy we have to pay them properly.'[20] Wilson himself, devoted to The Queen and always chivalrous in her interest, managed to defuse the issue by promising an All-Party Select Committee of Enquiry into royal finances, which was set up in June 1971. This was the first thorough investigation of royal finances.

In his preliminary statement to the Select Committee, Lord Cobbold said that

contrary to the impression which seems generally to have been given by the Press, The Queen is not asking for a pay rise. On the contrary Her Majesty has offered to forego Class I of the Civil List in future, and thus accept a reduction of £60,000 a year from the income to which her Privy Purse is entitled under present legislation. The remainder of the Civil List includes no element of 'pay to The Queen'. Expenditure under Classes II and III represents what we have termed 'Head of State Expenditure'. If it is the wish of Parliament that the Monarchy should be maintained at its present standards, increase of expenditure is inevitably dictated by the decrease in the purchasing power of the currency.[21]

As for the annuities paid to members of the royal family, they, said Lord Cobbold, 'can only be regarded to a small extent as "personal pay". The bulk of the Annuities goes to meet the necessary expenses of Members of the Royal Family under heads similar to Classes II and III, in carrying out their public duties.'

He explained that The Queen's possessions, public and private, can be divided into four categories:

1. The Royal Palaces, Crown Jewels, and Royal Collections, which are inalienable. 2. The Privy Purse, which is fed from Civil List Class I and Duchy of Lancaster revenues, which is at Her Majesty's disposal and controlled by the Keeper of the Privy Purse on her behalf. 3. The Sandringham and Balmoral Estates, which are Her Majesty's personal inheritance, and are similarly controlled on her behalf by the Keeper of the Privy Purse. 4. Her Majesty's other private possessions.[22]

In the first category,

The Royal Collection is regarded as covering all pictures and works of art purchased or acquired by all Sovereigns up to the death of Queen Victoria, and also certain property acquired by Sovereigns and their Consorts since the death of Queen Victoria, which was specially allocated to the Royal Collection. This, of course, covers the vast bulk of the contents of the Royal Palaces. The Royal Collection is regarded as passing in right of the Crown from Sovereign to Sovereign and, therefore, inalienable by the Occupant of the Throne. There are two very minor variations. Items of minor importance, surplus to the Collection, are occasionally sold to raise funds for the purchase of other items of special interest to the Collection. Further, certain very minor works and duplicate items once owned privately by Queen Victoria are occasionally disposed of as presents to the Commonwealth or for similar purposes.[23]

The Royal Philatelic Collection, the Royal Library and the Crown Jewels, Lord Cobbold continued, are all inalienable. The Queen does not regard them as being at her free personal disposal.

Except for personal current expenditure the funds derived from the Privy Purse and from the Duchy of Lancaster have been allocated over the past twenty years

(a) to create a pension fund for past and present employees of The Queen and her family not otherwise provided for.

(b) for the upkeep and improvement of The Queen's Sandringham and Balmoral Estates, on which, for obvious reasons, there had been scarcely any capital expenditure in the war and early post-war years.

(c) for assistance to Members of the Royal Family in meeting their official expenses.

(d) for charitable subscriptions and donations.

(e) for welfare and amenity purposes for the Staff of the Royal Household.

(f) to create a contingency reserve. This reserve has been heavily drained to meet the Civil List deficit in the most recent period pending the present review.[24]

There was enough money in that reserve to cover the Civil List deficit to the end of 1971 but not for the whole of 1972. This explains Prince Philip's remark that they were going into the red.

Speaking on behalf of The Queen, Lord Cobbold declared that

Her Majesty has been much concerned by the astronomical figures which have been bandied about in some quarters suggesting that the value of these funds may now run into fifty to a hundred million pounds or more. She feels that these ideas can only arise from confusion about the status of the Royal Collections, which are in no sense at her private disposal. She wishes me to assure the Committee that these suggestions are wildly exaggerated. Her Majesty also wishes me to state that the income from these private funds has been used in some part to assist in meeting the expenses of other Members of the Royal Family; owing to the progress of inflation, they have, in many cases, heavily outrun the Annuities granted by Parliament to cover such expenses at the beginning of the Reign.[25]

Questions from the Committee to Lord Cobbold ranged from the cost of the Chapel Royal and Choir School, to medals of the Royal Victorian Order, and why the Royal Gardens had suddenly gone into surplus. The reply to the latter was that they were making a small profit from the sale of mushrooms, flowers, etc.

When the organization of the Palace came under scrutiny, Lord Cobbold told the Committee of the work of the Treasury team set up at the instigation of Prince Philip in 1962. Lord Cobbold further explained that when he came to the Palace in 1963

there was something still of a feeling, though not as much as there had been earlier, that it was just an honour to serve The Queen, which indeed it still is, but people need not bother quite so much about what they were paid. That has disappeared a lot during the Reign, but it has been one of my preoccupations to get rid of that and see that from top to bottom people are properly paid, and I hope that I can say we have succeeded in that, with great help from the Chancellor's Department and the Civil Service Department. We have reviewed the whole of the salaries and wages from top to bottom in the last few years.[26]

The Committee were surprised to learn that there were 208 unpaid appointments at the Palace. Lord Cobbold explained that some, like the Swan Keeper, were 'purely hereditary', and that there were extra gentlemen ushers and extra equerries who helped out, for example, at garden parties and investitures, who were people who had served The Queen in other capacities. Some were called upon only four or five times a year. 'They are happy to do it and they regard it as a service to The Queen, the Crown and indeed to the State.' In reply to Joel Barnett MP, Cobbold explained that the expenses of those members of the royal family who did not receive annuities were helped 'to some extent from her own private money'.[27]

It was stated that the Palace is not only the official headquarters of the state; it is also a home, and therefore it is sometimes difficult to distinguish between public and private expenditure. When in doubt, it is The Queen who usually foots the bill. Harold Wilson, helpful as ever, pointed out that The Queen often paid for her official uniforms.

She was, as Joel Barnett succinctly observed, in fact, subsidizing the taxpayer. So she had also done this by 'paying expenses' of other members of the royal family.

What clearly emerged from the Committee's investigation was that the Palace was looking for about £450,000 a year at the end of 1972 to deal with the deficit. The Committee was able to recommend to the House an increase in the Civil List, subject to a review in ten years' time. There should be a fixed sum payable annually, with allowances for inflation. At the end of the ten-year period a report would be prepared by a Committee of Royal Trustees, composed of the Prime Minister, the Chancellor of the Exchequer and the Keeper of the Privy Purse, to oversee expenditure on the Civil List.

However, only three years later, when a Labour government was in power, the Royal Trustees reported to the Treasury, expressing concern at the steep rises in inflation and increases in wages and prices. Therefore on 12 February 1975 Wilson laid before the House a request for a rise in the Civil List from £980,000 to £1,400,000. This caused a fierce outcry from the Labour left, led by the ever-watchful William Hamilton, who produced powerful ammunition in his book *The Queen and I*. The fact that The Queen did not pay income tax concerned MPs of all political persuasions. Michael Stewart warned of 'a steady and growing concern about the royal immunity from tax'.[28] In spite of the argument of Denis Healey, the Chancellor of the Exchequer, that 'the real issue was whether humbly paid men and women on the royal staff should get the rate for the job',[29] 89 Labour MPs voted against the increase and 50 deliberately abstained. Nevertheless the Bill was passed.

More crucial changes in the funding and administration of Buckingham Palace were made as a result of a thorough investigation at the end of the 1980s, under the direction of the Lord Chamberlain, Lord Airlie, and Michael Peat.

The Earl of Airlie, was a banker: he had been chairman of Schroders. At a time when the cost of running the royal palaces was much in question, a practical knowledge of finance was of more importance than the diplomatic and military skills of his predecessors. Steeped in tradition though he is – his grandmother was Mabell Countess of Airlie, Lady of the Bedchamber to Queen Mary – Lord Airlie has been the prime mover in the recent reorganization of the administration and financing of the Palaces.

After six months' observing, he began a thorough survey of the royal Household and called in the accountants Peat Marwick McLintock, who were already acting as auditors at the Palace, to do a comprehensive survey. Michael Peat was brought in, with the new title of Director of

Finance and Property Services, before becoming Keeper of the Privy Purse in 1996.

Michael Peat, at forty-six, brought an acute intelligence, financial experience and considerable energy. With European business qualifications, he had worked with his father's firm as auditors at the Palace and was therefore already aware of the situation. With the co-operation of Lord Airlie and the consent of The Queen, Peat transformed the Palace administration.

In July 1990 the Conservative government, at that time led by Margaret Thatcher, established a ten-year agreement by which a figure was set, based on the average for the previous decade. The report of the Royal Trustees considered this 'would not only be in keeping with the dignity of the Crown, but in tune with modern financial practice'.[30] Instead of an annual argument about The Queen's finances, her Civil List income was increased by more than 50 per cent. This assumed a 7½ per cent inflation rate so that the surplus at the beginning of the ten-year period would cover the later shortfall. The total set was an annual £7.9 million from 1 January 1991. This meant that for the future the Palace would be in control of its own expenditure. This settlement received support from the Opposition. In fact, since future inflation and price rises had been overestimated the result turned out to the advantage of the Palace. Any surplus goes to the Treasury, and is not retained by the royal Household.

The second fundamental change was in the administration of the royal Household. Until 1991 the Department of National Heritage provided 'Grant-in-Aid' for the upkeep of Buckingham Palace and the other occupied Palaces. These services were managed by the Property Services Agency for the Department of National Heritage.

After 1991, the Department of National Heritage still remained answerable to Parliament for the funding of Property Services, but the Lord Chamberlain is now responsible for 'all aspects of the management and administration of the Queen's Household'. The Permanent Secretary of the Department of National Heritage is responsible for the accounting of 'the prudent and economical administration of the funds provided by Grant-in-Aid'.[31]

In the Memorandum of Understanding of 1 April 1991 the royal Household's objectives were set out.

a) to maintain the Palaces as buildings of State to a standard consistent with the Household's operational requirements and with the royal architectural and historic status of the buildings.
b) to that end to organise and obtain works and other property services in the most economic and effective way to achieve financial and other performance targets.[32]

As a result of this reorganization, and with the management of the Palace now the responsibility of the Lord Chamberlain and his colleagues, considerable savings have been made – not without 'blood and tears' – by energy-saving measures and reducing staff numbers. A small group of professional staff in the royal Household under Michael Peat took responsibility for the maintenance of services.

The question of the payment of Parliamentary annuities to the royal family was also settled in 1992. When The Queen came to the throne, the Civil List Act made provision for the expenditure incurred by The Queen's cousins, the Dukes of Gloucester and Kent, and Princess Alexandra, when on official duties for The Queen. However, from 1976 The Queen had herself reimbursed the Treasury for these expenses.

From 1991, Parliamentary annuities, including those reimbursed by The Queen, were fixed, like The Queen's Civil List, for a period of ten years. Queen Elizabeth The Queen Mother had been granted £643,000; the Duke of Edinburgh, £359,000; the Duke of York, £249,000; Prince Edward, £96,000; the Princess Royal, £228,000; Princess Margaret, £219,000; and Princess Alice, widow of the Duke of Gloucester, £87,000. The expenses of other members of the royal family were to be met by The Queen. The Prince of Wales has his own income from the Duchy of Cornwall.

In February 1992, Lord Airlie told a press conference, 'The Queen asked me to look at the feasibility of paying tax.'[33] By November 1992 the study was almost completed and preparations were being made to announce a plan for The Queen's taxation, when a fire broke out at Windsor Castle on 20 November. Public sympathy for The Queen, seen on television in headscarf and mackintosh among the ruins, waned when Peter Brooke, the Heritage Secretary, offered the consoling assurance that the government would foot the bill for repairs. The suggestion that the taxpayer should pay a bill that would run into millions raised again the question of The Queen's personal wealth. The announcement of The Queen's offer to pay tax, planned for January 1993, was now brought forward.

On 26 November 1992, Prime Minister John Major announced that The Queen and the Prince of Wales were to pay income tax on their private incomes from 1993. The £900,000 Civil List payments to five members of the royal family would be ended. Michael Peat explained in a television interview that

The Queen would return to the Treasury the Civil List money voted to all members of her family except herself, her mother and her husband. Adjustments would also be made to the contributions made by the Prince of Wales to the Treasury from the profits of the Duchy of Cornwall. Tax would not be paid on public assets or the royal train, royal yacht or the Queen's flight. Money paid by the Queen to her mother or husband would be tax deductible. No inheritance tax would be paid on bequests to the next Sovereign but tax would be paid on private assets: bequests to the Queen's other children would not be exempt from inheritance tax.[34]

The Windsor fire caused one of the most significant changes in the history of Buckingham Palace. In 1993, to help pay for the rebuilding of Windsor Castle, the State Rooms of Buckingham Palace were, for the first time, opened to the paying public for two months each summer.

The settlement of 1992 helped to defuse the arguments over Palace finances. Subsequently, a number of economies have been introduced. The grace and favour residences occupied by pensioners are being gradually phased out. From April 1994 new staff and staff transferring into residential accommodation have been charged 16.7 per cent of their salaries in rent. As a result of the measures introduced in 1991–2 the royal Household hopes to reduce the 'annual amount of the Grant-in-Aid to £15 million by the end of the decade. If this is achieved more than £70 million will have been saved since . . . the Royal Household assumed responsibility for property services in the occupied Palaces on 1st April 1991.'[35]

Despite these changes there are still wildly misleading estimates published about The Queen's private income. As the Keeper of the Privy Purse writes,

The Queen's personal income, derived from her personal investment portfolio, is used to meet her private expenditure. The Queen's private funds, as for any other individual, remain a private matter. However the Lord Chamberlain said in 1993 that estimates of £100 million and upwards were 'grossly overstated'.[36]

The Queen's private finances and those of many members of the royal family are dealt with still mostly by Coutts & Co. When in December 1978 The Queen opened their new bank in the Strand, she said

Members of my family, for generations, have had to acknowledge the wisdom and prudence of the advice they have received from Coutts . . . even if they have not *always* been grateful for it. Advice is, however, always easier to accept if it is delivered with that old-fashioned courtesy for which this institution is renowned and backed up by authority and expertise.[37]

The Queen was referring to the fact that Thomas Coutts himself had had the unenviable task of rescuing George IV and his brothers time and again from their vast debt. Without his aid the extravagant George IV could not have bequeathed such a magnificent collection to the Crown.

Buckingham Palace, like the other occupied Palaces, is now administered by the heads of the six departments under the chairmanship of the Lord Chamberlain. He 'oversees . . . the implementation of common procedures and policies and involves himself with all senior appointments to the Household'.[38] He still undertakes ceremonial duties and is the link between The Queen and the House of Lords.

Each head of the six departments is responsible for his own area and has direct access to The Queen. The Lord Chamberlain's regular meetings with the six heads strengthen their sense of a common purpose.

This structure works. Like the Commonwealth, it depends for its success on the combination of independence, co-operation and mutual understanding. As the present Lord Chamberlain says, 'The inspiration comes from the top, the Queen herself.'[39]

The heads of departments are: the Private Secretary, the Keeper of the Privy Purse, the Master of the Household, the Comptroller of the Lord Chamberlain's Office, the Crown Equerry and the Director of the Royal Collection.

The Private Secretary is assisted by a Deputy Private Secretary and Assistant Private Secretary. He is also responsible for the Buckingham Palace Press Office, with its Press Secretary, Deputy and two assistants. He is the Keeper of the Royal Archives, which are in the care of the Librarian of the Royal Library at Windsor Castle.

The Keeper of the Privy Purse is The Queen's Treasurer, responsible for The Queen's Civil List. Among his many responsibilities is the care of the Royal Philatelic Collection established by King George V. He is assisted by the Director of Property Services, who is responsible for the refurbishment of buildings and utilities (gas, water, electricity and telephones), for the gardens and for fire prevention. The fire prevention department has become increasingly important since the fire at Windsor Castle and is under a Director of Fire, Health and Safety.

The Master of the Household has a large and varied department, responsible for staff and domestic arrangements, The Queen's official entertaining, the Court Post Office, security, and the oversight of visitors to such ceremonies as the Changing of the Guard.

The Lord Chamberlain's Office is not to be confused with that of the Lord Chamberlain himself. The Comptroller of this department arranges state visits, presentation of credentials, garden parties, royal christenings, weddings and funerals.

The Crown Equerry is in charge of the Royal Mews, arranges transport on ceremonial occasions and provides cars or horses for members of the royal family.

The Director of the Royal Collection heads a department which co-ordinates the work of the Surveyor of The Queen's Pictures, the Surveyor of The Queen's Works of Art, and the Librarian of the Royal Library. The Royal Collection of pictures and works of art is in his care. He has overall responsibility for all items in the Royal Collection, including restoration, hanging and security, for initiating and assisting research into the history of the Royal Collection and for making it accessible to the public, either by display in the State Apartments or in The Queen's Gallery, or by loans to exhibitions.

The Royal Collection

One of the most important results of the reorganization of the Buckingham Palace royal Household at the end of the 1980s was the fundamental change in the administration of the Royal Collection.

In 1987, this department was set up, with its own offices in Stable Yard House, St James's Palace. It is run by a Director, assisted on the curatorial side by the Surveyor of The Queen's Pictures, the Deputy Surveyor of the Queen's Works of Art and the Librarian, and on the financial side by the Managing Director of Royal Collection Enterprises and a Finance Director. Together they manage 'the conservation, presentation, cataloguing and research, and relations with the public'. The Director of the Royal Collection, in collaboration with the Keeper of The Privy Purse, plans the budget of the Royal Collection department and meets with other departmental heads at the Lord Chamberlain's monthly meetings. He, like the other heads of department, has direct access to The Queen. From 1993, the income from opening the Palaces to the public and from the commercial activities of Royal Collection Enterprises has been administered by the Royal Collection Trust, chaired by the Prince of Wales.

To care for such an immense collection demands exceptional qualities of scholarship and expertise, and also of practical common sense. The first Director, Sir Oliver Millar, was succeeded on his retirement in 1988 by Sir Geoffrey de Bellaigue, who in turn was succeeded in 1996 by Hugh Roberts. All three directors have written works of high academic and specialist interest; they have modestly left unsigned many of their scholarly contributions to catalogues of exhibitions in The Queen's Gallery and elsewhere.

In the past the care of the Royal Collection had depended very much on the interest of the monarch. Charles I, that most discriminating of the royal collectors, had appointed the Dutch expert Abraham Van der Doort as overseer 'of all our pictures'. As Sir Oliver Millar wrote, his 'job description' might well be applied to the Surveyorship today: 'he was to prevent the pictures from being damaged or defaced, he was to order marke & number them to keep a Register of them & dispatching them. He was to organise the makeing & copying of pictures.'[40]

Charles II had 'a Keeper and Surveyor' of his pictures, Parry Walton, who was retained by William III and Queen Mary, and was followed by his son, Peter, as Surveyor and Keeper of Pictures.

George III had taken great care of his books and pictures and appointed his favourite painter, Benjamin West, as his Surveyor, cleaner and repairer. In the reign of George IV, William Seguier combined the post with that of director of the new National Gallery. His was a mammoth task, involving the supervision of the frequent moving of George IV's immense collection. Queen Victoria and Prince Albert had been horrified by the neglect of the paintings at Windsor under William IV; even so the appointment of Surveyor was still considered to be 'an honorary one with very slight duties attached to it'.[41] Their Surveyor, Richard Redgrave, considered that the work had to be carried out with 'more earnestness than had yet been brought to bear upon it'.[42] He ruined his eyesight in compiling a record of over 1,900 of the pictures in the Collection.

The importance of the Surveyor's task was still not recognized, and Sir Lionel Cust managed to combine it with the directorship of the National Portrait Gallery. It was with great reluctance that Kenneth Clark agreed to King George V's insistence that he should combine his work as Director of the National Gallery with the Surveyorship of the King's Pictures, recognizing that it was an impossible task for one man. The National Gallery was his main concern and he spent little time at the Palace.

His successor was Anthony Blunt, Surveyor of the King's and subsequently of The Queen's Pictures from 1945 to 1972. An art historian of great distinction and an inspiring lecturer, he was from 1947 to 1974

Director of the Courtauld Institute and was preoccupied with the definitive catalogues he and others were preparing of part of the collection of the Old Master drawings at Windsor.

His curious history meant that he did not often visit Buckingham Palace or attend meetings with his colleagues. On 23 April 1964 Blunt confessed to MI5 that he had been recruited, while under the influence of Guy Burgess at Cambridge, as a spy for the Russians. During the war, as the fourth man in an espionage ring, he had passed on a great deal of classified information to his paymasters. However, The Queen was advised through Sir Michael Adeane to retain his services as Surveyor. Blunt retired in 1972 and the story was concealed from the public until 1979, when the Prime Minister, Margaret Thatcher, made it known to Parliament. Blunt was succeeded by Sir Oliver Millar, who, as the first full-time Surveyor, had the immense task of organizing the department on a new basis. A distinguished art historian and an authority on the work of Sir Anthony van Dyck, he is remembered by all who worked with him for his scholarship and infectious enthusiasm for the paintings in his care.

Now that the department had responsibility for the overall maintenance and surveillance of the Collection, as Sir Oliver wrote, 'the collection provides its custodian with a unique and never wholly soluble problem. Apart from damaging atmospheric conditions and ... the effects of central heating ... there are many hazards. Workmen have sometimes not realized the delicacy of the paintings.'[43]

Labels have been stuck to the surfaces of pictures, electricians have altered picture lights when still on the pictures. The interference of members of the Surveyor's team has to be tactfully organised ... a flask of healing oil is as important a part of a Surveyor's kit as his torch and measure: especially when he finds painters at work in a room that has four great pictures by Stubbs still hanging on the wall.[44]

Sir Oliver tactfully does not mention that since the Palace is both museum and family home, children are an additional hazard. So, too, were the problems caused both to the Director of the Royal Collection and to the Master of the Household by the summer opening of Bucking-

ham Palace and the fact that work on conservation, repairs and redecoration has to be done when The Queen is not in residence. However,
the work of the department has been made infinitely easier now that it
is independent and that the six heads of the royal Household departments
meet regularly and can discuss problems constructively.

The Royal Collection is already one of the greatest in the world. 'There
are 7,000 paintings, 3,000 miniatures, 30,000 Old Master drawings and
watercolours, over 100,000 prints and hundreds of thousands of *objets
d'art.*'[45] It represents, as the Prince of Wales has written, the individual
tastes and interests of successive sovereigns. Many of the paintings in
the Picture Gallery at Buckingham Palace are reminders of George III,
a King who encouraged artists. George IV bequeathed to the Royal
Collection some of the world's finest paintings. It is to him that we owe
the magnificent collection of Dutch, Flemish and French paintings in
Buckingham Palace, at a cost that could not be countenanced today.
Rembrandt's *The Ship Builder and his Wife*, for example, is said to have
cost him 5,000 guineas.

Although The Queen has not felt the need to find and bring back
the best of European art in the way that George III and George IV
did, she has, however, added to the Collection sculpture, silver, drawings,
portraits and watercolours of distinction.

The Queen's contribution in other areas has followed the example of
Queen Mary and has encouraged the care, conservation and proper
organization of the collection, authorizing the setting up of the Royal
Collection department for this purpose. The love of order which Crawfie
and Queen Mary noticed in the little girl is still present in The Queen.

Loans are frequently made to exhibitions and museums, and above
all thousands of visitors to the summer opening of the Palace have been
able to enjoy seeing superb pictures in their traditional settings.

To walk through the Picture Gallery is to walk back through history.
Here the young Princesses, Elizabeth and Margaret, watched with
Crawfie while the treasures brought back from their wartime hiding
were unpacked; here King George VI and Queen Elizabeth heard the
Blitz shake the Palace walls; here in the First World War Queen Mary
defied fate and put a new glass roof over the Picture Gallery; here Queen

Victoria and Prince Albert danced and entertained the crowned heads of Europe; here George IV planned a magnificent home for his beloved collection of pictures. Here on this site, in 'the Queen's House' of George III and Queen Charlotte, the young Queen had her suite of rooms and from her windows had looked out and planned the King's surprise birthday party. Here the Duchess of Buckingham, robed in black, had sat in solemn state and mourned on each anniversary of the execution of her grandfather, Charles I.

Van Dyck's 'Great Peece' portrait of the sad-eyed Charles I with his French wife Henrietta Maria and his eldest children, his son Charles, who became Charles II, and his daughter Mary, dominates one wall. The portrait was painted in the old Whitehall Palace: behind the King, across the Thames, clouds gather over Westminster Hall, where later he would be condemned to death.

Walking among the portraits of kings and queens one is so often reminded that

> The glories of our blood and state
> Are shadows, not substantial things;
> There is no armour against Fate;
> Death lays his icy hand on Kings:
> Sceptre and Crown
> Must tumble down
> And in the dust be equal made
> With the poor crookèd scythe and spade.[46]

Here in the Palace is Queen Charlotte, a slender girl at her Coronation, painted with such humanity by Allan Ramsay; and here, plump and sad, she is as Sir William Beechey saw her in her middle age. Here is *The Apotheosis* by Benjamin West of George III's two beloved sons Princes Alfred and Octavius, who died young. In the Throne Room hangs Angelica Kauffmann's portrait of George III's sister, Augusta, Duchess of Brunswick, an unhappy wife and mother of Caroline of Brunswick, George IV's notorious wife. Like the portrait of his other sister, the tragic Queen of Denmark, they are reminders of the sad lot of many a royal bartered bride.

The portrayal of royal families through the ages is in itself a fascinating study. At Windsor the happiness of Queen Victoria and Prince Albert in their early days of marriage still shines from the Winterhalter portraits. One recalls Laurits Regner Tuxen's immense family group of 1887, which was painted as she wished, not 'stiff and according to etiquette, but prettily grouped'. Here Queen Victoria is indeed the 'Grand Mother of Europe' and Albert's bust looks down on their international family.

Buckingham Palace holds not only some of the finest paintings in the world but also superb furniture. There is a fascinating history behind many of the *objets d'art*. The magnificent commode in the Green Drawing Room, for instance, with *pietre dure* plaques, has a tragic opera story. It originally belonged to Marie Joséphine Laguerre, a singer at the Paris Opera, described as 'a priestess of love', who died young 'exhausted by excess of every kind'.

Many items have made interesting journeys before settling in the Palace – ivory chairs from India, superb porcelain from Sèvres. One of the most spectacular examples is the table known as the 'Table of the Grand Commanders'. Made for Napoleon, it was given to George IV, then Prince Regent, by Louis XVIII, the restored King of France. Painted in the form of cameo reliefs, it represents the twelve commanders of historical times surrounding Alexander the Great in the centre. It was one of George IV's most prized possessions.

Visitors who walk through the State Rooms may well be overwhelmed by the superb paintings, the exuberance of George IV's French furniture, the soaring pillars of marble, the glowing colours of carpets and furnishings, all reflected again and again in the mirrored doors. It is easy to miss the details, the delicate work of the craftsmen and sculptors – such as the handles of the great entrance gates, wrought in the shape of little cherubs, or the elegant urns of Coadestone on the outside walls of the Palace, or the beautiful capitals of the moulded pillars of the great double portico at the Grand Entrance, or, high above, panels in Coadestone celebrating the victories of Nelson and Wellington on sea and land.

Inside the Palace no one can miss Nash's superb ceilings. Here the richness of the gilded ornaments is held in the balance and harmony of the design. However, much of the detail and beauty of the plaster decorations – the work of Thomas and Alfred Stothard, Francis Bernasconi or William Pitts – is too high up to be appreciated. So too, some of the most exquisite workmanship in the Palace is underfoot. The parquet floor in the Music Room, inlaid with satinwood, rosewood, tulipwood, mahogany and holly, has few equals in the country. Designed by John Nash and made by Thomas Seddon, it cost £2,400 – a fortune at the time. It has survived the dancing feet of many a young Prince and Princess who took their lessons there.

The care and conservation of this vast collection is an immense task. Much of the specialist work is now undertaken in the workshops at Marlborough House, while the majority of the paintings are cleaned and conserved in the Royal Collection studios in St. James's Palace.

The work of the craftsmen of the past may be unnoticed by the casual visitor, but it is much admired by those who today are responsible for the conservation of the Palace. Great care is taken to preserve even fragments of past workmanship. In the 1980s pieces of a stained-glass window, shattered during the war, were found in store. The window had been erected by Queen Alexandra in 1905 in memory of her beloved eldest son, Eddy, who had died aged twenty-eight. It had been hung on the Ministers' Stairs and represented the Prince as a knight in shining armour – a somewhat improbable image of that lethargic Prince. Until recently the pieces had not been reassembled – perhaps Queen Mary had not wished to be reminded of her first fiancé. Though incomplete, it has been restored and lent to the stained glass museum in Ely Cathedral, where it can now be seen.

It is interesting that John Nash's reputation stands high today among those who work on the fabric of the Palace. The beauty of his designs is appreciated; so is his practical ability. Today's fire prevention officer claims that Nash was ahead of his contemporaries and of the present day in the precautions he took against fire. And how delighted Nash would be to know that his much criticized Palace has stood the test of time, wartime bombing and the tramp of thousands of feet during the summer opening! The building is regularly monitored to detect signs of movement. So far, there are none.

A Queen for All Seasons

Perhaps one of the greatest achievements of Queen Elizabeth II's reign has been that she has used the Palace as never before, opening it to many millions of people from all walks of life. In addition to the three garden parties a year, thousands more are received at investitures, official receptions and conferences. During the summer opening, up to seven thousand a day walk through the State Rooms and into the Palace gardens.

The Queen has allowed television cameras into Buckingham Palace, bringing it into millions of sitting rooms. Thanks to television, millions have been able to see The Queen in many of her different roles. She is seen driving out of the Palace gates in the State Coach, crowned and glittering in full regalia, for the State Opening of Parliament, or in evening dress, wearing dazzling tiara and jewels, at banquets and receptions at Buckingham Palace. She is seen at her desk, working at the red boxes of official documents, or with Prince Philip on 'walkabouts' in towns and villages at home and abroad. Now she appears, distressed, at the scene of such disasters as that at Aberfan; or radiant, with her family at christenings in the white and gold rooms of the Palace, or, with them, waving from the balcony to the crowds in the Mall. Now the camera catches her relaxed, in tweeds, walking her corgis in the Palace garden. Viewers have heard the bagpipes played at nine each morning under her Palace windows and remember pictures of Highland dancing at Balmoral and of The Queen in the tartan of her clan striding over the moors.

These glimpses, however, cannot convey the full extent of The Queen's working life. Prime Ministers, visiting heads of state and all who work with her pay tribute to her dedication and sheer professionalism. The red boxes come to her daily wherever she may be, containing briefs for meetings or visits, reports from Parliament or abroad, and documents to be signed. The Queen deals with them promptly and thoroughly. Often, after a long day's official work, she works on the boxes before going to bed.

*

In 1995, on the fiftieth anniversary of VE Day, the victory in Europe, once again thousands thronged the Mall to cheer The Queen, Prince Philip and the royal family as they made their traditional appearance. As wartime songs rang across the Park, there were many who remembered the courage of King George VI and Queen Elizabeth, who had braved the bombs with the people of London. Viewers caught the unforgettable moment when Queen Elizabeth The Queen Mother, then ninety-five, gave her characteristic wave as she sang with the crowds the wartime song 'Wish me luck as you wave me goodbye'.

In August, on the fiftieth anniversary of VJ Day, the victory over Japan, there was a significant change. The Queen took the salute at the foot of the memorial to Queen Victoria; and Prince Philip joined the veterans of the war in the Far East for the march past The Queen, walking beside the daughter of the late Lord Mountbatten. He has never forgotten his service in the Far East, when he was second-in-command of the destroyer HMS *Whelp*, nor that he was with his uncle Lord Mountbatten for the signing of the Japanese surrender in Tokyo Bay on 2 September 1945.

The Coronation made Queen Elizabeth II a star on the world stage, but she has never played to the gallery. When her friends have encouraged her to smile more, she has replied that she smiles and smiles until her face aches, but that in repose her expression is naturally solemn. When deeply moved she can appear impassive. She remembers her grandfather King George V's reply to the same criticism: 'Sailors don't smile on duty.' So the radiance of her sudden unexpected smile is all the more dazzling.

Without seeking applause, The Queen has earned it. She has made remarkably few mistakes in her long reign. She has inspired the admir-ation even of staunch republicans, who concede that she is a hard-working professional. Even her one-time critic, Lord Altrincham, now John Grigg, could write with approval, 'no breath of scandal has ever touched her . . . she behaves decently, because she is decent'.[48]

As for those who work for her, their praise is warm and unanimous. The late Sir Michael Adeane, her Private Secretary for nineteen years, described her to the present writer as 'pure gold'. Others who have come to the Palace from the services or business declare that they have never met a more supportive boss or colleague. In times of crisis she is, they say, a rock, a 'still centre', in a turbulent world. For the royal Household, Buckingham Palace is, without question, 'The Queen's House', in which they are proud to serve.

In the past Buckingham Palace has undergone many transformations, not always for the better. The modern challenge has been to organize efficiently a vast building that has so many different functions. The Palace has '19 state rooms, 52 bedrooms, 188 staff bedrooms, 92 offices and 78 bathrooms. Four hundred and fifty people work in the Palace and 40,000 are entertained there every year.' On state occasions it is the setting for magnificent displays of traditional ritual, yet it has also to be the modern headquarters of the Head of State – now with a site on the Internet. It has to house treasures and be a family home; and it opens its doors to the public.

Throughout the ages it has been fiercely criticized by some for its architecture and cost. For long periods it was certainly underused, such as during George III's illness, for example, and Queen Victoria's widowhood. In the past it has been badly organized and slow to be reformed.

But the Palace has endured. Neither harsh words nor enemy bombs have destroyed it, because it has fulfilled a deep-seated need – to have a focus, above party politics, which can in time of crisis or celebration unite the nation. The importance of a focal point for the expression of national joy or grief was powerfully illustrated by the scenes outside the royal palaces after the death of Diana, Princess of Wales. Vast seas of flowers surrounded the gates of Buckingham Palace, as well as those of Kensington Palace, as lines of mourners sought to share their sorrow. It is, too, the setting for honouring all kinds of people, from the simplest to the highest. An investiture at the Palace, conducted with time-honoured formality, means a great deal to the recipients. An invitation to one of the summer garden parties is a valued recognition of the service of a wide range of people from all over the country and the world. It would be difficult to find a better site for those occasions when there is a need to celebrate together. It has been a significant focal point over the years, when millions of people have lined the Mall to watch royal processions or crowded around Queen Victoria's Memorial to cheer the royal family on the balcony.

Buckingham Palace has come to represent an important part of our history, in which not only kings and queens, but also architects and artists, craftsmen and women, have all had their roles. The knowledge of those deep roots brings a sense of stability and security in a changing world.

Notes

PROLOGUE

1. *Gentleman's Magazine*, June 1863, vol. xxxiii, p. 311.
2. Horace Walpole, *Letters*, Clarendon Press, Oxford 1905.

CHAPTER ONE

1. It was removed by George III. Quoted Clifford Smith, *Buckingham Palace*, Country Life Ltd., 1931.
2. Walford, Edward, *Old and New London.*, 8 vols., Cassell Peter & Galpin, London, 1897.
3. *ibid.*
4. See Bruce Graeme, *The Story of Buckingham Palace*, Hutchinson & Co., 1928.
5. *ibid.*
6. Quoted Clifford Smith, *Buckingham Palace*, from Charles Gatty, *Mary Davies and The Manor of Ebury.*
7. See Bruce Graeme, *The Story of Buckingham Palace.*
8. Sir Charles Sedley, *The Mulberry Garden*, 1675.
9. John Evelyn, *Diary*, vol. 2, 10 May 1654, ed. William Brag, J. Dent & Sons, 1907.
10. Samuel Pepys, *Diary*, vol. 2, 5 April 1669, ed. H. Wheatley, 8 vols., G. Bell & Sons Ltd., London, 1924.
11. Samuel Pepys, *Diary*, vol. 2, 10 July 1660.
12. John Evelyn, *Diary*, vol. 2, 29 March 1665.

13. Thomas Macaulay, *History of England*, ed. Henderson, Routledge, 1909.

14. Comte de Gramont, *Memoirs*, transl. Peter Quennell, London, 1930.

15. Samuel Pepys, *Diary*, vol. 2, 10 July 1666.

16. Samuel Pepys, *Diary*, vol. 2, 24 June 1667.

17. John Evelyn, *Diary*, vol. 2, 1 August 1672.

18. John Evelyn, *Diary*, vol. 2, 6 November 1679.

19. John Evelyn, *Diary*, vol. 2, 26 October 1683.

20. John Evelyn, *Diary*, vol. 2, 17 April 1673.

21. John Evelyn, *Diary*, vol. 2, 21 September 1674.

22. See Clifford Smith, *Buckingham Palace*.

23. John Dryden, *The Poems of John Dryden*, ed. James Kinsley, 4 vols., Clarendon Press, 1903–5.

24. Quoted Clifford Smith, *Buckingham Palace*, from the Surveyor General's Report, 1698.

25. Thomas Macaulay, *History of England*.

26. *ibid.*

27. Quoted Clifford Smith, *Buckingham Palace*, from *A New View of London*, 1708.

28. John Sheffield, letter to Duke of Shrewsbury. *Complete Works*, 2 vols., 1740.

29. Quoted Clifford Smith, *Buckingham Palace*, from vol. 1, p. 117.

30. Horace Walpole, *Letters*, 8 vols., Clarendon Press, Oxford.

31. Alexander Pope, *The Character of Katherine, late Duchess of Buckingham and Normanby*, M. Cooper 1764.

32. B. M. Original Papers, vol. 1 1743–84 Folio 9; B. M. Original Papers, General Meeting, vol. 1., 2 April 1754, GM29.

CHAPTER TWO

1. It was removed by George III. Quoted Clifford Smith, *Buckingham Palace*, Country Life Ltd., 1931.

2. Horace Walpole, *Letters*, to Sir Horace Mann, British Envoy at Florence.

3. *ibid.*

4. Quoted E. S. Turner, *The Court of St James*, Michael Joseph, 1959, from *Court & City Register*.

5. *The Diaries of Mrs Lybbe Powys*, ed. E. J. Climenson, Longman, 1899.

6. Horace Walpole to Sir Horace Mann. Quoted Bruce Graeme, *The Story of Buckingham Palace*, Hutchinson & Co., 1928.

7. Duke of Buckingham, Letter to Duke of Shrewsbury, *Works*, vol. 2, 1753.

8. See John Brooke, *King George III*, Constable, 1972.

9. Sir Joshua Reynolds, source unknown.

10. John Thomas Smith, *Nollekens and His Times: the Life of the Sculptor Joseph Nollekens*, Turnstile Press, 1949.

11. Quoted Clifford Smith, *Buckingham Palace*.

12. Megan Aldrich (ed.), *The Craces*, John Murray and Brighton Pavilion, 1990.

13. Quoted Clifford Smith, *Buckingham Palace*, from Whitley, 'Artists and Their Friends in England 1700–1799'.

14. Quoted Clifford Smith, *Buckingham Palace*.

15. Sophie von la Roche, *Sophie in London*, transl. Clare Williams, Jonathan Cape, 1933.

16. Horace Walpole, letter to Sir Horace Mann, 1762. Quoted Clifford Smith, *Buckingham Palace*.

17. *The Diaries of Mrs Lybbe Powys*, March 23 and 27 1767, ed. E. J. Climenson, Longmans, 1899.

18. E. S. Turner, *The Court of St James*.

19. Mrs Charlotte Papendiek, *Court and Private Life in the Time of Queen Charlotte*, ed. Mrs Kernon Delves Broughton, Richard Bentley & Son, 1887.

20. Sophie von la Roche, *Sophie in London*.

21. J. T. Smith, *Nollekens and His Times*, 1949.

22. Mme D'Arblay, *Diary and Correspondence of Fanny Burney*, ed. G. F. Barrett, 6 vols., 1904.

23. Mrs Charlotte Papendiek, *Court and Private Life in the Time of Queen Charlotte*.

24. Mme D'Arblay, *Diary and Correspondence of Fanny Burney*.

25. *London Chronicle*, May 1764.

26. Journals of the House of Commons, 11 February 1780.

27. Nathaniel Wraxall, *Historical Memoirs*, ed. H. Wheatley, vol. ii, 1884.

28. Mrs Charlotte Papendiek, *Court and Private Life in the Time of Queen Charlotte*.

29. Mme D'Arblay, *Diary and Correspondence of Fanny Burney*.

30. Mrs Charlotte Papendiek, *Court and Private Life in the Time of Queen Charlotte*.

31. *Gentleman's Magazine*, 1802.

32. William H. Pyne, *A History of the Royal Residences*, vol. 3, L. P., 1819.

33. Quoted Bruce Graeme, *The Story of Buckingham Palace*, Hutchinson and Co., 1928, from Holt's *Life of George III*.

34. *Letters of Princess Charlotte 1811–1817*, ed. A. Aspinall, Home and van Thal, 1949.

35. *Memoirs of Baron Stockmar by his Son, Baron E. von Stockmar*, ed. F. Max Müller, 2 vols, Longmans, Green & Co., 1872.

36. Olwen Hedley, *Queen Charlotte*, John Murray, 1975.

37. Richard Rush, diary of 17 February 1818, *Memoranda of a Resident at the Court of London*, 1833.

38. Quoted Olwen Hedley, *Queen Charlotte*, from Mme D'Arblay (Fanny Burney), *Diary and Correspondence of Fanny Burney*.

39. *ibid.*

40. Princess Lieven, *The Private Letters*, John Murray, 1934.

CHAPTER THREE

1. King George IV to John Nash, quoted Clifford Smith, *Buckingham Palace*, Country Life Ltd, 1931.

2. Mrs Arbuthnot, *The Journal of Mrs Arbuthnot*, 1820–1832, 2 vols. Macmillan & Co., 1950.

3. Quoted John Summerson, *The Life and Work of John Nash*, Allen & Unwin, 1935.

4. *The Times*, 23 January 1826.

5. Mrs Arbuthnot, *The Journal of Mrs Arbuthnot*.

6. John Nash to Sir John Soane, 18 September 1822, quoted John Summerson, *The Life and Work of John Nash*.

7. *The Times*, May 1825.

8. *The Times*, June 1825.

9. Quoted John Summerson, *The Life and Work of John Nash*.

10. *The Literary Gazette*, 4 September 1826.

11. *Fraser's Magazine*, 1830.

12. John Summerson, *The Life and Work of John Nash*.

13. Professor Richardson, quoted Clifford Smith, *Buckingham Palace*.

14. John Summerson, *The Life and Work of John Nash*.

15. Quoted in Alison Kelly, *Mrs Coade's Stone*, Self Publishing Association Limited, 1990.

16. 'Obituary of Mrs Coade, Inventor of Coade Stone', *Gentleman's Magazine*, 1821.

17. Alison Kelly, *Mrs Coade's Stone*.
18. *The Times*, 10 March 1826.
19. *The Times*, 5 November 1827.

CHAPTER FOUR

1. Lord Holland, *Holland House Diaries*, ed. A. D. Kriegal, Routledge & Paul, 1977.
2. *Report of House of Commons Select Committee*, October 1831.
3. John Summerson, *The Life and Work of John Nash*, Allen & Unwin, 1935.
4. Lord Holland, *Holland House Diaries*.
5. Robert Huish, *Memoirs of George IV*, ed. Kelly, 2 vols., London, 1831.
6. Thomas Creevey, *The Creevey Papers*, 14 March 1831, ed. Sir Herbert Maxwell, John Murray, 1903.
7. Philip Ziegler, *King William IV*, Collins, 1971.
8. John Martin Robinson, *Royal Palaces: Buckingham Palace*, Michael Joseph, 1995.
9. Thomas Creevey, *The Creevey Papers*.
10. William Hazlitt, quoted Claire Tomalin, *Mrs Jordan's Profession*, Viking, 1994.
11. Lord Holland, *Holland House Diaries*.

CHAPTER FIVE

1. Quoted Bruce Graeme, *The Story of Buckingham Palace*, Hutchinson & Co., 1928.
2. *Leaves from the Greville Diary*, ed. Morrell, Eveleigh Nash & Grayson, 1929.
3. *Memoirs of Baron Stockmar by his Son, Baron E. von Stockmar*, ed. F. Max Müller, 2 vols., Longmans, Green & Co., 1872.
4. Elizabeth Longford, *Victoria R.I.*, Weidenfeld & Nicolson, 1964.
5. Princess Lieven, *The Private Letters*, John Murray, 1934.
6. Lord Holland, *Holland House Diaries*, ed. A. D. Kriegal, Routledge & Paul, 1977.
7. Lord Holland, *Holland House Diaries*.
8. Michael Joyce, *My Friend H: the Life of John Hobhouse, Lord Broughton*, John Murray, 1948.
9. Queen Victoria, *Queen Victoria's Letters: a Selection from Her Majesty's Correspondence* (see Bibliography).
10. Queen Victoria, 7 May 1839, *Journal* (see Bibliography).

11. Queen Victoria, 9 May 1839, *Journal.*

12. Queen Victoria, *Letters.*

13. Queen Victoria, 29 May 1839, *The Girlhood*, ed. Viscount Esher, 2 vols., John Murray, 1912.

14. *ibid.*

15. Baron Stockmar to Prince Albert, quoted Robert Rhodes-James, *Albert, Prince Consort*, Hamish Hamilton, 1983.

16. Baron Stockmar to Queen Victoria, *Memoirs of Baron Stockmar by his Son, Baron E. von Stockmar.*

17. *ibid.*

18. Dowager Duchess of Gotha, quoted Robert Rhodes-James, *Albert, Prince Consort.*

19. Louise, Duchess of Coburg, Prince Albert's mother, June 1820, quoted Robert Rhodes-James, *Albert, Prince Consort.*

20. Quoted Robert Rhodes-James, *Albert, Prince Consort.*

21. Baron Stockmar to Prince Leopold, quoted *ibid.*

22. Queen Victoria, 18 May 1836, *Journal.*

23. Prince Albert to a friend, 1838, quoted Robert Rhodes-James, *Albert, Prince Consort.*

24. Prince Leopold to Baron Stockmar, quoted Robert Rhodes-James, *Albert, Prince Consort.*

25. Queen Victoria, 11 October 1839, *Journal.*

26. Queen Victoria, 15 October 1839, *Journal.*

27. Prince Albert to Baron Stockmar, 16 October 1839, *Letters*, ed. K. Jagow, John Murray, 1938.

28. Prince Albert to Baron Stockmar.

29. Queen Victoria, address to Privy Council, 23 November 1839. Quoted Elizabeth Longford, *Victoria R.I.*

30. Queen Victoria to Prince Albert, quoted Elizabeth Longford, *Victoria R.I.*

31. Prince Albert to Duchess Caroline of Saxe-Gotha-Altenberg, 12 February 1841, *Letters.*

32. Quoted Bruce Graeme, *The Story of Buckingham Palace.*

33. Mendelssohn, Felix Bartholdy, to his mother, 9 July 1842, *Letters 1833–1847*, ed. Jacob, 1863.

34. Queen Victoria, 31 December 1843, *Journal.* Quoted Christopher Lloyd, *The Royal Collection*, Sinclair-Stevenson.

35. Queen Victoria, *Letters.* Quoted Elizabeth Longford, *Victoria R.I.*

36. Quoted Sir Oliver Millar, *Victorian Pictures in the Collection of Her Majesty The Queen*, Cambridge University Press, 1992.

37. *ibid.*

38. *Memoirs of Baron Stockmar by his Son, Baron E. von Stockmar.*

39. *ibid.*

40. *ibid.*

41. Prince Albert to Stockmar, 18 January 1842, quoted Robert Rhodes-James, *Albert, Prince Consort.*

42. *Memoirs of Baron Stockmar by his Son, Baron E. von Stockmar.*

43. *ibid.*

44. *ibid.*

45. *ibid.*

46. *ibid.*

47. *ibid.*

48. John Pudney, *The Smallest Room*, Alan Sutton, 1984.

49. *ibid.*

50. *Memoirs of Baron Stockmar by his Son, Baron E. von Stockmar.*

51. Boswell, James, *Boswell's Journal 1762–1763*, ed. F. A. Pottle, Heinemann, 1950.

52. Prince Albert to his father, May 1842, *Letters.*

53. *The Times*, December 1840.

54. *The Times*, 17 March 1841.

55. *The Times*, 23 March 1841.

56. Charles Dickens, *The Letters*, ed. Storey, Pilletson and Easson, vol. 3, Oxford University Press, 1993.

57. Quoted Elizabeth Longford, *Victoria R.I.*

58. *Memoirs of Baron Stockmar by his son, Baron E. von Stockmar.*

59. *The Times*, 24 June 1842.

60. E. S. Turner, *The Court of St James*, Michael Joseph, 1959.

61. *ibid.*

62. *The Times*, April 1841.

63. Queen Victoria to Sir Robert Peel, 10 February 1845, *Letters.*

64. Annual Register, June 1845.

65. Anonymous, quoted Bruce Graeme, *The Story of Buckingham Palace.*

66. *The Times*, 13 August 1846, including a letter from the architect, Blore, confirming the need for Palace improvements.

67. Letter from 'Sphinx', *The Times*, 24 August 1846.

68. Clifford Smith, *Buckingham Palace.*

69. *The Builder*, August 1846.

70. Queen Victoria, 10 June 1849, *Journal*.

71. Quoted Hermione Hobhouse, *Thomas Cubitt*, Macmillan, 1971.

72. *ibid.*

73. Robert Rhodes-James, *Albert, Prince Consort*.

74. Quoted *ibid.*

75. Queen Victoria, 28 February 1854, *Journal*.

76. Queen Victoria to King Leopold, 27 February 1855, *Letters*.

77. Frieda Arnold, *My Mistress the Queen*, Transl. Sheila de Bellaigue, Weidenfeld & Nicolson, 1994.

78. G. Tyack, *Sir James Pennethorne and the Making of Victorian London*, Cambridge University Press, 1992.

79. Thomas Cubitt, quoted Hermione Hobhouse, *Thomas Cubitt*.

80. *ibid.*

81. Quoted Clifford Smith, *The Story of Buckingham Palace*, from *The Builder*, May 1856.

82. Queen Victoria, 8 May 1856, *Journal*.

83. Queen Victoria to Lord Clarendon, 25 October 1857, *Letters*.

84. Elizabeth Longford, *Victoria R.I.*

85. *Punch*, quoted Bruce Graeme, *The Story of Buckingham Palace*.

86. *Memoirs of Baron Stockmar by his Son, Baron E. von Stockmar*.

87. Prince Albert to Bertie. His last letter to his son. Quoted Robert Rhodes-James, *Albert, Prince Consort*.

88. Queen Victoria, 1874, *Journal*, quoted Elizabeth Longford, *Victoria R.I.*

89. Queen Victoria to King Leopold, 20 December 1861, *Letters*.

90. Queen Victoria to King Leopold, 26 December 1861, *Letters*.

91. *Memoirs of Baron Stockmar by his Son, Baron E. von Stockmar*.

92. Queen Victoria, 3 February 1865, *Journal*.

93. Queen Victoria to Princess Alice, 26 July 1874, quoted Elizabeth Longford, *Victoria R.I.*

94. Queen Victoria to her daughter Vicky, February 1868, Kronberg Letters, quoted Elizabeth Longford, *Victoria R.I.*

95. *Memoirs of Baron Stockmar by his Son, Baron E. von Stockmar*.

96. Quoted E. S. Turner, *The Court of St James*, from *Manners & Rules of Good Society*.

97. *ibid.*

98. John Bright, quoted E. S. Turner, *The Court of St James*.

99. Queen Victoria, 20 June 1887, *Journal*.

100. Lady Monkswell, *A Victorian Diarist*, John Murray, 1994.

101. *ibid*.

102. Dorothy Laird, *Queen Elizabeth, The Queen Mother*, Hodder & Stoughton, 1966.

103. Quoted James Pope-Hennessy, *Queen Mary*, Allen & Unwin, 1959.

104. *ibid*.

105. *ibid*.

106. Prince George, Duke of York to Princess Mary, Duchess of York, quoted James Pope-Hennessey, *Queen Mary*.

107. Queen Victoria, 22 June 1897, *Journal*.

108. Elizabeth Longford, *Victoria R.I.*

CHAPTER SIX

1. Lord Esher, *Journals and Letters*, Nicholson and Watson, 2 vols., 1934.

2. James Pope-Hennessy, *Queen Mary*, Allen & Unwin, 1959.

3. *The Times*, obituary of Edward VII, May 1910.

4. HRH The Duke of Windsor, *A King's Story*, Cassell, 1951.

5. Sir Philip Magnus, *King Edward VII*, John Murray, 1903.

6. Lord Esher, *Journals and Letters*.

7. *ibid*.

8. Sir Lionel Cust, *King Edward VII and His Court*, John Murray, 1930.

9. *ibid*.

10. *ibid*.

11. *ibid*.

12. *ibid*.

13. *ibid*.

14. Sir Philip Magnus, *King Edward VII*.

15. *ibid*.

16. James Pope-Hennessy, *Queen Mary*.

17. Quoted *ibid*.

18. John Martin Robinson, *Buckingham Palace*, Michael Joseph, 1995.

19. Quoted Sir Philip Magnus, *King Edward VII*.

20. Sir Lionel Cust, *King Edward VII and his Court*.

21. Sir Philip Magnus, *King Edward VII*.

22. Sir Lionel Cust, *King Edward VII and His Court*.
23. *ibid.*

CHAPTER SEVEN

1. J. R. Clynes, *Memoirs*, 1924–1937, Hutchinson, 1937.
2. Quoted James Pope-Hennessy, *Queen Mary*, Allen & Unwin, 1959.
3. Mabell, Countess of Airlie, *Thatched with Gold*, ed. Jennifer Ellis, Hutchinson, 1962.
4. *ibid.*
5. HRH The Duke of Windsor, *A King's Story*, Cassell, 1951.
6. *ibid.*
7. *ibid.*
8. *ibid.*
9. *ibid.*
10. *ibid.*
11. *ibid.*
12. Queen Mary to King George V, quoted James Pope-Hennessy, *Queen Mary*.
13. Kenneth Rose, *King George V*, Weidenfeld & Nicolson, 1983.
14. Queen Mary to the Grand Duchess of Mecklenburg-Strelitz (her aunt), 26 February 1911, quoted James Pope-Hennessy, *Queen Mary*.
15. Queen Mary, quoted James Pope-Hennessy, *Queen Mary*.
16. Kenneth Rose, *King George V*.
17. HRH The Duke of Windsor, *A King's Story*.
18. Kenneth Rose, *King George V*.
19. *ibid.*
20. *The Times*, October 1913.
21. *The Times*, 1 November 1913.
22. James Pope-Hennessy, *Queen Mary*.
23. Quoted James Pope-Hennessy, from Queen Mary, 4 June 1914, *Diary*.
24. Kenneth Rose, *King George V*.
25. Royal Archives, George V CC 62/94. Report by Charles Allom of the firm White Allom, describing in detail the work done at Buckingham Palace 'under the personal supervision of Queen Mary'.
26. Royal Archives, George V CC 62/94.
27. Royal Archives, Queen Mary to the Marquess of Cambridge, February 1925. Quoted James Pope-Hennessy, *Queen Mary*.

28. James Pope-Hennessy, *Queen Mary*.

29. James Pope-Hennessy, *Queen Mary*.

30. Quoted Kenneth Rose, *King George V*, King George V, 4 August 1914, *Diary*.

31. Kenneth Rose, *King George V*.

32. *The Times*, 8 September 1914.

33. Charles Allom Report, Royal Archives, George V CC 62/94.

34. John Martin Robinson, *Buckingham Palace*, Royal Palaces, Michael Joseph, 1995.

35. Royal Archives, George V CC 62/94.

36. Mabell, Countess of Airlie *Thatched with Gold*.

37. *ibid.*

38. King George V to Queen Mary, Royal Archives, George V CC 4 163.

39. James Pope-Hennessy, *Queen Mary*.

40. *ibid.*

41. Mary Agnes Hamilton, *Mary MacArthur*.

42. *ibid.*

43. James Pope-Hennessy, *Queen Mary*.

44. *ibid.*

45. Queen Mary to Grand Duchess of Mecklenburg-Strelitz, 24 March 1916, quoted James Pope-Hennessy, *Queen Mary*.

46. Quoted James Pope-Hennessy, *Queen Mary*, Queen Mary, December 1916, *Diary*.

47. James Pope-Hennessy, *Queen Mary*.

48. *ibid.*

49. *ibid.*

50. Mabell, Countess of Airlie, *Thatched with Gold*.

51. *ibid.*

52. HRH The Duke of Windsor, *A King's Story*.

53. *ibid.*

54. Lord Esher, *Journals and Letters*, Nicholson and Watson, 2 vols., 1934.

55. Harold Nicolson, *King George V: His Life and Reign*, Constable, 1952.

56. *ibid.*

57. Sir Henry Channon, *Diaries*, Weidenfeld & Nicolson, 1967.

58. Dorothy Laird, *Queen Elizabeth, The Queen Mother*, Hodder & Stoughton, 1966.

59. *ibid.*

60. *ibid.*

61. Kenneth Rose, *King George V.*

62. J. R. Clynes, *Memoirs.*

63. Kenneth Rose, *King George V.*

64. *ibid.*

65. Mabell, Countess of Airlie, *Thatched with Gold*, quoting Lord Salisbury, House of Lords, Hansard, May 1926.

66. *ibid.*

67. Kenneth Rose, *King George V.*

68. *ibid.*

69. *ibid.*

70. *ibid.*

71. Harold Nicolson, *King George V: His Life and Reign.*

72. Mabell, Countess of Airlie, *Thatched with Gold.*

73. E. S. Turner, *The Court of St James*, Michael Joseph, 1959.

74. Mabell, Countess of Airlie, *Thatched with Gold.*

75. *ibid.*

76. *ibid.*

77. *ibid.*

78. HRH The Duke of Windsor, *A King's Story.*

79. Kenneth Rose, *King George V.*

80. *ibid.*

81. *ibid.*

82. Sir Henry Channon, *Diaries.*

83. Harold Nicolson, *King George V: His Life and Reign.*

84. James Pope-Hennessy, *Queen Mary.*

85. HRH The Duke of Windsor, *A King's Story.*

86. *ibid.*

87. Duchess of Windsor, *The Heart Has Its Reasons*, Michael Joseph, 1956.

88. *ibid.*

89. Michael Bloch (ed.), *Wallis & Edward, Letters 1931–1937: the Intimate Correspondence of the Duke and Duchess of Windsor*, Weidenfeld & Nicolson, 1986.

90. Duchess of Windsor, *The Heart Has Its Reasons.*

91. Mabell, Countess of Airlie, *Thatched with Gold.*

92. Kenneth Rose, *King George V.*

93. *ibid.*

94. J. R. Clynes, *Memoirs 1924–1937*.
95. Quoted James Pope-Hennessy, *Queen Mary*, from Queen Mary, *Diary*.
96. *ibid.*
97. HRH The Duke of Windsor, *A King's Story*.
98. *ibid.*

CHAPTER EIGHT

1. Michael Bloch (ed.), *Wallis & Edward, Letters 1931–1937: The Intimate Correspondence of the Duke and Duchess of Windsor*, Weidenfeld & Nicolson, 1986.
2. HRH The Duke of Windsor, *A King's Story*, Cassell, 1951.
3. James Pope-Hennessy, *Queen Mary*, Allen & Unwin, 1959.
4. HRH The Duke of Windsor, *A King's Story*.
5. Mabell, Countess of Airlie, *Thatched with Gold*, ed. Jennifer Ellis, Hutchinson, 1962.
6. James Pope-Hennessy, *Queen Mary*.
7. HRH The Duke of Windsor, *A King's Story*.
8. *ibid.*
9. Quoted James Pope-Hennessy, from Queen Mary, *Diary*.
10. *ibid.*
11. *ibid.*
12. HRH The Duke of Windsor, *A King's Story*.
13. *ibid.*
14. *ibid.*
15. *ibid.*
16. Sir Henry Channon, *Diaries*, Weidenfeld & Nicolson, 1967.
17. HRH The Duke of Windsor, *A King's Story*.
18. *ibid.*
19. Michael Bloch (ed.), *Wallis & Edward, Letters 1931–1939*.
20. Mabell, Countess of Airlie, *Thatched with Gold*.
21. *ibid.*
22. HRH The Duke of Windsor, *A King's Story*.
23. *ibid.*
24. Philip Ziegler, *Diana Cooper*, Hamish Hamilton, 1981.
25. HRH The Duke of Windsor, *A King's Story*.
26. *ibid.*

27. Sir Henry Channon, *Diaries*.

28. *ibid.*

29. HRH The Duke of Windsor, *A King's Story*.

30. Sir John Wheeler-Bennett, *King George VI: His Life and Reign*, Macmillan, 1958.

31. HRH The Duke of Windsor, *A King's Story*.

32. *ibid.*

33. *ibid.*

34. Frances Donaldson, *Edward VIII*, Weidenfeld & Nicolson, 1974.

35. Quoted Frances Donaldson, *Edward VIII*.

36. *ibid.*

37. Sir Henry Channon, *Diaries*.

38. *ibid.*

39. Baldwin's statement in the House of Commons, Hansard, 16 December 1936.

40. Sir Henry Channon, *Diaries*.

CHAPTER NINE

1. King George VI to Lady Airlie, in Mabell, Countess of Airlie, *Thatched with Gold*, ed. Jennifer Ellis, Hutchinson, 1962.

2. Dorothy Laird, *Queen Elizabeth, The Queen Mother*, Hodder & Stoughton, 1966.

3. Sarah Bradford, *King George VI*, Heinemann, 1989.

4. Queen Elizabeth The Queen Mother, private conversation.

5. HRH The Duke of Windsor, *A King's Story*, Cassell, 1951.

6. HRH Duke of Windsor, BBC broadcast from Windsor, 12 December 1936.

7. Sir John Wheeler-Bennett, *King George VI: His Life and Reign*, Macmillan, 1958.

8. Quoted Sir John Wheeler-Bennett, *King George VI*, from King George VI, *Diary*.

9. HRH The Duke of Windsor, *A King's Story*.

10. Sir John Wheeler-Bennett, *King George VI*.

11. *ibid.*

12. Mabell, Countess of Airlie, *Thatched with Gold*.

13. HRH Princess Margaret, private conversation.

14. Marion Crawford, *The Little Princesses*, Cassell, 1950.

15. *The Times*, 12 October 1938.

16. Royal Archives, G. VI., PS3317.

17. Mabell, Countess of Airlie, *Thatched with Gold*.

18. *ibid.*

19. Marion Crawford, *The Little Princesses*.

20. *ibid.*

21. *ibid.*

22. Kenneth Campbell, *Campbell Smith & Co., A Century of Decorative Crafts-manship 1873–1973*, published 1973; printed Land Humphries.

23. Mabell, Countess of Airlie, *Thatched with Gold*.

24. Marion Crawford, *The Little Princesses*.

25. Mabell, Countess of Airlie, *Thatched with Gold*.

26. Quoted James Pope-Hennessy, *Queen Mary*, Allen & Unwin, 1959, from Queen Mary, 12 May 1937, *Diary*.

27. HRH Princess Elizabeth, 12 May 1937, 'The Coronation', Royal Library, Windsor.

28. Marion Crawford, *The Little Princesses*.

29. HRH Princess Elizabeth, 12 May 1937, 'The Coronation'.

30. Sir Henry Channon, *Diaries*, Weidenfeld & Nicolson, 1967.

31. *ibid.*

32. Frances Donaldson, *Edward VIII*, Weidenfeld & Nicolson, 1974.

33. Mrs Eleanor Roosevelt, *This I Remember*, Harper & Row, New York, 1938.

34. HM King George VI, BBC broadcast, 3 September 1939.

35. Sir John Wheeler-Bennett, *King George VI*.

36. HM King George VI, BBC broadcast, 25 December 1939.

37. Sir John Colville, *The Fringes of Power: 10 Downing Street Diaries 1939–1955*, Hodder & Stoughton, 1985.

38. Dorothy Laird, *Queen Elizabeth, The Queen Mother*.

39. Sir John Wheeler-Bennett, *King George VI*.

40. *ibid.*

41. Queen Elizabeth The Queen Mother, private conversation.

42. Winston Churchill, House of Commons, 20 August, 1940.

43. King George VI to Queen Mary, 11 September 1940, Royal Archives, Geo V CC 12/134.

44. Royal Archives, G.VI. P.S. 4920/1.

45. King George VI to Queen Mary, 14 September 1940, Royal Archives, George V, CC 12/136.

46. Queen Elizabeth to Queen Mary, 13 September 1940, Royal Archives, George V, CC 12/135.

47. Sir John Wheeler-Bennett, *King George VI*.

48. HRH Princess Margaret, private conversation.

49. Dorothy Laird, *Queen Elizabeth, The Queen Mother*.

50. Sir John Wheeler-Bennett, *King George VI*.

51. Dorothy Laird, *Queen Elizabeth, The Queen Mother*.

52. Sir John Wheeler-Bennett, *King George VI*.

53. Royal Archives, Geo V. CC 62/123.

54. Chief Superintendent Metropolitan Police, Douglas Lightwood; article in *London Police Pensioner*, December 1994, p. 24. Details of this raid are also contained in an unpublished article by PC Alan Graham, later to be a member of the Royal Protection Unit, based at Clarence House.

55. Quoted Sir John Wheeler-Bennett, *King George VI*.

56. HRH Princess Elizabeth, BBC broadcast, 13 October 1940.

57. Queen Elizabeth to Queen Mary, 19 October 1942, Royal Archives, George V CC 13/26.

58. Mrs Eleanor Roosevelt, *This I Remember*.

59. *ibid*.

60. Mrs Eleanor Roosevelt, *On My Own*, Harper & Row, New York, 1958.

61. Royal Archives, GV CC 13/64.

62. Royal Archives, 25 September 1943, GV CC 13/64.

63. Marion Crawford, *The Little Princesses*.

64. *ibid*.

65. HRH Princess Margaret, private conversation.

66. Queen Elizabeth to Queen Mary, 25 September 1943, Royal Archives, GV CC 13/64.

67. Marion Crawford, *The Little Princesses*.

68. Quoted Sir John Wheeler-Bennett, *King George VI*.

69. *ibid*.

70. Marion Crawford, *The Little Princesses*.

71. *ibid*.

72. Sir John Wheeler-Bennett, *King George VI*.

73. Mr Clement Attlee, conversation with author.

74. Sir John Wheeler-Bennett, *King George VI*.

75. *ibid*.

76. *ibid*.

77. Royal Archives pp G.VI 7009.

78. *ibid.*

79. *ibid.*

80. Royal Archives, pp G.VI 7009 1947.

81. *ibid.*

82. Hansard, *Report of Proceedings of the House of Commons*, 31 March 1947, p. 261.

83. Sir John Wheeler-Bennett, *King George VI*.

84. Mabell, Countess of Airlie, *Thatched with Gold*.

85. HRH Princess Elizabeth, broadcast from South Africa, 21 April 1947.

86. Quoted Sir John Wheeler-Bennett, *King George VI*, from Queen Mary's Collection, Royal Archives.

87. Mabell, Countess of Airlie, *Thatched with Gold*.

88. *ibid.*

89. King George VI to Queen Mary, 14 September 1947, quoted Sir John Wheeler-Bennett, *King George VI*.

90. Aneurin Bevan, quoted Kenneth Rose, *King George V*, Weidenfeld & Nicolson, 1983.

91. Sir John Colville, *The Fringes of Power*.

92. Mabell, Countess of Airlie, *Thatched with Gold*.

93. *ibid.*

94. Sir John Colville, *The Fringes of Power*.

95. *ibid.*

96. *ibid.*

97. *ibid.*

98. Marion Crawford, *The Little Princesses*.

99. Sir John Colville, *The Fringes of Power*.

100. Marion Crawford, *The Little Princesses*.

101. *ibid.*

102. *ibid.*

103. King George VI to Princess Elizabeth on her honeymoon, quoted Sir John Wheeler-Bennett, *King George VI*.

104. Sir John Wheeler-Bennett, *King George VI*.

105. *ibid.*

106. Quoted Sir John Wheeler-Bennett, *King George VI* from King George VI's address to the Conference of Commonwealth Prime Ministers, Buckingham Palace, 27 April 1949, Memorandum by Sir Alan Lascelles.

107. *ibid.*
108. HRH Princess Margaret, private conversation.
109. James Pope-Hennessy, *Queen Mary.*
110. King George VI to a friend, quoted Sir John Wheeler-Bennett, *King George VI.*
111. Winston Churchill, source unknown.
112. HRH Princess Margaret, private conversation.
113. Ben Pimlott, *The Queen: A Biography of Queen Elizabeth II*, HarperCollins, 1996.
114. *ibid.*
115. Lord Charteris, private conversation.
116. *ibid.*
117. Mabell, Countess of Airlie, *Thatched with Gold.*
118. Winston Churchill in the House of Commons, Hansard, 11 February 1952.
119. Clement Attlee, Labour Leader of the Opposition, Hansard, 11 February 1952.
120. *ibid.*

CHAPTER TEN

1. Mabell, Countess of Airlie, *Thatched with Gold*, ed. Jennifer Ellis, Hutchinson, 1962.
2. Quoted Sarah Bradford, *Elizabeth: A Biography of HM The Queen*, Heinemann, 1966.
3. Hansard, 25 March 1953.
4. Mrs Eleanor Roosevelt, *On My Own*, Harper & Row, New York, 1958.
5. Ben Pimlott, *The Queen: A Biography of Queen Elizabeth II*, HarperCollins, 1996.
6. Lord Cobbold, statement to the All Party Select Committee, Hansard, 21 June 1971.
7. Private conversation.
8. Elizabeth Longford, *Victoria R.I.*, Weidenfeld & Nicolson, 1964.
9. Professor Harold Laski, *The Fortnightly*, December 1942.
10. *ibid.*
11. *ibid.*
12. Ben Pimlott, *The Queen: A Biography of Elizabeth II.*
13. Author reminiscence.

14. Quoted Sarah Bradford, *Elizabeth: A Biography of HM The Queen.*

15. Author reminiscence.

16. Lady Solti to Edna Healey, private letter.

17. *ibid.*

18. Quoted Sarah Bradford, *Elizabeth: A Biography of HM the Queen.*

19. Quoted Ben Pimlott, *The Queen: A Biography of Elizabeth II.*

20. *ibid.*

21. Hansard, *Minutes of the All-Party Select Committee of Enquiry into Royal Finances*, 21 June 1971.

22. *ibid.*

23. *ibid.*

24. *ibid.*

25. *ibid.*

26. *ibid.*

27. *ibid.*

28. Hansard, 12 February 1975.

29. *ibid.*

30. Report of the Royal Trustees, July 1990.

31. Memorandum of Understanding, 1 April 1991.

32. *ibid.*

33. Lord Airlie to Press Conference, quoted Ben Pimlott, *The Queen: A Biography of Elizabeth II.*

34. Michael Peat, television interview, quoted Ben Pimlott, *The Queen: A Biography of Elizabeth II.*

35. Press conference 1994, Lord Airlie's address.

36. Royal Finances, second edition, 1995.

37. Edna Healey, *Coutts & Co., Portrait of a Private Bank*, Hodder & Stoughton, 1993.

38. Official Report, the Lord Chamberlain.

39. Interview with Lord Airlie, the Lord Chamberlain.

40. Sir Oliver Millar, 'Surveyors Past and Present', *The Queen's Pictures: The Royal Collection through the Ages*, ed. Christopher Lloyd, National Gallery Publications, 1991.

41. *ibid.*

42. *ibid.*

43. *ibid.*

44. *ibid.*

45. Elspeth Montcrieff, 'Utility and Delight', *Apollo*, October 1991.

46. James Shirley, *Death the Leveller*, 1659.

47. Elspeth Montcrieff, *Apollo*, October 1991.

48. Quoted Ben Pimlott, *The Queen: A Biography of Elizabeth II*, from *The Sunday Times*, 29 May 1977.

Select Bibliography

Airlie, Mabell, Countess of, *Thatched with Gold*, ed. Jennifer Ellis, Hutchinson, London, 1962.

Albert, Prince Consort, *Letters*, ed. K. Jagow, John Murray, London, 1938.

Aldrich, Megan, *The Craces*, John Murray and Brighton Pavilion, London, 1990.

Arnold, Frieda, *My Mistress the Queen: Dresser to Queen Victoria*, transl. Sheila de Bellaigue, Weidenfeld & Nicolson, London, 1994.

Aspinall, A. (ed.), *Letters of Princess Charlotte, 1811–1817*, Hume and van Thal, London, 1949.

Barker, Felix and Jackson, Peter, *2000 Years of a City and its People*, Cassell, London, 1974.

Battiscombe, Georgina, *Queen Alexandra*, Constable, London, 1969.

Beaton, Cecil, *Photobiography*, Odhams Press, London, 1957.

Bloch, Michael (ed.), *Wallis & Edward, Letters 1931–1937, the Intimate Correspondence of the Duke and Duchess of Windsor*, Guild Publishing: Weidenfeld & Nicolson, London, 1986.

Blunt, Wilfred, *On Wings of Song*, Hamish Hamilton, London, 1974.

Bradford, Sarah, *Elizabeth: A Biography of HM The Queen*, Heinemann, London, 1966.

Bradford, Sarah, *King George VI*, Heinemann, London, 1989.

Briggs, Asa, *Victorian Cities*, Allen & Unwin, London, 1953.

Brooke, John, *King George III*, Constable, London, 1972.

Buckingham, John Sheffield, *Complete Works, London*, 2 vols., London, 1740.

Callaghan, James, *Time & Chance*, Collins, London, 1987.

Campbell, Kenneth, *Campbell, Smith & Co. 1873–1973*, privately printed, London, 1973.

Channon, Sir Henry, *The Diaries*, Weidenfeld & Nicolson, London, 1967.

Clark, Kenneth, *Another Part of the Wood*, John Murray, London, 1974.

Clynes, J. R. *Memoirs, 1924–1937*, London, Hutchinson, 1937.

Colville, Sir John, *The Fringes of Power: 10 Downing Street Diaries 1939–1955*, Hodder & Stoughton, London, 1985.

Colvin, H. M. (ed.), *History of The King's Works*, 6 vols., HMSO, London, 1973.

Crawford, Marion, *The Little Princesses*, Cassell, London, 1950.

Creevey, Thomas, *Papers*, John Murray, London, 1912.

Cust, Sir Lionel, *King Edward VII and His Court*, John Murray, London, 1930.

D'Arblay, Mme, *Diary and Correspondence of Fanny Burney*, ed. G. F. Barrett, 6 vols., London, 1904.

Dickens, Charles, *The Letters of*, ed. Storey, Tillotson and Easson, vol. 7, Oxford University Press, Oxford, 1993.

Donaldson, Frances, *Edward VIII*, Weidenfeld & Nicolson, London, 1974.

Dryden, John, *The Poems of John Dryden*, ed., James Kinsley, 4 vols., Clarendon Press, Oxford, 1958.

Esher, Lord, *Journals and Letters*, 2 vols., Nicholson & Watson, London, 1934.

Evelyn, John, *The Diary of*, ed. William Bray, 2 vols., J. M. Dent & Sons, London, 1907.

The Farington Diary, 8 vols., Hutchinson, London, 1922–8.

Fitzgerald, Percy, *The Life and Times of William IV*, Tinsley Bros., London 1884.

Gatty, C. T., *Mary Davies and The Manor of Ebury*, 2 vols., Cassell, London, 1921.

Greville, Charles, *Leaves from the Greville Diary*, ed. Philip Morell, Eveleigh, Nash & Grayson, London, 1929.

Gloag, John, *Georgian Grace*, A. & C. Black, London, 1956.

Harris, J. and Snodin, M. (eds.), *Sir William Chambers* (exhibition catalogue), Courtauld Gallery, with Yale University Press, London, 1996.

Harris, J., de Bellaigue, G., and Millar, O., *Buckingham Palace*, London, 1968.

Healey, Edna, *Coutts & Co.: The Portrait of a Private Bank*, Hodder & Stoughton, London, 1992.

Hedley, Olwen, *Queen Charlotte*, John Murray, London, 1975.

Hibbert, Christopher, *The Court of St James*, Weidenfeld & Nicolson, London, 1979.

Hibbert, Christopher, *The Biography of a City*, Penguin Books, Harmondsworth, 1980.

Hobhouse, Hermione, *Thomas Cubitt*, Macmillan, London, 1971.

Howarth, David (ed.), *Art & Patronage in the Caroline Courts*, Cambridge University Press, Cambridge, 1993.

Howell-Thomas, Dorothy, *Duncannon, Reformer and Reconciler*, Michael Russell, Norwich, 1992.

Huish, Robert, *Memoirs of George IV*, ed. Kelly, 2 vols., London, 1831.

Huish, Robert, *History of the Life of William IV*, London, 1837.

Joyce, Michael, *My Friend H: the Life of John Cam Hobhouse, Lord Broughton*, John Murray, London, 1948.

Kelly, Alison, *Mrs Coade's Stone*, Self Publishing Association Ltd, London, 1990.

Kriegal, A. D. (ed.), *The Holland House Diaries*, Routledge & Paul, London, 1977.

Lacey, Robert, *Majesty*, Hutchinson, London, 1977.

Laird, Dorothy, *Queen Elizabeth, The Queen Mother*, Hodder & Stoughton, London, 1966.

Lane, Peter, *Prince Philip*, Robert Hale, London, 1980.

Lascelles, Sir Alan, *In Royal Service*, Hamish Hamilton, London, 1989.

Lieven, D., Princess, *The Private Letters*, John Murray, London, 1934.

Lloyd, Christopher, *The Royal Collection*, Channel 4 and Sinclair-Stevenson, London, 1992.

Lloyd, Christopher, 'The Picture Gallery Today', *Apollo*, London, September 1993.

Longford, Elizabeth, *Victoria R.I.*, Weidenfeld & Nicolson, London, 1964.

Lytton, Lady, *Court Diary*, ed. Mary Lutyens, Hart Davis, London, 1964.

Macaulay, Thomas, *History of England*, ed. Henderson, Routledge, London, 1907.

Macmillan, Harold, *At the End of the Day*, Macmillan, London, 1973.

Magnus, Philip, *King Edward VII*, John Murray, London, 1964.

Marie Louise, HRH Princess, *My Memories of Six Reigns*, Evans Bros., 1856.

Martin, S. Theodore, *The Life of HRH The Prince Consort*, 5 vols., Smith, Elder & Co., 1875.

Martin Robinson, John, *Royal Palaces: Buckingham Palace*, Michael Joseph, London, 1995.

Maxwell, Sir Herbert (ed.), *The Creevey Papers*, John Murray, London, 1903.

Mendelssohn, Felix Bartholdy, *Letters 1833–1847*, ed. Jacob, London, 1863.

Millar, Sir Oliver, *Victorian Pictures in the Collection of HM The Queen*, Cambridge University Press, Cambridge, 1992.

Morell, Philip (ed.), *Leaves from Greville Diary*, Eveleigh Nash & Grayson, London, 1929.

Pimlott, Ben, *The Queen: A Biography of Elizabeth II*, HarperCollins, London, 1996.

Plumb, F. and Weldon, H., *Royal Heritage*, BBC, London, 1977.

Pope, Alexander, *The Character of Katherine, Late Duchess of Buckinghamshire & Normanby*, M. Cooper, London, 1746.

Powys, Mrs Lybbe, *The Diaries of*, ed. E. J. Climenson, Longman, London, 1899.

Pyne, W. H., *Royal Residences*, vol. 3, London, 1819.

Rhodes-James, Robert, *Albert, Prince Consort*, Hamish Hamilton, London 1983.

Roberts, Jane, 'Sir William Chambers & George III', *Sir William Chambers* (exhibition catalogue), ed. J. Harris and M. Snodin, Courtauld Gallery, London, 1997.

Roche, Sophie von la, *Sophie in London*, transl. Clare Williams, Jonathan Cape, London, 1933.

Roosevelt, Eleanor, *This I Remember*, Hutchinson, London, 1938.

Roosevelt, Eleanor, *On My Own*, Hutchinson, London, 1950.

Rose, Kenneth, *King George V*, Weidenfeld & Nicolson, London, 1983.

Rose, Kenneth, *Kings, Queens & Courtiers*, Weidenfeld & Nicolson, London, 1985.

Rush, Richard, *Memoranda of a Residence at the Court of London*, USA, 1833.

Russell, J., 'King George III's Picture Hang at Buckingham House', *Burlington Magazine*, London, 1987.

Sedley, Sir Charles, *The Mulberry Garden*, London, 1675.

Smith, Clifford, *Buckingham Palace*, Country Life Ltd., London, 1931.

Smith, J. T., *Nollekens and His Times*, Turnstile Press, London, 1949.

Stockmar, Baron E., *Memoirs of Baron Stockmar by his Son, Baron E. von Stockmar*, ed. F. Max Müller, 2 vols., Longmans, Green & Co., London, 1872.

Stow, *Survey of the Cities of London and Westminster*, 2 vols., Dent & Sons, London, 1956.

Strong, Roy, *Royal Gardens*, BBC Bks Conrad Octopus, London, 1992.

Summerson, John, *Georgian London*, Penguin Books, Harmondsworth, 1945.

Summerson, John, *The Life and Works of John Nash*, Allen & Unwin, London, 1935.

Tait, A. A., *Robert Adam: the Creative Mind*, The Gallery, London, 1997.

Tomalin, Claire, *Mrs. Jordan's Profession*, Viking, London, 1994.

Turner, E. S., *The Court of St James*, Michael Joseph, London, 1959.

G. Tyack, *Sir James Pennethorne and the Making of Victorian London*, Cambridge University Press, Cambridge, 1992.

Victoria, HM The Queen, *The Girlhood*, ed. Viscount Esher, 2 vols., John Murray, London, 1912.

Victoria, HM The Queen, *Queen Victoria's Journal: a Selection from Her Majesty's Diaries 1832–1840*, ed. Viscount Esher, 2 vols., John Murray, London, 1912.

Victoria, HM The Queen, *Queen Victoria's Letters: a Selection from Her Majesty's Correspondence 1837–1861*, ed. Benson and Esher, 1st series, 3 vols., John Murray, London, 1907. 2nd series, *1862–85*, ed. G. Buckle, 3 vols., John Murray, London, 1907. 3rd series, *1886–1901*, ed. G. Buckle, 3 vols., John Murray, London, 1930.

Walford, Edward, *Old and New London*, Cassell Peter & Galpin, London, 1897.

Walpole, Horace, *Journal of Visits to Country Houses*, Walpole Society Annual, 1927.

Walpole, Horace, *Letters*, ed. Mrs Paget Toynbee, 8 vols., Clarendon Press, Oxford, 1903–5.

Walpole, Horace, *Memoirs and Portraits*, Batsford, London, 1822–5.

Wheeler-Bennett, Sir John, *King George VI: His Life and Reign*, Macmillan, London, 1958.

White, Christopher, *Dutch Pictures in the Collection of H.M. The Queen*, Cambridge University Press, Cambridge, 1952.

Windsor, HRH The Duchess of, *The Heart Has Its Reasons*, Michael Joseph, London, 1956.

Windsor, HRH The Duke of, *A King's Story*, Cassell, London, 1951.

Wraxall, Nathaniel, *Historical Memoirs*, ed. H. B. Wheatley, 5 vols., 1884.

Wright, Patricia, *The Strange History of Buckingham Palace*, Alan Sutton, Gloucestershire, 1996.

Ziegler, Philip, *King William IV*, Collins, London, 1971.

Ziegler, Philip, *Crown & People*, Collins, London, 1978.

REFERENCES

Hansard
Journal of the House of Lords
The Annual Register

ENCYCLOPAEDIAS

Chronicle of the 20th Century, Jacques Legrand, Paris, 1988.
Chronicle of The Royal Family, Chronicle Communications, London, 1991.
Dictionary of National Biography, Oxford University Press, Oxford, 1975.
Oxford History of The British Monarchy, ed. John Cannon and Ralph Griffiths,
    Oxford University Press, Oxford, 1988.
Royal Encyclopedia, Macmillan, London, 1991.

PERIODICALS

Apollo
Burlington Magazine
Fortnightly Review
Gentleman's Magazine
Punch
The Times, Sunday Times, et al.

Index

CP and P at the end of entries refer to either the colour plate insets or the black and white plate inset.

Charlotte, Queen 1–2n, 28–81, 135, 152, 154–5, 222, 388 **CP3, CP11, CP14**
  children 37, 50, 52, 54, 71, 75–7 **CP3, CP16**
  during Regency period 70–80
  George III's birthday, xv, 72 **CP5**
  given 'Queen's House', xvi
Charteris, Martin 335, 351, 369
Chartists 162
Chatham, 1st Earl of (Pitt the Elder) 63
Chatsworth 106
Cheam school, Surrey 313
chimneys *see* fireplaces
china 45, 45n, 47, 84, 346–7, 367
  Chelsea service 44–5, 367 **CP12**
  see also art(s)
Chinese Chippendale Room 223, 230
Chinese influence 38, 44, 83, 98–9, 160, 230
Chinese Room 183, 268, 301
Chipp, Mr: owner of Mulberry Garden 9, 10, 11
Chippendale Room 222
Christian IX, King of Denmark 183
Christian VII, King of Denmark 67–8
Christie family: sale 45
Church of England: monarch as Head 342
Churchill, Sir Winston 247–8, 316, 318
  2nd World War 295, 296, 300, 303, 308–9, 314
  and the Duke of Windsor 270, 272, 275, 276–7, 278, 292, 296
  Elizabeth II 326, 335, 340
  George VI 292, 296, 333–4, 335–6
Cipriani, G. B. 46–7 **CP6**
cistern 35
Civil List 48
  Elizabeth II and family 325–6, 373, 374, 377–81, 383
  George III 49–50, 64–6, 69, 70
  George V 257
  George VI 325–6, 328
Civil War 4, 5, 7, 8–10, 12, 16
Claremont, nr Esher 74, 80
Clarence, William, Duke of *see* William IV
Clarence and Avondale, Albert Victor, Duke of (Eddy) 185–6, 187 **P10**
Clarence House 101–2, 299–300, 330, 331, 335, 338
Clarendon, Earl of (Lord Chamberlain to Edward VII) 193, 201
Clarendon, Earl of (Lord Chamberlain to Elizabeth II) 340
Clark, Charles 217
Clark, Sir James 126, 144
Clark, Kenneth 385
Clarke, Sir Charles 126
Cleveland, Duchess of (Barbara Villiers) 14
Clifden, Nellie 173, 174
clocks and watches 46, 48, 84, 231–2, 287 **CP9**
Clynes, J. R. 246–7, 253–4, 262
Coade, Eleanor, and Coade stone 95, 96–7, 389–90
Cobb, of Vile & Cobb 42–3
Cobbold, Lord (Lord Chamberlain) 346, 351–2, 373–8
Coburg, Dukes of: royal descendants 130
Coburg, Ernest, Duke of 114, 129–30, 132
Coburg, Frederick, Duke of 130, 225
Coburg, Louise, Duchess of 131
Colville, John 296, 317, 326–8, 328n

Committee for Women's Training and Employment 235–6, 237
Commonwealth 331–2, 342, 351, 352, 358
  monarch's role 360–62
Commonwealth Institute 361
Communism: revolutions in Europe 162–3
Comptroller of the Household 359
Comptroller, Lord Chamberlain's Office 346, 383
Conroy, Sir John 80, 113–5, 119, 123, 126
Constantine, Grand Duke of Russia 130
Constantine I, King of Greece 312–3
Conyngham, Lord (1837) 115, 125
Cooper, Sam 387
Cooper, Sir Simon, *ix–x*
Cope, Sir Arthur **CP23**
Cotes, Francis **CP4**
Counsellors of State 359
Court 340–41
  Edward VII 193–4
  Elizabeth II 340, 342–3, 355
  George III 55–62, 77
  George V 251–6
  Victoria 121, 122, 151–2, 180–82
  see also Headquarters of State; Royal Household
Court of St James 363
courtyard 35, 39, 71, 92, 94, 159, 161
Coutts & Co 86, 382
Coutts, Angela Georgina (later Baroness Burdett-Coutts) 144, 234
Coutts, Thomas 38, 43, 49–50, 144, 382
Coward, Noël 309, 326
Cowes: regatta 204
Crace, Edward 44
Cranfield, Lionel 4
Crawford, Marion 286–9, 295, 310–11, 312, 314–6, 339
  'The Little Princesses' 332–3
  wedding of Elizabeth II 327–8, 329
Creevey, Thomas, 103, 110–11
Crewe, Lady (1914) 236
Crimean War 163–5, 170, 173
Crimond: 'The Lord is My Shepherd', 327–8, 328n
Crimson Drawing Room 38–9, 71
Cripps, Sir Stafford 325–6
Croggan, William 97
Cromwell, Oliver 4, 9
  see also Civil War
Crossman, H. B. S. 374
Crown Equerry 383
Crown Jewels 375
Cubitt, Thomas 152, 157, 159–61, 165–8
Cumberland, Ernest, Duke of 31, 76, 116
Cumberland, Henry Frederick, Duke of 68
Cumberland Gate: Marble Arch 161
Cust, Sir Lionel 194–200, 205, 206, 207, 221, 231, 385
Cuyp, Aelbert 84

Dagmar, Dowager Empress of Russia 204, 212, 225
Dalton, Hugh 318, 325
Dalton, Richard 39–40, 44
Dartmouth College 312, 313
David, Prince *see* Windsor, Duke of
Davies, Alexander and Mary (daughter) 10, 11
Davies, Ernest 321
Dawson of Penn, Lord (surgeon) 248–9, 262

28 DAYS